THE DAUGHTERS OF THE AMERICAN REVOLUTION
AND PATRIOTIC MEMORY IN THE TWENTIETH CENTURY

Simon Wendt

UNIVERSITY PRESS OF FLORIDA

Gainesville · Tallahassee · Tampa · Boca Raton

Pensacola · Orlando · Miami · Jacksonville · Ft. Myers · Sarasota

25 24 23 22 21 20   6 5 4 3 2 1

Library of Congress Cataloging-in-Publication Data
Names: Wendt, Simon, author.
Title: The Daughters of the American Revolution and patriotic memory in the
twentieth century / Simon Wendt.
Description: Gainesville : University Press of Florida, 2020. | Includes
bibliographical references and index.
Identifiers: LCCN 2020016903 (print) | LCCN 2020016904 (ebook) | ISBN
9780813066608 (hardback) | ISBN 9780813057613 (pdf)
Subjects: LCSH: Daughters of the American Revolution—History—20th
century. | Women—United States—History. | United
States—History—Revolution, 1775–1783—Societies, etc.
Classification: LCC E202.5.A7 W46 2020 (print) | LCC E202.5.A7 (ebook) |
DDC 369/.13509—dc23
LC record available at https://lccn.loc.gov/2020016903
LC ebook record available at https://lccn.loc.gov/2020016904

The University Press of Florida is the scholarly publishing agency for the State University System
of Florida, comprising Florida A&M University, Florida Atlantic University, Florida Gulf Coast
University, Florida International University, Florida State University, New College of Florida,
University of Central Florida, University of Florida, University of North Florida, University of
South Florida, and University of West Florida.

University Press of Florida
2046 NE Waldo Road
Suite 2100
Gainesville, FL 32609
http://upress.ufl.edu

FOR FANJA

Contents

Figures

Acknowledgments

The generous support of many individuals and institutions made this book possible.

Manfred Berg in particular—as a scholar, adviser, and mentor—has influenced my growth as a historian in innumerable ways and deserves thanks for supporting this project from the very beginning.

Several fellowships have been critical to the completion of this study. A Jolanta and Soheyl Ghaemian Travel Fund fellowship, a research fellowship from the Schlesinger Library in Harvard University's Radcliffe Institute for Advanced Study, and a research fellowship from the German Historical Institute in Washington, DC, provided crucial financial support to complete the archival research. A writing fellowship from the Historisches Kolleg in Munich allowed me to complete the first version of the manuscript.

A number of colleagues read drafts of the study and made valuable suggestions for revisions. I am grateful to the following people for their insightful comments: Manfred Berg, Christoph Cornelißen, Andreas Fahrmeir, Kristin Hass, Jürgen Müller, and Susanne Opfermann.

In addition, Styles Sass deserves thanks for copyediting parts of an early version of the manuscript.

Other colleagues offered support and encouragement during the long and arduous process of researching and writing the book. During my five years at the University of Heidelberg, the following people offered assistance, friendship, or both: Danijela Albrecht, Cord Arendes, Isabelle Deflers, Frank Grüner, Detlef Junker, Cornelia Logemann, Wilfried Mausbach, Katja Patzel-Mattern, Carla Meyer, Jörg Peltzer, Bernd Schneidmüller, Kilian Schultes, and Alexander Vazansky. I am also grateful for critical support from my colleagues at the Institute of English and American Studies at Goethe University Frankfurt. I owe a huge debt of gratitude to Christa Buschendorf, Bernd Herzogenrath, Linda Hess, Rieke Jordan,

Stephan Kuhl, Magda Majewska, Regine Vatanasomboon, Britta Viebrock, and Johannes Völz. I would also like to thank Heike Bungert, Michael Butter, Volker Depkat, Steve Estes, Norbert Finzsch, Philipp Gassert, Hans-Werner Hahn, Isabel Heinemann, Michael Kimmel, Martin Klimke, Jürgen Martschukat, Christof Mauch, Francesca Morgan, Jörg Nagler, Anke Ortlepp, Torsten Riotte, and Britta Waldschmidt-Nelson.

At the University Press of Florida, Sian Hunter deserves special thanks for gracefully ushering this book through the review and publication process.

Finally, friends and family supported me throughout the decade that it took to finish this study. I am ever grateful for Brian Behnken's friendship and support. When things looked bleak, Brian cheered me up. He also offered sound advice when I was trying to find the right press for this book. My father, Volker, my brother, Hannes, and my sister, Meike, were there when I needed them. My in-laws, Pierrette Razafimbelo and Hans-Joachim Riedel, have shown great patience when confronted with the unusual working hours of a historian who is frantically trying to finish a book, and they deserve a big thanks for helping out when life was difficult. Fara Riedel and Martin Lüthe also helped in numerous ways. My children, Marie and Mio, are too little to understand what it means to write a book, but I am grateful for their patience while waiting, too many times, for Daddy to return from the library. My final and most important thanks go to my wife, Fanja Riedel-Wendt. I could not and would not have completed this project without her love and unwavering support. This book is dedicated to her.

Introduction

In 1914 a member of a Washington, DC, chapter of the Daughters of the American Revolution (DAR) expressed her indignation at citizens' lack of knowledge about the role of women in the American Revolution. Recounting a conversation with her young son about his eighth-grade history textbook in an article for the *DAR Magazine,* Grace D. Johnson was shocked to hear her son say, "'Well, mother, I don't see why you ladies make such a fuss about the American Revolution. The women didn't do anything worth putting in our history books.'" Examining the book that was used in the capital's public schools, Johnson was incensed that it blatantly ignored women's contributions to American independence. "It seems to me," she concluded, that America's youth "should be as familiar with the deeds of our heroines as with those of our heroes."[1]

This anecdote hints at the importance of the Daughters of the American Revolution in the history of US nationalism. A closer look at the DAR's activism reveals that especially prior to World War II, its white middle-class members played a vital role in private citizens' efforts to both bolster patriotism and guard the nation's gender and racial boundaries through commemorative practices. In fact, from the perspective of the Daughters, their nationalist project was inextricably intertwined with gender and race. As suggested by Grace Johnson's story, they engaged in patriotic activism long believed to be the domain of men and deliberately challenged male-centered accounts of US nation-building. At the same time, their tales about the past helped reinforce traditional notions of femininity and masculinity, reflecting a strongly held belief that any challenge to these traditions would jeopardize the nation's stability. In a similar fashion, the organization frequently voiced support for inclusive civic nationalism but deliberately used memory to consolidate Anglo-Saxon whiteness and to keep the nation's racial divisions in place. The history of America's largest patriotic hereditary women's organization testifies to white female conservatives' remarkable agency in US nationalism and explains the tenacity of a particular nationalist ideology that deemed ingrained gender and race hierarchies vital to America's unity and progress.

By shedding light on these intricacies, this book bridges several interrelated historiographical gaps. First, it provides new insights into the ways that a considerable number of white middle-class women tried to mold historical memory in twentieth-century America. While we know much about southern elite women's endeavors to pay tribute to the former Confederacy and the antebellum South, a national perspective has been largely missing in studies on memory and gender.[2] This study also sheds fresh light on the social, political, and cultural activism of white female conservatives and their contributions to US nationalism. A number of historians have probed nationalist women's organizations, including the DAR, but they tend to concentrate on the groups' anticommunist activism and rarely examine how related views on gender and race changed over time.[3] Finally, this is the first monograph to examine the history of the Daughters of the American Revolution and their efforts to keep alive the memory of the nation's past.[4] Those few studies that address the DAR's interpretations of US history either focus on the late nineteenth century or merely hint at the complexity of its commemorative campaigns.[5] This book provides the most comprehensive account of what can arguably be called one of the most influential women's organizations in US history and adds much to understanding the entangled histories of memory, gender, race, and nationalism in twentieth-century America and beyond.

Given its focus on the multilayered meanings of patriotic memory, this study is not a traditional organizational history. Rather it is a cultural history that sheds light on the various ways in which the DAR's interpretations of the past were entangled with and strengthened entrenched ideas about gender, race, and the nation in the present. At the same time, it shows how these ideas informed the organization's social and political activism. This particular perspective is based on the premise that memory is not merely a minor aspect of US nationalism and related ideas about gender and race but rather an integral part of the complex process through which people come to believe these constructs to be real and relevant. Similarly, this book focuses on one particular organization because only a detailed analysis of how historical actors understood and tried to shape the world around them will allow a fuller grasp of the significance of their actions. Broad-based comparative approaches might reveal the general contours of this story, but they do not suffice to explain how what Benedict Anderson has called an "imagined community" became a lived reality.[6] As this study is national in scope, it pays much attention to the tensions between national and regional memory, examining how the Daughters reconciled the distinct collective memories that existed in the Northeast, the Midwest and West, and the South in their efforts to create and bolster national unity. Moreover, to thoroughly examine the impact of the organization's activism, it combines analyses of national, regional, state, and local campaigns, since the DAR's national headquarters in Washington, DC, tended to set the organization's ideological tone but gave much freedom to state organizations and its thousands of local chapters to pursue their own projects.[7]

In many ways, the DAR's founders created a unique organization, which testified to both white women's growing activist prowess in the late nineteenth century and private groups' increasing interest in the American past and boosting US citizens' patriotism. Founded in 1890 by white veteran clubwomen as a form of protest against the decision of the patriotic organization Sons of the American Revolution (SAR) to bar women, the DAR's explicit purpose was "to perpetuate the memory and spirit of the men and women who achieved American independence" as well as "to foster true patriotism and love of country." The Daughters sought to accomplish these two goals through commemoration, historical preservation, and education.[8] Women, the organizers believed, had a key role to play in this endeavor. For one thing, they considered women to be more patriotic than men because of their alleged ability to feel the sentiment of national allegiance more deeply and strongly than men, who seemed to be patriotic only during wars and failed to commemorate the valor of the nation's fallen soldiers in peacetime.[9] The Daughters believed themselves to be the best teachers of national loyalty because they were convinced that patriotic sentiment and women's sphere—the home and the family—were indivisibly entangled. In fact, they considered the family the most important source of national loyalty. In their view, it was from the home that patriotic sentiment took hold of the nation's citizens, especially its future generations of intrepid soldiers who would willingly give their lives for the nation. Consequently, American mothers had a patriotic duty to inculcate in their children a steadfast allegiance to the United States, which together with the Daughters' efforts to commemorate the nation's heroic past would help the organization put into practice its lofty motto "Home and Country."[10]

By evoking "Home and Country" as the basis of US nationalism, the DAR's leaders upheld the idea of "Republican Motherhood" and staunchly defended it at a time when a growing number of critics questioned its validity. First formulated during the American Revolution, Republican Motherhood idealized the educated and self-reliant mother who forwent her own ambitions to devote all of her energies to raising a future generation of virtuous citizens and supporting her husband in the process of nation-building. While they were barred from equal citizenship and political participation, women's domestic virtues as wives and mothers were regarded as the backbone of the republic. Throughout the nineteenth century, this politicized ideal of domesticity became the yardstick for feminine perfection among white middle-class Americans. This ideal intersected with the similarly dominant middle-class concept of "true womanhood" in which women ideally would be confined to the home and required to remain modest as well as sexually pure. For true women, motherhood and submissive wifehood were believed to be the epitome of femininity.[11] Only Republican Motherhood and true womanhood, the Daughters insisted, would safeguard the family, the home, and the nation.

What differentiated the DAR from similar women's associations was its focus on patriotic memory and restrictive membership requirements. Following the example of the SAR, the Daughters admitted only those women who could prove lineal descent from American patriots who actively contributed to the cause of the American Revolution. Acceptable ancestors were mostly men, including members of the Continental Army, civil officers, and the signers of the Declaration of Independence, but the descendants of women who "rendered material aid to the cause of independence" or served as nurses were also encouraged to apply.[12] The DAR's relative exclusivity and prestige as well as a growing public interest in genealogy around 1900 proved powerful recruiting tools among America's white middle and upper classes. By 1915 the DAR boasted a membership of almost 100,000, with more than 1,500 chapters in all forty-eight states and several other countries. These numbers dwarfed similar ancestral women's organizations such as the Colonial Dames, whose focus on commemorating colonial America and more stringent membership requirements increased its exclusivity but diminished its influence. The DAR's membership also surpassed that of the United Daughters of the Confederacy, a southern women's organization that was founded in 1894 to commemorate the former Confederacy and its fallen heroes. By the late 1920s the Daughters of the American Revolution had almost 200,000 dues-paying members, which made it the country's largest patriotic women's organization.[13]

The DAR's organizational structure served to create a very homogeneous membership roster, which was composed almost exclusively of white middle-class Protestants. Led by a national Board of Management, it was a highly centralized association, although chapters and state organizations were granted considerable autonomy. The board was composed of the president general, national officers such as the historian general, and state regents for each state or territory. The board admitted new members, granted charters to new chapters, and determined the national organization's policies, which it put to a vote before the chapter regents and other delegates at the DAR's annual Continental Congress in Washington, DC. None of these various officers received a salary; for that reason only women of means could afford to accept such positions. The DAR's high dues and initiation fees had a similarly selective impact on the composition of the rank and file. Especially the organization's leadership posts were extremely time-consuming and required a high level of education and administrative experience. Most members had completed high school, and a considerable number held college degrees. After marriage, they focused on rearing their children and could afford to stay at home because many of them were married to affluent businessmen, politicians, or educators. The Daughters clearly moved within privileged social circles and regarded themselves as part of America's female elite.[14]

Although the DAR's founding generation included a number of liberal clubwomen, the organization became increasingly conservative after 1914. This development was the result of a conspicuous ideological shift during World War I. In its early years, the Daughters supported many campaigns associated with Progressivism, including settlement houses and laws restricting child labor. But in the wake of the Great War, the organization experienced a process of radicalization that led its leaders to strongly support military preparedness and antiradicalism while adamantly opposing government intervention on behalf of the downtrodden. For the rest of the twentieth century the DAR warned that socialism and communism would destroy the American nation, a fear that influenced the Daughters' views on virtually every aspect related to their activism, including memory, immigration, and feminism.[15] In a similar fashion, reflecting the organiza-

Figure I.1. Members of the Daughters of the American Revolution in front of DAR headquarters, 1919. Courtesy of Library of Congress Prints and Photographs Division, Harris & Ewing Collection, LC-H261-30167.

tion's emphasis on Republican Motherhood and true womanhood, many members opposed the woman suffrage movement, rejecting claims that the right to vote constituted a form of female empowerment. They also scoffed at the New Woman, denouncing her independence and seemingly unfeminine style and manners as unpatriotic and selfish. Even after World War II, the Daughters continued to oppose feminist calls for full gender equality.

While this study attempts to do justice to the DAR's long and complex history, it focuses on the Daughters' most visible commemorative activities between 1890 and 1945, when the organization was most influential. Chapter 1 examines the DAR's gendered interpretations of patriotism and its efforts to commemorate the American Revolution. It explores the organization's turn toward antiradicalism in the post–World War I era and analyzes its impact on their remembrance of colonial and Revolutionary America in the interwar period. Although the Daughters countered male-centered histories of the War of Independence by insisting that Revolutionary women had been as heroic as men, they generally affirmed traditional gender dichotomies and used memory to defend gender hierarchies in the present. In the Daughters' tales about the past, female patriots neither abandoned their feminine identity nor questioned their relative lack of political power in the new nation, remaining mere supporters of their husbands. Men, moreover, remained more prominent in DAR commemorations, which praised martial masculinity and suggested that male Revolutionaries were the real agents of historical change. The Daughters thus inadvertently helped to perpetuate the one-sided accounts of America's struggle for independence they had pledged to revise, and they argued that any challenge to such time-honored gender dichotomies would disrupt the American nation.

Chapter 2 scrutinizes the efforts of the DAR in the Midwest and West to commemorate western expansion during the antebellum era. It reveals that the organization used the memory of western pioneers and explorers to maintain strict racial boundaries of national inclusion while simultaneously upholding traditional gender binaries within white America. Most of the DAR's activism in the Midwest and West revolved around marking the trails that pioneer families and explorers used to reach the region prior to the Civil War. But in stark contrast to the remembrance of the American Revolution, women were conspicuously absent from the tales the Daughters offered prior to the 1920s. Western Daughters highlighted primarily the heroic accomplishments of pioneer men, whom they regarded as masculine warriors for their violent resistance against Native Americans. Only the organization's post–World War I Madonna of the Trail campaign focused on the memory of pioneer mothers, but as with the Revolution, female pioneers' heroic determination was interpreted as part and parcel of women's natural instincts as wives and mothers. In the end, the Daughters primarily praised white men as advance guards of white civilization and US nation-building, much of which revolved around violently subduing America's Indigenous population.

Chapter 3 presents the organization's peculiar fascination with American Indians and its various efforts to commemorate white-Indian friendship and Indian patriotism. It also looks at the close connections between the Daughters' interpretations of Native peoples' past and the DAR's attempts to improve Indians' lives in the present. By sanitizing and romanticizing America's history of racial violence and colonial conquest, the Daughters justified white nation-building and white supremacy while further consolidating notions of Anglo-Saxon whiteness. Daughters across the nation commemorated what they regarded as cordial collaboration between the two groups, loyal Indian support during America's wars, and Indians' ostensible willingness to cede their ancestral homelands to the United States. Native warriors were most prominent in the DAR's cheerful reading of the Indigenous past, but Indian women also played an important role because they were believed to have an inherent propensity to seek interracial friendship and to assist white male nation-builders. This tendency to distort or ignore the history of racist subjugation while nostalgically exoticizing Indian culture allowed the Daughters to become seemingly genuine supporters of Indian welfare, education, and citizenship in the present.

Chapter 4 analyzes the ways the DAR ignored African American citizens and their contributions to US nation-building in the context of Civil War memory as well as the fears of racial intermixture harbored by its members. It examines the Daughters' efforts to "Americanize" new immigrants and their excessive admiration for "racially pure" Appalachian mountaineers. It also gives a brief account of the infamous 1939 controversy over black opera singer Marian Anderson's request to perform in the DAR's concert hall in Washington, DC. In contrast to the organization's fascination with Indians, African Americans remained virtually invisible in its stories about the nation's past. This deliberate amnesia, together with their opposition to racially "suspect" immigrants, support for restrictive immigration legislation, and profuse praise for Anglo-Saxon mountaineers, reflects a deeply felt conviction that patriotism and whiteness were inextricably intertwined. From the DAR's perspective, the United States was a white nation whose racial integrity had to be preserved.

To shed light on the continuities and discontinuities in the Daughters' interpretations of the nation and its past, the book's final chapter and the conclusion explore the organization's post–World War II history, a period that saw major challenges to its conservative vision of America's "imagined community." Despite these challenges, the DAR's views on race, immigration, gender, and the nation's past remained virtually unchanged. The Daughters continued to embrace ethnic nationalism, opposing racial integration and liberalization of America's immigration laws, and upheld the very same ideals of femininity and masculinity they had emphasized prior to 1945. Against the backdrop of these continuities, it was not surprising that the organization regarded the social movements of the 1960s, including the civil rights movement, the anti–Vietnam War movement, and Second Wave feminism, as a grave danger to the nation. Although the DAR began to admit black members in 1977 and finally acknowledged African Americans' patriotic contributions to American independence in the 1980s, its public rhetoric of civic tolerance frequently belied the DAR's conservative views on race and gender. In the twenty-first century the organization continues to attract many new members including a number of black women, which is likely the result of its more democratic membership policy and increasingly egalitarian perspective on America's cultural memory. Yet tensions between civic and ethnic nationalism, while less visible, remain and are unlikely to dissipate in the years to come.

In each chapter, theoretical insights from political science, sociology, cultural studies, and gender studies help in delineating the complex interconnections of nationalism, race, gender, and memory in the DAR's activism. Although scholars of nationalism continue to debate its origin, definition, and evolution, this study draws on some of their key findings. Nationalists generally claim that a unique and sovereign nation exists, that its members have a common destiny as well as a national homeland, and that the nation trumps all other collective and individual loyalties. Although the nation is an imagined community that is actively constructed by various elite and non-elite groups, people come to believe in its existence because constant iterations of this construct permeate public discourse as well as their daily lives. Convinced that the nation is real, its members constantly debate the question of who belongs to it and who does not. Scholars have long differentiated between civic and ethnic nationalism to analyze the inclusionary and exclusionary functions of nationalist ideologies. In terms of civic nationalism, people are accepted as members of the nation because they pledge allegiance to its political institutions and values regardless of their perceived race or ancestry. In the case of ethnic nationalism, membership qualifications are tied to a specific racialized ancestry and notions of national culture that are purportedly shared by all members of the nation. Consequently, even if people who are considered an alien race have formal citizenship, they are not necessarily deemed legitimate members of the national community.[16] Critics of this analytical framework have faulted its dichotomous perspective, arguing that ancestry, while certainly overlapping with race, can also connote kinship hierarchies that do not necessarily preclude national membership. These cautionary exhortations are important, not least when studying the DAR, an organization that put immense emphasis on genealogy. However, the analytical categories of civic and ethnic nationalism continue to have much explanatory value since US nationalist ideology has constantly veered between these two poles in ambiguous and often contradictory ways.[17]

The Daughters of the American Revolution insisted that the United States was a unique nation that deserved undivided loyalty from its members. They regarded themselves and other white middle-class Protestants who could trace their ancestry to the nation's founding as the only true Americans and felt that they had an obligation to inculcate patriotism in fellow citizens and noncitizens. Given this idealization of and belief in white supremacy, the DAR's members were staunch ethnic nationalists who regarded African Americans and most other nonwhite people as a danger to the nation's racial purity. Despite this strong commitment to ethnic nationalism, the organization occasionally voiced support for civic nationalism, suggesting that immigrants and even American Indians could become members of the nation if they adopted the same political and cultural values that the Daughters deemed so essential to national unity. Ultimately, though, the DAR positioned itself squarely in the ethnic nationalist camp.

If nationalism is a relational construct intertwined with race, it is similarly entangled with gender, a term that can be defined as a fluctuating process through which dichotomous views of masculinity and femininity are performatively produced, practiced, and naturalized as stable and fixed.[18] The nation tends to be imagined as a brotherhood of heterosexual men who frequently incorporate women into national discourse as potent patriotic symbols but simultaneously restrict their active participation in nation-building. More importantly, nationalism depends on and perpetuates gender difference. National membership frequently is limited to purportedly appropriate notions of femininity and masculinity, which are deemed crucial to national unity and stability. Strengthening the idea of fixed gender identities also helps nationalism to be perceived as similarly stable, natural, and unchanging. In nationalist discourses of the nineteenth and twentieth centuries, three major themes contributed to this symbiotic process of naturalization: heroism, motherhood, and the family. Manly warrior heroes had long been hailed as embodiments of strong masculinity, but by the early nineteenth century, their heroism was increasingly linked to the willingness to sacrifice their lives for the nation.[19] Mothers also became crucial to such gendered interpretations of nationalism. Men regarded women's ability to bear children and inculcate them with the nation's norms and values as a patriotic service; they praised women as the biological and cultural reproducers of the nation while at the same time expecting them to accept a subordinate position. Ideals of the patriarchal family cemented such nationalized gender dichotomies. Nationalists portrayed the family as both the smallest unit of and a metaphor for the nation. In this interpretation, men's dominance over women and children as their providers and protectors was portrayed as a natural hierarchy that symbolized social and political hierarchies within the nation. Women's roles as obedient wives and mothers were not only regarded as a reflection of a seemingly natural gender order but also as essential to national cohesion.[20] Thus, nationalism shaped people's political identities but also helped regulate gender identities and gender relations.

The DAR's gendered interpretations of the nation were highly ambiguous, since they deliberately challenged but simultaneously helped to perpetuate gender difference and male privilege. The founding of the DAR itself was a form of political protest that questioned men's patriotic monopoly, and the organization's insistence that women needed to play a key role in inculcating patriotism reflected the same ideological thrust. As Francesca Morgan has rightly argued, the Daughters and other female nationalists created a "self-consciously women-centered nationalism" that actively countered men's efforts to reduce women to passive nationalist symbols and pushed the boundaries of "woman's sphere."[21] Yet, the DAR's challenge to male-centered nationalism revolved around a staunch belief in nineteenth-century notions of gender difference and the fear that any challenge to the hierarchies entailed by this belief would disrupt the nation's patriotic equilibrium. The DAR thus fully embraced the idea that women were the biological and cultural reproducers of the nation who proved their loyalty by raising virtuous citizens and accepting the gendered status quo.

Historical memory plays a crucial role in the construction and naturalization of race, gender, and the nation. It can be understood as selective interpretations of the past that shape and frame individual and collective identities, norms, and values in the present. Nationalists generally use it to create unity and solidarity, claiming that the nation's populace has a common past and a common destiny. Despite such efforts to downplay difference and conflict, there are multiple memories that are constantly debated, contested, and reinterpreted, reflecting power struggles among various elite groups and institutions that vie for political and cultural authority.[22]

Similarly important in this struggle to determine the true version of the nation's past, nationalists cannot simply expect the masses to accept their particular interpretations. Instead, they need to incorporate competing collective memories that are circulating in vernacular culture to succeed in their efforts to strengthen people's allegiance to the nation. Historians are therefore confronted with the dual challenge of reconstructing elite groups' attempts to create a collective national memory while trying to comprehend, in the words of Alon Confino, "how the nation-state came to be a vernacular memory."[23]

Egyptologist Jan Assmann's conceptual distinction between "communicative memory" and "cultural memory" can help in comprehending the tensions and multiple interconnections between elite and vernacular memories of the nation. "Communicative memory" stands for "living memory," which is passed on orally within families or towns as part of everyday life; it reaches back only eighty to one hundred years and vanishes with the death of the last person who remembers the past. Cultural memory, by contrast, is a formalized and lasting form of collective memory. It is deliberately preserved by experts and elite groups such as politicians, historians, and the DAR to strengthen collective identities in the present through monuments, narratives about the past, and commemorative rituals. These two forms of memory are far from dichotomous or static. Instead, they are inextricably entangled because the memories of families, towns, regions, and the nation tend to be connected with and are fused into what is presented as the coherent collective memory of one single imagined community. Similarly, although there might be a dominant cultural memory in society, there are always competing cultural memories as well as multiple communicative memories that become part of a dynamic process through which elite and non-elite groups strive to consolidate or to attain cultural, social, and political power. Consequently, elites have to draw on the various forms of vernacular communicative memory that exist in society to make the nation's cultural memory meaningful, but local communities' living memories can also become the wellspring of a lasting cultural memory.[24]

Especially between 1890 and the 1940s, the Daughters used historical memory as a key means not only to foster citizens' and non-citizens' patriotism but also to convince them as well as the Daughters themselves that the nation's stability depended on appropriate gender roles and rigid gender hierarchies. As with its nationalist ideology, the DAR's commemorative messages were ambivalent. The organization questioned white men's preeminence in traditional accounts of US history and argued that the past could not be fully comprehended if women were excluded. Still, the Daughters' countless monuments, memorial markers, patriotic ceremonies, and publications buttressed rather than challenged entrenched gender hierarchies in the present. The DAR claimed only an auxiliary role for women in US nation-building and exhorted female citizens to heed their ancestors' modest example. More importantly, although the DAR's raison d'être purportedly centered on women, the organization gave much more room to the memory of heroic men and in doing so reinforced the idea that male soldiers, generals, explorers, and pioneers were the true agents of national progress.

With regard to patriotic memory and race, the DAR was less equivocal than it was toward gender. Until the 1980s, the Daughters' interpretations of the nation's past completely ignored African Americans. Combined with the organization's focus on the memory of white soldiers' valor, this deliberate amnesia helped its leadership soothe sectional tensions among its members, a considerable number of whom were southerners who glorified the Confederate States of America. Unlike black citizens, American Indians actually received much praise from the Daughters and could even attain heroic status if they proved their loyalty toward the nation. However, the organization's interpretations of Indigenous peoples' past and present ultimately remained paternalistic affirmations of white superiority. The DAR's keen interest in Americanizing immigrants during the first four decades of its existence also reveals much about the members' racialized understanding of memory and nationalism, since they believed that white old-stock citizens such as the white mountaineers of Appalachia had a seemingly inborn love of country that was passed on to succeeding generations through ancestry and communicative memory. Since new immigrants from southern and eastern Europe were believed to lack this racial capacity for patriotism, the DAR deemed it crucial to familiarize them with the cultural memory of the nation so that they might possibly be transformed into loyal citizens.

The Daughters' memorial campaigns are also revealing because they testify to the complex dialogue between nationalized communicative and cultural memory in the organization's attempts to make the abstract idea of the nation seem real and relevant. For DAR members themselves, the communicative memory of the American Revolution that had been passed on within their families and local communities strengthened their patriotic pride and confirmed their belief that they were part of an Anglo-Saxon elite that had a particular duty to inculcate patriotism in others. They also drew on such family memories to create the heroic cultural memory that they believed would boost people's allegiance to the nation, recording the reminiscences of their mothers and grandmothers, naming chapters after patriotic ancestors, and honoring Real Daughters, DAR members whose fathers had actually fought in the War of Independence. The remembrance of western pioneers reflected the same powerful interrelationship. Since midwestern and western Daughters could not establish direct commemorative links between the American Revolution and their local communities, they used the history of western expansion to connect their own and other citizens' communicative memories to white America's cultural memory. The DAR also drew on the long-ignored communicative memories of aging pioneers and other local residents to reconstruct what they interpreted as a seamless story of heroic nation-building. Tens of thousands of citizens witnessed the ritualized dedication ceremonies the Daughters staged as the hundreds of monuments and markers were placed along old pioneer trails. These memorials made nationalism meaningful because local people's family histories were presented as crucial building blocks of the nation's history. A closer look at the organization's memorial campaigns thus sheds light on the intricate process through which white female elites tried to make the nation a vernacular memory. Studying these campaigns also reveals that it took a complex dialogue between communicative and cultural memory to make the nation and accompanying notions of gender and race seem stable, natural, and unchanging.

It is difficult to measure the impact of the DAR's nationalist activism, let alone gauge to what degree citizens and noncitizens fully accepted the messages the organization wanted to convey in its commemorative campaigns. Especially prior to the 1940s, the Daughters did expose hundreds of thousands of people to their gendered and racialized ideas about national loyalty, including members of the youth auxiliary Children of the American Revolution and generations of students who participated in their essay contests and later in their national Good Citizenship campaigns, as well as hundreds of white, Indian, and immigrant communities. Many of the organization's commemorative rituals would not have been possible without the cooperation of local communities, suggesting that the Daughters confirmed and strengthened existing ideas about gender, race, and the nation among many white citizens. Some Indians and immigrants might have been affected by the idea of friendship and Americanization, but it is conceivable and even likely that many others welcomed the DAR's attention and support while having no qualms about dividing their loyalties between tribal nations, foreign nations, and the United States. Although it is hard to assess people's responses to the Daughters' campaigns, DAR members certainly reinforced their own allegiance toward the nation as well as the conviction that white Anglo-Saxon Protestants like themselves should police its boundaries.

1

"Woman Proved Herself Man's Helpmate"

Nationalism, Gender, and the Memory of the American Revolution

In a letter to the editors of the *Washington Post* that appeared on July 12, 1890, Mary S. Lockwood vented her indignation against the Sons of the American Revolution (SAR), a patriotic organization that had been founded fifteen months earlier. Commenting on a recent SAR meeting in Washington, DC, Lockwood lamented that the Sons commemorated "a one-sided heroism" that left no room for women in their praise of Revolutionary patriots. She asked why "the patriotism of the country" was not "broad enough to take women in, too" and opined that it was "an opportune time to bring forward some of the women of '76 before the sires" became "puffed up by vain glory." She then recounted the story of Hannah Arnett, who in 1776 shamed her husband and other men who had agreed to side with the British rather than fight for the newly founded United States. According to Lockwood, Arnett denounced them as unmanly traitors who cowardly kissed "'the feet that have trampled upon us.'" This "leaven of courage, manliness and resolution," Lockwood wrote, eventually resolved the men "to spurn the offered amnesty" and to take "a solemn oath to stand by their country through good days and bad, until freedom was written over the face of this fair land." Lockwood was incensed over the fact that the valorous service of these male patriots was so widely remembered while the memory of Hannah Arnett had unjustly faded into oblivion.[1]

Lockwood's angry indictment articulated the sentiment of a small group of Washington's white middle-class clubwomen who resented the general disregard for women's patriotic contributions to the American Revolution and the SAR's decision to bar female members during its first national meeting in Louisville, Kentucky, in April 1890. Two of these women, Eugenia Washington and Flora Adams Darling, had already considered founding a rival organization that would give the women of the American Revolution their due, and they heartily applauded Lockwood's letter. While corresponding with Lockwood about their previous plan, they received unexpected assistance from William O. McDowell, a co-founder of the SAR, who supported female membership. In reaction to Lockwood's *Washington Post* letter, he issued a public call in the same newspaper on July 21, 1890, to form a National Society of the Daughters of the American Revolution. A number of women, among them Eugenia Washington and another clubwoman named Ellen Hardin Walworth, responded to McDowell's call and met to discuss further steps. To attract more members, Washington placed another call for organization in the *Post* on August 17, and several hundred responded. After drawing up a constitution with the help of McDowell, a group of eleven women and four men met at the home of Mary Lockwood on October 11, 1890, to establish the National Society Daughters of the American Revolution (DAR).[2]

The DAR's founding opened a new chapter in the history of white women's relationship to US nationalism and their role in the construction and dissemination of patriotic memory. The DAR's efforts to rescue from oblivion the memory of white women's heroic contributions to the American Revolution were just as groundbreaking as their assertion of female agency in American nation-building. Yet, their gendered memorialization of the revolutionary era was fraught with ambiguity. A closer look at the Daughters' activities reveals a paradox: although the DAR deliberately countered male-centered accounts of the War of Independence, insisting that Revolutionary women had been as heroic as men, it generally affirmed entrenched gender hierarchies and used memory to uphold them. In the Daughters' tales about the past, female patriots neither abandoned their feminine identity nor questioned their relative lack of political power in the new nation. White men, moreover, remained more prominent in DAR commemorations, which praised martial masculinity and suggested that male Revolutionaries were the real agents of historical change. Since such stories about the Revolution's manly men tended to outnumber stories about women and reached larger audiences, the Daughters inadvertently helped to perpetuate the one-sided accounts of America's struggle for independence they had pledged to revise.

World War I became a watershed moment in the DAR's nationalist activism because the conflict exacerbated dichotomous interpretations of gender and the nation. Like other organizations that embraced antiradicalism during and after the Great War, the Daughters warned of the pernicious impact of "un-American" ideologies, including socialism, feminism, and pacifism. In particular their dire predictions that socialism and feminism would destroy the nation by undermining traditional notions of femininity and the family reflected strongly held beliefs in established gender binaries without which America was believed to be doomed. These fears also affected the Daughters' commemoration of colonial America and the American Revolution in the 1920s and 1930s. Members fiercely resisted attempts to question the Revolutionary generation's heroism or to dismiss its significance because they believed that both interpretations would play into the hands of un-American radicals. Traditional notions of martial masculinity were crucial elements of their interpretations of the past, although the Daughters continued to praise heroic women as an ideological antidote to the menace of feminism and socialism.

Although the DAR's nationalist activism continued to reach many Americans in the 1930s, including hundreds of thousands of students who entered into the DAR's newly established Good Citizenship competitions, the DAR's influence on the cultural memory of the American Revolution gradually dwindled in the interwar period. Due to a combination of criticism of the organization, the growing importance of the federal government in commemorating the American past, and the increasingly difficult challenge to make meaningful connections between the communicative memory and cultural memory of the Revolution, their remembrance of colonial America took less conspicuous forms, was largely confined to DAR circles, and generally lacked the impact of previous campaigns. By the end of World War II, the Daughters were less visible than they had been in the early twentieth century, but their activism had left a lasting imprint on the memory of the War of Independence and conservative interpretations of what it meant to be American.

Roots: Memory, Nationalism, and Women's Activism in the Nineteenth Century

The DAR's goal to strengthen people's allegiance to the United States by commemorating the American struggle for independence while simultaneously highlighting women's heroic contributions to that struggle can be seen as the result of two converging developments that first manifested in the late 1860s and gained momentum during the 1870s and 1880s. The first of these developments was the increasing importance of patriotic memory; the other was the emergence of women's sustained social and political activism.

While the patriotic remembrance of the American Revolution might be expected to have been an essential ingredient of US nation-building in the nineteenth century, neither the past nor patriotism played a significant role in American citizens' lives prior to 1861. For much of the period between the Revolution and the Civil War, the mindset of most Americans, in the words of Michael Kammen, was one of "simplistic present-mindedness and future orientation."[3] Focused on mobility and advancement in a rapidly expanding nation and unfettered by sharply defined social hierarchies or traditions of pedigree, most Americans trusted that their country's progress would continue indefinitely. The past seemed utterly irrelevant in their efforts to actively shape the future. Consequently, US history was rarely taught in the nation's schools, and historic sites were seldom considered important enough to be preserved. There was an unspoken understanding that in a republic of virtuous citizens, the people themselves should commemorate the history they deemed significant.[4]

Between 1776 and 1861, a few citizens actually did dwell on the past, striving above all to salvage the memory of the American Revolution through art, fictional and nonfictional writings, and celebrations of historical anniversaries. Yet the purpose of such forms of commemoration largely tended to revolve around fostering morality rather than patriotic remembrance. Of course, the War of Independence did become an important symbol of US nationalism, and subsequent wars fired the country's patriotism. But the observance of the Fourth of July and similar patriotic holidays was rather inconsistent, and the memory of America's military heroes, with the exception of George Washington, tended to be short-lived. Even the national flag, which had become an omnipresent symbol of the United States by the late nineteenth century, was rarely on public display prior to the 1860s. Most US citizens felt stronger allegiances to their towns, states, or regions than to the abstract concept of the nation, and they were suspicious of giving the federal government too much political power. Thus, prior to the early 1860s, notions of a common past and loyalty toward the United States were in an inchoate state, and the rare efforts of private groups to strengthen patriotic memory were characterized by disagreement and fragmentation.[5]

Only the Civil War fundamentally changed Americans' relation to their nation and its past, although the war's effects would not become fully visible until the late nineteenth century. Southern secession and the subsequent founding of the Confederate States of America forced both sides to ponder the importance of national loyalties and the role of a common past in the process of fostering such loyalties. The expansion of federal power during the war also served to erode some of the opposition to the idea that the nation-state could play a larger role in citizens' lives. After the South's defeat, the victorious Union was compelled to translate its particular vision of the nation into a symbol that would be meaningful to all Americans. At the same time, northerners and southerners had to come to terms with a bloody conflict that had killed almost 800,000 people. Despite the ambiguous and conflicting memories that were subsequently constructed, the nation's past took on unprecedented importance during the postwar period and became the foundation of citizens' allegiance to the United States in the twentieth century. Memorial Day was probably one of the most important building blocks in this process. It began shortly after the Civil War as part of localized commemorative campaigns that allowed both sides to honor and grieve for their fallen soldiers. By 1900 the holiday had become a ritualized medium of national reconciliation and southern pride that was observed across the country.[6]

The Civil War also fostered patriotic memory because the brutal conflict and its legacy called into question the notion that America's progress would continue indefinitely. After four years of carnage, a growing number of citizens nostalgically looked back at the colonial period and the American Revolution, believing that those times had been more amicable and virtuous than the present. The economic depression of the 1870s further eroded people's confidence in the traditional mantra of progress. The various anniversaries of revolutionary events that were observed during this decade became a final source of inspiration for white middle-class organizations' commemorative activism. The centennial of American independence in 1876 in particular reflected the growing importance of memory and its patriotic uses. In the wake of the popular celebrations, white citizens established numerous historical societies as well as ancestral patriotic organizations such as the Sons of Revolutionary Sires, the predecessor of the SAR, to honor the Revolution's heroes. By the early 1880s, moreover, there was an increasing fascination with all things colonial, including antique furniture, silver, and other artifacts, that became a nationwide craze in the following decade. Those who had proposed to commemorate Revolutionary patriots and historic spots were no longer regarded as backward-looking eccentrics but could proudly regard their efforts as a service to the nation. Despite these encouraging developments, patriotic memory had not yet become part of the cultural mainstream, and the US government continued to show little interest in the country's past, leaving private middle-class organizations virtually free rein to shape the nation's cultural memory.[7]

White elite women played a significant role in these various movements to keep alive the memory of the American past.[8] Especially in the South, dozens of Ladies' Memorial Associations spearheaded campaigns to commemorate the former Confederacy and its fallen heroes. Initially regarding the remembrance of the Civil War as a social obligation and as a continuation of their loyal service during the war, southern white women founded Ladies' Memorial Associations as early as 1865 and quickly shifted the focus from grieving to celebrating Confederate soldiers' valor. These campaigns were the first public enunciations of the Lost Cause ideology, which reinterpreted the Confederacy's defeat as an unrecognized victory. Through dedicated fundraising and lobbying campaigns around 1900, these elite women were able to shape the content and form of Confederate memory. Although they contributed to the commemorative dominance of the male warrior hero, they carved out a new space for themselves in the public sphere and repositioned women's roles vis-à-vis men and the nation. The founding of the United Daughters of the Confederacy in 1894 consolidated white women's cultural authority in southern society. While northern women were not as quick to organize as their southern sisters, they also engaged in campaigns to keep alive the memory of the Civil War in the auxiliaries of male veterans' organizations, among them the Woman's Relief Corps and the Ladies of the Grand Army of the Republic, both of which were founded in the 1880s.[9]

Southern women's assertive role in the memorialization of the Civil War reflected and bolstered a new phase of female social, cultural, and political activism that also began in the 1860s and 1870s. The roots of such activism can be traced to the first three decades of the nineteenth century. Although most of these female activists accepted prevailing notions of true womanhood, numerous women used that ideology to expand their roles in society. In particular, they drew on dominant assumptions about women's seemingly inherent compassion and moral superiority over men to argue that woman's sphere extended to virtually all aspects of society affecting women and children. As a result, antebellum America saw the proliferation of thousands of local, regional, and national women's associations that worked diligently for moral reform, temperance, and the abolition of slavery. These efforts allowed women to become active outside the home, to exercise rights that were denied them as wives, to engage in political activities such as lobbying and petitioning, and to assume leadership positions in a world that had traditionally been led by men. Just as important, it made them keenly aware of their shared identities as women and the limitations that were placed upon them as a group. Especially their involvement in the abolitionist movement reminded them of these limitations and led some women to call not just for an extension of a woman's sphere but for women's civil rights. On the eve of the Civil War, then, a large number of white female citizens argued that women's unique feminine qualities gave them the right to become a moral compass of society through an extension of the domestic sphere. A smaller number of female activists felt that while women's moral superiority made them different from men, they deserved the same rights that male citizens claimed as their prerogative.[10]

Although the Civil War did little to change the idea of separate gender spheres, it served as a significant catalyst in further extending women's influence and ushered in a new phase of female activism. During the war, the widespread efforts of the Union and the Confederacy to instill loyalty allowed many northern and southern women to demonstrate their patriotism by serving as war nurses or by organizing local relief efforts. As in the past, they entered the public sphere by cloaking their work in the ideology of true womanhood and related assumptions about women's sense of nurturing and propensity toward selfless service. After the war, many women built on those gains by combining such gendered stereotypes with novel social science approaches to society that among other things enabled them to enter medical fields that had long been male domains. The Civil War also set precedents by forcing student-starved colleges to enroll women, a trend that led to the founding of women's colleges and coeducational institutions of higher learning after 1865. In the following decades, many of these colleges' graduates joined the ranks of newly established women's associations and contributed to their successes. The postwar movement for woman suffrage, too, gained new momentum. As a result, in 1869 the two activists Elizabeth Cady Stanton and Susan B. Anthony created the National Woman Suffrage Association, which in 1890 merged with the rival American Women's Suffrage Association into the National American Woman Suffrage Association. Most female citizens continued to reject the militant idea of gender equality, but the almost two million women who had become part of the women's club movement by the late 1880s redefined the idea of "woman's sphere" and appeared eager to further challenge traditional gender boundaries in the future.[11]

Gendering Nationalism and Memory: The DAR and Its Goals

Only the growing importance of patriotic memory and the flourishing of women's activism in the late nineteenth century created the preconditions for the unparalleled type of organization that the founders of the Daughters of the American Revolution established. Like the Ladies' Memorial Associations and the Ladies of the Grand Army of the Republic, the DAR's founders felt that women had a right and an obligation to keep alive the memory of the American past and to strengthen people's national loyalty. But unlike these sectional organizations, the DAR had a vision to bolster the patriotism of the entire nation through the unifying cultural memory of the American Revolution. The founders' decision to counter the SAR's snub with an all-female rival organization as well as their forceful argument about women's important role in the War of Independence demonstrated white clubwomen's growing self-confidence as well as their organizational and political skills. The DAR's founders were battle-hardened veterans of the clubwomen's movement and applied their experiences to this new type of patriotic women's association. Mary Lockwood, for instance, had been a member of the Woman's Relief Corps and led a temperance society in Washington, DC. Mary Desha, who hailed from Kentucky, worked as a clerk in the US Department of the Interior and had served as a nurse in the Confederate Army during the Civil War. Ellen Hardin Walworth was the most highly educated of the founders, having earned a law degree from New York University before securing an administrative position with the US government.[12] The DAR's founders thus benefited from traditions of women's cultural, social, and political activism, but they went beyond that activism by creating a new type of national organization that was meant to demonstrate white elite women's profound allegiance to the United States of the past and the present.

The DAR's relative exclusivity, its deliberate efforts to recruit national female leaders who were associated with America's political elite, and the growing popularity of genealogy around 1900 made DAR membership a much-coveted badge of social distinction among America's white middle and upper classes. The prestige associated with its admittance of only descendants of patriots who had contributed to the success of the American Revolution was enhanced by the DAR's ability to recruit the wives of prominent politicians for the office of president general. The DAR's first president general was Caroline Scott Harrison, the wife of President Benjamin Harrison. She was followed by Letitia Green Stevenson, the wife of Vice President Adlai E. Stevenson during the administration of Grover Cleveland. Their names lent an enormous public status to the new organization.[13] The presidential prestige of Caroline Harrison and Letitia Stevenson lured thousands of women to join the new organization, as many of them drew vicarious pleasure from being associated with such prominent names. During her tenure, Harrison initiated White House receptions during the Daughters' annual meeting in Washington, DC, allowing DAR delegates to actually shake hands with the president of the United States. Such elitist rituals were an important part of the DAR's appeal, but the growing fascination with the memory of colonial America and a similarly widespread obsession with genealogy during the 1880s and 1890s also contributed to the organization's popularity. Especially elite women in the urban Northeast became fixated on their family trees, valuing it as an important means to enhance their social status. The Daughters, together with numerous other hereditary associations that were founded in the late nineteenth century, encouraged women to transform what had long been a private leisure activity into a public badge of honor that reassured old-stock Americans of their class and racial identity during an unsettling era of economic depression and large-scale immigration. As a result of its ability to serve various interests among white middle-class women, the DAR grew quickly, especially in the Northeast and Midwest, and soon surpassed the membership of the SAR.[14]

If the Daughters agreed that they were worthy representatives of American society's upper echelons, they also shared a general understanding that memory and patriotism were inextricably linked. From their perspective, knowing one's past was an essential ingredient of national progress and patriotism. Forcefully rejecting antebellum traditions of present-mindedness and future orientation, DAR leaders insisted that only the memory of the nation's ideals and accomplishments would enable Americans to understand the present and shape the future. Knowing and appreciating the accomplishments of America's heroes and heroines, moreover, would instill in citizens a desire to emulate their patriotic example. The Daughters generally believed that there was no more compelling inducement to develop lasting allegiance to the United States than studying its history and the patriotic contributions of one's ancestors to that history.[15] Their nationalist ideology thus revolved around the idea that America's citizens shared a common destiny that spanned past, present, and future, and they regarded the cultural memory of the nation's heroic past as a crucial element of their efforts to strengthen people's belief in this ostensibly seamless continuity.

Although a growing number of Americans agreed that the nation's past was worth commemorating, the DAR's patriotic vision occasionally clashed with nineteenth-century traditions of present-mindedness, leading many a commentator to criticize the new organization. During the first three decades of its existence, reporters, clergymen, and other pundits repeatedly accused the organization of being a "mutual admiration society."[16] Many of these critics suggested that the Daughters practiced a form of elitist "ancestor worship" that was a veiled attempt to gain social status. Disparagements of this nature were certainly not a complete fabrication, but the Daughters indignantly repudiated them. Reacting to critics' taunts in 1918, President General Anne Rogers Minor proclaimed that the DAR had not been "organized simply to scrape the moss from the monuments of the dead lest they be forgot." Instead, their efforts "to perpetuate the noble qualities" of their ancestors would help the DAR to exert a beneficial "educational, moral and spiritual influence" among its members and American citizens more generally.[17] The Daughters hoped that the ultimate result of their influence would be a more patriotic populace.

When it came to the question of who should instill patriotism, the organization's leaders argued that women, due to the nature of their sex, were best suited for this important task. National allegiance, in the words of Mrs. C. B. Bryant, who addressed fellow Daughters at the Nashville centennial of 1897, was as much "of the heart" as it was "impulse" and "nature," thus making patriotism essentially "a woman's virtue."[18] More importantly, the Daughters believed patriotism, the home, and the family to be inextricably intertwined, a belief that reflected the continuing cultural dominance of the nineteenth-century middle-class ideal of Republican Motherhood. Encapsulated in the DAR's motto "Home and Country," this ideal called upon mothers to devote their lives to raising virtuous citizens as a patriotic service to the nation.[19]

But in the years that followed the DAR's founding, the emergence of so-called New Women reflected a gradual erosion of this ideal. These college-educated and economically independent women tended to post-pone marriage and motherhood, engaged in seemingly unfeminine hobbies such as tennis, and preferred functional garb to the traditional, cumbersome dresses of middle-class women.[20] Although the DAR probably counted a number of such women among its members, the organization's leaders believed that the New Woman seriously jeopardized the United States. In 1895, during the Massachusetts DAR's annual meeting in Boston, the regent of the Old Colony Chapter spoke for many members when she declared, "In these days, when the new woman is so much to the front, with schemes of advancement and glorification of the sex, the Daughters of the American Revolution desire to stand proudly as representing the old woman . . . to whom home and country stand first."[21] A year later, President General Mary Foster made it clear that she fully concurred with this view at a celebration of George Washington's birthday when she insisted that only "old-fashioned womanliness" would enable women "to train the children in the ways of true patriotism." Foster said women should be "content to be loving wives and mothers, making in our homes loyal husbands, brothers, and citizens."[22] Sharing such convictions, many of the organization's officers accused self-assertive and ambitious New Women of unpatriotic selfishness. DAR leaders expressed the staunch belief that true patriotism required maternal self-sacrifice and republican virtue that could be transmitted to the next generation only by true women.[23]

The DAR's male supporters were probably just as disturbed by the challenges that the New Woman seemingly posed to American patriotism, as these men repeatedly confirmed the Daughters' belief that the nation was in dire need of loyal republican mothers. During DAR meetings, which frequently featured male speakers including historians, clergymen, military officers, and politicians, men praised the idea of Republican Motherhood and the Daughters for their ardent efforts to uphold it. Addressing the annual meeting of the Massachusetts DAR in 1900, the secretary of the city of Lowell's Board of Police, Joseph Smith, declared, "The mothers of America must plant in the hearts of their children the seeds of a genuine patriotism . . . for on the teachings of the American mother depends the perpetuity of the republic."[24]

Three years later, the pastor Sam W. Small reiterated the Daughters' arguments about women's crucial role in teaching patriotism when he addressed an audience at a welcome meeting for the DAR in the Georgia House of Representatives in Atlanta. Men, he said, could not be safely entrusted with raising America's future citizens, since their love of country was strongest only during times of war. Women's "patriotic fire," by contrast, would burn eternally and make them the ideal purveyors of the "supreme and nation-saving work" of instilling patriotism in American children.[25] Journalists sometimes echoed such gendered sentiments. In 1910 the editors of the *Washington Post* lauded the DAR for inspiring "the growing generation with every-day enduring patriotism" and asserted that women laid "the foundation stone of American character."[26] Although a younger generation of American women challenged traditional notions of femininity, the Daughters and their male supporters remained stalwart defenders of these traditions.

Heroines and Helpmates: Commemorating the Women of the Revolution

The DAR's commemoration of the American Revolution reflected the organization's interrelated goals of calling attention to the patriotic contributions of women to the struggle for independence while stressing the crucial role of wives and mothers in inculcating national loyalty. In the late nineteenth and early twentieth centuries, women were largely absent from academic histories and the public memory of the Revolutionary period. It was primarily due to the Daughters that such traditional male-centered accounts were challenged. In trying to salvage the history of revolutionary women, the DAR continued efforts that had begun before the Civil War. Between 1848 and 1850 the writer Elizabeth Ellet published the three-volume study *Women of the American Revolution,* which reconstructed women's experience through letters, diaries, and family memories. After the Union's victory in 1865, though, such books were hard to find. Most female historians worked in obscurity at the local level and wrote for publications in their hometowns, collected historical relics, or taught history in public schools. In the 1880s and 1890s, a few writers interspersed traditional tales of male heroism with glimpses into the lives of colonial women. But with the increasing professionalization of history in the late nineteenth century, accounts written by men entailed a bias against ostensibly unofficial sources that had been produced by women; such male historians' works contributed to the marginalization of female voices in academic as well as popular accounts of the Revolutionary era.[27]

The Daughters bemoaned the absence of narratives that acknowledged the courage of the women who had contributed to American independence, and they deliberately countered the dominance of male soldiers, generals, and presidents in the memory of the Revolution. History in general, they said, could not be fully comprehended if men were the sole protagonists. "To ignore the feminine element . . . in the study of history," DAR officer Janet Elizabeth Richards declared to fellow Daughters in 1892, "would be to sacrifice much of the true significance of the story—to miss the complete meaning of the whole."[28] Heeding Richards's words, many DAR chapters regularly devoted their monthly meetings to such topics as "The Influence of Women, or Woman in History" and "The Heroic Women of the American Revolution." Some chapters even staged colorful historical pageants for fellow Daughters and other clubwomen in which members personified the historically significant women they so admired. Meanwhile, the national DAR initiated essay competitions and awarded prizes to members for the best biographical sketches of female patriots.[29]

In the Daughters' historical imagination, most visible in the thousands of articles they wrote for the organization's magazine,[30] wives and mothers in particular became crucial pillars of American nation-building since they instilled virtue and patriotism in their children, sustained their husbands in times of crisis, and sometimes even took up arms to defend the nation. To highlight women's important auxiliary roles, the Daughters recounted countless intrepid deeds that had been or were believed to have been performed by women during the Revolutionary period; in effect, DAR members created a specifically female type of heroism that revolved around women's seemingly inherent instincts as wives and mothers.

Above all, the DAR praised colonial women's propensity for self-sacrifice and selfless service to others. In many of the stories the Daughters told in the DAR's own publications as well as in newspaper articles and letters to editors, women cared for the sick and the wounded during the War of Independence. In most stories, it was a wife's or a mother's love that compelled her to brave unspeakable dangers. In one often-repeated story, a woman named Kerenhappuch Turner rode on horseback from her home in Maryland to North Carolina to help her son, who had been severely wounded during the Battle of Guilford Court House. The Daughters also highlighted women's ability to endure tremendous privations in order to support their husbands and American independence. Numerous articles stressed women's heroic willingness to suffer silently in the face of poverty, social isolation, and British harassment.[31] In 1916 an article in the *DAR*

Magazine detailed the life of Hanna Morrill Whitcher, who followed her husband, Chase, into the wilderness of New Hampshire during the days of the Revolution and bore eleven children. The author asked her readers to consider Whitcher's tremendous courage and self-sacrifice. "Although *his* is the name recorded in the Revolutionary rolls," she asked, "is not the woman who endured hardships, poverty and loneliness in a mountain wilderness, that her husband might go into battle for the cause of freedom, as much of a heroine in her own way?"[32] Through such stories the DAR asked contemporary Americans not only to acknowledge colonial women's heroism and patriotism but also to reconsider the male-centeredness of heroism more generally.

Even though the Daughters asserted that Revolutionary women had proven their patriotism through virtuous support for their sons and husbands, they also praised deeds that went beyond traditional female duties, among them women's active role in anti-British boycotts and fundraising drives for the Continental Army. In addition, DAR publications lauded women's skills in maintaining and managing farms or plantations in the absence of men. Others received praise for destroying their own property, including houses and crops, before it could fall into enemy hands. Still other women were eulogized for braving many a danger when warning leaders of the Continental Army of imminent British attacks or serving as spies.[33]

During the American Revolution, a few women went even further, diverging from traditional gender roles by taking up arms to defend the United States. To the Daughters, these women were particularly praiseworthy since their stories clearly contradicted traditional accounts of the War of Independence. Some women were said to have donned the uniforms of their fathers or husbands to deceive and scare off approaching British troops.[34] Others were eulogized for taking over the positions of their fallen husbands on the battlefield. The memory of these intrepid female citizens lingered in many American communities during the nineteenth century, but the DAR's campaigns elevated them to a new level of patriotic fame. Margaret Corbin was singled out for special acclaim. From the DAR's inception, the organization repeatedly praised this unlikely heroine who in 1776, during the Battle of Fort Washington in New York, first assisted her husband, James, in cleaning and loading his gun before taking over his position after James was killed by British bullets. Eventually, Corbin was wounded by British gunfire but recovered from her injuries and later received a congressional pension for her military service. Especially to

Daughters in the state of New York, Margaret Corbin was a subject of local pride. As early as 1902, shortly after the 125th anniversary of the Battle of Fort Washington, the Mary Washington Colonial Chapter placed a bronze tablet on a wall in Holyrood Episcopal Church near the old fort to commemorate Corbin's bravery. Although the Daughters expressed so much admiration for Corbin, their stories made clear that it had been loyalty toward her husband and the nation, not a quest for gender equality, that motivated her to take on manly duties for the duration of the battle. From the DAR's perspective, Corbin abandoned neither the tenets of true womanhood nor the duties of Republican Motherhood.[35]

A similar interpretation could be seen in the commemoration of Deborah Sampson, who in 1782 disguised herself as a man and enlisted in the Continental Army as a common soldier under the name Robert Shurtliff. It was primarily because of the DAR's efforts that her memory lived on in the late nineteenth and early twentieth centuries. In 1897 DAR members from Sampson's hometown, Brockton, Massachusetts, formed the Deborah Sampson Chapter and placed bronze tablets on buildings in Brockton and in two other communities. And in the organization's monthly magazine, a number of articles sang her praises in subsequent years. Although the memory of Sampson could be interpreted as a challenge to the Daughters' efforts to affirm traditional gender dichotomies, those members who commemorated her were quick to point out that her military service had in no way undermined her feminine identity.[36]

Nancy Hart was another Revolutionary heroine the Daughters praised for her patriotism. Especially in her home state of Georgia, many members memorialized her. Hart was remembered for capturing a group of British soldiers who had invaded the Hart family's cabin and forced Nancy to cook dinner for them. She was lionized in local and regional lore for killing two of the attackers and holding off the rest at gunpoint until her husband arrived. Her memory lay dormant during the second half of the nineteenth century but was rekindled after the founding of DAR chapters in Georgia. In 1901 Georgian Daughters claimed they had visited Hart's grave, even though it remained unclear whether she had actually existed. By 1906 the state's Eberton Chapter had located and purchased the cabin that was believed to have been the Hart family's home. In the following years, Daughters produced historical tableaux as well as pageants that incorporated Hart's story into seemingly accurate portrayals of Georgia's history.[37] Daughters also wanted state officials to acknowledge Hart's bravery. In 1916 the organization's Piedmont Chapter presented the oil painting *Nancy Hart Capturing the Tories* to the state of Georgia, which duly accepted it and stated that it was "just and proper that the memory and deeds of one of Georgia's most noted Revolutionary citizens should be perpetuated by the State."[38] In the Daughters' accounts of the War of Independence, Hart became a shining symbol of heroic female patriotism in forcefully countering male-centered accounts of the American Revolution. At the same time, the DAR viewed Corbin, Sampson, and Hart as exemplars of traditional femininity.

But the DAR's research on Revolutionary heroines was more than a challenge to the dominant memory of American independence; it also became a powerful source of patriotic pride for many of the Daughters themselves because the history they uncovered was so closely linked to their own ancestry and the communicative memories that were shared within their families, hometowns, and states. Numerous members related stories from the Revolutionary period that their mothers, grandmothers, or other relatives had told them, and they did so at chapter meetings and in public speeches as well as articles they wrote for DAR publications. Such communicative memories had been told and retold within families since the Revolution but gained new significance once the Daughters attempted to make them part of America's national cultural memory. In many cases, these family memories were the only accounts of certain events that had survived for the historical record. This was especially true for the history of colonial America. Tracing their ancestry and researching the lives of their forebears thus took on powerful meanings that pertained to individual, regional, and national identities.[39]

The links between genealogy, memory, and nationalism in the DAR's efforts to highlight women's contributions to the American Revolution were probably most explicit in the selection of chapter names. Hundreds of chapters honored female patriots by adopting their names. Daughters in East Orange, New Jersey, organized the Hannah Arnett Chapter, while members in Massachusetts founded a Margaret Corbin Chapter. The women thus honored had lived in the towns or regions where the chapters that bore their names were organized, and in a number of cases, they were ancestors of the chapters' organizing regents or other founding members.[40] While establishing such personal connections to the past was particularly common in the Northeast, where most revolutionary events had taken place, Daughters across the country attempted to link their own family histories to those of their hometowns, their states, and the nation, strengthening the idea that white women had made crucial contributions to US nation-building.

The DAR's veneration for Real Daughters, the living daughters of men who fought the British in the War of Independence, served a similar purpose, as those members were regarded as embodiments of the heroic female spirit of 1776. Once the Daughters began to actively recruit such women, they were surprised to find out how many of them were still alive. By 1915 the organization had admitted 731 Real Daughters, 93 of whom were still alive. Many of them actively participated in local chapters' activities, and some even became charter members of new chapters. The DAR made strenuous efforts to find these elderly women, extensively reported about them, honored them with gold souvenir spoons, lobbied the US Congress to provide federal pensions for those who lived in poverty, and ultimately financed such pensions itself after its lobbying had proved unsuccessful.[41] The organization's resentment over this neglect was a result of the genuine belief that these female patriots were crucial links between the past and the present. For that reason, the Daughters considered their memories a precious good that needed to be recorded as long as they were still alive. Local chapters frequently asked them to share recollections of people who had been closer to or even part of the Revolution: their parents and grandparents. At a meeting of the Quaker City Chapter of Philadelphia in 1898, a silver-haired, 106-year-old Sarah Terry, whose father had fought in George Washington's army, was introduced as the chapter's newest member and promptly entertained fellow Daughters with stories her parents had told her. The daughters or granddaughters of these honorees frequently interviewed them and wrote down their reminiscences, which were subsequently read to local chapters or published in the DAR's monthly.[42]

Through these various means, the Daughters made clear their conviction that the women who participated in the Revolution had been just as heroic as the soldiers and generals of the Continental Army. In the words of DAR member Nellie V. Mark, these female patriots had demonstrated not only "passive physical courage," purportedly the only type of bravery that women could muster, but also the "active courage . . . of their convictions." Writing in 1899 in the organization's *American Monthly Magazine*, Mark confidently stated, "To whatever line of heroism men may point, there also we will almost surely find a woman deserving of the same cross of honor."[43]

Although the DAR paid tribute to Corbin, Sampson, Hart, and numerous other Revolutionary heroines, the organization did so within the confines of dominant gender hierarchies, which allowed women to be supporters but denied them the political rights that would have made them true members of the nation. In the Daughters' interpretation of the American Revolution, women remained men's auxiliaries and never abandoned their traditional feminine identity.

At a meeting of the DAR's Minneapolis Chapter in 1897, one of its members, Jennie J. B. Goodwin, spoke to this general interpretive framework when drawing the following conclusion about women's role during the Revolution: "So, in the great struggle of our country for freedom, woman proved herself man's helpmate, as God intended her to be. Not hers to bear the musket, wield the sword, or charge with bayonet upon the field of battle, but a true patriot, wife and mother was woman, who in thousands of instances . . . has performed astonishing deeds of heroism that have won for woman a place of honor in the history of our Nation."[44] In the DAR's historical imagination, even those women who took up arms to defend the American nation did so primarily as a result of their unselfish love for sons and husbands, although these feelings were inextricably intertwined with their love of country. The Daughters passionately argued for the need to acknowledge their female ancestors' patriotism, but they did not deduce from these narratives that women were or should aspire to become men's equals.

Commemorating Revolutionary Soldiers and Martial Masculinity

The DAR's attempts to counter the male-centered memory of the American Revolution was even more ambiguous because the bulk of its commemorative activities glorified men; in doing so the DAR reaffirmed powerful traditions of martial masculinity and suggested that men were the true agents of historical change and nation-building. From the Daughters' perspective, the most patriotic Americans were the soldiers of the Continental Army who willingly sacrificed their lives for the nation and the political and military leaders whose wise leadership helped them win the War of Independence. Stories about these heroic men outnumbered narratives about women, and they were disseminated more widely and reached larger audiences. Ironically, then, the Daughters helped to bolster the very same male-centered accounts of the Revolutionary period they had vowed to correct. Just as importantly, their tales about the late eighteenth century underscored the idea that membership in the nation was dependent on conforming to closely circumscribed gender roles.

In its efforts to exalt the Revolution's male heroes, the DAR did strive for more inclusiveness that reflected the gradual democratization of military heroism in the late nineteenth century. Prior to the Civil War, the recognition of heroism on the battlefield had been confined to the higher echelons of the military hierarchy, but after 1865, this honor was increasingly extended to ordinary servicemen and linked to the idea of the nation.[45] The DAR furthered this development by arguing that the 250,000 rank-and-file soldiers and sailors who fought for American independence were just as praiseworthy as their high-ranking leaders. Arkansas State Regent Mrs. John McClure spoke for many when she stressed in 1909, "That hero worship which gives all credit to the general is not satisfying to the wives and mothers of this country, whose husbands and sons are entitled to the same meed of praise and to the same remembrance as he who wore the epaulette."[46]

True to such democratic sentiment, the Daughters published numerous stories about ordinary soldiers, marked thousands of their long-forgotten graves, and erected dozens of monuments in their honor. A few of these men were well known and received more praise than others, but in general, DAR members as well as the male historians who occasionally contributed articles to the organization's publication recounted heroic deeds that had never been recorded. To honor these unsung heroes, hundreds of chapters in the Northeast, Midwest, and South searched for the graves of the Continental Army's rank-and-file members to mark, restore, and maintain them.[47] To the Daughters, these graves were sacred places that they believed had much to teach the present-day generation, especially children. A DAR member from Georgia wrote in 1910 about the state's efforts to locate and mark these gravesites: "The burial places of the revolutionary soldiers in our state . . . and the memory of the men who achieved American independence should be held in the highest honor. These graves should each be a hallowed spot, where children are taken to learn of heroism and the reward which comes from patriotic service."[48] By the beginning of World War I, thousands of such graves bore the DAR's simple bronze markers.

Despite its proclaimed goal to counter elitist traditions in American hero worship, the DAR did much to bolster those very traditions by putting considerable emphasis on the heroic leadership of Revolutionary generals, governors, US presidents, and the signers of the Declaration of Independence. On the pages of the organization's magazine, heroic leaders received ample acclaim, and hundreds of chapters were named after them. But in the DAR's tributes to those intrepid leaders, one man towered above women, common soldiers, generals, and statesmen. That man was George Washington. Although Washington's image underwent a gradual process of democratization between the end of the Civil War and World War II, efforts to humanize "the Father of the Country" and traditional portrayals of America's first president as a godlike paragon of republican virtue continued to exist side by side. This "dualism of commonness and distinction" could also be seen in the DAR's interpretations of the first president of the United States.[49] DAR members celebrated Washington's birthday as well as his wedding day. DAR officer Emily Nelson Ritchie McLean argued that it was "womanly to celebrate not only the battles, but the love affairs, of history."[50] Even with this more thorough look into Washington's private life, the Daughters had no doubt that he was the most heroic leader that ever lived. As one historian has observed, in American schoolbooks of the nineteenth century, George Washington bore "more resemblance to Jesus Christ than to any human being."[51] If Washington was no Jesus to the DAR, he probably was a close second.

The large number of historic buildings and house museums that the DAR purchased and renovated between the 1890s and the 1920s likewise highlighted the accomplishments of America's white male elite during the Revolutionary period. Prompted in part by the centennial of the Revolution in 1876, a historic house movement gained momentum in the 1880s to preserve dilapidated buildings that were associated with the founding era.[52] As part of the movement, Daughters across the country identified and purchased historic buildings and transformed them into museums or chapter homes. In other cases, wealthy benefactors donated buildings to the organization, while some chapters were even able to save decaying historic edifices by lobbying local and state authorities to cooperate in financing their restoration. The vast majority of these buildings were located in the original thirteen colonies and associated with elite men's efforts to build, defend, and lead the United States. Many houses had been residences of governors and generals. Other edifices had belonged to wealthy and powerful white families who made names for themselves during the Revolutionary period.[53]

The Daughters' efforts to collect historic relics from the colonial and Revolutionary periods were also characterized by a penchant for elitist memory. The national DAR amassed numerous objects of historical interest and exhibited them at the organization's headquarters in Washington, DC; northeastern chapters frequently organized their own exhibits of colonial and Revolutionary artifacts. These activities reflected a general craze for all things colonial during the Progressive Era as well as private citizens' efforts to use historic preservation for patriotic purposes. Like the DAR, organizations such as the Boston-based Society for the Preservation of New England Antiques were convinced that historic objects from the Revolutionary period would instill in exhibition visitors a greater loyalty toward the nation. Some of the exhibits proved extremely popular and were viewed by thousands of citizens. The items the public could see in DAR exhibits tended to reveal more about America's Revolutionary leaders than about the Continental Army's rank and file. They included Samuel Adams's sword cane, a gavel made from a tree that grew above the grave of Patrick Henry, and a silver watch that was presented to Colonel Daniel Hitchcock by General Nathaniel Greene. In 1902 the national DAR's Relics Committee even displayed what it claimed to be several of George Washington's teeth that had purportedly been preserved by the general's personal dentist.[54]

The organization's determination to promote American history among the nation's youth promoted an understanding of America's revolutionary past that also tended to highlight political history and the accomplishments of the nation's male elite. Almost every DAR chapter as well as DAR state organizations offered prizes to the best students in local high schools and staged essay contests for high school and college students with awards for the best essays on topics from the colonial and Revolutionary periods. Tens of thousands of students participated in the contests and were given topics that echoed the DAR's emphasis on the accomplishments of officers, generals, and statesmen.[55]

Regardless of whether they commemorated common soldiers or generals, the Daughters generally affirmed traditions of martial masculinity and linked this gendered ideal to US patriotism. In doing so, they bolstered long-held gender dichotomies and suggested that America's greatness as a nation depended on these very same binaries. While locating the graves of soldiers served to highlight their manly heroism, the DAR's commemorations of the battles that the Continental Army fought against the British foe became the ultimate expression of its veneration for white warrior heroes. Especially in the Northeast, many chapters gathered annually to celebrate battle anniversaries. During the receptions that accompanied these festive events, participants would attentively listen to talks explaining the historical context of the battles. Members also spent many hours researching the exact locations of old battlefields and cooperated with towns and cities to incorporate the memory of these places into festivities that involved entire communities. Some of the celebrations drew enormous crowds of spectators and exposed tens of thousands of Americans to the idea that true patriotism required manly valor on the battlefield.[56] In hundreds of American towns and cities, the Daughters thus created what Edward Tabor Linenthal has called "prime examples of sacred patriotic space where memories of the transformative power of war and the sacrificial heroism of the warrior are preserved."[57] From the perspective of the Daughters, a man's patriotism hinged on his ability and willingness to conform to the masculine values that military valor entailed.

Underscoring the relational nature of gender ideologies, such affirmations of what it meant to be a patriotic American man could also be observed in tales of the past that were actually meant to praise the accomplishments of women. Mary Lockwood was the first Daughter to do so in her 1890 *Washington Post* article on Hannah Arnett.[58] Her tribute to Arnett for prodding her husband and his friends into patriotic action by denouncing them as pitiable cowards indirectly confirmed a martial ideal of manhood that the Daughters repeatedly invoked around 1900. At the organization's 1892 annual meeting, DAR member Janet Elizabeth Richards recounted the experience of one patriotic woman from New Jersey who, during the American Revolution, called after her departing husband, "Remember to do your duty! I would rather hear that you were left a corpse on the field, than that you played the part of a coward!"[59] Five years later, in a speech at the celebration of the Nashville Centennial in 1897, Mrs. C. B. Bryant evoked the example of Spartan mothers in ancient Greece, claiming that American women had followed the example of their ancient predecessors during the Revolutionary War when urging men to prove their manhood. "It was the Spartan mothers," Bryant exclaimed, "with their proud injunctions to their loved ones: 'Bring back your shield or else be brought back upon it,' that for centuries" had made Sparta so strong and that should inspire female citizens to emulate their example.[60] Such gendered ideas meshed well with some articles on the importance of manly patriotism that male historians published in the DAR's *American Monthly Magazine*. Writing in 1912 about the lessons of Valley Forge, the historian Henry S. Curtis lauded the idea of erecting a mausoleum on the spot of the Continental Army's most trying months of the American Revolution. Such a monument, he wrote, would strengthen boys' patriotism and teach them "to honor the Spartan spirit of endurance, and to despise the effeminacy" that the "modern life of luxury" had fostered among the country's citizens.[61]

Such assessments reflected widespread concerns around 1900 over what many men perceived as a crisis of masculinity. Their insecurities stemmed from a number of factors including the assertiveness of the New Woman, the meaninglessness of white-collar work, and the idea that modernity threatened to sap men's virility. In this context, the DAR's activities became significant because the organization staunchly upheld what Raewyn Connell has called "hegemonic masculinity," a dominant ideal of white heterosexual masculinity that leads to the oppression of women and so-called marginalized masculinities, especially homosexual and nonwhite men. While very few men are actually able to live up to that ideal, it serves as a model to determine what is manly and what is not.[62] Scholars of masculinity have generally argued that men themselves produce hegemonic masculinity in homosocial environments such as all-male associations, but women's role in this process should not be underestimated since men most certainly paid attention to what women believed constituted true manhood. The Daughters' suggestion that those men who refused to heroically serve the nation on the battlefield were unmanly cowards might thus have had a considerable impact on members' families as well as on US society more generally.

Only very few Daughters criticized the glaring contradictions between the DAR's goal to emphasize women's contributions to American history and the fact that so many of its commemorative campaigns confirmed rather than challenged the male-centeredness of the Revolution's memory. Probably the most explicit critique came in 1903 when the Kentuckian suffragist Kate Woolsey resigned from the DAR, citing her frustration with what she regarded as a betrayal of its founding principles. In a letter to the organization's leadership, which she also sent to the Associated Press, Woolsey wrote, "When I joined the Daughters of the American Revolution, I was under the impression that the fathers of the republic intended to include my sex as units of power in the government. I have since learned the error of such belief and it is on this account that I sever my relations with you." Woolsey found it unbearable "to belong to a society, the purpose of which is chiefly to honor the fathers of a government who have repudiated and disinherited my sex."[63]

Woolsey's public condemnation was an exception, however, as were statements that questioned the DAR's ideal of martial manhood. At the national DAR meeting in 1910, in a response to the address of President General Julia Green Scott, a member named Mrs. John R. Walker argued that mothers should teach their sons "to be good citizens rather than soldiers" and "to battle for good laws and social conditions."[64] But in general, the Daughters neither shared Woolsey's disdain for hero worship nor pondered Walker's suggestion that manhood did not revolve solely around military service. From their perspective, patriotic manhood and martial heroism were inextricably linked.

Serving the Nation in the Present: The DAR's Patriotic and Social Activism during the Progressive Era

Although the Daughters were occasionally accused of spending too much time reflecting on the past, they were very much concerned about current affairs and vied to emulate their ancestors' patriotism in the present. The DAR's nationalist and social activism around 1900 was another facet of the organization's determination to show that women were and had always been crucial contributors to US nation-building, but it reflected some of the same gender ambiguities that characterized its remembrance of the Revolution. One example of the DAR's patriotic activism in the present was its service during the Spanish-American War. On the eve of the conflict with Spain in 1898, the Daughters sought to demonstrate their devotion to the United States by establishing an officially sanctioned Hospital Corps of nurses to aid the war effort. Thousands of Daughters volunteered and served in field hospitals across the country. Meanwhile, numerous chapters raised funds for the war effort, organized Thanksgiving dinners for soldiers, or dispatched supplies to troops in Cuba. During a war that millions of American men viewed as a direly needed affirmation of their manhood, the Daughters demonstrated women's skills as auxiliary organizers but also as active contributors to the war effort, which they believed bolstered their argument that female citizens could be as heroic as men.[65] The DAR's recording Secretary General Alice Pickett Akers proudly proclaimed at the Continental Congress of 1899, "Since the day of the call to arms against our Spanish foe to the signing of the protocol of peace, the Daughters of the American Revolution have, by their untiring effort and energy, proven themselves scarcely second in heroism to the soldiers at the front."[66] Reiterating their argument about the largely unacknowledged courage of women during the American Revolution, the Daughters perceived themselves as worthy heirs of their patriotic forebears' legacy.

The DAR's tireless efforts during the first decade of the twentieth century to erect its impressive headquarters, Memorial Continental Hall, in Washington, DC, reflected similar convictions about the significance of women's accomplishments. Shortly after the organization's founding, its members began to discuss plans to build an administrative building that would also serve as a means to commemorate the Revolution's heroines and heroes. In the ensuing years, thousands of Daughters contributed to the building fund, and the US Senate allowed the DAR to purchase a parcel of the capital's monument lot between D Street and New York Avenue Northwest. After the DAR acquired the site in 1902, ground was broken the same year, and the cornerstone was laid in 1904.[67] During the ceremonies that accompanied the laying of the cornerstone, the Daughters made clear their belief that opening Memorial Continental Hall would mark a turning point in American women's relation to the nation. "It will, when completed," President General Cornelia Cole Fairbanks told a sizeable audience in 1904, "symbolize the work, the contributions, the beliefs of thousands of the patriotic women of the republic."[68] From the perspective of DAR leaders, the new building would once more prove women's patriotic devotion to the American republic, whose survival depended as much on female citizens' nationalist sentiments as it did on men's martial prowess and leadership. When Memorial Continental Hall was finally completed in 1910, it became one of the most conspicuous symbols of women's patriotic activism in America. The three-story, marble building contained 35,000 square feet and featured a large memorial portico supported by thirteen marble columns representing America's original thirteen colonies. Its auditorium had almost 2,000 seats, making it one of the largest in the capital. At the time, it was the costliest and largest building that had been built by a women's organization in the United States.[69]

Although the Daughters used their patriotic wartime service and Memorial Continental Hall to claim active roles in American nation-building,

Figure 1.1. Memorial Continental Hall, DAR headquarters, Washington, DC, ca. 1915. When it was completed in 1910, it was the costliest and largest building that had been built by a women's organization in the United States. Courtesy of Library of Congress Prints and Photographs Division, National Photo Company Collection, LC-F82-152A.

they did not regard their activism as a rationale to challenge gender inequality. Given the Daughters' emphasis on patriotic motherhood, alliances between the DAR and women's rights organizations would have been conceivable. After all, by 1900, the women's rights movement had abandoned earlier demands for full gender equality and instead pragmatically used sex-specific arguments that revolved around nineteenth-century ideas of separate spheres. Like their predecessors, American suffragists argued not only that women were different from men but that their maternal inclination toward caring for others would make them more responsible voters. Motherhood was crucial to this line of reasoning. It was men's aggressive and selfish competitiveness, they claimed, that had led to many of the social problems American society faced during the Progressive Era. Women, by contrast, would use their innate inclination toward caring for others to right these wrongs at the ballot box. From the suffragists' perspective, politics were as much about the family and the home as about the economy and warfare.[70] Some Daughters, including the organization's co-founder Mary S. Lockwood, sympathized with the cause of woman suffrage, but many members, especially the organization's leaders, vehemently rejected the franchise for women because they had a starkly different understanding of women's role in US society and the political implications of gender difference.[71]

The skeptics were part of a female antisuffrage movement that emerged in the 1880s and reached its peak during the 1920s, when the influential National Association Opposed to Woman Suffrage, founded in 1911, boasted several hundred thousand middle-class members. The antisuffrage organization and its allies argued that women could not be entrusted with making wise political decisions because they were not rational enough to choose the right political leaders. They also voiced fears that suffrage would take away the type of female nonpartisanship believed to be crucial to influencing male politicians to protect women and children through legislation. Finally, female antisuffragists denounced women's rights activists as unpatriotic egotists who flagrantly ignored their duty to home and country. Beneath these arguments lay deep-seated fears of losing social status and political influence.[72]

Numerous DAR leaders agreed with antisuffragists' dire predictions and probably harbored similar fears. They publicly embraced the antisuffrage cause and argued that women were able to wield indirect political influence that they claimed was just as powerful as the ballot. If women wished to win political office, many of them argued, they had the opportunity to do so in their women's associations. Some members also put forward arguments that an earlier generation of antisuffragists had used. Margaret B. Downing said women were "too emotional, too easily swayed by personal feelings to receive the right of suffrage for many years at least."[73] A number of Daughters even took on leadership positions in the antisuffrage movement. Against this backdrop, DAR leaders sought to suppress frictions that regularly flared up between supporters and opponents of woman suffrage within the organization. They convinced delegates at the DAR's 1914 Continental Congress to pass a resolution that prohibited "the mentioning of any subject thought likely to cause angry feeling among the Daughters," including women's right to vote. In line with this gag rule, the Daughters did not publicly embrace the Nineteenth Amendment until almost one year after its passage.[74]

Prior to World War I, female participation in the Progressive movement encountered much less opposition from the DAR than did the women's rights movement because the Daughters tended to focus on aspects of Progressivism that did not fundamentally challenge America's gender order. Those members who joined the Progressive movement supported its argument that women had a duty to engage in "municipal housekeeping" to combat such evils as corruption, crime, and poverty, which they regarded primarily as consequences of male self-interest. Progressive Daughters also believed that the nation-state had an obligation to ensure the well-being of mothers and children by passing legislation that would provide pensions for widowed mothers and end child labor, among other initiatives. To accomplish these goals, the DAR joined forces with Progressive organizations such as the General Federation of Women's Clubs and tirelessly lobbied state legislatures as well as Congress. In 1909 the DAR officially endorsed Progressive demands for a federal Children's Bureau, which was created in 1912.[75] Unlike woman suffrage, then, Progressivism caused fewer tensions within the DAR because it allowed members to base their arguments for social improvements on the same gendered binaries that the Daughters championed in their commemorative campaigns.

The Daughters' firm belief in the vital role of the traditional nuclear family in American nation-building reflected these ideals and explains why the Daughters so adamantly rejected the practice of polygamy in the Church of Jesus Christ of Latter-Day Saints. The Mormon Church had long been disparaged for practicing polygamy, which its founder, Joseph Smith, made a prerequisite for salvation since the church's beginning in 1830. After the Mormons settled in Utah Territory in the 1840s, their leader Brigham Young heeded Smith's exhortations, taking almost sixty wives and defending the practice until his death in 1877. During the 1880s, growing anti-Mormon sentiment finally led the US Congress to pass legislation that enabled courts to prosecute men who entered into plural marriages, putting enormous pressure on the Church's leadership to end the practice. In 1890 Mormon leaders finally renounced polygamy, but they never annulled existing plural marriages and continued to condone the practice after Utah gained statehood in 1896.[76]

Like other patriotic women's organizations, the Daughters regarded polygamy as a violation of American laws and a grave danger to the nation. In a resolution the Daughters passed during their 1904 Continental Congress, the DAR described polygamy as "a crime against the government and the United States" because it degraded women and destroyed the home, which they deemed "the bulwark of the nation's safety."[77] Subsequently, they unsuccessfully lobbied members of Congress to ostracize Mormon congressmen and senators and denied DAR membership to polygamists, their descendants, and those who supported the practice. As late as 1915, the Daughters railed against Mormons but eventually welcomed them in the interwar period after the Church's leadership vowed to end polygamy for good.[78]

By 1914, then, the Daughters claimed a highly visible role in patriotic and social activism, demonstrating to the American public that women of the present contributed as much to America's nationalist project as had their Revolutionary ancestors. Yet, as in their commemorative campaigns, the Daughters made clear their conviction that the nation would be gravely endangered if traditional gender dichotomies were to be altered.

Fighting the Un-American: World War I and Antiradicalism

World War I marked a conspicuous shift in the Daughters' nationalist rhetoric and strengthened their dichotomous interpretations of gender and the nation. This shift occurred as 1914–1918 saw the emergence of a powerful antiradical movement that received much of its support from white middle-class women and made antifeminism a central pillar of its ideological thrust. A confluence of developments contributed to the surge in female antiradicalism. The beginning of the Great War led to an upsurge in patriotism and suspicions of subversive ideologies. When the United States finally entered the war in 1917, female patriots supported the efforts of the US government and patriotic civic organizations to fight disloyalty within American society. The second event that led to the birth of the antiradical movement was the Russian Revolution of 1917, which deeply disturbed male and female antiradicals alike because they regarded Bolshevism as a thoroughly alien ideology that jeopardized America's institutions and values. Finally, congressional passage of the Nineteenth Amendment brought a large number of female antisuffrage activists into the antiradical camp, where they contributed to its strongly antifeminist agenda during the 1920s. Among the most prominent antisuffragist groups to turn to a patriotic focus was the National Association Opposed to Woman Suffrage; its name was changed to Woman Patriots, and its members sought to prevent feminist ideas from gaining traction among female voters.[79]

The DAR became a vocal member of this movement and explicitly linked antiradicalism, military preparedness, and antifeminism in its nationalist rhetoric. In the eyes of the Daughters, these three themes were inextricably intertwined since they deemed any type of change in America's entrenched gender hierarchies detrimental to the country's political system, and vice versa. DAR leaders generally agreed with their male counterparts that those perceived as un-American radicals sought to abolish the foundations of the nation, including the US government, patriotism, private property, and the family.[80] Nothing less than a strong military and constant vigilance would save America from total destruction. As a consequence of its antiradicalism, the organization abandoned much of its Progressive agenda. By the mid-1920s the DAR rejected Progressives' calls for the federal government's involvement in domestic affairs, severed relations with Progressive organizations, argued that only military preparedness would help America secure peace, and strengthened alliances with other right-wing patriots.[81]

Since the DAR's membership was comprised primarily of white middle-class women, the fight to save the American nation certainly reflected fears of class warfare, but the gender dimensions of its antiradicalism were even more pronounced. The Daughters asserted that the patriarchal family and the American nation were inextricably intertwined. The stability of both, the DAR and its allies said, depended on clearly defined notions of masculinity and femininity as well as rigid relations of men and women to the state.[82] Against the backdrop of this strong belief, the organization repeatedly warned of the dire consequences that so-called un-American ideologies would have for the United States. Socialism seemed the most dangerous one because it was believed to destroy the most sacred foundation of the nation: the American home. Many DAR leaders warned that un-American radicals would ultimately seek to erase traditional gender differences and take away the privileges that the Daughters thought protected women and the family under America's form of government. But in the eyes of DAR leaders, other un-American "isms" that challenged America's gender order were just as perilous to the nation. Feminism was seen as a threat because its advocacy of female autonomy, gender equality, and self-fulfillment struck at the very heart of patriarchy, but the organization's leaders considered pacifism just as treacherous, warning that pacifists would leave the American nation defenseless in the face of foreign foes and suggesting that pacifism would undermine the ideal of the manly citizen soldier.[83]

As early as 1919, the DAR issued a report on the organization's work during World War I that warned of "the avowed defense-destroying pacifist" who endangered America's ability to protect itself against hostile nations.[84] Reflecting the critique's gender dimensions, DAR leaders repeatedly taunted pacifists as "cowards" or "weaklings" who displayed "selfish fear for personal safety" rather than masculine loyalty toward the nation.[85] The Daughters and their nationalist allies insisted that women had an obligation to affirm long-standing traditions of martial masculinity, as it would protect the United States against the menace of un-Americanism. A few members opposed militarism and advocated less martial solutions to political conflicts during the 1920s, but many Daughters appeared to feel that their allegiance to the United States in times of national crisis required undivided support for military valor.[86]

The Daughters' vocal antiradicalism gained them much acclaim from politicians, representatives of the military, and the editors of the *Washington Post*,[87] but not everyone praised the organization during the 1920s. Especially liberal activists and like-minded pundits railed against the DAR; their criticism testifies to the contested nature of US nationalism during a period when patriotic orthodoxy was pitted against liberal voices demanding a candid discussion about America's national ideals. The so-called blacklist affair is a case in point. The controversy was the result of DAR leaders' efforts in 1928 to ban speakers they considered un-American from appearing before its chapters. Quickly dubbed blacklists, the documents named dozens of well-known liberal organizations and individuals including African American civil rights activist W. E. B. Du Bois and settlement house worker Jane Addams. Helen Tufts Bailie, a liberal writer from Massachusetts and a member of both the DAR and the blacklisted Women's International League for Peace and Freedom, launched a well-prepared campaign to protest the blacklists and to initiate liberal reforms within the DAR. Bailie founded a DAR Committee of Protest and wrote a number of widely published essays to criticize what she considered a violation of the freedom of speech as well as the organization's undemocratic policies. Her activism proved unsuccessful, however, as the DAR's leadership forced her Committee of Protest to disband and expelled Bailie and some of her allies.[88]

As suggested by this detractor's ouster, the DAR's national leadership brooked no dissent and quickly silenced any internal protest. Consequently, those who disagreed with the organization's national leaders or aired their grievances publicly were either censured or expelled. Others quit in protest.[89] The historian Francesca Morgan has argued that despite protest letters from numerous chapters and a wave of resignations during and after the blacklist controversy, the DAR's antiradical agenda was supported by a majority of its members. The organization's impressive growth in the 1920s suggests that its liberal critics might indeed have been a minority. In 1923 the *Washington Post* reported that so many women were eager to join the DAR that the organization had established special facilities to process the numerous membership applications. Meanwhile, the organization's Board of Management held a special meeting to grant charters to sixteen new chapters with a combined membership of 1,600. By April 1931 the DAR had more than 172,000 members in 2,431 chapters in the United States and other countries including Cuba, Canada, and China.[90]

The Memory of the American Revolution in the Interwar Period

If World War I marked the emergence of a powerful antiradical movement of which the DAR became an integral part, the Great War and the subsequent economic boom of the 1920s also affected the ways Americans and the Daughters remembered the nation's past. With regard to the general role of historical memory in US society, the period from 1918 to 1929 was characterized by a strained rivalry between debunkers, traditionalists, and the present-minded. The first group was largely composed of academic historians who challenged traditions of triumphant hero worship and espoused nuanced interpretations of the past that gave more room to long-term structural explanations and ethnic minorities. Although this New History approach had been firmly established in college curricula by the early twentieth century, it became a subject of public debate after 1918, when traditionalists began to scrutinize debunkers' influence on history textbooks in American schools. These traditionalists continued to uphold the heroic cultural memory that organizations such as the DAR had struggled so strenuously to create in the preceding three decades. They nostalgically idealized the social and political order that they claimed had characterized the country in the past, and their emotionally charged efforts to commemorate it pushed notions of American national uniqueness to an unprecedented level. Biographies of historical figures became immensely popular, as did efforts to preserve the homes of famous Americans including Alexander Hamilton. Even the federal government began to take an interest in the traditionalist cause, as could be seen in the decision of the US Congress to provide $400,000 for the Pilgrim Tercentenary in 1921 in Plymouth, Massachusetts. The third group cared neither for nostalgia nor for iconoclastic reconsiderations of the American past. Instead, its adherents stressed the heroic accomplishments of contemporary businessmen, athletes, and explorers as living proof of American progress and modern civilization.[91]

The Daughters were squarely in the traditionalist camp and fiercely resisted attempts to either demythologize America's Revolutionary past or dismiss its significance. In the battle against New History debunkers, the organization fired its first salvos as early as 1910, when DAR co-founder Mary Lockwood blasted independent scholar James Henry Stark's study on Loyalists during the American Revolution. Lockwood minced no words when commenting on Stark's critiques of some of the very same men the DAR worshipped as national heroes. "I wish someone would wipe up the floor with Stark and his history," she bluntly told the *Washington Post*.[92] After World War I, the Daughters deemed the New History even more sacrilegious because they believed that such critical interpretations played into the hands of socialists, pacifists, and other un-American radicals. Along with their antiradical allies, the DAR staunchly defended traditions of unquestioning hero worship, arguing that unfavorable assessments of US history were factually inaccurate but also would undermine the patriotism of America's youth.[93]

To protect young citizens from the pernicious effects of the debunkers' historical distortions, the Daughters began to scrutinize numerous history textbooks and called upon publishers to take seriously their duty to teach allegiance to the United States. In 1923 the DAR's Continental Congress passed a resolution on textbooks that encapsulated the organization's belief in the patriotic significance of traditionalist history in the country's schools. The "heroic story" of the nation's founding, it stated, "should be preserved unsullied and transmitted unimpaired, to our children in the public schools, as their rightful heritage, and for the perpetuation of wholesome national spirit based upon right conceptions of the vital doctrines and traditions of American democracy." To the Daughters, any publication that defamed or ignored the nation's "heroic forefathers" and misrepresented "the consecrated causes for which they struggled" were unsuitable for educational use.[94] From this perspective, the didactic function of the past trumped any effort to achieve a more balanced or nuanced interpretation of US history. In the DAR's view, the cultural memory of colonial America and the American Revolution needed to instill a firm belief in the greatness of the nation's heroes; without such a belief, a truly patriotic populace would not be possible.

Consequently, the Daughters and their allies examined numerous textbooks to expose publications they believed sowed the seeds of disloyalty among American children; they vociferously protested pro-British, pacifistic, and other purportedly un-American histories of the United States. They also suspiciously eyed teachers who failed to glorify the Founding Fathers, statesmen, and military leaders in their classrooms.[95] In 1928, President General Grace Brosseau reminded DAR members how important such vigilance was in keeping "America American." Many historians, she charged, suggested that America was "hopelessly wrong on all counts!" Brosseau warned that high school teachers and college professors who taught that type of history would receive "substantial and undeserved returns on their investments in disloyalty."[96] The efforts of the Daughters and their supporters were relatively unsuccessful in the end, and many of the books they deemed unpatriotic remained in use in public schools throughout the interwar period. Yet, these setbacks notwithstanding, many white middle-class Americans clung to traditional tales of heroism and patriotism.[97]

If debunkers' demythologization eroded young citizens' allegiance to the nation, as the Daughters repeatedly warned, indifference to the past was just as pernicious. In the face of what they perceived as a communist conspiracy undermining the foundations of the American nation, they considered its cultural memory more important than ever. Especially the ideals that had been formulated during the nation's founding era needed to be cherished and remembered to safeguard the United States. At the organization's 1922 Continental Congress, President General Anne Rogers Minor urged members to "lose no time in exposing the poisonous doctrines of socialism that are spreading everywhere and trapping the unwary under the guise of a false Americanism or some apparently innocent and desirable reform. . . . This menace cannot prevail against our country if we remain true to the principles of the fathers and founders, but this is no reason for minimizing or underestimating its grave and sinister aspects." The DAR, she said, was called upon to defend the United States as truly as their ancestors had done in 1776.[98] Writing three years later in the *National Republic* about the Daughters' role in American society, President General

Lora Haines Cook likewise stressed that there was a dire "need for every true American to stand united against the red menace which on every hand is striving to break down the ideals which actuated the founding fathers of our great republic."[99]

In their fight against historical revisionism and indifference, the DAR continued to put heavy emphasis on male heroes. As they had done in their pre–World War I commemorations, the Daughters paid great tribute to the Revolutionary era's social elite including the signers of the Declaration of Independence and well-known generals. Throughout the 1920s, male historians and DAR members published articles in the organization's monthly magazine about George Washington, Thomas Jefferson, and other "Men Who Thought Out the Revolution," as one headline called them. Some DAR chapters honored them by putting bronze plaques near historic places where the men had performed deeds that made them famous. In 1923 the General Knox Chapter of Thomaston, Maine, launched a campaign to rebuild the old home of its namesake, General Henry Knox, who also served as secretary of war during the War of Independence. Its members had labored for eight years to raise $10,000 and hoped to obtain another $15,000 from the state of Maine. Their plan was to rebuild the structure that had been destroyed in 1871, using the original plans and drawings of the house. In a similar fashion, other Daughters continued their efforts to save the edifices that had some connection to the heroes of the Revolution. The DAR carried on its endeavor to commemorate the Revolution's ordinary soldiers as well. Stories about them frequently appeared in the *DAR Magazine,* and chapters across the country tirelessly searched for and marked their moss-covered graves.[100]

But America's early female patriots remained important in the DAR's historical imagination not only as having been unjustly ignored but also as representing an antidote to the menace of un-American radicalism, especially feminism. In their search for female role models, the Daughters honored women of the American Revolution but also found much to admire in the pre–Revolutionary period. The "Pilgrim Mothers," as the first female settlers in colonial America were called, were seen as the epitome of the gendered virtues that contributed to American nation-building. "Like the Pilgrim Mothers," Minor exclaimed at the Pilgrim Tercentenary of 1920 in Provincetown, Massachusetts, "we must be filled with the same spirit of service to the common cause, the same faith, courage and unselfish devotion that led them into a strange world and enabled them to build the homes that they have transmitted to us to preserve."[101] Five years later, Minor and her successor Lora Haines Cook reiterated this message during a commemorative event in Plymouth, Massachusetts. Expressing her dismay at feminist attacks "upon the family as a unit and as an institution," Cook exhorted women to follow the example of the early female settlers who had served their country by concentrating on their roles as "helpmates and mothers." Cook warned that feminism, if not contained, would "lead the innocent and the foolish into the dangerous morasses of emotional license and depravity and make of them standard bearers of Bolshevistic and Communistic propaganda."[102] To the Daughters, preserving the memory of these female ancestors remained crucial to safeguarding the American nation because its stability depended on the same gendered principles that had governed colonial America.

With regard to the women of the Revolution, the Daughters' remembrance was characterized by much continuity with their past positions. Especially in the Northeast and those southern states that had been part of the original thirteen colonies, DAR state organizations and local chapters invested countless hours of research and fundraising to honor their memory. In 1926, after researching the location of Revolutionary gunner Margaret Corbin's grave, the New York State DAR obtained official permission to remove the heroine's remains from her grave at Highland Falls, New York, and have them reinterred in the US Military Cemetery at West Point. At her new burial site, the Daughters erected a granite monument that bore a large bronze tablet with a relief depicting a woman firing a cannon and a text relating Corbin's heroic deed. On April 14, 1926, the monument was dedicated with full military honors.[103] Recent forensic investigations have revealed that the remains that were reinterred at the West Point Cemetery do not belong to a woman, but to an unknown man. The location of Margaret Corbin's grave remains unknown.[104]

Georgian Daughters likewise labored on to keep alive the memory of Nancy Hart, the woman who was said to have armed herself to capture several British soldiers in her cabin in the state's piney woods. During the second half of the 1920s, the DAR managed to win the support of state authorities and convince the State Highway Board to cooperate with the organization in finding a highway that could be named after the intrepid heroine. In 1927 a Nancy Hart Highway Committee chose a route that connected the towns Hartwell and Augusta, and it was subsequently designated as Nancy Hart Memorial Highway. A year later, chapters in the area

Figure 1.2. Memorial for Margaret Corbin at West Point Cemetery. The DAR erected the memorial in 1926 to honor Corbin, who became famous for manning her husband's gun during the Battle of Fort Washington in the American Revolution. Wikimedia Commons, photographer: Ahodges 7, https://commons. wikimedia.org/wiki/File:Margaret_Corbin_Memorial,_West_Point_Cemetery,_ United_States_Military_Academy.jpg, license: https://commons.wikimedia. org/wiki/Commons:GNU_Free_Documentation_License,_version_1.2.

where Hart was believed to have lived placed markers along the route. By the early 1930s, motorists might pass ten such memorials on their journey through the Peach State. Along with these efforts, in 1931 the Nancy Hart Chapter of Milledgeville and the Stephen Heard Chapter of Elberton bought and later presented to the Georgia DAR a five-acre tract of land in Elberton County that they claimed was the site where Nancy Hart's cabin stood during the Revolution. The property was later transformed into a memorial park that featured a replica of the cabin. While competing versions of Hart's story continued to circulate, DAR members seemed interested in perpetuating a portrayal of the Georgia heroine that strengthened ideas of Republican Motherhood and true womanhood in the present; they lauded her as a republican inspiration for American mothers and downplayed tales that undermined her femininity.[105] Their efforts meshed well with statements by the DAR's national leaders who in the 1920s unceasingly stressed women's essential role in US history as wives and mothers. Vice President General Elizabeth C. Barney Buel wrote that for the Daughters, there would be no history without "the home, the wife, [and] the mother." Writing in 1924 in the *DAR Magazine*, Buel insisted that the male "makers of history" would be helpless without their wives' "faithful support."[106] In the 1920s, the Daughters continued to remind their audiences that the nation's past as well as its present and future hinged on time-honored gender dichotomies that revolved around wifehood and motherhood.

During the Depression and World War II, the DAR's anticommunist and commemorative campaigns continued on parallel and frequently overlapping tracks. As during the 1920s, political change as well as an altered commemorative landscape affected the Daughters' activism and contributed to the organization's waning visibility in mainstream discourse. The DAR's ideological convictions remained unchanged, notwithstanding its more subdued political rhetoric after 1930. The organization's decision to reconsider its anticommunist agenda during the Great Depression stemmed primarily from previous campaigns' ineffectiveness as well as communist activists' ability to redefine themselves as America's allies in the fight against European fascism. It was also the result of a less confrontational style of leadership. When Massachusetts native Edith Scott Magna was elected president general in 1932, journalists wrote of a "New Deal" for the DAR because Magna toned down the organization's antiradical rhetoric.[107]

Yet what some regarded as the DAR's New Deal was more about style than substance, as the Daughters' warnings against un-American subversion continued unabated throughout the 1930s. What did change was the organization's strategy to counter the perceived menace. While much of the DAR's previous antiradical activism had revolved around alerting America's entire population to the purported dangers posed by socialism, feminism, and pacifism, it now focused on those its leaders considered most susceptible to these ideologies: America's youth.[108] Given the Daughters' belief in Republican Motherhood, children had always been among the prime targets of their nationalist ideology. Already during the 1890s, the Daughters created the Children of the American Revolution (CAR) to prepare members' sons and daughters for the patriotic duties of citizenship. CAR was open to those between the ages of twelve and twenty-one who were descended from patriots of the American Revolution. It was incorporated in 1895 and put much emphasis on inculcating the type of cultural memory the Daughters thought would help children understand the importance of patriotism.[109] The numerous historical essay contests that DAR chapters sponsored and their efforts to monitor the contents of history textbooks in America's schools served a similar purpose.

During the first half of the 1930s, the Daughters stepped up their efforts to transform America's youth into loyal citizens. Through the DAR's Junior American Citizens (JAC) clubs, which were open to children between six and fourteen years of age regardless of their ancestry, race, or creed, the Daughters hoped to teach patriotism through such means as historical pageants, readings, and sightseeing trips to historically significant places. Unlike Children of the American Revolution chapters, which were led by DAR members, the JAC clubs operated under the auspices of the Daughters but were directed by trained teachers.[110] The DAR's Good Citizenship Medal and Good Citizenship Pilgrimage were probably even more influential. Established in 1932 and 1934, respectively, the two campaigns targeted hundreds of thousands of pupils all across the nation. In the case of the Good Citizenship Medal, the Daughters asked public as well as private grammar schools and junior high schools to select students who exemplified "those qualities of character which will result in worthy citizenship, the exercise of its privileges and responsibilities, and the development of a higher type of manhood and womanhood."[111] Unlike the Good Citizenship Medal, the Good Citizenship Pilgrimage award was conferred only upon female high school seniors. In a complicated selection process that differed from state to state, contestants were judged on their dependability, service, leadership, and patriotism. Eventually, only one student from each state was selected every year and won a trip to the nation's capital, where awardees were officially honored at the DAR's annual meeting.[112] In the following decades, tens of thousands of American children and teenagers competed for these two awards by trying to conform to the standards of patriotism the DAR had established. Through their involvement in the selection process, the peers and teachers of the award winners confirmed and taught the Daughters' interpretations of national loyalty and the nation's history.

The participation of thousands of schools in the DAR's campaigns to instill patriotism in America's youth indicated at least tacit approval of its nationalist ideology and might have influenced numerous students, but the organization's educational activities did not save the DAR from continuing public scorn. As in the 1920s, the Daughters were frequently lambasted and even ridiculed for their uncompromising anticommunism, most famously by the artist Grant Wood, whose 1934 painting *Daughters of the American Revolution* caricatured the organization as austere reactionaries. Not surprisingly, the Daughters felt unjustly defamed by Wood and like-minded critics; they frequently cited as evidence of their continued significance the close cooperation with various government agencies and committees that investigated subversive radicalism.[113]

Commemorating the nation's Revolutionary past continued to be as important to the Daughters as the hunt for un-American radicals, but their remembrance took less conspicuous forms and lacked the impact of earlier campaigns. In part, the diminishing visibility of the DAR's commemorative activities stemmed from the changes that historical interpretations of colonial America and the American Revolution underwent during the 1930s, although it is likely that many members applauded those changes. Widespread economic hardship as well as the New Deal rekindled people's interest in America's heroic past, largely silenced the debunkers, and brought unprecedented federal support for commemorative activism. Particularly military and political heroes were once more in vogue, soothing feelings of economic insecurity and reflecting a yearning for traditional values that could guide a crisis-ridden nation. The era's most significant transformation of patriotic memory was probably the unparalleled involvement of state authorities and the federal government in preserving the nation's cultural memory. Especially the Roosevelt administration's New Deal programs fostered historical research in compilations of regional folklore, historical documentaries, and historical surveys. In a similar fashion, the National Park Service metamorphosed into a key institution in the process of preserving historic sites such as national monuments and battlefields. Never before had Washington taken such an avid interest in the nation's history and its patriotic uses in the present.[114]

Despite the unprecedented attention that state legislatures and the US government paid to patriotic memory, most commemorations of the American Revolution would not have been possible without politicians' collaboration with private groups. Neither the 1931 sesquicentennial of America's victory in the Battle of Yorktown nor the bicentennial of George Washington's birthday in 1932 would have become a nationwide celebration had it not been for close alliances between the federal government, state legislatures, local communities, and various private groups and individuals. The Daughters continued to be part of these alliances and became sought-after advisers. In the Washington bicentennial, President General Lora Haines Cook became one of only two female members of the federal planning committee. The Daughters also played important roles in thousands of local George Washington bicentennial celebrations across the country. In 1931 the organization's chapters frantically planned events to memorialize the nation's first president, frequently assisting special bicentennial committees in their respective communities. In these celebrations, hundreds of historical pageants, tableaux, essay contests, colonial balls, and other events were planned to remind people of the greatness of "the Father of the Country."[115]

Although the Daughters tried to remain relevant in the commemorative discourse on the American Revolution, their heyday as preservers of its cultural memory had passed. Between 1935 and 1945, the organization continued to demand official recognition of Revolutionary women's patriotic contributions to American independence and stressed the importance of selfless wifehood and motherhood while simultaneously praising the heroic accomplishments of men. But most of these commemorative efforts were confined to DAR circles, decreased in number, and no longer reached as many communities. The organization's receding prominence was not only due to the federal government's unprecedented role in preserving and disseminating America's cultural memory. It probably also stemmed from the increasing difficulty for members to make meaningful connections between the Revolution's communicative memory and cultural memory. In many ways, the year 1943 marked the ultimate end of this interrelationship. On December 1 of that year, the organization's last living Real Daughter, Annie Knight Gregory, died only a few months after celebrating her hundredth birthday in Williamsport, Pennsylvania. Her father, Richard Knight, had joined the Continental Army as a nine-year-old and was seventy-seven years old when Annie was born. Gregory had been the last of 757 Real Daughters whom the DAR managed to recruit between 1890 and World War II. Shortly after her death, the committee that only in 1940 had changed its name to Real Daughters and Granddaughters dropped "Real Daughters" from its name.[116] Her death certainly did not end the DAR's efforts to boost citizens' patriotism, but it marked the end of an era of patriotic memory that the Daughters had actively shaped for more than four decades.

2

"A Long and Mighty Race of Heroic Men"

Remembering the Pioneers and American Nation-Building

In 1901 the members of a joint SAR-DAR essay contest committee in Denver, Colorado, discussed suitable topics that could be assigned to generate interest in American history among the state's high school students. While the Sons suggested topics from the Revolutionary period, the Daughters preferred essays on Colorado's history between the Revolution and the mid-nineteenth century. In the eyes of the committee's female members, as chairwoman Julia H. Platt wrote in a report, "the history of our own State affords topics which are fresher, and which are fully worthy of attention." Platt argued that Colorado's early history constituted "a fine example of the manner in which America has expanded," while the territorial period was "an equally fine example of American state building."[1] In the end, the Sons yielded to the Daughters' demands. "Colorado from the Earliest Time to 1855" became the topic of the 1901 essay competition; it was followed in 1902 by "Territorial Days of Colorado."[2]

Western and midwestern Daughters' seemingly surprising focus on the commemoration of the nation's expansion in the postrevolutionary era was a direct result of the close interrelations between communicative memory, cultural memory, and nationalism in the organization's activism. Although the DAR experienced its fastest growth in the urban Northeast, where local chapters were able to mark or preserve numerous reminders of the region's colonial and Revolutionary past, the organization also attracted many members in the Midwest and West. In those regions the American Revolution had left virtually no physical legacy, which prevented members from creating commemorative links between the nation's founding and their states or local communities. The regions' Daughters therefore devoted much of their time to the history of western explorers, frontiersmen, and pioneers because it allowed them to connect their own and other citizens' communicative memories of territorial expansion to the heroic cultural memory they believed would strengthen Americans' loyalty toward the nation. Remembering this history also allowed them to soothe a general sense of insecurity among white middle-class Americans over the closing of the western frontier, economic hardship during the 1890s, and the fundamental changes brought about by modernity in general. The Daughters' efforts to study and preserve the western past received a boost after 1903 when the national DAR began to encourage chapters to study local and state histories. As a result, the number of chapters in the West and Midwest increased considerably in the first two decades of the twentieth century.[3] By 1925 almost half of the DAR's 2,071 chapters and upward of one third of its more than 150,000 members resided in those regions.[4]

The DAR's pre–World War II commemorative campaigns in the West and Midwest reveal that the organization worked hard to maintain racial boundaries of national inclusion while simultaneously upholding traditional gender binaries within white America. Most of these campaigns revolved around marking the trails that pioneer families and explorers used to reach the regions prior to the Civil War. But in stark contrast to the DAR's remembrance of the American Revolution, women were conspicuously absent from the tales the Daughters offered prior to the 1920s. Western Daughters highlighted primarily the heroic accomplishments of pioneer men whom they regarded as masculine warriors for their violent confrontations with Native Americans. Those who lost their lives in these conflicts were honored as patriotic martyrs who had advanced the causes of the nation and white civilization.

Only their post–World War I Madonna of the Trail campaign focused on the memory of pioneer mothers. This new focus was the consequence of the national DAR's failure to convince the US government to build the National Old Trails Road, a highway that would have connected the various routes of the old pioneer trails. Only after its defeat did the Daughters commit themselves to erecting twelve identical statues in twelve trail states to pay tribute to the pioneer mother. The project reflected the same ambivalence that characterized the Daughters' tributes to Revolutionary women. The organization imagined the pioneer mother as a resolute figure who was ready to defend her loved ones with arms, but as happened in the Revolution, her seemingly unfeminine militancy and heroic determination were interpreted as part and parcel of women's natural instincts as wives and mothers. In many ways the DAR's Madonna of the Trail became the Margaret Corbin of Western Expansion, ready to provide selfless service to her husband and the nation while refraining from transgressing traditional gender boundaries.

But the Madonna of the Trail campaign remained an exception in the organization's memorialization of western expansion. Other commemorations that took place in the region during the 1920s and 1930s generally reaffirmed the primacy of male pioneers and explorers and wedded it to the advance of the nation and white civilization. Numerous local projects emphasized a notion of nationalism that revolved around male heroism, conflicts with the "savage foe," motherhood, and Anglo-Saxon whiteness. The Daughters not only marked the sites of the first house, first church, or first school in their respective communities but also paid homage to the first white men to set foot in the territories where those communities were later established as well as to the first white settlers and first white babies there. The DAR's commemorative campaigns in the West and Midwest were explicitly racial projects that consolidated American founding myths about manly Anglo-Saxons who conquered the North American continent.

What made the organization's activism in the West and Midwest particularly significant was that its members repeatedly tapped the region's cultural memory and the living communicative memories that lingered in local communities to make the abstraction of the white nation meaningful for ordinary people and the Daughters themselves. During the dedication ceremonies for markers and monuments, which the DAR organized with counties, local communities, elderly pioneers, and their descendants, people's communicative memories were integrated into nationalist rituals that were witnessed by a great number of local citizens.

Memorializing Manly Men: Marking Pioneer Trails during the Progressive Era

Western Daughters' eagerness to commemorate their region's past was entangled with a number of developments that altered public perceptions of the West in the late nineteenth century. Probably the most important of these developments was the widespread frontier anxiety that gripped many Americans in the 1890s. This concern about the perceived closing of the western frontier, the boundary that divided settled from unsettled territory, began in the 1870s but received new impetus in 1890 when the US Census Bureau officially declared that the entire continent had been settled. Blatantly ignoring the fact that the West had long been inhabited by Native Americans who were dispossessed of their homelands, this announcement was premature, since the process of settling the region continued well into the early twentieth century. But in the eyes of scholars, most prominently among them the historian Frederick Jackson Turner, the development was real and reason for grave concern. In his famous 1893 lecture "The Significance of the Frontier in American History," Turner argued that what he regarded as the advancing line of civilization had forged America's unique national character by fostering democratic thinking, sturdy individualism, and a spirit of enterprise among the white pioneers who had settled in the Midwest and West. In what later generations of historians have demonstrated to be a flawed reading of the past, Turner lamented the end of this incubator of American identity because it would no longer strengthen the country's national character or serve the function of a safety valve for millions of American citizens and immigrants who relied on it to escape the Northeast's crowded cities.[5]

Turner's concerns were voiced by many other pundits and received new urgency in the face of a severe economic depression, subsequent clashes between urban workers and middle-class entrepreneurs, protests by impoverished western farmers, and the arrival of millions of new immigrants from southern and eastern Europe. Theodore Roosevelt, the historian-turned-politician who served as a colonel during the Spanish-American War, became governor of New York, and later was the twenty-sixth president of the United States, painted a similarly nostalgic picture of the West's bygone era and regarded its passing as a grave danger to white Protestants like himself. He interpreted the region as a battlefield on which white Anglo-Saxon men had heroically struggled against and successfully subdued Indian savages. To Roosevelt, the legacy of this victorious race war was now in peril. Not only was the frontier closed, but a new wave of immigrants and dwindling birth rates among white, old-stock Americans threatened the power of the very same group that had conquered the West. Roosevelt's two-pronged solution was to pay homage to pioneers' heroic masculinity and to use America's imperialist ventures in Cuba and the Philippines as ersatz frontiers that would preserve the nation's unique character. Echoing pre–Civil War voices that had deemed it America's "Manifest Destiny" to conquer the North American continent, Turner and Roosevelt conveyed a general sense of insecurity among white Protestants who feared the potentially harmful implications of the frontier's passing.[6]

The white western pioneers whom Turner and Roosevelt lionized as the virtuous backbone of the republic likewise nostalgically reminisced about their experiences prior to the frontier's passing, albeit for different reasons. During a period when the rural Midwest and West were undergoing a gradual but inexorable transformation into urban and industrialized landscapes, hundreds of thousands of the regions' early settlers thought back to their onerous westward treks and the deprivations they had faced after their arrival, contrasting their experiences with the comfort and prosperity of modern-day America. Their communicative memories of the close-knit communities they had created helped them cope with a growing sense of irrelevance and purposelessness in the face of fundamental social change. Much of their nostalgic reminiscing took place within hundreds of Pioneer Societies and Old Settler Associations that were founded between the 1870s and 1890s. At their meetings, organizations such as the Society of Montana Pioneers (1884) celebrated the hardships their members had endured and the many accomplishments they had achieved. Beginning in the 1880s, quite a few of their members wrote books and articles to share their recollections with other Americans. In some states, old pioneers received commemorative support from their children. In California, especially the Native Sons and Daughters of the Golden West (1875) sought to make their pioneer heritage part of the region's and nation's cultural memory. With the help of newspapers and magazines, these various developments and organizations made more and more white Americans aware of their western heritage and animated them to commemorate it.[7]

The centennial in 1904 of the famous Lewis and Clark expedition can be seen as one direct result of these multilayered efforts to commemorate the western past in the face of modernity's ambivalent impacts on American society. Between 1804 and 1806, US President Thomas Jefferson's private secretary, Meriwether Lewis, and his friend William Clark explored the huge Louisiana Territory between St. Louis, Missouri, and the Pacific coast that France had sold to the United States in 1803. The expedition's centennial rekindled citizens' interest in this adventurous journey and prompted them to organize celebrations that portrayed the two explorers' exploits as a rationale for territorial expansion in North America and beyond. Alongside numerous newspaper and magazine articles, the Lewis and Clark Centennial Exposition and Oriental Fair in Portland, Oregon, wistfully recalled the golden age of the West but simultaneously lauded modern industrial progress and imperial expansion. The Lewis and Clark centennial thus soothed frontier anxieties by honoring white male explorers for their role in American nation-building and by offering a justification for ersatz frontiers abroad.[8]

Western DAR members were undoubtedly influenced by this commemorative phenomenon and labored ardently to keep alive the memory of western pioneers during the Progressive Era. Despite the DAR's pledge to challenge male-centered accounts of the American Revolution, pioneer women were largely absent from its remembrance of the West prior to World War I.[9] Most of the Daughters' commemorative efforts before the 1920s centered on the heroism of pioneer men and revolved primarily around the trails they traveled to reach the West. Two trails gained particular prominence in DAR campaigns: the Santa Fe Trail and the Oregon Trail. The Santa Fe Trail was established in 1821 as a trade route to transport goods from Franklin, Missouri, to Santa Fe, New Mexico. After the Mexican-American War and the US annexation of what is now the Southwest, tens of thousands of settlers from the East used the 900-mile trail to reach what was then called the Far West. The Oregon Trail began at Independence, Missouri, and had long been used by Native Americans. In 1811, a commercial expedition traveled on it for the first time. Eventually, the Oregon Trail covered almost 2,000 miles. It followed the route of the Santa Fe Trail to Gardner, Kansas, where it branched off to the northwest, repeatedly traversing some of the Santa Fe Trail areas before ending in Washington Territory on the Pacific coast. The Oregon Trail became an essential travel route for new settlers but also played a vital role during the Gold Rush of 1849 and subsequent waves of migration. After the Civil War, as the railroad became the preferred mode of transportation, these two trails were abandoned and largely forgotten.[10]

Daughters from the West and Midwest deemed it imperative to mark these trails to rescue from oblivion the vanishing communicative memories of the pioneers who had traveled them but also to establish a more permanent cultural memory that would strengthen people's allegiance to the nation. Between 1906 and 1909, when the regions' DAR state organizations discussed ways to pay tribute to the pioneers, arguments such as the one put forward by Mrs. Charles Oliver Norton, the regent of the Fort Kearny Chapter in Kearny, Nebraska, convinced many fellow Daughters of the importance of marking the two trails. Speaking at the Nebraska DAR state conference in 1908, Norton said the need to commemorate the Oregon Trail was "urgent, in the extreme, for soon the memory of living man will not be ours to give advice and assistance and we are in danger of losing all signs of this once most famous of the trans-continental roads, save in the few mentions of it in printed texts."[11]

Western Daughters warned that the lessons old pioneers could teach subsequent generations of American citizens would vanish with them unless the DAR transformed their recollections into a national cultural memory. More importantly, memorializing explorers' and early settlers' heroic deeds would help people cope with the challenges of modern life and strengthen American patriotism.[12] In an article that appeared in 1909 in the DAR's monthly magazine, Norton voiced her belief that the pioneers' heroic example would lead younger generations of Americans to become more patriotic citizens. "The value of a noble past is inestimable in leading our future citizens to heights of aspiration and emulation," Norton wrote, "and we must not allow our past to slip away from us, but talk our history, teach our history and live surrounded by its memorials." She was convinced that keeping "the memories of the heroic past fresh in the minds of our people" would fan patriotic fervor and ensure national stability.[13]

In their efforts to memorialize the region's past and stress its importance for American patriotism, the Daughters regarded male pioneers as the primary harbingers of civilization and American nation-building. Fusing traditions of Manifest Destiny with the ideas of Frederick Jackson Turner, the Daughters imagined a rugged and strong American man who pushed forward in the name of civilization regardless of the obstacles he faced. In 1907 a Mrs. W. E. Stanley explained to the readers of the DAR's *American Monthly Magazine* that only "the hardiest pioneers dared undertake this dangerous journey and brave the privations and suffering incident to the route."[14] It was due to these dangers, another article in the magazine stated, that the pioneers had acquired "a grim fearlessness that knew nothing but the thrill of success or the deep oblivion of death."[15] The Daughters frequently described the pioneers as strong, rugged, simple, and sincere. Some Daughters even likened them to valorous soldiers who fought a strenuous battle in their struggle to win the West, making it all the more important to commemorate the trails they had traveled. These interpretations meshed well with the memories of the pioneers themselves, who in their published and unpublished reminiscences stressed that the frontier had molded the region's society along with that of the nation.[16]

The Kansas DAR took the lead in working toward the Daughters' goal of marking the Santa Fe Trail, first discussing the project during a state conference in late 1902, then placing the first markers in 1907. In the following six years, Daughters in Colorado, New Mexico, and Missouri followed the Sunflower State's example.[17] For the Oregon Trail, it was the Nebraska DAR that erected the first monument along the historic route in 1910; the project was emulated by state organizations of Nebraska, Colorado, Wyoming, New Mexico, Washington, and Oregon. By the end of World War I, hundreds of Santa Fe and Oregon Trail markers dotted the landscape between Missouri and the West Coast. In every state where the two trails were marked, DAR state conferences established special trail committees that labored diligently, sometimes for several years, to research and publicize their histories, to find their exact routes, and most importantly, to raise funds to finance commemorative trail markers. The trail committees distributed thousands of leaflets, postcards, images, and maps of the trails to familiarize the region's residents with their histories. Local newspapers frequently assisted the DAR by publishing articles about the organization's work and the bygone days of the trails. In Kansas the publicity campaign also targeted the state's public schools. Furnished with a special Trail Day program by the Daughters, teachers were asked to observe that special day on January 29, 1906, the state's anniversary.[18]

The DAR's campaigns elicited considerable public interest in the two trails as well as in the organization's efforts to preserve their memory. The organization managed to convince various political institutions, private groups, and individuals to support the projects financially. Most of the money for the markers came from state legislatures, some of which provided the Daughters with $1,000, while others gave as much as $3,000. Counties as well as town and city councils frequently covered costs such as the setting of the heavy markers, while railroad companies agreed to transport them free of charge. DAR state organizations and local chapters raised additional money from private groups and individuals, sometimes receiving assistance from the Sons of the American Revolution. In Kansas the DAR's supporters even included hundreds of children who had been asked to give one penny each during the Trail Day celebration at the state's schools, resulting in a contribution of almost $700.[19]

Much of the enthusiasm and money that western Daughters generated through their Santa Fe Trail and Oregon Trail campaigns were results of the organization's efforts to tap both the hidden cultural memory of the

West that had been preserved by archivists and historians and aging pioneers' communicative memories that lingered in numerous communities. Especially the process of locating the trails and significant historic spots along them involved close cooperation between the Daughters, who sought to establish a national cultural memory, state historical societies and state engineers as the professional preservers of such cultural memory, and numerous old pioneers who were the keepers of the West's communicative memories. In almost all of the states where the DAR marked the Santa Fe and Oregon Trails, its trail committees either sought the assistance of state historical societies or became part of joint committees that state legislatures established as part of the bills that appropriated funds for the markers. These committees brooded over old government maps and discussed the research of curators and archivists to locate the trails. In several cases, professional archivists or historians used archival materials and old maps to create new maps that showed their exact routes.[20]

Although archivists and historians played an important role in these trail committees, many of them received or actively solicited the assistance of elderly pioneers to help them find the trails and identify significant historic spots where the markers should be placed. They thus drew on the communicative memories that had lingered in western communities after the end of the wagon days in order to create the heroic cultural memory they deemed so vital to the nation's survival. Throughout the West, the DAR's publicity campaigns generated a deluge of letters from old settlers who volunteered accounts of their adventurous journeys and advice on how to find the trails, while many Daughters also attempted to track down and contact pioneers to acquire more detailed information. In Kansas, the DAR encouraged schoolchildren to interview old pioneers in their respective communities when preparing essays for the organization's Trail Day essay contest. Such efforts generated unprecedented interest in the history of the settlement of the West that previously had primarily been confined to discussions within families and pioneer societies.[21] Mrs. T. A. Cordry of the Kansas Santa Fe Trail Committee wrote about this phenomenon in 1915: "The enthusiasm grew all over the route of the Trail, and great interest was taken in the history gathered from the old settlers, who were aroused as though from the sleep of ages to tell of their experiences while traveling the old Trail."[22]

In some campaigns, the Daughters relied almost exclusively on pioneers' memories to confirm the conclusions that archivists and historians had drawn from their scholarly research. For example, in the Washington DAR's campaign between 1914 and 1916 to mark the Oregon Trail, an early settler named George H. Himes and General Hazard Stevens, who had traveled the trail in the mid-1850s on horseback as an Internal Revenue collector for the US government, became crucial authorities. Himes, who had come to Olympia, Washington, in 1853, suggested marking former relay stations where settlers had changed horses and stayed for a respite from the arduous journey. Hazard Stevens was frequently consulted to confirm the correct locations of these relay stations and other historic spots; he did so by relying on his personal memory and official maps he had drawn during the 1850s. Praising his contributions to their campaign in Washington State, the chairwoman of the state's DAR trail committee reported in 1916 that Stevens's clear and accurate memory, together with the official maps he created, cleared many doubtful points as to the trail's exact route. The committee was grateful "to have its findings pronounced correct by General Stevens."[23]

Once the trails' routes and special historic spots such as relay stations, camping places, old taverns, and crossings had been documented and agreed upon, the Daughters, with the assistance of counties and local communities, proceeded to place markers along the trails. Their design tended to be rather unremarkable. The majority of them were five-foot granite boulders or concrete monuments that bore simple inscriptions such as "Santa Fe Trail, 1822–1872" (the latter year marking the opening of the Santa Fe Railroad) and "Oregon Trail 1844," which called attention to the year the first settlers camped in Oregon territory. The monuments' simplicity was primarily a consequence of financial considerations rather than aesthetic preferences. Choosing more affordable materials and little ornamentation allowed DAR state organizations to purchase and place a larger number of markers. In Kansas alone, the Daughters' frugality, combined with the generosity of the state as well as that of numerous counties, cities, towns, and individual citizens, allowed them to place ninety-eight monuments by 1914. Ultimately, several hundred markers dotted the landscape along the two trails.[24]

Occasionally the joint fundraising campaigns of DAR chapters, counties, and local communities allowed for more elaborate marker designs that hinted at their intended commemorative meanings. In 1915 the Oregon Trail Chapter of Hebron, Nebraska, the Nebraska Historical Society, the State of Nebraska, and the citizens of Hebron County and Thayer

Figure 2.1. DAR marker in Kearny County, Kansas. The DAR placed hundreds of markers like this along the Santa Fe Trail during the Progressive Era to commemorate American pioneers who traveled to the Midwest and West before the Civil War. Wikimedia Commons, photographer: Ammodramus, https://commons.wikimedia.org/wiki/File:Indian_Mound_(Kearny_Co_KS)_DAR_marker_1.JPG, Public domain: https://creativecommons.org/publicdomain/zero/1.0/deed.en.

County erected an eight-foot, red granite boulder whose squared top bore a detailed carving of a covered wagon drawn by a yoke of oxen. A longer inscription gave details about its route and the people who traveled the trail until the railroad ended the pioneer era. The narrow side of the stone showed a carved modern-day automobile, hinting at the impressive technological developments that had taken place since the covered wagon days.[25] State line markers, which tended to be joint projects between two DAR state organizations, were also larger and had longer inscriptions, although specially designed monuments were rare. The Washington State DAR chose one of the most ornate designs for a state line monument; it secured the services of local sculptor Alonzo Victor Lewis to design an eight-foot granite fountain with a large bronze tablet. In 1917 the fountain was placed near the pedestrian entrance on the west side of a bridge over the Columbia River. It was composed of a central granite shaft that was paired by two smaller stones, each of which had a bronze buffalo skull attached to its front. The polished shaft bore a large bronze tablet that depicted the female allegorical figure the Spirit of the Trail, which led a trek of covered wagons drawn by oxen toward the setting sun in the West. The top of the tablet, which was ornamented by additional buffalo skulls, bore the inscription "To the Pioneers of the Oregon Trail 1844." Lewis's bronze tablet was most likely inspired by John Gast's 1872 painting *American Progress*, featuring a female allegorical figure guiding American settlers who, together with the telegraph and the railroad, bring civilization to the dark and primitive West.[26] Western Daughters thus implicitly praised the idea of Manifest Destiny and regarded nineteenth-century pioneers as the agents of white civilization and US nation-building.

While a handful of markers hinted at the cultural memory the Daughters sought to convey, it was especially the ceremonies accompanying the dedications of these monuments that allowed the organization to expose tens of thousands of citizens to its interpretation of western expansion. On hundreds of wooden stages that were erected next to the markers before their dedication, Daughters drove home the nationalist message. They praised the valor of heroic male pioneers whom they considered the trailblazers of white civilization, and they stressed the significance of the men's patriotic example for the present generation of citizens.[27] But the Daughters also repeatedly linked the commemoration of these men's heroism to the need for national unity and patriotism. At the unveiling of an Oregon Trail monument in Omaha, Nebraska, state regent Mrs. Oreal S. Ward explained, "By placing these monuments as visible evidences of heroic deeds and hard-won victories before the present and future citizens of the United States, we may foster in their hearts the desire to give their best to the service of their country, and the inspiration may come to them to strive for the higher patriotic ideals of American citizenship."[28] The numerous male orators the DAR invited to speak at the unveilings, including governors, mayors, and judges, as well as the journalists who reported on the ceremonies, reinforced the idea that male pioneers' heroism needed to be remembered in order to strengthen citizens' allegiance to the nation.[29]

Communicative memory proved essential to making such nationalist abstractions meaningful to the people who attended the celebratory events. It was through the involvement of old pioneers and their descendants and repeated references to their memories that the Daughters were able to connect loyalty to families, towns, states, and regions with loyalty toward the

Figure 2.2. Elaborate Oregon Trail monument near Hebron, Nebraska, 1916. The DAR's Oregon Trail Chapter erected the monument in 1915, in cooperation with the Nebraska Historical Society, the state of Nebraska, and residents of Hebron County. Reprinted from Nebraska Society of the Daughters of the American Revolution, *Collection of Nebraska Pioneer Reminiscences* (Cedar Rapids, IA: Torch Press, 1916).

nation. Old settlers had already assisted the DAR in locating the trails and historic spots along the trails, and once the exact locations of the markers had been agreed upon, the DAR continued to depend on their cooperation. In Johnson County, Kansas, the Old Settlers' Association agreed to place the markers that had been chosen for the locale and promised to make it the central event of Old Settlers' Day on September 8, 1907. Aging settlers and their descendants became prominent features in the dedication ceremonies. In the eyes of the Daughters, they embodied the past that was commemorated, which is why they asked these elderly citizens to share their reminiscences of the covered-wagon days with audiences across the West. In Washington State, General Hazard Stevens spoke about his experiences in the 1850s at almost every of the ten marker dedication ceremonies in 1916. At one such event in the town of Tumwater, the chaplain P. D. Moore, who was a pioneer resident of Olympia and a member of the Pioneer and Historical Society of Thurston County, had been invited by the DAR to give the invocation. On that occasion, the dedication ceremonies were scheduled to coincide with reunions of old pioneers and their descendants. Even if they were not asked to participate in the ceremonies, old pioneers were almost always among the large audiences that witnessed the events, sometimes even traveling to the dedications from other western states.[30] What made the Daughters' activism in the region significant was that the nation and its past became meaningful to those who attended DAR dedication ceremonies because the history of their families was presented as a crucial building block in the history of the nation. Family history and national history appeared to become one.

Surprisingly—and in stark contrast to the DAR's stated goal to correct male-centered accounts of the past—the Daughters invited almost no pioneer women to share their recollections of the western past during dedication ceremonies. In part, this inattention might have reflected women's marginalized role in early pioneer societies. These organizations occasionally praised the sacrifices female pioneers had made but initially barred women from full membership before eventually merging with women auxiliaries. Women frequently recorded their reminiscences of the journey to the West, but male pioneers tended to dominate the institutionalized commemoration of western expansion; their dominance might explain why Daughters asked mostly men to advise them in their efforts to find the trails' original routes. In light of the DAR's ambiguous remembrance of the American Revolution, which praised women's heroism but regarded them as mere helpmates, the lack of enthusiasm for the accomplishments of pioneer women certainly also stemmed from the implicit understanding among its members that men, albeit supported by loyal wives and daughters, had been the most important agents of territorial expansion.[31]

The DAR's close cooperation with old pioneers and local communities shaped the commemorative themes that ran through the dedication ceremonies; the events were consistently linked to the region's communicative memories and generally confirmed the organization's nationalized interpretations of the western past. Probably the most dominant theme was the pioneers' struggle against the "savage foe," as Indians were routinely called in articles and speeches. In their tales about the challenges that settlers met on their long journeys, Daughters stressed the courage and perseverance that was required of male pioneers when being attacked by cruel warriors and risking capture or death. Writing in 1910 in the *American Monthly Magazine,* a member of the Fort Kearny Chapter of Nebraska opined that "it was the Indian, whose stealthy step or startling war-cry set the blood of the pioneer running like icy water through his veins. For the red man showed no respect for the dead and left his victim mutilated, a thing of horror, unburied on the plains."[32] The Daughters thus fully subscribed to the myth of the frontier that held that American civilization and democracy had only been possible through the conquest of the continent and the removal of its Indigenous population. Richard Slotkin has demonstrated that the history of the American nation was seen as being inextricably intertwined with the idea of the "savage war," which implied that there could be no peaceful coexistence between "primitive natives" and "civilized" Europeans. In this interpretation of racial conflict on the frontier, Native Americans were regarded as the initiators of war and the only obstacles to the creation of a virtuous republic; they could thus justifiably be subdued and displaced to make room for the superior Anglo-Saxon. The trail markers' dedication ceremonies frequently served as ritualized reminders of this violence, as many monuments were erected at locations where Indians had killed pioneer families. The Daughters and old pioneers regarded those who perished during conflicts with America's Indigenous population as heroic martyrs in the struggle to build a white nation.[33]

In October 1908 a Santa Fe Trail marker was placed on the grounds of a ranch on the outskirts of Burdick, Kansas, that was raided by six hundred Cheyenne warriors in 1863.[34] Ten years later, Nebraska's Kit-Ki-Ha-Ki Chapter used one of the final dedications of Oregon Trail markers to commemorate an "Indian massacre" that took place in Nuckolls County in 1864 and left two white men dead. Once more drawing on people's communicative memories to make the nation's cultural memory meaningful, three survivors of that Indian attack were present at the dedication ceremony.[35] The theme of Indian violence and white suffering permeated numerous published and unpublished pioneer reminiscences that were penned between the 1880s and the 1920s. In these memoirs the savage war took center stage, and the authors lionized the white conquerors who, despite being victimized by Native Americans, emerged victorious.[36]

Although white and Indian conflict was a prominent theme in the DAR's remembrance of western expansion, it occasionally intersected with other, seemingly contradictory messages that testify to the complexity of the region's memory. For example, cooperation between Indians and the US government or white settlers was occasionally commemorated as well. In Council Grove, Kansas, a Santa Fe Trail memorial bore an inscription that explained how the local Osage tribe signed a treaty with the United States near the town in 1825 allowing white settlers to travel the Santa Fe Trail. One of the pioneer settlers who spoke at the dedication ceremony lauded the tribe for living up to its promises and refraining from attacks on white settlers.[37] The idea of white and Indian friendship and cooperation dominated the DAR's commemoration of the Native American past but remained marginal in the marking of western trails.

In general, the dedication ceremonies confirmed the thrust of the Daughters' major argument about white men's primacy as nation-builders. Male explorers who blazed the trails before the arrival of white settlers took on a particularly prominent role in the interpretations of the past that were offered during these events. Since many markers were placed only a few years after the 1904 centennial of the famous Lewis and Clark expedition, a number of granite boulders marked spots where the two discoverers had camped on their way to the Pacific. Kit Carson, the famous adventurer, trapper, scout, and soldier, was also occasionally lavished with praise. Such was the case in Trinidad, Colorado, where the DAR dedicated the last of the state's thirty Santa Fe Trail monuments with the assistance of Carson's sons, daughters, and granddaughters.[38] While men like Lewis, Clark, and Carson were portrayed as preparing the ground for western expansion, the pioneers who followed them were sometimes lauded for initiating the process of establishing the new territories' political sovereignty. In Washington State, Daughters and local citizens assembled in 1916 near the town of Kelso to dedicate an Oregon Trail marker that commemorated an 1852 meeting of the state's pioneers who petitioned the US Congress to organize the Territory of Washington. One of the men on the platform was Edward Huntington, who had attended the meeting, together with three generations of his descendants.[39]

The Daughters' extensive publicity campaigns and collaborations with political officials and interested citizens on the local, regional, and state levels ensured that tens of thousands of citizens across the West were exposed to the organization's patriotic interpretations of the nation's past. In almost every state where Santa Fe and Oregon Trail memorials were dedicated, hundreds and sometimes thousands of local residents attended the ceremonies. In many towns the dedication ceremonies became the largest event of the year.[40] In Franklin, Missouri, 2,000 people welcomed the members of the organization's Santa Fe Trail Committee, and older residents told the Daughters that "the dedication was the biggest event recorded in the history of the town since the arrival of the steamboat Independence from St. Louis in 1819."[41] Approximately 3,000 people attended the unveiling of an Oregon Trail monument in Grand Mound Prairie, Washington, in October 1916.[42]

While it is difficult to know how many people accepted or internalized the messages the Daughters sought to convey, it is likely that a large number of people were able to link the communicative memories of their families, towns, and regions with the patriotic cultural memory of the nation. The nationalist rituals that preceded or concluded each ceremony— among them the singing of the "Star Spangled Banner" and "America" as well as the recitation of the Pledge of Allegiance—certainly reminded them of the patriotic significance of the people and events that were being memorialized.[43] A journalist's report on the dedication of an Oregon Trail marker at Woodland, Washington, in 1916 suggests that the DAR's commemorative rituals did have a considerable impact on people's identities as US citizens. "Never in the history of the town," he wrote, "has so much interest been shown in a public event, and one could not but help going away from the place feeling better, feeling more patriotic and feeling more than one possibly has at any time in the past that the great work accomplished by the pioneers has not been fully appreciated by those who are enjoying the fruits of it in the peaceful possession of the lands opened up by these same pioneers."[44]

Although the Daughters' commemorations of American pioneers around 1900 were most visible in the Midwest and West, DAR state organizations and local chapters in the South and Southwest also marked a number of pioneer trails. While these campaigns tended to focus on the pre–Revolutionary period, they stressed the same themes that dominated western Daughters' tributes to the past. In Texas and Louisiana, the Daughters marked the Camino Real, also called the Old San Antonio Road, a 1,000-mile trail that the Spanish Crown began in the seventeenth century to connect its numerous missions and military posts in what was then New Spain. Especially the Texas DAR embraced the state's Spanish heritage, but the Daughters used it primarily to illustrate western civilization's progress in general and white Anglo-American civilization's superiority in particular.[45]

In North Carolina and Tennessee, the Daughters confirmed western Daughters' interpretation of territorial expansion as a process that was initiated by heroic explorers. In both states, they focused on the memory of Daniel Boone, the pioneer explorer, hunter, and scout who in the mid-1770s explored the region between the future states of North Carolina and Kentucky before founding one of the first white communities west of the Appalachian Mountains.[46] Surely influenced by the many tales about his adventures, in 1914 and 1915, the North Carolina and Tennessee DAR commemorated Boone's activities in their states by erecting several commemorative granite boulders that resembled the ones that were placed on western trails and the Camino Real.[47] The Daughters' admiration for Boone extended beyond the states through which he had traveled, reflecting important links between southern and western Daughters' remembrance of America's pioneers. As early as 1906, Daughters in Iowa City, Iowa, had founded a Daniel Boone chapter whose membership was composed entirely of Boone's descendants, including his granddaughter. In Missouri the DAR erected a monument on the grave of Boone and his wife, Rebecca Bryan.[48] To the Daughters, Boone was yet another exemplar of strong, white masculinity. A 1916 report on the marking of his trail in North Carolina called him the "foremost Pioneer of a long and mighty race of heroic men who gave their lives to win that golden country called the West."[49] Southern as well as western Daughters thus upheld dominant notions of white masculinity that they believed were indivisibly entangled with what it meant to be a patriotic man.

"Loyal to Their Men": The National Old Trails Road, Pioneer Mothers, and the Madonna of the Trail

It was only after World War I that the DAR began to explicitly honor pioneer women because of the organization's failure to transform its regional achievements into an enduring national memorial. In 1912 the successful efforts of western Daughters to memorialize the Santa Fe and Oregon Trails inspired the national DAR to make the marking of the old trails a national project. Following the lobbying of Daughters from Missouri, the organization's leaders established the National Old Trails Committee, which fervidly lobbied state governments as well as the US Congress to build an "ocean-to-ocean highway" that would connect five historic pioneer trails as a lasting national memorial to the pioneers.

Two women from the DAR's Kansas City, Missouri, Chapter, Elizabeth Butler Gentry and Hope Casey Van Brunt, initiated this movement, which began at the state level before becoming a national DAR project. Both women had been instrumental in marking the Santa Fe Trail in their state and established the Missouri DAR's Good Roads Committee in 1911 to coordinate their campaign for a national memorial highway. The committee emerged against the backdrop of the good roads movement, a nationwide effort of white middle-class citizens during the Progressive Era to build or improve the nation's many deplorable roads. But the committee went further than this movement because it lobbied the governor of Missouri and the state legislature for appropriations to transform unpaved old trails into modern roads as an explicit homage to the pioneers. Its ultimate goal was to connect all major routes that the pioneers had taken on the continent by building a National Old Trails Road highway.[50] This commemorative project, as Gentry explained their intentions, would bolster patriotism by joining "the hands of all women living along these trails to forge a human chain across the continent: a chain with links of patriotism, history, and sentiment."[51]

Gentry and Van Brunt proposed to build this national highway on five historic trails that would connect Washington, DC, and San Francisco: the Old National Road or Cumberland Road, Boone's Lick Road, Kearny's Road, Santa Fe Trail, and Oregon Trail. The latter two had been western settlers' primary routes, while the other three trails had served mostly as military roads or connections between new western settlements. At the DAR's 1912 annual meeting, Gentry's and Van Brunt's Good Roads Commit-

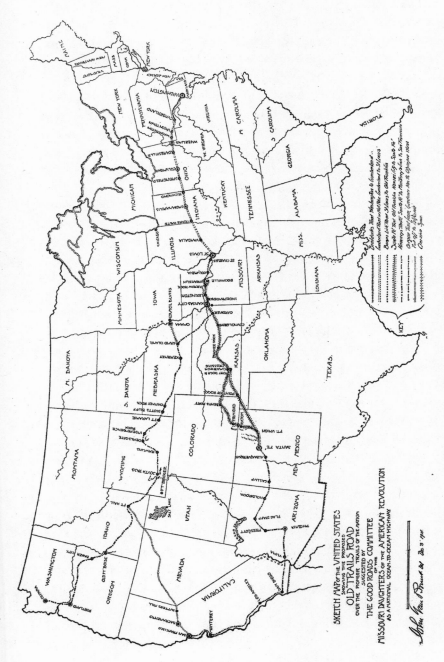

Figure 2.3. Map of the DAR vision for a National Old Trails Road, 1913. The memorial road was to be a national highway connecting all major routes that pioneers traveled to reach the Midwest and West. The Daughters launched the ambitious project in 1912 but failed to obtain funding for the highway. Their successful Madonna of the Trail campaign was an outgrowth of the project. Reprinted from *American Monthly Magazine*, April 1913, 162.

tee proposed to add George Washington Road—which had been a military road from Cumberland, Maryland, to Braddock, Pennsylvania, during the French and Indian War—to emphasize the highway's patriotic symbolism. In order to include the nation's capital as well as Baltimore, Philadelphia, and New York, the Daughters extended Braddock's trail by adding the large cities that George Washington had visited during his inaugural journeys as president of the United States. Ultimately, the proposed highway would have stretched 6,000 miles from coast to coast. The National Old Trails Road was thus an attempt to establish a national cultural memory but also a prime example of what Eric Hobsbawm has termed "invented traditions," since the Daughters constructed various fictitious historical and geographic continuities to boost their nationalist message.[52]

As they had done during the Santa Fe Trail initiative, Gentry and Van Brunt launched an impressive publicity campaign that targeted fellow Daughters, state historical societies, politicians, Missouri citizens, and the good roads movement. The Missouri DAR's Good Roads Committee invited fellow Daughters in each of the twenty trail states to assist in the effort. All but three DAR state organizations responded enthusiastically and pledged their support; the initiative brought together Daughters from states that included Virginia, Pennsylvania, Wyoming, and Washington. In each of the trail states, DAR state organizations and chapters used strategies that had proven successful in previous campaigns; they established contacts with state historical societies and lobbied members of the US Congress to vote for the National Old Trails Road bill that was introduced by Missouri Representative William P. Borland in early 1912.[53] Missourians in particular responded with great interest to the DAR's project. To support the Daughters, five hundred of them assembled in Kansas City in April 1911 to form the National Old Trails Road Association. By the end of 1912 the Missouri-based association had built an impressive network of 7,000 supporters in twelve states. The Daughters found new allies also by aligning themselves with the good roads movement whose advocates lobbied for federal financial assistance in building and improving America's roads.[54]

In April 1912, after it had become clear that Van Brunt and Gentry's campaign was gaining considerable momentum, the national DAR decided to support Missouri Daughters' efforts by establishing the National Old Trails Road Committee (NOTRC), which took over the work of the Missouri Good Roads Committee under the same leadership. The new committee received immediate encouragement and support from an unexpected corner. William Cody, the organizer of the widely popular Wild West shows who was known to most people as Buffalo Bill, supported the DAR's efforts by giving the NOTRC a historic stagecoach for its collection of trail relics. Given these nationwide lobbying efforts and endorsements by prominent organizations and individuals, Gentry and her followers were hopeful that Congress would pass the memorial highway bill.[55]

The same month that the National Old Trails Roads Committee was established, the Daughters were given an opportunity to present their project before the congressional Committee on Agriculture, to which the bill had been referred. At the hearing, Representative William Borland and an array of DAR officers from western and midwestern states sought to convince the committee members of the importance and potential benefit of a memorial highway. Gentry presented the DAR's main arguments, which reflected the organization's adroit attempt to adapt to the changing commemorative landscape during the first decade of the twentieth century. Through the introduction of affordable cars such as Ford's Model T, tourism had begun to reshape the ways America's cultural memory was presented to the public. More and more middle-class Americans were becoming acquainted with America's battlefields, monuments, and other reminders of the country's past during motor trips across newly built or improved highways.[56] Gentry incorporated the early signs of this development into her argument, promoting the National Old Trails Road as a boost to both American patriotism and the emerging tourism industry. She pointed out that the proposed highway would have practical effects as well, as it would help farmers market their products and make it easier for their children to attend school. In the end, however, neither the DAR's massive lobbying campaign nor Gentry's eloquent arguments about the road's political, economic, and social benefits swayed the committee, and its members declined to recommend the bill for an official vote in Congress. Although a determined Representative Borland reintroduced it twice in the following years, in 1913 and 1918, the US Congress never passed the National Old Trails Road bill.[57]

Two major factors probably contributed to the DAR's failure to win federal support for its national memorial highway project. First, during the Progressive Era, commemorative projects continued to be primarily financed by private groups, with occasional financial assistance from towns, counties, and state legislatures. The federal government rarely contributed to such campaigns and remained reluctant to do so until the late 1920s.

Probably just as important, the DAR's National Old Trails Road bill faced stiff competition from the good roads movement, which proposed and sponsored dozens of bills that were intended to fund new roads or improve existing ones.[58] Although the Daughters had highlighted the proposed highway's practical benefits, they could not hide the fact that the project's primary purpose was commemorative. And the National Old Trails Road would have been extremely expensive, which probably made it seem superfluous in the eyes of many legislators.

Despite this defeat, the Daughters refused to give up and patiently continued their National Old Trails Road project at the state and local levels. In almost every trail state, DAR chapters cooperated in marking the route of the memorial road for American motorists. Given their scarce resources, thousands of members took it upon themselves to paint four-inch red, white, and blue stripes on virtually every telegraph and telephone pole that lined the various trails in their respective communities. Above the colored bands they placed the name National Old Trails Road and the DAR insignia. In some towns, local people assisted the Daughters in painting the poles. A few DAR chapters even placed granite boulders beside certain sections of road.[59]

In contrast to the Daughters' unsuccessful lobbying efforts at the national level, governors and state legislatures proved much more responsive to their pleas. In Kansas the DAR's cooperation with the state's Good Roads Association generated enough funds to transform sections of the Santa Fe Trail into a dirt road. And in Missouri the governor and the state legislature agreed to build a state highway on certain sections of the Santa Fe Trail and the Oregon Trail. This road, christened the Missouri State Highway, was dedicated in October 1911. In Washington State, Daughters faced the least opposition to their endeavor because the routes of Washington's state highway and Pacific Highway were virtually identical with the Oregon Trail, making them easy to designate as the National Old Trails Road.[60]

Although federal support for the national highway eluded them, the NOTRC's chairwoman, Elizabeth Butler Gentry, felt that its work had made important progress. At the DAR's 1915 Continental Congress, she proudly announced that the National Old Trails Road was "open across the Continent," which meant that all trails that made up the memorial highway could be used by motorists. In addition, red, white, and blue painted bands now marked almost the entire distance from the capital to San Francisco and would help tourists find the historic route.[61] In light of this success, Gentry was confident that the road could now serve its patriotic purpose, instilling in younger generations the lessons of the pioneers' accomplishments. To her, actually seeing the historic spots that had been marked along the old trails was superior to reading history books in school. Gentry also argued that simply working on the project had served a patriotic purpose by bringing together Daughters from across the country.[62]

As with the American Revolution, then, the DAR's remembrance of western expansion was intended to strengthen the patriotism of the entire populace, but its effect on the nationalist convictions of the organization's members was probably much more profound. While a few tourists might have visited the historic places the Daughters marked along the National Old Trails Road, the project appears to have been of greater importance to the Daughters themselves, who labored assiduously to mark the route and felt that they were part of a truly patriotic endeavor. In contrast to the marking of the Santa Fe and Oregon Trails, which exposed thousands of ordinary citizens to their patriotic message, the efforts of the Daughters to mark and establish a national memorial highway primarily boosted their own nationalism.

Despite Gentry's attempts to emphasize the NOTRC's successes, many Daughters were dismayed by the limited national visibility of that work and pondered alternative forms of commemoration that would allow them to reach a larger number of citizens. Consequently, the National Old Trails Road Committee proposed to replace the temporary markers on telephone poles along the route with more permanent markers; that idea was endorsed by the national DAR in 1914.[63] Three years later the committee presented the design for iron markers that would be placed on those telephone poles where color bands had already faded, and the Continental Congress voted to finance 3,050 such markers. Even though World War I impeded the NOTRC's fundraising activities, its members hoped that the end of the military conflict would help them raise enough money to complete the project.[64]

By 1924, however, the new chairwoman of the National Old Trails Road Committee, Arlene Nichols Moss, acknowledged the impracticality of the original proposal and suggested another way to commemorate the National Old Trails Road. In a letter to DAR state regents she explained that many places along the road were characterized by "an over-abundance of markers," which made it implausible to purchase more than 3,000 identical markers. Rather than contribute to pointless memorial inflation, Moss proposed to "place markers of more pretentious proportions along this Highway at certain chosen spots that might well be commemorated for sake of historical interest."[65] In April 1924 the DAR's Continental Congress followed Moss's recommendations and resolved to erect twelve identical monuments "of dignified and pretentious proportions" that would "definitely mark an historical spot" and be placed in twelve states through which the Old Trails Road passed. The states included Maryland, Indiana, Missouri, Colorado, Arizona, and California; the extent reflected the DAR's continuing efforts to build a nationalized cultural memory and more patriotic citizenry.[66]

What distinguished the new campaign from similar pre–World War I endeavors was its focus on the memory of pioneer women. The National Old Trails Road Committee and its predecessor had actually long demanded greater appreciation for women's contributions to western expansion, but DAR leaders and local communities apparently ignored their appeals. "History," Gentry wrote in 1911, "has failed to record the pioneer women who braved the unknown wilderness or desert, succored their children and inspired their men, dauntlessly; who held the forts built by the men, and made homes and planted the civilization of the frontier."[67] And although Gentry appeared to reaffirm earlier male-centered accounts by likening frontiersmen and pioneers to the heroes of Homer's epics of ancient Greece, she repeatedly stressed that the proposed national highway was a memorial to both men and women. More importantly, the NOTRC made women a visible part of cultural memory. The committee's official emblem was the *Madonna of the Trail,* a watercolor painted by the American artist and illustrator Percy Van Eman Ivory; the piece was first published as "A Madonna of the Prairies" in the December 1909 issue of the middle-class monthly *Century Illustrated Magazine.* The picture showed a weary mother holding her sleeping baby inside a covered wagon on its way toward the West. Opposite the woman, two rifles lean against the canvas wall. Through the opening of the canvas cover one can see a man who holds the reins of a horse that pulls the wagon. As part of their fundraising efforts, the committee sold gilded Madonna of the Trail pins in red, white, and blue bands of enamel with the name of the road in gold lettering. The committee also seems to have made sure that the memory of pioneer women was discussed at least occasionally at gatherings of its supporters.[68] Although the memory of female pioneers was largely ignored in the DAR's official commemorative campaigns prior to the 1920s, the leadership of the National Old Trails Road Committee apparently sought to make sure that male pioneers were not the only heroes who were honored for their patriotism.

These attempts to salvage the memory of pioneer women culminated in the Madonna of the Trail statue, which the national DAR accepted in 1927 as the official design for the twelve identical monuments that were to be placed on historic spots along the National Old Trails Road. The statue was conceived by NOTRC chairwoman Moss and designed by the German St. Louis-based sculptor August Leimbach in accordance with Moss's ideas. Leimbach created an impressive ten-foot likeness of a pioneer mother clad in a homespun skirt, boots, and a bonnet. Determinedly looking toward the horizon on her way toward the West, she cradles an infant in her left arm while holding the shaft of a rifle in her right hand. A young boy clings to her skirt. The front of the monument's six-foot base bore the inscriptions "Madonna of the Trail" and "NSDAR Memorial to the Pioneer Mothers of the Covered Wagon Days." With its two-foot-tall foundation, the Algonite stone statue towered eighteen feet above the ground.[69] In the design depicting an armed and resolute mother, the monument's visual language reflected the Daughters' admiration for Margaret Corbin and other heroines of the American Revolution who had taken up arms to defend themselves, their husbands, and the nation. As in the remembrance of the Revolution, the DAR's patriotic message tended to be at odds with the visual militancy the statue appeared to convey.

Once more, the Daughters used elaborate dedication ceremonies to expose American citizens to their gendered and racialized interpretations of the Madonna of the Trail. Jointly organized by the DAR, local towns and chambers of commerce, private associations, and individual citizens, the dedication ceremonies began in July 1928 in Springfield, Ohio, and concluded in April 1929 in Bethesda, Maryland. Local, regional, and national memories were closely entwined in these festive events and fused into one coherent narrative of national unity and progress. Reiterating previous commemorative messages, the ceremonies and the parades that preceded them presented the history of the National Old Trails Road as a triumph of Anglo-American civilization. Featuring frontiersmen, cowboys, miners, Native Americans, and in California, Mexican Americans, the colorful processions' message revolved around technological progress in transportation and the subduing of nonwhite people.[70] In Springerville, Arizona,

MADONNA OF THE TRAIL

N·S·D·A·R· MEMORIAL
TO THE
PIONEER MOTHERS
OF THE
COVERED WAGON DAYS

Figure 2.4. Madonna of the Trail, Wheeling, West Virginia. The Daughters of the American Revolution erected twelve such statues in as many trail states in the Midwest and West between 1928 and 1929 to honor pioneer mothers. Courtesy of Library of Congress Prints and Photographs Division, West Virginia Collection within the Carol M. Highsmith Archive, LC-DIG-highsm-31941.

members of the Apache tribe were invited to perform "their weird Devil Dance," and the Arizona monument's inscription paid tribute "to the Pioneers of Arizona and the Southwest who trod this ground and braved the dangers of the Apaches and other Warrior Tribes."[71] In Upland, California, the Daughters included the subjugation of Mexicans in this tale of triumph over uncivilized peoples; the town's parade, in the words of the *Los Angeles Times* reporter, "pictured the early days of the western country and told in story form the tale of the Indians and Mexicans fleeing before the resolute men of '49."[72]

In Colorado and Pennsylvania, however, the Daughters also paid tribute to the pioneers' benevolence toward Native Americans and instances of interracial cooperation.[73] Only the monument's unveiling in Illinois departed from these themes, putting much emphasis on the memory of the state's native son Abraham Lincoln. Yet the contrast was not as stark as one might expect because the slain president had long been remembered as a humble man who came from a pioneer background and remained anchored in the mindset of the Midwest's early settlers. The Daughters adopted this interpretation and could easily utilize Lincoln's image to stress the importance of national unity in the context of western expansion.[74]

Flag salutes and the singing of patriotic songs during the dedication ceremonies were meant to intensify people's love of country. Occasionally, public interest in the Madonna of the Trail monuments was so great that the crowds who attended the dedications even surpassed the ones that had flocked to marker dedications during the Progressive Era. While the Arizona DAR ceremony managed to attract only a few hundred onlookers, the dedications and parades that were organized in other trail states tended to be witnessed by several thousand people and in Vandalia, Illinois, even by 10,000. According to the DAR, the parades reflected the idea that the old trails were "the true index of a Nation's progress" as well as "the life-history of a people," that is, Anglo-Saxon America.[75]

Although these nationalist rituals generally repeated earlier commemorative themes, the Daughters broke new ground by focusing on the memory of pioneer mothers. On the one hand, this was accomplished on a symbolic level through the ten-foot likeness of the resolute pioneer mother itself. In addition and in stark contrast to their pre–World War I campaigns, the Daughters asked old pioneer women or their descendants to pull the ropes that uncovered the monuments. In Springerville, Arizona, that honor went to ninety-three-year old Liza Rudd, the oldest resident settler of the valley where the town was established.[76] But the DAR also explicitly hammered home the message of women's important role in settling the West in dozens of speeches that preceded the unveilings. Arlene Moss in particular lauded female pioneers' heroism, emphasized their contributions to American nation-building, and implored her audiences to let the women's example inspire them to become more patriotic citizens. Before the unveiling of the twelfth statue, in Bethesda, Maryland, in April 1929, Moss said, "We are at last paying tribute to the silent and patient 'Madonnas of the Trail'—brave in their sacrifice, loyal to their men, following them trustfully, carrying the coming race in their arms."[77]

Six months earlier Moss had explained to the huge crowd in Vandalia, Illinois, that this ability to silently endure the privations of the journey while supporting their husbands and nurturing their children was due to women's inherent qualities as mothers. Moss contended that Americans needed to keep alive this spirit and dedicate themselves "to the great ideals of the past, to an abiding faith in our nation . . . [and] to steadfastly upholding our institutions."[78] As in the remembrance of the Revolution, the Daughters applauded pioneer women's selfless service to others as well as their loyalty toward the nation and their men but refrained from any argument that would compromise women's femininity or call for more gender equality as a reward for their heroism.

Local communities and the male speakers the Daughters invited to the Madonna statue dedications embraced this emphasis on patriotic maternalism. Many of the monument inscriptions that communities selected in cooperation with the DAR revealed the same notions of seemingly natural gender binaries that Moss invoked in her speeches. In Albuquerque the Daughters sponsored a contest for the best inscription that was initiated through local newspapers before the monument's dedication in September 1928. The two local women who won the contest clearly empathized with the DAR's message. One inscription read, "Into the primitive West. Face upflung toward the sun. Bravely she came. Her children beside her. Here she made them a home. Beautiful Pioneer Mother!" The other inscription stated, "To the Pioneer Mother of America, through whose courage and sacrifice the desert has blossomed, the camp became the home, the blazed trail the thorofare."[79] The Madonna of the Trail monument in Wheeling, West Virginia, bore a similar inscription. "To the Pioneer Mothers of our Mountain State," it read, "whose courage, optimism, love and sacrifice made possible the National Highway that united the East and the West."[80]

The politicians, businessmen, historians, and other male speakers who gave orations during the celebrations likewise lauded female pioneers' maternal qualities and linked these qualities to the narrative of national progress and unity.[81] However, not all communities followed this pattern. The inscriptions of some monuments such as the one in California made references to men rather than women, remembering the first group of American settlers who entered California in 1826.[82]

The DAR was certainly not the first organization to honor American pioneer mothers, but the Madonna campaign stood out because of its unparalleled emphasis on pioneer mothers' patriotic significance.[83] From the Daughters' perspective, women were by nature ordained to be mothers and supporters of their husbands not only within the family but also within the American nation. Confirming their gendered interpretations of colonial America and the American Revolution, the Daughters regarded pioneer mothers as icons of traditional notions of wifehood and motherhood, which the organization regarded as a powerful antidote to feminists and others they perceived as radicals and believed to jeopardize the United States. The DAR exposed thousands of citizens to this message, reinforcing dichotomous interpretations of gender and the nation, while reassuring its members that the nation's future would be secure if the memory of patriotic motherhood was kept alive.

Remembering "White Space": The Daughters
and the Pioneer Past during the 1920s and 1930s

Although many Daughters regarded the Madonna of the Trail statues as the crowning achievement of a campaign that had begun almost two decades earlier, it was not the only commemorative project that focused on the remembrance of explorers and pioneers during the 1920s, nor would it be the last prior to World War II. Dozens of western and midwestern chapters paid tribute to what they interpreted as harbingers of white civilization. They did so by financing and dedicating monuments, and many Daughters also worked hard to prevent the communicative memories of western settlers from fading into oblivion by interviewing parents and grandparents who had made the trek, writing down and sometimes publishing their life stories, and sharing these stories with fellow Daughters. In these narratives, the voices of women were heard far more frequently than in the Daughters' public commemorations, and they were more than mere family reminiscences. Rather, they linked each Daughter through their ancestors to the imagined community of the American nation. That community was white, Protestant, and Anglo-Saxon, something the Daughters had certainly implied before but highlighted much more explicitly in the local and regional forms of remembrance that took place in the 1920s.

Despite the efforts of the National Old Trails Road Committee to put more emphasis on women's contributions to American nation-building in the West, the great majority of the DAR's smaller commemorative projects continued to praise a small pantheon of male pioneers and explorers, chief among them Meriwether Lewis and William Clark. Numerous chapters continued to mark spots where the famous expedition had either put up camp or made discoveries from 1804 to 1806. Daniel Boone also remained popular among the Daughters. Pioneer men were likewise honored, as in 1927 in Columbus, Nebraska, where the DAR Platte Chapter erected an arresting sixteen-foot monument that bore in relief an armed frontiersman to mark the northern section of the Oregon Trail. Women, by contrast, received virtually no such public recognition. The only exception to this general rule was the Pioneer Mothers' Memorial Cabin, the replica of an old blockhouse in Champoeg that the Oregon DAR completed in 1931.[84] The Daughters thus perpetuated dominant notions of masculine valor and reaffirmed white men's preeminent role in the American nation's expansion.

As during the Progressive Era, western Daughters who portrayed the pioneers as national heroes of white civilization during the interwar period deliberately linked this abstract idea to local communicative memories. Throughout the Midwest and West, DAR chapters called attention to the first signs of white civilization in their respective communities by marking the sites of the first house, first church, or first school. As part of the efforts to mark local historic sites, a number of chapters also sought to save old log cabins that were to be demolished.[85] In many instances the Daughters established explicit connections between education, Christianity, and the progress of white civilization. Such was the case in 1930 when the California State DAR placed a boulder on the El Monte High School grounds to commemorate the pioneers' arduous journey to the West and to mark the site of California's first schoolhouse and first Protestant church.[86] Mrs. James E. Babb reported about the marking of the Lapwai Mission near Lewiston, Idaho, in 1924, that what the buildings represented—Christianity, home, and education—constituted "the three basic elements of civilization" and thus of the American nation.[87] In the

1920s, chapters in California added technological innovation to these three basic elements when marking the sites of the state's first telegraph station, its first water-operated gristmill, and Oakland's Old Railway Station, where the first overland train had arrived in 1869. In California in particular, the Daughters left a lasting legacy by contributing a list of the state's historic spots to the three-volume *Historic Spots of California,* which complemented an earlier inventory that had been written by the pioneer organization Native Sons of the Golden West.[88]

If Christianity, the home, education, and technological advancement were regarded as crucial building blocks of the nation, local commemorative projects of the 1920s revealed that the Daughters deemed whiteness an equally essential element of American nation-building. By the end of World War I, the idea of Anglo-Saxon superiority had been clearly established, and whiteness was consolidated during the Jazz Age.[89] The Daughters contributed to this consolidation through their remembrance of western expansion. A considerable number of chapters commemorated the first white men to enter what would become US states as well as local communities' first white babies and first white settlers regardless of whether they were US citizens or of Anglo-Saxon descent. In the Daughters' racialized interpretations of the past, Spanish Catholics were white enough to be included in their tributes to white nation-building. In 1923 Utah's Spirit of Liberty Chapter erected a monument to perpetuate the memory of the first white man to enter the future state, a Spanish priest named Father Escalante, who camped in the Utah Valley in 1776.[90] Five years later, California's Santa Barbara Chapter placed a boulder next to the city's courthouse to honor the Spanish officer Gaspar de Portolá and his soldiers, "the first white men to march through the wilderness of California," who had camped near that spot in 1769.[91] As the historian David Glassberg has aptly observed, in 1920s California, historical space was primarily "white space."[92]

To other DAR chapters, the first white children born in their communities and the first white settlers also seemed worth remembering. In 1928 the John Crawford Chapter of Oakland, Michigan, placed a bronze tablet at the birthplace of the first white children who were born in Oakland Township. That same year, the state's Lucinda Hinsdale Stone Chapter marked the site of the first permanent white settlement in Kalamazoo County, while another Michigan chapter marked the spot where the county's first white settler had built his log cabin one hundred years earlier.[93] DAR member

Catherine Cate Coblentz's articles entitled "The First Babies in the Midwest" and the "First Far Western Babies," both of which were published in 1941 in the *DAR Magazine*, testify to the tenacity of such racialized ideas about western expansion. After enumerating the various white newborns in such states as Minnesota, North Dakota, and Wyoming in the first half of the nineteenth century, Coblentz explained in the article on western babies that the "early mixture of Spanish blood with the Indians of Mexico and the northern continent" made "it impossible to ascertain when the first child of white parentage may have been born in New Mexico."[94] True American history, such explanations suggested, began only with the birth of truly white children, their acclaim for early Spanish explorers notwithstanding. The DAR's commemorative campaigns in the Midwest and West thus became significant exercises in racial boundary-making that restricted national membership to old-stock Anglo-Saxons.

But during the 1920s and 1930s, western and midwestern Daughters also engaged in much less visible campaigns to honor the pioneers by attempting to save the communicative memories of pioneers and their descendants. These efforts had already begun prior to World War I in such places as Minnesota, Kansas, and Nebraska, but they expanded during the interwar period across the western United States. Already in 1913 Lucy Wilder Morris, a member of the DAR's National Committee for the Preservation of Historic Spots, called Minnesota's pioneers "living repositories of history" who were "passing daily, taking their stories with them." For Daughters, Morris said, it was therefore imperative to record their stories.[95] The Michigan DAR was among the first state organizations during the 1920s to exhort its chapters to collect the reminiscences of old settlers. By 1922, Daughters in that state had compiled 550 biographical sketches of Michigan pioneers. Some DAR chapters published oral histories they collected, but most of them were never made public.[96]

Mirroring northeastern members' experience with the commemoration of the American Revolution, these largely unnoticed efforts to salvage pioneers' living memories allowed western Daughters to discuss among themselves the significance of families' communicative memories for the nationalized cultural memory they deemed so important. In 1925 the historian of Michigan's Coldwater Chapter asked early pioneer families from the region to share their reminiscences with the chapter's members. The letters these families sent to the Daughters in response to the request were read and discussed in some of the chapter's monthly meetings. On a number of occasions the Daughters used their own family memories to highlight women's important contributions to western expansion, but discussions about women's accomplishments continued to oscillate between the attempt to counter male-centered interpretations of the region's past and the conviction that America's gendered status quo needed to be maintained. In the early 1920s in Deerfield, Ohio, the Western Reserve Chapter's historian, herself the great-granddaughter of the first pioneer to settle in the town in 1799, told members about the life stories of the region's early pioneer families. Her account put much emphasis on these families' female members and stressed the same maternalistic message that the DAR's Madonna of the Trail campaign would emphasize a few years later. In a volume of collected life stories of pioneer women of Genesee County, Michigan, which was published six years after the last Madonna statue was erected, the state's Daughters similarly highlighted the campaign's emphasis on pioneer women's heroic qualities while suggesting that men remained the true agents of western history.[97] In the eyes of the Daughters, regardless of whether they commemorated the western past in public spaces or discussed its significance among themselves, white pioneer women, like the women of the American Revolution, remained mere auxiliaries whose greatest patriotic contribution was their maternal loyalty toward male nation-builders.

In the late 1930s, using the new medium of radio, a number of Daughters sought to share with fellow citizens at least some of the gendered lessons they recognized in pioneer women's biographies. In 1938 the Daniel Newcomb Chapter from Yankton, South Dakota, broadcast a number of talks on historical subjects pertaining to the history of the state. Many of these talks, which were part of a series of broadcasts that marked South Dakota's fiftieth anniversary, focused on the state's pioneers, and the Daughters could use them to share the family histories with others while stressing the important role they believed women had played in the settling of the West. In one story about a pioneer woman named Sarah Wood Ward, her daughter Margaret shared with listeners the Ward family's memories and recounted the life story of her mother, who had come to Dakota Territory in 1868 as the wife of a missionary. Her life, she said, was a testament "that the early pioneer women were heroes no less than the men" because they had "kept their fears, sorrows and homesick moments locked in their hearts and carried on without faltering." These women, Margaret Ward told her audience, "were not in the public eye as were the men, but, by their quiet, unselfish devotion to those men of early Dakota, they, as well, should go down in history as builders of our state."[98] Other DAR broadcasts on early pioneer life in Dakota Territory offered similar interpretations and confirmed the general thrust of the organization's nationalist ideology, which continued to veer between challenging and reaffirming men's preeminence.[99]

Western Daughters' various local, state, and national efforts to instill patriotism through memorializing the pioneers prepared the ground for and intersected with projects that were initiated by western and midwestern state governments as well as the US government. All of these authorities gradually expanded their roles in the commemoration of America's western past in the 1920s and 1930s in seeking to actively shape its content to strengthen citizens' allegiance to the United States. Like the Daughters, politicians took seriously the importance of local communities' communicative memories and incorporated them into such celebrations as state anniversaries, the Oregon Trail centennial, and the sesquicentennial of the first white settlement in the Northwest Territory. Once more, World War I marked an important historical turning point. Prior to the Great War, patriotic and commemorative campaigns were launched and financed primarily by private associations such as the DAR. After 1914 the federal government became more and more involved in the creation and dissemination of a nationalized cultural memory to counter social antagonism that was believed to jeopardize national unity. Western and midwestern state governments became allies in these efforts to shape people's collective memory of the nation's past as well as the lessons they should learn from it. The pioneers became a key symbol in these campaigns. During the state centennial celebrations of Indiana and Illinois in 1915 and 1918, respectively, officials allowed local communities to incorporate communicative memories of the pioneers into their celebrations while they also urged them to link the celebrations to the larger idea of the nation. Yet, mirroring similar developments within the commemoration of the American Revolution, state officials were glad to accept the assistance of the DAR and other private associations when organizing such large-scale events. During the 1930s DAR chapters actively contributed to the programs of Wisconsin's tercentennial, Michigan's centennial, and the diamond jubilee of Dakota Territory.[100]

By the early 1930s the memory of the pioneers had become an important element of America's national cultural memory and served important functions during the Great Depression. The nation's unprecedented economic crisis and the human suffering it caused revived not only a general interest among Americans in their country's past but also a growing curiosity about the lives of pioneer men and women who faced great privations during their arduous journeys to the West. The nation's severe economic crisis also sparked debates about the role of the federal government in society and led a number of people to question the values that organizations such as the DAR had promoted in their commemorative campaigns; chief among them was the idea of constant progress. Federal officials, keen on using the memory of the pioneers to soothe people's discontent, portrayed them as symbols of patriotic perseverance who never abandoned their loyalty to the nation despite the seemingly insurmountable obstacles they faced.[101]

On the eve of World War II, the DAR was no longer a major player in the commemoration of western expansion; that status mirrored their dwindling significance as preservers of the memory of the American Revolution. But the seemingly eternal patriotic truths they had promoted year after year in their nationwide campaigns are likely to have had a lasting impact that contributed to the persistence of interpretations of the past that glorified white Anglo-Saxon men as the advance guards of western civilization and American nation-building.

3

"Let Us Clasp Hands, Red Man and White Man"

The DAR and the American Indian

On the evening of April 20, 1921, DAR member and US Congresswoman Alice Robertson was ready to address several thousand fellow Daughters at the organization's thirtieth Continental Congress in Washington, DC. Next to Robertson stood Tsianina Redfeather, a young Creek-Cherokee mezzo soprano who was among the most successful Native American singers of the first third of the twentieth century. Wearing a beaded buckskin dress and moccasins, Redfeather was more than the meeting's musical highlight; she was held up as the epitome of a civilized and cultured Indian. The singer was born in 1892 on Oklahoma Territory's Creek Indian reservation and educated in the state's government-run Indian College, where her musical talent quickly became apparent. Oklahoma native Alice Robertson was so impressed by her performances that she helped the young girl hone her skills as a piano player and singer in Denver, Colorado. Once there, Redfeather caught the attention of the famous white "Indianist" composer Charles Wakefield Cadman. Taking her under his wing, he made Redfeather the main attraction of his extremely popular "Indian Music Talk," which enthralled audiences across the country with traditional Native American and Indianist songs. While impressed with her musical talent, the Daughters were probably even more moved that the young singer had interrupted her successful career in 1917 and 1918 to voluntarily serve with the American Expeditionary Forces in Europe. Following a call by General John J. Pershing, who had asked American entertainers to boost US soldiers' morale, she accompanied Pershing's troops when they crossed the Rhine River to occupy Germany.[1]

Alice Robertson and other speakers who gave talks at the DAR's Continental Congress that night in 1921 regarded the young singer's fascinating career as proof that Indians deserved official citizenship and white support. Thomas L. Sloan, president of the Society of American Indians, exclaimed that Tsianina Redfeather was a "hundred per cent American singer" who did everything she could to "enlist the sympathy and to create a proper and thorough understanding of the real Indian character" among white citizens. Sloan then recounted Indian soldiers' heroic service during the Great War to lend force to his argument that America's Indigenous population had been wronged and finally deserved justice.[2] One of the resolutions the delegates passed during their meeting reflected the DAR's commitment to Sloan's cause. In it the Daughters stated, "The North American Indian is not an alien in our midst, but the original American," and pledged "to secure wise and timely legislation, both State and Federal, for Indian welfare and protection."[3]

The Daughters' admiration for Redfeather and vows to help the "original American" secure federal assistance attest to the organization's peculiar fascination with Native Americans and the pre–World War II efforts to integrate them into their nationalist ideology. Memory was crucial to this endeavor, since the Daughters' remembrance of western pioneers created a major predicament. On the one hand, their riveting stories of the Santa Fe and Oregon Trails celebrated Anglo-Saxon whiteness and the defeat of the savage foe. On the other hand, the organization's leaders were eager to integrate Indians into the DAR vision of a united nation and to transform them into loyal patriots. The Daughters' ambiguous solution to this predicament was the memorialization of white-Indian friendship and cooperation. By sanitizing and romanticizing America's history of racial violence and colonial conquest, the Daughters justified white nation-building and white supremacy while consolidating notions of Anglo-Saxon whiteness.

Reflecting a general concern for the "vanishing Indian" among white middle-class Americans after the US armed forces had crushed the last remnants of Indigenous resistance, Daughters across the nation commemorated what they regarded as cordial collaboration between the two groups and loyal Indian support for white nation-building. During the Progressive Era, most of the Daughters' commemorations of the Indigenous past revolved around treaties in which tribes had agreed to cede their ancestral homelands to the United States as well as Native military support for the US armed forces during and after the American Revolution. Loyal mixed-race chiefs who had signed the treaties and the Indigenous commanders of pro-American warriors received particularly lavish praise.

While Native warriors were most prominent in the DAR's cheerful reading of the Indigenous past, Indian women also played an important role because they were believed to have an inherent propensity to seek interracial friendship and to assist white nation-builders. Tapping white citizens' memory of loyal Indian princesses in American history, the Daughters amplified the idea that Native women simply could not resist the masculine charm of white explorers, gladly supported them in their mission to conquer the continent, and readily served as mediators between the races. The Creek-Cherokee singer Tsianina Redfeather became the Daughters' twentieth-century equivalent of the loyal Indian princess. Based on this belief in Indian loyalty together with concerns that the Indigenous population had become a vanishing race, the Daughters extensively studied Indian culture, "played Indian," and picked Indian names for their chapters; they also had no qualms about the prospect of Indian DAR members or interracial marital unions.

Yet, their Indian-related campaigns were as much about remembering particular aspects of Indigenous peoples' past as they were about omitting or distorting others. Occasionally the Daughters voiced criticism of the injustices Indian tribes had suffered at the hands of the United States, but they continued to engage in imperialist nostalgia, which was characterized by stereotypical portrayals of the Indigenous past and the erasure of the memory of violence and displacement. The DAR's amnesia was a crucial element in its efforts to increasingly focus on the present, as can be seen in their calls for Indian citizenship and their attempts to transform Indigenous men and women into patriotic citizens through financial assistance and education. By 1945 the Daughters were certain of Indians' patriotic loyalty and began to interpret Indian culture as an integral part of US culture that needed to be preserved for posterity. Indians' designation as the first real Americans and the tales of the country's purportedly strong tradition of white-Indian friendship had thus become part of the DAR's nationalist ideology, which oscillated between inclusionary civic nationalism and paternalistic ethnic nationalism.

Loyal Chiefs and Devoted Princesses: Commemorating the Indian Past around 1900

The Daughters' concerns about and fascination with Indians was inextricably intertwined with the consequences of a watershed year in Anglo-American and Native American history: 1890. That year, US troops massacred almost three hundred Lakota Sioux near Wounded Knee, South Dakota, crushing the last remnants of Indian military resistance in the American West. In the eyes of white citizens, Wounded Knee was the final battle for territorial and political sovereignty in North America. Not long after that fateful event, the US Census Bureau not only officially declared the western frontier to be closed but also reported a precipitous decline in the Indian population, from more than 400,000 in 1850 to fewer than 250,000 in 1890. In the wake of this announcement, scholars began to speak of "the vanishing Indian," expecting the continent's Indigenous population to die out and become absorbed into the country's white citizenry.[4]

This moment of final military defeat and momentous demographic decline marked the beginning of a new phase in white-Indian relations. While hastening efforts to integrate Native Americans into US society physically and symbolically, that integration perpetuated racist stereotypes and generally was meant to destroy Indigenous cultures. Government officials and white middle-class reformers had long pondered "the Indian problem." They felt that the hundreds of reservations that tribes had been forced onto across the nation in the nineteenth century were detrimental to the goal of Americanizing the Indigenous population, as these isolated communities fostered Indian identity and values. Already in the 1870s, government officials had begun to advocate a two-pronged strategy to counter such tendencies: imposed individualization and acculturation. To disrupt Native traditions of collective ownership and tribal government, which were seen as obstacles to Indians' transformation into industrious and patriotic individuals, federal legislation was designed to prod Indian men to become independent farmers. The Dawes Severalty Act of 1887 divided tribal land into 160-acre plots and promised US citizenship to those who worked the plots and abandoned their Indian ways. Despite the resistance of Indians to imposed assimilation and the ability of some to adapt to the new conditions that the new law created, the law's devastating effects soon became apparent. Through a provision that allowed the United States to sell tribal land to non-Indian individuals and railway companies, Indian tribes lost almost half of their land by the end of the nineteenth century. In addition, many Native men who accepted the government's offer frequently received less fertile land and struggled to survive. White reformers' second strategy—acculturation—in effect sought to destroy Indigenous cultures. Indian norms and values were seen as preventing the aboriginal population from becoming a productive part of American civilization. Reeducation of Indian children in private and government-run boarding schools was seen as a key formula to Americanize this minority. By 1900 almost 50 percent of all Indian youths attended such schools, where they were forced to abandon their tribal names, languages, cultures, and religions. Although the schools had the unintended effect of fostering a pan-Indian identity among the various tribes whose children attended them, they also traumatized many students.[5]

After 1890 these two strategies were pursued with greater determination than ever, although many scholars suggested that they might be necessary only for a limited time since the vanishing Indian would eventually be absorbed into the white population. Although American Indians were regarded as an alien race and were believed to be inferior to white Anglo-Saxons, white Americans condoned the prospect of racial amalgamation because the relatively small number of Native Americans was not expected to excessively pollute the white race. During an era when white citizens feared racial intermixture and increasingly defined membership in the nation in terms of Anglo-Saxon whiteness, interracial marriages were certainly not openly advocated, but as Patrick Wolfe has convincingly argued, they were "consistent with the logic" of the goal of settler colonialism to "replace the natives on their land."[6]

Yet, the bloody Wounded Knee massacre and concerns about Indians' diminishing numbers also prompted efforts among white middle-class Americans to symbolically integrate Native Americans into US society, a phenomenon primarily reflected in an increasing fascination with the Indian past. Images of Indigenous culture proliferated in books and magazines. Indian arts and artifacts became sought-after commodities, and anthropologists exhorted white America to study and preserve such examples of Native cultural practice before people's knowledge about them was gone forever. Meanwhile, white citizens flocked to Indian performances in the Southwest and Midwest to see seemingly authentic Indigenous culture. Tens of thousands also attended the extremely popular Wild West shows of William Cody. Better known by his stage name, Buffalo Bill, he staged vivid morality plays that echoed the DAR's tales of pioneers' heroic battles against savage Indians but also suggested that they were brave warriors whose virtues were worth emulating. Scholars and promoters of tourism held up these virtues—among them the idea that Indians lived in harmony with nature—as examples of aboriginal people's primitive authenticity and promoted it as an antidote to the overcivilization of modern America.

Around 1900, such notions of primitivism led many middle-class Americans to join voluntary associations such as the Improved Order of Red Men that organized leisure activities that mimicked what were believed to be Indian customs. In fact, playing Indian became a minor craze among white citizens around 1900 and allowed them to romanticize the Indian past while downplaying the role of white people in the violent subjugation of the country's Indigenous population.[7]

Fascination with Indian history became part of what Renato Rosaldo has called "imperialist nostalgia," which propelled the incorporation of American Indians into nationalist cultural memory prior to World War II. Rosaldo finds that colonizers and their descendants tended to display sentimentality for the supposedly traditional cultures of colonized peoples that they deliberately and violently transformed or eradicated. Accordingly, during an era when US imperialism transcended the nation's territorial boundaries, more and more white citizens nostalgically pondered the consequences of their imperialist ventures at home but also incorporated Indian traditions into their own cultural memory as a form of self-justification. Although entrenched images of the savage foe or the ignoble savage continued to be part of the white imagination, they were increasingly accompanied by the long-standing trope of the noble savage and images of the dignified first Americans; the Native American came to be seen as a national icon and was believed to deserve support despite his backwardness.[8]

Prior to 1918, the DAR's efforts to commemorate the Indian past revolved largely around the various attempts by white middle-class citizens to symbolically and physically integrate the country's Indigenous population into the nation. As indicated by western Daughters' campaigns to honor nineteenth-century pioneers, their remembrance was not without contradictions. Despite the DAR's purported concern for Indians' dire situation, the savage foe continued to be part of the organization's nationalized cultural memory, as may be seen in markers that memorialized "Indian massacres," buildings and fortifications that had provided protection against Indian attacks, and battles between US soldiers and Native warriors.[9] The commemorative specter of the ignoble savage thus continued to influence non-Indian views on the aboriginal past and operated in tandem and in tension with his noble counterpart.

Despite these reminders of racial warfare, during the Progressive Era most of the DAR's commemorative projects and publications pertaining to Native Americans' past focused on friendship and cooperation between them and whites. Emphasizing Indian loyalty and goodwill toward the United States and white settlers, the DAR constructed a narrative of national unity that was largely devoid of racial violence; it allowed the Daughters to imagine Indians as important auxiliaries to US nation-building in the eighteenth and nineteenth centuries. Treaties in which Indians had ceded tribal lands to the United States and loyal chiefs who had signed them took center stage in the Daughters' memorializations. By the 1880s, Native American tribes had been coerced or tricked into signing almost 370 treaties with the US government. These documents tended to force them to cede most of their lands and stay on small reservations thousands of miles from their ancestral homelands. In many cases, moreover, Washington failed to honor even those agreements. Through the process of forced displacement, most Indian tribes lost their legal status as dependent nations within the United States and became official wards of the state whose lives were closely controlled by agents from the federal Bureau of Indian Affairs.[10]

From 1900 through the end of World War I, Daughters across the nation commemorated the signing of US treaties with tribes and hailed them as symbols of both white victory and interracial friendship. In 1917, for instance, the Captain Christopher Robinson Chapter of Crawford, Nebraska, dedicated a commemorative granite boulder at Fort Robinson to call attention to the final peace treaty the Sioux signed under Chief Red Cloud in 1876. Almost 1,500 Nebraskans witnessed the dedication ceremony, including fifty representatives of the various Sioux tribes that lived on the nearby Pine Ridge Indian Reservation in South Dakota. In her presentation speech at the dedication, the chapter's regent, Anna Cross, contrasted what she called a "wilderness" with the "marvelous changes" that had taken place since 1876. More importantly, referring to Indian soldiers' role in World War I, Cross proudly proclaimed, "To-day our red brother and our white brother stand side by side in the struggle for peace, liberty, and democracy." Elaborating on modernity's beneficial effect on Nebraska and Indians' splendid patriotism, Cross voiced her hope that the memorial might "bring to the minds of all a just appreciation of the true character and rights of the Indians."[11]

In their endeavors to celebrate these treaties, the Daughters lavished particular praise on the loyal, mixed-race Indian chiefs who signed them and sometimes paid with their lives for doing so. White citizens tended to have ambivalent feelings about Indians of mixed racial heritage. Many viewed them with suspicious hostility, while others pitied them for being unwanted wanderers between two cultures. Still others regarded them as heralds of racial integration.[12] But in the eyes of the Daughters, they were primarily symbols of Indian loyalty toward the white man and the United States. Even when the chiefs had not died at the hands of fellow tribe members for what most viewed as treason, the Daughters constructed tales of martyred mixed-blood chiefs who had given up their lives for the progress of Indian-white friendship and US nation-building. In 1911 the Abiel Fellows Chapter of Three Rivers, Michigan, marked the grave of Sauganash, a British-Potawatomi chief who in 1833 signed a treaty as a representative of the United Nation of Chippewa, Ottowa, and Potawatomi, ceding their tribal lands to the United States in exchange for money and federal land in the far West. Although Sauganash died a natural death in 1841, the chapter claimed that fellow Potawatomi Indians had murdered him as retribution for his actions and his friendship with Michigan's first white settlers.[13]

Daughters in Georgia constructed a similar memory to give credence to their idea of white-Indian friendship. Also in 1911, Atlanta's Piedmont Continental Chapter marked the site where in 1825 Creek Indians and the state of Georgia had signed the second Treaty of Indian Springs; in it the tribe surrendered its lands to the state and accepted financial compensation as well as federal land west of the Mississippi. The dedication exercises, which were attended by several hundred people, took place in a historic building that reportedly belonged to William McIntosh, the Creek-Scottish chief who had negotiated and signed the treaty. During the ceremony, speakers did not dwell on the history that McIntosh had been opposed by a majority of Creeks and was considered a traitor. The Creek National Council had threatened any member with death who sold tribal lands to foreigners without permission of the council. A bribe eventually persuaded McIntosh to take the chance. He and some of his allies signed the agreement, but McIntosh had no time to enjoy the fruits of his scheme. On orders of the Creek National Council, he was assassinated shortly after putting his signature on the document.[14] But in the eyes of the Daughters, McIntosh was a heroic martyr who deserved special acclaim for mustering the courage to risk his life for white-Indian amity. Consequently, Daughters considered purchasing and marking the McIntosh residence. In her address to the Georgia DAR's state convention in March 1912, DAR officer Cornelia Alfriend appealed to fellow members to pay homage to McIntosh, "the highly cultured, dignified, half-breed chief, in whose veins some of the best blood of our native state" flowed. Alfriend said McIntosh was "loyal to the red man and as true to the white," which motivated him to advocate the signing of the treaty despite death threats from "a few disaffected braves." Given that Indians in Georgia in 1912 "enjoyed peace and prosperity" because "of his foresight and courage," she argued that McIntosh should be included in the pantheon of loyal chiefs who were murdered for collaborating with the United States.[15]

Four years after Alfriend's words of praise for William McIntosh, the Major Isaac Sadler Chapter of Omaha, Nebraska, unveiled a bronze tablet it had placed in the city's Fontenelle Hotel to honor the building's French-Omaha namesake. Logan Fontenelle was a fur trader who had served as an interpreter in negotiations over tribal land between the Omaha and the United States in 1853. A year later, the negotiations led to a treaty in which the Omaha agreed to cede four million acres of land to the US government. Fontenelle was among the treaty's signers. There is continuing debate among historians over whether he was an official or de facto chief of the Omaha tribe; having a white father made such ascendancy difficult, but government officials certainly regarded him as such in the 1850s. Only a year after signing the agreement, Fontenelle was killed during a hunting trip that turned violent when he and his fellow hunters were confronted by a group of hostile Sioux.[16] To the Nebraska Daughters, this mixed-blood man, much like Sauganash and McIntosh before him, was more than an Indian official who paved the way for Nebraska Territory to become a state. In the words of the author of the Nebraska DAR's official history, Fontenelle "was the connecting link between savagery and civilization in this part of Nebraska." Since he was the only member of the Omaha delegation who could speak and write English, "his was the only authentic signature on the document, the others being merely the mark of the signatory Indians." In addition, the Daughters asserted that Fontanelle had planned to educate the members of the Omaha tribe, alleviate their poverty, and contain the spread of alcoholism among the tribe's members. To highlight his important place in the nation's history, the DAR draped the tablet it dedicated at the Fontenelle Hotel with a US flag that was purportedly given to the Omaha chief by President Franklin Pierce after the treaty was signed in Washington, DC.[17]

While paying much attention to these treaties, the Daughters also lionized certain tribes and their leaders for supporting the US military in the eighteenth and nineteenth centuries. In 1910 the North Carolina DAR placed a monument on Cherokee Chief Junaluska's grave near the town of

Robbinsville to honor him and his warriors, who in 1814 assisted General Andrew Jackson and his troops in defeating the Creek nation. And in 1912 and 1916, Daughters in Maine dedicated two markers to commemorate Native Americans' "loyal service" during the American Revolution. Unlike most Native American tribes that sided with the British because they rightly feared that an American victory would only accelerate white territorial expansion, the Penobscot and Passamaquoddy became the colonists' allies and contributed to their victory during the War of Independence. While the Daughters lauded Junaluska for turning the tide of the fateful Battle of Horse Shoe Bend "at the peril of his life," the Maine DAR praised Indians for being "uniformly faithful" despite "many inducements to the contrary."[18] Rather than becoming savage foes, these tribes actively contributed to American independence and the young nation's expansion, which made them praiseworthy in the eyes of the Daughters.

What differentiated such expressions of gratitude for Indian loyalty during America's past military conflicts from the commemorations of white-Indian treaties and the mixed-blood chiefs who signed them was the participation in these events of many descendants of the honored Indian warriors. During the ceremonies that accompanied the marking of sites where treaties had been signed, only a few, if any, Native people attended. This was not surprising since they constituted celebrations of the Indigenous population's defeat and subjugation. Thus, if they participated, their involvement was not necessarily voluntary. In the commemoration of the Treaty of 1876 between the US government and the Sioux in Crawford, Nebraska, fifty representatives of various Sioux tribes from the Pine Ridge Reservation had been brought to the event and were not allowed to address the audience.[19]

When the DAR memorialized Native warriors' valor in North Carolina and Maine, by contrast, local Indians appear to have been much more interested in taking part in the ceremonies that paid homage to their ancestors. Despite the Daughters' willingness to give Indians a prominent role in these ceremonies, however, they made sure that the Indians' involvement would not run counter to the overarching message of patriotic cooperation. At the dedication of the Junaluska monument in Robbinsville, the North Carolina DAR asked two Indian girls to remove the two American flags that draped the fenced memorial boulder and allowed several Cherokees to sing the song "Blessed Home" in their tribal language. They also asked the Cherokee pastor Armstrong Cornsilk to give the event's principal address, an honor that was acceptable to the southern audience because of his seemingly unquestionable loyalty toward the United States and the white South. In 1861 Cornsilk had enlisted in the Confederate Army and served until the end of the Civil War. Upon his return to western North Carolina, he became a Baptist preacher and a spiritual leader of the approximately two hundred Cherokees who continued to live in the vicinity of Junaluska's home.[20]

At the dedication ceremony, more than fifty years after the chief's death, Cornsilk reminisced about his friend in Cherokee. His talk, which was translated by an interpreter into English for the largely non-Indian audience, certainly pleased the Daughters since it focused on Indian-white friendship and made no mention of racial warfare or the forced removal of the Cherokee nation in the 1830s. The pastor stressed that the audience had assembled at Junaluska's grave "as friends and brothers and sisters." After expressing the tribe's appreciation for the chief's military valor and reminiscing about his kindness, Cornsilk said he was glad "we have this beautiful monument. It shows Junaluska did good, and it shows we all appreciate him together."[21] In North Carolina the Daughters were thus willing to acknowledge Indians' patriotism and encouraged their participation in the commemoration of Indian valor, but they also adeptly sought out particular Indian communicative memories to legitimize their particular version of America's nationalized cultural memory. The DAR's effort to shape the nation's cultural memory about Indians was as much about forgetting as it was about remembering the past.

In Maine the Daughters also encouraged tribal participation in the events that wedded the memory of Indian heroism with white nationalism. During the 1912 dedication of a monument in honor "of the Penobscot and other tribes of Maine for their loyal service during the Revolutionary War" in the cemetery of Oldtown Island, where a few of the tribe's members still lived, a chorus of Indian children sang "America," waving small American flags during their performance. In traditional tribal garb, another group of Indian children performed an "Indian dance" to the tune of "Battle Hymn of the Republic." As in North Carolina, a few representatives of the Penobscot were allowed to address the large audience that had assembled, although no evidence has survived as to the content of their talks. According to a DAR report, the Native visitors "expressed much pleasure" at this event, but the Daughters were probably even more pleased because they believed that the monument would boost Indian patriotism. Writing in the *American Monthly Magazine*, Maine DAR member Mrs. S. L. Board-man regarded the monument "as a daily reminder to the Indian youth of the bravery and fealty of their forefathers, as well as an incentive to the patriotism we . . . are so desirous to inculcate."[22]

Four years later, the Hannah Weston Chapter of Machias, Maine, emulated the North Carolina DAR's example in tapping the communicative memory of the Passamaquoddy to celebrate Indian patriotism in the American Revolution. While white citizens rarely mentioned Indian military assistance to the colonists during the Revolutionary Era, the Passamaquoddy of the Pleasant Point reservation on Mount Desert Island had honored the almost two hundred tribal members who had fought and died for the United States by burying them in the reservation's ancient cemetery. The tribe also surrounded it with an "ornamental wire fence" and, placing a large flagpole in the center of the sacred site, symbolized their patriotic service by hoisting a large American flag. It was in this cemetery where in June 1916 the Daughters unveiled a granite boulder to honor those members of the tribe who had fought for the United States. As in previous events, they asked tribe members to participate in the ceremony. Indian children dressed in traditional costumes and carried small American flags while singing "Speed our Republic." The 103-year-old Socis Joseph, a well-respected tribal elder, was given the honor of unveiling the monument. The audience, which consisted of numerous Passamaquoddy clad in tribal attire, then listened to Louis Mitchell, a member of the tribe who had represented it in the Maine state legislature from 1880 to 1911. In 1887 Mitchell gave a much-noticed speech to fellow legislators in which he criticized the state's refusal to honor the hunting and fishing rights that had been promised to the tribe in a number of treaties. But during the DAR dedication ceremony, these grievances were not a prominent part of his English-language talk on the history of the Passamaquoddy. Instead, he and non-Indian speakers focused on lauding the valor of the tribe's warriors during the War of Independence. In the eyes of the Daughters, the event "was a genuine 'Indian Day'" and "the most unique patriotic entertainment ever held in this section, among this most easterly tribe of peaceful Redmen."[23] Integrating Indians into its nationalist rituals thus bolstered the DAR's stance that Indigenous people accepted colonial subjugation and felt strong allegiance to the United States.

Although most of the campaigns that commemorated Indian patriotism and interracial cooperation during the Progressive Era focused on Indigenous men, the Daughters repeatedly suggested that Indian women had offered white Americans the most genuine friendship. In the Daughters' historical imagination, Native women were and had always been naturally inclined toward reconciliation with white male settlers and explorers. As early as 1897, DAR member Flora Clarke Huntington explained in the organization's magazine that there had been "many incidents that could be mentioned of the beauty, bravery, courage, shrewdness, and devotion of the Indian women" who might have been "treacherous on the warpath" but "never betrayed a friend." "If once you gained the gratitude of the dark-eyed dusky women," Huntington stressed, "they would risk any danger, at the perils of their own lives, to save the life of the white man."[24]

In this exoticized view of Indigenous women, the Daughters were influenced by and further contributed to the white cultural memory of the Indian princess. This figure had its origins in various mythologized renderings of the life of Pocahontas, the young daughter of Indian Chief Powhatan who purportedly saved the life of the explorer John Smith in Virginia in 1607 and thus ensured the survival of the first permanent British settlement in North America. Philip Deloria contends that in these tales, "Indian women, linked to the land itself, gave themselves metaphorically to colonizing white men, engendering a peaceful narrative of cross-cultural harmony in which whites became Indigenous owners of the continent through sexualized love and marriage stories such as that of Pocahontas."[25] Already in the eighteenth century the romanticized accounts of this Indian girl's courageous deeds and her subsequent marriage to white colonist John Rolfe had become part of America's national origin myth. Pocahontas's concern for Smith seemed to legitimize colonial conquest, while her matrimony with Rolfe symbolized Indigenous people's consent to displacement and dependence. Although this favorable image competed with that of the villainous "savage squaw," her voluntary support for white men made Pocahontas a legitimate and noble princess in the eyes of many Anglo-Americans.[26]

The Daughters fully subscribed to this origin myth and incorporated it into their nationalist ideology. Writing in 1907, the organization's honorary vice president general, Jane S. Owen, called Pocahontas "the Mother of an Empire." Reflecting upon the remarkable character of the young woman, Owen was "proud to claim her as one of ourselves" because she had been "the first, and while she lived, the only reliant friend of the first English colony on American soil through the saving of its leader from death." In

Owen's reading, Pocahontas "was the first and only one to sympathize with their sufferings," the "first American Indian to speak the English language, the first to accept the Christian faith, the first of her race to marry in that faith," and she gave "birth to the first blood uniting the Anglo-Saxon and American races."[27] Only by helping white men and by fully assimilating into Euro-American culture could Pocahontas expect admiration from the Daughters. More importantly, the Native American girl was deemed praiseworthy because she showed so much affection for John Smith, the embodiment of white male superiority.[28] Once more, women—even Indigenous women—were deemed meritorious, but white men remained the true agents of American nation-building.

In their gendered interpretations of America's aboriginal past, some Daughters drew on regional variations of white lore about other kind-hearted Indian princesses. In 1899 women of Anderson, South Carolina, founded the Cateechee Chapter, commemorating a Choctaw girl who, according to local memory, was a slave of Cherokee Chief Kuruga in the first half of the eighteenth century. Like Pocahontas, she gave in to the advances of a white Englishman. She braved unspeakable perils to warn her lover, Allan Francis, and other white settlers at Fort Cambridge of an impending Cherokee attack and eventually "remained with her white friends and became the wife of Allan Frances [sic], beloved and honored by all."[29] Ella Cox Cromer, the regent of the Andrew Hamilton Chapter of Abbeville, South Carolina, explained sixteen years after the Cateechee Chapter's founding, it mattered little that the story was generally believed to be a legend. "I firmly believe in this romantic episode," Cromer wrote, "and think it should be treated as a real part of Abbeville's history, and it should be treasured as such by her people, who now possess a birthright to the land once occupied by the Cherokees."[30] To the Daughters, communicative memory thus trumped historical scholarship and was reinterpreted as a justification for the removal and subjugation of America's original inhabitants. It was through such tales of Indian women's affection for white men that the Daughters reaffirmed entangled notions of masculinity and white supremacy.

Unlike Cateechee, the Shoshone woman Sacajawea, who played a central role in the famous Lewis and Clark expedition, did exist and became the Daughters' most revered Indian heroine because they regarded her as the epitome of Indigenous women's patriotic loyalty. As the wife of a French fur trader, Sacajawea joined the expedition and took along her infant son on the journey as she helped the two explorers safely navigate Indian territories and cultures. In the wake of the Lewis and Clark centennial of 1904, many Americans, especially white middle-class women, began to reconsider Sacajawea and her role as a guide and interpreter during the dangerous journey. For the woman suffrage movement, Sacajawea became, in the words of Michael Hefernan and Carol Medlicot, "a real, flesh-and-blood historical character," who had been "an active agent" in one of American history's most pivotal moments.[31] In 1902, Oregon suffragist Eva Emery Dye published a fictionalized account of the expedition in which Sacajawea played a heroic role. Resulting from Dye's fundraising efforts, a larger-than-life bronze statue of the Indian expedition member was dedicated in 1905 on Women's Day during the Lewis and Clark Centennial Exposition in Portland, Oregon. In the opening address at the dedication ceremony, women's rights activist Susan B. Anthony lauded Sacajawea as a heroic role model who exemplified why women were entitled to the same rights enjoyed by men.[32]

While the DAR could not have agreed more with suffragists' argument that Sacajawea epitomized female agency in the history of the American West, its members fundamentally disagreed with the assessment of the meaning of her agency in the present. From the perspective of women's rights activists, women like Sacajawea deserved equal rights because of their patriotic service to the nation in the past and the present.[33] In the eyes of the Daughters, by contrast, the young Shoshone was primarily a paragon of Indian virtue, loyalty, and interracial friendship. A thirteen-ton memorial boulder that the Montana DAR erected in 1914 in the town of Three Forks testifies to this particular interpretation of her role in history. The inscription on the bronze tablet mounted on the monument stated, "In patriotic memory of Sacajawea, an Indian woman whose heroic courage, steadfast devotion, and splendid loyalty in acting as guide across the Rocky Mountains made it possible for the Lewis and Clark Expedition . . . to occupy so important a place in the history of this republic."[34] Not long after the unveiling of the Montana memorial, Daughters in Wind River, Wyoming, erected a concrete monument at what was believed to be Sacajawea's grave, and a DAR chapter in Idaho marked the spot where reportedly she was born.[35]

Cherokee mezzo soprano Tsianina Redfeather, whom the Daughters invited in 1921 to perform at that year's Continental Congress, became the Daughters' twentieth-century equivalent of the Indian princess.[36] Linking the memory of loyal Indian women with the expectation of Indigenous people's national allegiance in the present, the Daughters essentially regarded Redfeather as a modern-day Sacajawea who had demonstrated her loyalty to the United States, apparently accepted the Indigenous population's subjugation, and became a cultural mediator between whites and Indians. After all, she was a Christian, received a western education in a government school, supported the US armed forces during World War I, and refrained from condemning Anglo-Americans for racial violence and the forced removal of the Cherokee and other tribes. Yet, Redfeather did not necessarily subscribe to the Daughters' paternalistic interpretations of the past. In her autobiography, she later reflected on the irony of her support during World War I for the United States, a country that had destroyed the continent's Indian societies and cultures with impunity. In fact, although her attitudes toward white citizens changed over time, she admitted to despising them and their tendency to distort Indigenous history. While she was aware that her musical performances tended to reinforce entrenched racial stereotypes, Redfeather considered her concerts a chance to challenge racist notions of Indian backwardness. It is difficult to determine whether the young singer's efforts had the intended effect, but she certainly contributed to expressions of sympathy for Indians' plight among white concertgoers and the press. The Daughters, however, were unaware of the mezzo soprano's conflicting loyalties and regarded her as yet another paragon of Indigenous women's devotion to the United States.[37]

Within the DAR, the organization's tributes to Native American patriotism even rendered acceptable the prospect of Indian membership and interracial marriage. A few Daughters proudly claimed to be descendants of Pocahontas, and in 1905 the DAR's annual meeting was addressed by Carrie F. Adams, who had Cherokee ancestors. At the time, Adams was believed to be the only member of Indian origin. Her husband, Richard C. Adams, was a Delaware Indian who was descended from Captain White Eyes, an officer in the Revolutionary Army, and represented his tribe in negotiations with the US government over material claims before the Dawes Commission in the 1880s. As a DAR regent of Indian Territory in Oklahoma, Carrie Adams encountered no opposition when she voiced her intention to recruit new Daughters among the state's Indigenous population.[38]

But the Daughters not only kept alive the memory of Indians' ostensible devotion to white settlers and the United States but also displayed a general nostalgic fascination with Native culture at a time when many

Figure 3.1. Cherokee mezzo soprano Tsianina Redfeather, ca. 1915. The Daughters admired Redfeather for both her musical talent and her patriotism. In the eyes of DAR members, Redfeather was a symbol of white-Indian friendship and Indian loyalty to the United States, two themes the organization emphasized in its commemoration of Indigenous peoples' past. Courtesy of Library of Congress Prints and Photographs Division, George Grantham Bain Collection, LC-B2-5179-10.

scholars spoke of the vanishing Indian. Like these scholars, DAR members believed that the Indigenous population would soon disappear, which was deemed a regrettable price that America needed to pay for the progress of white civilization.[39] The Daughters' interest in anything Indian could be seen in the numerous chapters that adopted Indian names, among them the Pocahontas Chapter and the Sacajawea Chapter. Other Daughters honored Indian men who had proven their friendship by helping white settlers. The namesake of the Waw-Wil-A-Way Chapter of Hillsboro, Ohio, organized in 1895, was a member of the Shawnee tribe "who befriended the early pioneers of Highland County" and gave "aid and assistance to them."[40] Some chapters, among them the Chinckchewunska Chapter of Newton, New Jersey, named themselves after the Indian words for their hometowns or after Indian villages in their vicinity. Still others were named after cultural groups among tribes that had lived in their regions. Indian chapter names proved to be so popular that they soon outnumbered those pertaining to Colonial America, the American Revolution, and the Early Republic. Daughters across the country also extensively studied Indian history and culture to preserve it for posterity. Before the 1920s, numerous Georgia chapters researched and discussed the meanings of the Indian names that had been given to the state's rivers and towns, and DAR officers exhorted fellow Daughters to study and preserve Indian languages and legends.[41]

In many of the DAR's projects, studying Indigenous peoples' past went hand in hand with playing Indian. In 1916 the Michigan DAR adopted a resolution asking the state's chapters to hold an "Indian Day" once a year to study Indigenous history and to "foster the sale of Indian baskets" to prevent the art of Indian basketry from dying out. Members of the Charity Cook Chapter of Homer, Michigan, observed its day by dressing in "picturesque Indian costumes," decorating their meeting house with Indian blankets, pottery, and baskets as well as the US colors, and listening to informal talks about Indian culture.[42] In historical pageants that the Daughters staged on numerous occasions, they and their guests also donned Indian garb to embody the legends they had studied, while, at the same time, praising the white settlers who had replaced the Indigenous population. In 1914 the Governor John Milledge Chapter of Dalton, Georgia, presented a historical pageant on the history of Whitefield County in the City Park school auditorium. More than twenty well-known Daltonians took on roles and put on Indian costumes to depict the Cherokee's history and the signing of the treaty of New Echota, in which the tribe ceded its lands to the United

States. To enhance the various scenes' effects, the costumed performers sang Indian songs in addition to "Home, Sweet Home."[43]

That same year, the Abiel Fellows Chapter of Three Rivers, Michigan, after studying the "games, manners and customs" of several of the state's tribes, staged a historical pageant entitled "The Coming of the Pioneer." Much of that pageant was devoted to the history of the Potawatomi, who were forced to cede their tribal lands to the region's early settlers. In the first part of the pageant, "The Forest Primeval," young children in Native dress performed the symbolic dance "The Spirit of the Wilderness," which was followed by a scene entitled "The Coming of the Pioneer: Nature Surrenders to Man." The second part presented the history of the region's Indian nations and their interactions with early white settlers; the final part closed the pageant with the history of the establishment of the townships of St. Joseph County.[44] These ritualized forms of becoming Indian reflected the Daughters' nostalgic fondness for Indian culture and helped them downplay the memory of racial warfare and forced removal.

Conserving and Preserving Indian Culture in the Interwar Period

After World War I, the DAR's interest in Indigenous America was characterized by both continuity and change. In many ways, the Great War bolstered the Daughters' interpretations of and efforts to preserve the Native past, as Indian soldiers' valorous service for the United States on European battlefields seemed to confirm the organization's emphasis on white-Indian amity and Indian loyalty. At the same time, the war led the DAR to gradually shift the focus of its activism to the Indian present, since its members believed that Native Americans needed white support to become truly patriotic citizens.

If the Daughters regarded Tsianina Redfeather as a modern-day incarnation of Pocahontas, they deemed the almost 13,000 Indian soldiers who fought for the United States during World War I worthy descendants of the aboriginal warriors who had defended America in the past. Indigenous servicemen had fought during the Civil War, but only after Wounded Knee in 1890 did government officials consider integrating larger numbers of them into white regiments. Some fought in the Spanish-American War in 1898. Many Anglo-American citizens regarded military service as a potential civilizing inspiration that would convince Indian soldiers of the benefits of US citizenship and national allegiance. Although there was draft resistance among some tribes, the thousands of Indians who volunteered and those who were subsequently decorated for their valor in combat seemed to confirm many white observers' belief that Native soldiers were willing to assimilate into US society. Their eagerness to serve also confirmed stereotypes about the seemingly biological basis of Native men's fighting abilities and suggested that they had adopted western ideals of the heroic citizen soldier who willingly sacrificed his life for the nation. Unbeknown to the Daughters and like-minded groups, however, Indians' motivations to fight for the United States were multiple and frequently contradicted the general idea of assimilation and undivided national loyalty. The Great War strengthened what Paul C. Rosier has called the "hybrid patriotism" of Indians who readily defended the United States but also viewed their service as an opportunity to protect the territory of their own tribal nations.[45]

But to the Daughters, Indian patriotism appeared to be neither hybrid nor divided. Instead, they were convinced that Indian men and women simply maintained traditions of patriotic loyalty that began with Pocahontas and continued during the American Revolution, while they also found expression in tribal nations' willingness to cede much of their land to the United States. It was against this backdrop of the memory of white-Indian friendship and Indian patriotism that the Daughters used their 1921 Continental Congress not only to quench their thirst for seemingly authentic examples of Indian culture by inviting Tsianina Redfeather but also to voice their support for Indian welfare and citizenship. During that conference, Redfeather's white mentor, Alice Robertson, forcefully spoke on behalf of Native Americans. She began by pointing out that less than 1 percent of the more than 17,000 Indians who had been called upon to register for the draft during the Great War asked for an exemption, thus outperforming all other ethnic groups including white citizens. The delegates fully supported her appeals to improve the situation of Indians and passed a resolution that pledged assistance for "Indian welfare and protection." In their pledge the Daughters declared that "the Indian has not yet been accorded full privileges of citizenship and full protection under the laws of the land, in spite of the fact that 10,000 Indian youths served under the colors in the great World War."[46] By the time the organization called for Indian citizenship rights, however, two-thirds of the Native population had already become citizens as a result of treaty stipulations or other provisions they had been promised in return for ceding tribal lands. Indian veterans of World War I could also apply for citizenship upon their return.[47]

Even if most Indians already were citizens by the early 1920s, the Daughters were nevertheless pleased when the US government officially granted citizenship to all members of tribal nations in 1924 because their new status seemed to provide more opportunities for incorporating them into the American nation. And yet, while the Indian Citizenship Act was designed to hasten assimilation, it still allowed state governments to bar Indians from voting. Native Americans continued to be wards of the federal government and could do little to prevent whites from illegally acquiring tribal land.[48] Despite these limitations, the Daughters hailed the new law and hoped it would help them in the citizenship campaigns they had launched in the early 1920s. Already in 1922, the California DAR established the Indian Citizenship Committee to "assist the Indians to become good citizens" and "to foster understanding and harmony" between Indians and white Americans.[49]

In those years, the national DAR and some state organizations stressed Indian citizenship and education. From 1922 to 1924, the organizers of the Continental Congress invited representatives of the American Indian Bureau as well as Indian and non-Indian speakers who headed educational facilities for Indian children to shed light on Indigenous America's dire situation. In these talks, Indians were portrayed as victims of neglect and exploitation but also received much acclaim. In the words of Commissioner of Indian Affairs Charles W. Burke, who spoke at the DAR's 1922 Continental Congress, Indians were "loyal, hospitable and full of abounding virtues."[50] Praise for their particular virtues was always combined with displays of seemingly authentic Indian culture. Like Tsianina Redfeather did in 1921, Native men and women wore traditional Indian garb when they were allowed to speak on behalf of Indian education during those meetings. Among them were Ho-Chunk educator Henry Roe Cloud and Nannie Muskrat, a young Cherokee student from the American Indian Institute; the speakers appealed to DAR delegates to help the Indigenous population. The Daughters did not shy away from condemning white authorities for treating Indians unfairly. Cooperating with other white middle-class organizations sympathetic toward Native Americans, DAR leaders repeatedly stated that Indians had been wronged.[51]

The DAR's more vocal criticism of past injustices toward Native Americans reflected changing attitudes among white middle-class reformers during the 1920s. Although many Progressive reform efforts waned after World War I, the movement to solve the so-called Indian problem gained visibility and influence. During a time when the Daughters along with other conservative and right-wing groups propagated 100 percent Americanism, some intellectuals and reformers called for more Indian political self-determination and cultural autonomy. They questioned complete assimilation and favored the preservation of Indian culture as an antidote to the detrimental effects of modernity. Most of the experts who wrote on the Indian problem focused on education because it was deemed crucial to help Indians help themselves in their struggle for advancement. The government-financed Merriam Report of 1928 confirmed reformers' previous findings and made several recommendations. It questioned allotment, asked to strengthen Indian family and community life, and regarded education as the best strategy for self-improvement, thus allowing Indians to eventually be absorbed into US society or at least to live on the margins of that society with a minimum standard of health and decency.[52]

Since the DAR's shift toward helping Indians in the present was inextricably linked to its particular version of America's cultural memory, it was not surprising that the organization extensively studied the Native past in the interwar period. Its work seemed even more urgent than before because of the widely held belief that Indians would soon disappear. This can be seen in the DAR's use of its Conservation and Thrift Committee to coordinate activities relating to Indians. The Daughters established the committee in 1919 to convince the American public of the need to conserve natural resources and America's wildlife, although it also sought to conserve people's "patriotic spirit" and the "ideals of our forefathers."[53] In 1921 its chairwoman, Arlene Moss, who would later become the driving force behind the Madonna of the Trail campaign, initiated this new line of work by offering a prize of $25 in gold for the best essay written by a Daughter on ten reasons Americans "should conserve and preserve" Indian "Life, Morals, Characteristics, Art and Tradition."[54]

The winning essay appeared in the July 1922 issue of the *DAR Magazine* and reflected the importance of memory in the Daughters' support for Native Americans. Relying on a number of historians' writings as well as her own interpretations of the Indigenous past, prize winner Myra H. Patch gave as the first reason the "Tardy Justice Toward the First Americans," who certainly had been "treacherous, revengeful and war-like" but who were also "loyal, grateful and peace-loving." According to Patch, Indian culture should also be preserved as an acknowledgement of their "Arts and Literature," which she believed were "at least the equal of Greeks, Teutons, and British Druids." Their music, too, deserved recognition because it was a distinct contribution to world music and American music. Echoing previous DAR campaigns, Patch argued that Indian culture should also be protected "In Gratitude for Their Help to the Explorers and Early Settlers of Our Country." In addition, Patch lauded their "Morals and Religion," which had been "the purest" prior to the onset of "the contaminating influence of the Whites."[55] In this romanticized version of Native American culture, which constructed an ahistorical image that was devoid of racial conflict and appeared to be applicable to all tribes, Patch's essay echoed both the DAR's focus on white-Indian friendship and a nostalgic longing for community values among conservative nationalists who suspected that people's allegiance to the United States would be undermined by industrialization, urbanization, and secularization.

As suggested in Patch's article, the commemorative themes that emerged in the Daughters' interpretations of Indian history changed little during the 1920s and early 1930s. The "savage foe" motif occasionally reappeared in the organization's interpretations of the past.[56] But the remembrance of conflict was frequently interspersed with expressions of admiration for the defeated enemy and tended to be counterbalanced by numerous tales of Indian loyalty. In 1929 the Montana DAR dedicated two tablets at the site of the Battle of Bear's Paw, fifteen miles south of Chinook. The tablets were set into a large monument of concrete and boulders that was erected to pay tribute to twenty-two army officers and enlisted men who were killed in the battle in 1877. The second tablet commemorated the surrender of Chief Joseph and his tribe of Nez Perce to the US Army that same year. "Chief Joseph," the tablet's inscription stated, "was a military genius, courageous and humane," keeping his word that he would "fight no more forever." Likening Joseph to famous European military commanders, the Daughters believed that this "Red Napoleon" exemplified "the very best of his people and in his character were found the highest attributes of his race."[57] In the face of Indians' defeat, the Daughters took on the role of magnanimous victors who conceded that Native men had heroic qualities, although their status tended to hinge on conceding defeat or helping white Americans build the nation.

More lavish praise was once again reserved for mixed-blood Indian leaders who played vital roles in the cession of tribal lands or Indian removal in the first half of the nineteenth century. Especially members of the Cherokee received much acclaim. In 1922 Daughters marked the home of Cherokee Chief John Ross in Rossville, Georgia, with a patriotic ceremony that involved no Native Americans.[58] Six years later, the Ocoee Chapter of Cleveland, Tennessee, asked a Cherokee named Esi Kalonieheiskie to unveil a monument in memory of "chief" Jack Walker, a prominent mixed-blood Cherokee who had fought for the United States under Andrew Jackson during the War of 1812 and was honored during the dedication ceremony as the "Greatest of his tribe and a servant of our government."[59] In the Daughters' estimation, Walker's service to the nation was his decision to travel to Washington, DC, in 1831 to advocate for Cherokee relocation without receiving permission from the Cherokee Tribal Council. This step made Walker many enemies among his fellow tribesmen; two of them murdered him in 1834. While it is not entirely clear whether the attack was a consequence of his advocacy for removal or merely a personal quarrel with his assailants, the Daughters suggested that he was another martyr who died for the cause of American nation-building.[60]

Chapters also commemorated treaties between Indigenous nations and the US government and marked spots where treaties were signed in southern, midwestern, and western states. These commemorations veered between fascination with Indian culture and hints of nostalgic remorse, which might explain why the Daughters asked Indians to participate in the events more frequently after 1918. In 1921, Michigan's Abiel Fellows Chapter made a "centenary Pilgrimage" along the old Indian trails across St. Joseph County to commemorate the Chicago Treaty of 1821, in which the Ottawa, Chippewa, and Potawatomi surrendered their lands to the United States. After a visit to the county's Nottawa-Sepee reservation, the Daughters sat down in the woods for a jovial basket dinner to which they had invited as guests of honor the Potawatomi Chiefs Samuel Mandoka and Pamp and their families. As with Tsianina Redfeather's clothing, the Daughters were excited that Mandoka wore traditional beaded buckskin clothing, moccasins, and a feathered headdress. According to a chapter report, the chief "told with true pride the story of the Pottawatomie nation" and "of the fine spirit in the hearts of the white friends, and of the gratitude in the hearts of the red brethren."[61] Once more, the Daughters' choice of their Indian guests helped them confirm their belief in the strong bond between whites and Native Americans in the past and the present. Such events also seemed to validate the idea that white Americans had been justified to violently subdue Indian tribes and take their lands.

Only a few years later, in 1926, the Lucinda Hinsdale Stone Chapter placed a large bronze tablet on a historic spot in Kalamazoo, Michigan, where 3,000 Potawatomi and Ottawa held their last council in 1840 before beginning the forced trek from their midwestern homelands to western reservations. Although the tablet's inscription suggested remorse at the forced departure of these two tribes, the Daughters also inserted yet another hint of white-Indian amity. As in the Abiel Fellows Chapter's pilgrimage, the large bronze plaque commemorated the Chicago Treaty of 1821 as well as the Treaty of 1833, recounting the "weird" and "mournful dramatic scene" that was caused by the two tribes' final council meeting before their departure. Noting their reluctance to leave the "homes of their ancestors," the text described how the departing Indians "passed single file before Judge Epaphroditus Ransom" and respectfully "doffed their ornamental headgear, elevated their right hand to say good bye."[62]

The Daughters probably drew on the region's white communicative memory to find such expressions of respect for Ransom, who they believed was deserving of such praise because he had issued a legal guideline that spared Catholic members of the Potawatomi from having to abandon their tribal lands. Once more using dedication ceremonies to link this communicative memory to their idea of a nationalized cultural memory, the Daughters not only invited two of Ransom's great-granddaughters to unveil the memorial but also asked Potawatomi Chief Samuel Mandoka to address the audience. His biography actually complicated the story the Daughters sought to tell. The sixty-two-year old chief was the descendant of a small group of Potawatomi who managed to escape from the US soldiers who were escorting their tribe to a reservation in Kansas. Eventually these escapees returned to Michigan to settle near the town of Athens. As a child, he had heard tales of the dreadful trek and his family's secretive return, but in 1926, he refrained from challenging the DAR's interpretations of the past. Donning traditional buckskin clothing, Mandoka told the white audience of the history of the Potawatomi and Ottawa after their forced removal but voiced no judgments of the past that would have offended his white listeners.[63] If Indian communicative memory served to confirm the Daughters' interpretations of Indian loyalty and white superiority, they happily incorporated it into their commemorative events.

Even though Indigenous women played a less visible role in the Daughters' post–World War I remembrance of Indigenous America, scattered evidence suggests that the trope of the loyal Indian princess still colored their view of the past. In a DAR-financed book about Coweta County, Georgia, that was published in 1928, its editors Mary G. Jones and Lily Reynolds claimed that "the Indian women loved the white men because they treated them with respect and chivalry." Jones and Reynolds surmised, "This may explain several very interesting manifestations in connection with the affairs between the whites and Indians: On so many different occasions white men, as in the case of Captain John Smith, were saved at the instant of execution, by chiefs' daughters." From the editors' perspective, romantic relationships between Indian women and white men as well as the proclivity of Indian women such as Pocahontas to save white men from Indian violence were due to Anglo-American men's chivalric manliness.[64] Pocahontas herself remained a staple of the DAR's tales about the Indian past, even in events that were only indirectly related to Indians. During the George Washington Bicentennial of 1932, Missouri's Kansas City Chapter staged a musical pageant that used a living portrait of a "typical Indian woman" who was identified as Pocahontas and was described as "loyal, fearless, [and] courageous to the point of ready personal sacrifice if need be to save the life of one who had shown kindness." In this pageant, Pocahontas was presented as the quintessential "friend of the White Man."[65]

The founding of the Princess Aracoma Chapter in Logan, West Virginia, in the early 1930s suggests that not only midwestern Daughters subscribed to such ideas about Native American women. According to local lore, Aracoma was the daughter of Shawnee Chief Cornstalk and fell in love with an English soldier named Boling Baker, who had deserted the British colonial army in western Pennsylvania in 1756. When Cornstalk's warriors apprehended the fugitive in Ohio, the girl persuaded her father to spare his life by making him a member of the tribe. Nine years later she married Baker and with him had six children, all of whom perished during an epidemic in 1776. Aracoma died in 1780 after sustaining fatal injuries during a battle between Shawnee warriors and armed settlers. Writing in 1938 in the DAR's monthly magazine, the Princess Aracoma Chapter's historian explained that the chapter's namesake was not "aggressive, nor did she store within her heart hatred for the white man. For the love of her husband she was willing to forgive and to die."[66] Once more, living white memories became the basis of the DAR's interpretations of US history. In large part, those memories were devoid of interracial hostility because Indigenous women were believed to be enamored with masculine Anglo-European men. Daughters viewed especially Indian women as accepting both white supremacy and their own subjugation.

In the late 1920s, commemorations of the Indian past remained immensely popular among the Daughters but drew smaller audiences, took place primarily within DAR ranks, and focused on general Indian history and culture rather than on white-Indian relations. Numerous individual chapters held Indian Days, immersed themselves in aboriginal culture by mimicking Indians, and marked local places believed to be important in Indigenous history.[67] In 1930, during a special meeting of Colorado's Pueblo Chapter, members sang Indian songs composed by Indianist white composer Thurlow Lieurance and performed a rain dance in costume; the chapter's regent, Mrs. Herman Woodworth Nash, served as Rain Priest, wearing a special "Thunderbird costume."[68] A year later, the Roanoke Chapter of Roanoke, Virginia, also devoted an entire day to studying Indian culture, during which members listened to papers on the "Life of Pocahontas" and "Souvenir Pipes of Peace" and observed a group of children who gave "a war dance around camp fires," "a scalping party," and an "attack with weapons and war yells."[69] In their attempts to preserve Indians' seemingly dying cultures, the Daughters concentrated on topics that allowed them to avoid controversial issues such as colonial conquest and forced displacement. Genuine expressions of appreciation for such cultural practices as Indian basket weaving afforded opportunities to laud Native artistic achievements without delving deeper into the controversial legacy of racial warfare.[70]

As during the Progressive Era and the Jazz Age, the DAR's endeavor to preserve and protect Indian culture during the Depression of the 1930s cannot be fully comprehended without considering changing federal policies toward America's original inhabitants. The Indian Reorganization Act of 1934, a New Deal initiative, reversed the US government's long-pursued plan to Americanize Indians through the elimination of the reservation system. The new approach was based on the belief that the reservations would actually help Indians survive. The law promoted Native political and cultural self-determination as well as the improvement of tribal economies. In particular, it reversed assimilationist policies that had sought to destroy Native culture by transforming Indian men into individual landowners. The new law instead allowed tribes to administer their territories and political affairs collectively as they had done for centuries. In addition, the act supported traditional Indian arts and Indian artists as part of the government's mission to revitalize Indigenous cultures. This so-called Indian New Deal envisioned only a limited form of cultural pluralism and involved special agencies to monitor tribal decisions. Moreover, almost 40 percent of

Indian tribes rejected the legislation because of their distrust of the US government. Yet, the Indian Reorganization Act did mark a turning point in Indian-white relations because it suggested that cultural self-determination applied not only to white Anglo-Saxons.[71]

Among white citizens, the Indian Reorganization Act was not without its critics, and the DAR's support for the new law was remarkable, given that its detractors portrayed the Indian New Deal as the scheme of communist conspirators. Members of the US Congress as well as prominent missionary organizations branded it as an un-American endeavor that would only buttress communist tribalism and Native religious practices.[72] Despite its vigorous campaign to root out communists during the 1930s, the DAR did not join this chorus of critics. During its Continental Congress of 1934, the DAR passed a resolution that explicitly endorsed the act, criticizing as un-American the "lamentably bad" conditions on Native American reservations "from the standpoint of health, education, social welfare and economics." According to the organization's leaders, these conditions were due to a long tradition "of depriving the Indians of the rights to govern themselves in local matters, to administer their property as free citizens, and to educate themselves efficiently." The Daughters were confident that the act would not only correct these injustices but also finally give Native Americans the rights that the Constitution "guaranteed to all American citizens."[73] The DAR endorsed the idea to grant Native Americans more self-determination; it also fully subscribed to the general understanding among white reformers that education would be the most important means of integrating Indians into the nation. Already in the 1920s and early 1930s, the Daughters had begun to implement such ideas in supporting the American Indian Institute as well as Indian colleges such as Bacone College in Muskogee, Oklahoma, an institution that exclusively trained Native Americans.[74] Convinced of Indians' loyalty and eagerness to adopt the white man's ways, the DAR was prepared to transform Indians into true Americans.

"Good Will and Cordial Fellowship": World War II and the American Indians Committee

As the DAR's remembrance of the Indian past turned inward and focused on Indigenous culture, the Daughters simultaneously stepped up their campaign for improved Indian welfare and education in the present to help them achieve their long-term goal for Indians to become devoted patriots. During the second half of the 1930s, the national DAR demonstrated its staunch commitment to incorporating Indians into US society by establishing a special committee to coordinate this aspect of the organization's activism. In 1936, as it became increasingly clear that Indians were no longer a vanishing race, the Daughters established an Indian citizenship section within the national Americanism Committee. Five years later, in October 1941, the DAR terminated the Conservation Committee's subcommittee on American Indians and established the National Committee on the American Indians, subsequently renamed American Indians Committee.[75] The purpose of the committee was "to help the American Indian secure educational advantages, especially for those who are desirous and capable of becoming leaders of their own race." To do so, it provided scholarships, loans, and other forms of financial assistance to Indian students, primarily to Indian girls.[76]

A few months before the committee was established, its first chairwoman, Leda Ferrell Rex, had already exhorted the heads of American Indians Committees in each state to learn more about the needs of Indian schools and their students and to consider supporting those who needed assistance. DAR chapters and state organizations across the country then began to raise funds for this purpose. As a result, they were able to offer fellowships to Indian schools, Indian colleges, and individual students. The New York DAR even launched four-year scholarships for Indian girls who enrolled in Cornell University's home economics program. The national committee also promoted adult education in Native arts and crafts at reservation community centers.[77] In fact, the Daughters regarded education as a key means to make Native people more patriotic. "The Daughters of the American Revolution," the national DAR explained in 1941, "are giving every possible assistance to help in the education of the American Indian in true Americanism, that he will have reason to love and respect and the desire to defend his country against all enemies."[78]

Although the new committee officially focused on education, it also coordinated and supported members' continuing desire to study and celebrate Indian cultures. Earlier efforts to do so were initiated to preserve the legacy of a purportedly vanishing society, but the American Indians Committee now promoted preserving living Indian cultures to protect America's heritage, praise Indians' cultural accomplishments, and support Indigenous communities. The Bureau of Indian Affairs had announced in the early 1920s that the vanishing race theory might be flawed. But only the agency's 1940 report, which demonstrated that Indian citizens numbered more than 360,000 and were reproducing at a higher rate than the non-Indian population, convinced the last skeptics.[79] By the time the American Indians Committee was established, the Daughters no longer believed in the vanishing race theory. More importantly, they began to view Indian culture as an integral part of US history and used the term "first real American" to express their admiration for Indigenous people's contributions to that history and American nation-building.[80]

To underline that Indian culture was alive and an integral part of US culture, the committee created a Living Indians Room in DAR Memorial Continental Hall in April 1942. In this room, Indian art as well as books on and images of Indian history and culture were on display to acquaint Daughters and visitors with what Leda Rex called "our first Americans."[81] Three years later, the committee's second chairwoman, Ramona Kaiser, made clear her conviction that one should no longer regard Indian culture as a sign of a primitive race that had to make room for American civilization, but as a symbol of American nation-building. In the November 1945 issue of the *DAR Magazine,* Kaiser stated, "The art of a people reflects the soul of a race—so, as believers in the perpetuation of all things truly American, we must preserve those things that symbolize the growth of our nation. Let us make the D.A.R. Living Indians Room a living tribute to a truly liberty-loving race: the American Indian."[82] Indians were thus no longer seen as a quaint but detrimental obstacle to national expansion; rather, their culture, although not necessarily their history, was reinterpreted as being part of the nation's progress. Seen in this light, studying Indian culture became as important as examining the American Revolution or western expansion because the Daughters had come to regard it as an integral part of America's nationalized cultural memory. Devoid of reflections on the violent legacies of white conquest, this sanitized interpretation of the past allowed the Daughters to envision a truly united nation.

Encouraged by the American Indians Committee, DAR chapters across the country explored Indian cultural traditions and pondered strategies to preserve them during the first half of the 1940s. From 1941 to 1943, dozens of Ohio chapters created special study programs that included guest speakers, papers by chapter members, and Indian songs and legends.[83] As a result of the committee's prodding, hundreds of chapters also regularly collected used beads and distributed them among Indian reservations to encourage handicraft and to help them find additional sources of income. The committee itself frequently sold Indian baskets and similar items to raise funds to support Indian education.[84] This fascination with the exotic "other" made it possible and even desirable for the Daughters to meet Native Americans. The American Indians Committee actively encouraged such encounters to motivate more members to support its goals. "Embrace every opportunity to meet Indians, especially young people," Leda Rex instructed state committee chairwomen in December 1941, "and try to promote the idea of having our members personally meet these people. This will win members to our cause." The committee also frequently invited Native artists to display and discuss their work at the DAR's headquarters in Washington.[85] In many cases, the committee's efforts to preserve Indian culture echoed the organization's ritualized commemorations of white-Indian friendship, since committee members, as Rex stressed in 1943, should "never lose an opportunity to contact and to carry good will to our Indian friends."[86]

As had been the case during World War I, the Daughters' belief in interracial friendship and cooperation seemed to be confirmed once more by the ostensible eagerness of Native men to fight for the United States after the Japanese attack on Pearl Harbor in December 1941. Very few tribes resisted the draft, and hundreds of Indians volunteered for military service. By the end of the war, more than 25,000 Indian men had served in the US armed forces. In addition, several hundred Native women had enlisted as war nurses. Numerous Indian servicemen received awards for heroism on the battlefield. This reinforced white stereotypes about Indigenous men as born warriors and strengthened the idea that they wanted to leave their reservations, abandon tribal cultures, and become full-fledged citizens. In yet another echo of the Great War, however, individual soldiers' reasons for joining the army as well as the consequences of their military service were complex. Although their exposure to a world beyond the reservation contributed to a process of detribalization, the war also allowed many tribes to renew their commitment to ancient warrior traditions and Indigenous identity by honoring returning veterans. But to the head of the DAR's American Indians Committee, such tribal rituals seemed to prove rather than counter the argument that Indians were loyal citizen soldiers. Noting approvingly in late 1943 that Sioux in South Dakota had danced the Sun Dance for 2,000 members of the tribe who were about to enter military service, Rex proudly proclaimed that Native Americans across the nation had gone "on the warpath against the Jap and the man they call the 'Moustache Smeller.'" There was no doubt in her mind that Indians' loyalty was "100 percent."[87]

Rex and fellow DAR leaders tirelessly praised Indians' devotion to the American war effort and felt confirmed in their conviction that white Americans and the descendants of the aboriginal population had become genuine friends despite the injustices that Indians had suffered at the hands of white America.[88] As in the DAR's commemorative campaigns, the Daughters used every available opportunity to show Native servicemen their appreciation. In July 1942 Rex organized an American Indians Committee open house for Indigenous members of the armed forces at the War Service Room in Memorial Continental Hall. More than fifty Native men and women attended the event, listening attentively to a speech delivered by President General Helena Hellwig Pouch, who, according to a report on the event, stressed the "good will and cordial fellowship" that she believed characterized relations between white Americans and the Indigenous population.[89]

While the committee paid tribute primarily to Indigenous servicemen, it also actively encouraged Native American women to enlist by financially supporting those tribal members who wanted to become war nurses. Doing so allowed the DAR to make contributions toward the war effort while simultaneously supporting Native communities.[90] In the following years, numerous DAR state organizations raised funds to finance Indian girls' training as nurses, and the *DAR Magazine* proudly reported about Indian graduates. In spring of 1943 the publication reported on "full blooded Cherokee" Mary Louise Whitewater, who had just graduated from the Hillcrest Memorial Hospital in Tulsa, Oklahoma. Having signed up for the Army's Evacuation Service, Whitewater was described as the "brave little Indian nurse" who was "sent forth with a blessing from the Indian Committee."[91]

After the Allied victory, the Daughters continued to call attention to the dismal plight of many Indians. Occasionally the Daughters admitted white wrongdoing with unprecedented candor and described the Indian past with more nuance than they had done before. Writing in the DAR's monthly magazine in September 1945, Hattie Starcher admitted, "The history of the Indian and the white man is a record of which no American has a right to be proud. With rare exceptions the white man treated the original Americans with contempt and treachery." Starcher argued that it should come as no surprise that Indians, who were "forced back inch by inch," attempted "to stave off the inevitable by massacre and guerilla warfare." She further explained that Native Americans were decimated and had lost "native skills" as well as "faith and dignity." She emphasized that Indians constituted a heterogeneous mix of different tribes; some were nomads on the Great Plains, while others had always lived in "permanent dwellings."[92] Still, such nuanced interpretations of the Native past that offered a frank discussion of white-Indian conflict remained rare, probably because they would have challenged the DAR's emphasis on interracial amity and cooperation.

Since they believed in the necessity of protecting Indian culture as well as Native Americans' rights as US citizens, the Daughters even applauded the beginnings of Indian political activism during World War II. In 1944, representatives of more than fifty tribes met in Denver to found the National Congress of American Indians, an intertribal organization that demanded federal protection for tribal property, civil rights, a higher percentage of Native employees in government agencies, and a dialogue between Indian leaders and the US government over decisions pertaining to the Indigenous population. White politicians praised the organization because it professed nonpartisanship and stood for moderate change. Appealing to the conscience of white America and trying not to offend public opinion, the National Congress of American Indians insisted that tribal cultural self-determination would not undermine Indians' allegiance to the nation.[93] In light of Native men's valorous service during World War II, American Indians Committee chairwoman Leda Rex supported the intertribal congress's demands and wrote that the organization promised "to be of tremendous importance to future Indian well-being." Rex described the National Congress of American Indians as "an attempt of Indians to help themselves through united effort, and as such it merits the support of every public-spirited D.A.R."[94]

By 1945, mirroring the trajectory of their earlier commemorations of the American Revolution and western expansion, the Daughters' remembrance of Native Americans was no longer as visible as it had been. But the idea of white-Indian friendship was stronger than ever. In the eyes of the American Indians Committee members, World War II provided final proof that the two races could amicably work together in a united effort to defend the American nation. "Now, as never before we need the Indian and they need us," Rex wrote in February 1942. "War is upon us and in it the Indians will play an important part. Let us clasp hands, Red Man and White Man . . . and united pledge ourselves to keep America forever AMERICAN."[95]

4

"Conserve the Sources of Our Race in the Anglo-Saxon Line"

African Americans, New Immigrants, and Ethnic Nationalism

Eighteen years after delegates of the DAR's Continental Congress lauded Tsianina Redfeather as a "hundred per cent American singer," the famous black contralto Marian Anderson stepped toward the microphone on the plaza of the Lincoln Memorial in Washington, DC. Unlike Redfeather, Anderson had never been asked to perform before a DAR audience. Neither had she received permission to give a benefit concert at Constitution Hall, the Daughters' large auditorium in the capital. Enforcing a "white artists only" policy that the DAR introduced in the early 1930s, its leaders refused to let the African American opera singer perform in the city's only concert hall that was large enough to accommodate the huge audience that a star of her stature regularly drew in Europe and North America. Neither thousands of protest letters nor the resignation of the organization's most famous member, First Lady Eleanor Roosevelt, swayed the DAR. With the help of the Roosevelt administration, civil rights activists managed to organize a free open-air concert in front of the memorial to the Great Emancipator. The recital took place on Easter Sunday 1939, and almost 75,000 white and black citizens came to hear Anderson sing. Millions of others could hear her voice on numerous radio stations that broadcast the concert live across the nation. Introduced by Secretary of the Interior Harold L. Ickes and observed by members of Congress and other high-ranking government officials, the black contralto began her concert with "America" and proceeded with arias as well as Negro spirituals. After Anderson's last song, the huge crowd erupted in thunderous applause.[1]

As indicated by the DAR's treatment of Marian Anderson, before World

War II there was a stark contrast between the Daughters' paternalistic fascination with Indians and their profound disregard for African Americans. Unlike America's Indigenous population, black citizens hardly appeared in the organization's interpretations of the nation's heroic past and were deemed a threat to its racial purity in the present. This deliberate amnesia, together with their ambivalent opposition to immigration and profuse praise for supposedly racially pure mountaineers, reflected the Daughters' deep conviction that patriotism and Anglo-Saxon whiteness were inextricably intertwined. From the DAR's perspective, the United States was a white nation whose racial integrity had to be preserved.

The Daughters' racist amnesia was due to an ideologically powerful combination of the DAR's strong ethnic nationalism, the racial dimensions of Civil War memory, and related ideas about whiteness. In the South many Daughters also belonged to the United Daughters of the Confederacy, a rival women's organization that countered the DAR's message of national unity by romanticizing the antebellum South and its defeat in the Civil War. To quell the occasional tensions that erupted over such competing memories of the war, the Daughters stressed the common military valor of southern and northern white soldiers as well as the patriotic lineages their female descendants shared. Creating a heroic cultural memory to boost American patriotism, then, was as much about remembering white heroism as it was about forgetting slavery and the existence of millions of black citizens, whom the Daughters deemed irrelevant to the nation's past, present, and future.

As for the millions of new immigrants who arrived on America's shores around 1900, the organization's reactions were more ambivalent, veering between civic and ethnic nationalism, but confirmed members' belief that the nation's stability and unity depended on white, old-stock citizens like themselves and the traditional gender dichotomies they upheld in their commemorative campaigns. Although many of the newcomers from such countries as Italy, Greece, and Russia seemed racially suspect, the Daughters initially believed they could be transformed into patriotic citizens if the organization succeeded in instilling in them white middle-class values—including proper notions of masculinity and femininity—and allegiance to their adopted country. The DAR therefore joined a nationwide movement to Americanize these European newcomers, familiarizing them with the history of the United States and its laws through lectures, publications, and patriotic children's clubs.

Although seemingly unprejudiced, these efforts to support immigrants on their path toward citizenship reflected the Daughters' racialized understanding of memory and patriotism. From their perspective, Americanization was imperative because the dwindling number of old-stock Americans prevented the inculcation of national allegiance through a combination of ancestry and communicative memory. The Daughters believed that white, old-stock Americans possessed an inborn love of country, while new immigrants purportedly lacked this inherent capacity for patriotism and therefore had to be familiarized with the nation's cultural memory through other means. By 1923, however, DAR leaders had grown frustrated with what they perceived as the limited impact of their Americanization campaigns. Consequently, they joined politicians and other patriotic organizations in calls for restrictive immigration legislation, applauding the passage of the National Origins Act of 1924 and the subsequent steep decline in immigration from eastern and southern Europe. The Daughters' fascination with the white mountaineers of the southern Appalachians similarly reflected their racialized understanding of patriotic memory and was entangled with the Daughters' fear of immigration. They regarded this large group of uneducated whites in isolated highland areas of the South as a crucial reservoir of untainted Anglo-Saxon patriotism and insisted that they would serve as an antidote to the influx of European newcomers.

During the 1930s the Daughters continued to believe that at least some immigrants could be transformed into loyal US citizens, but they remained indifferent to African Americans and showed their disdain by barring black artists from performing at its Constitution Hall in Washington, DC. Only Marian Anderson's request in 1939 to perform in the auditorium forced the Daughters to confront their racist amnesia and the question of whether citizens of color should be regarded as legitimate members of the nation. Despite the storm of criticism the Daughters endured because of their racist policies, they did not budge and asserted that barring Anderson had nothing to do with race. Although World War II challenged many of its racist assumptions, the DAR continued to uphold the idea that only white citizens could be "true" Americans.

"There Is Not a Drop of Negro Blood in My Family": Nativism, Racism, and Civil War Memory

The DAR's concerns about race during the Progressive Era were closely connected to angst among white middle-class Protestants over perceived threats to what they believed was a white nation. The arrival of millions of immigrants in particular added to these anxieties. Unlike earlier arrivals, who hailed from western European countries such as Ireland and Germany, the vast majority of the almost nine million newcomers who arrived in the United States between 1880 and 1900 came from Italy, Ukraine, and other countries in southern and eastern Europe. By 1915 their numbers had swelled to more than twenty million, almost one quarter of the US population. Beginning in the late 1880s, a growing number of white citizens called for immigration restriction and stricter naturalization requirements to protect the United States against the massive influx of these purportedly un-American newcomers. This expression of nativism had a long tradition in America, but the movement that emerged in the late nineteenth century differed from earlier manifestations of xenophobia because of its strong emphasis on the idea that the Anglo-Saxon race was pitted against other, inferior races that potentially threatened the unity and stability of the United States. To be sure, between 1890 and World War I, the impact of this movement was uneven, and public support for nativism was never unanimous. Only on the West Coast, where anti-Asian sentiment had run rampant since the arrival of the first Chinese immigrants after the Civil War, had nativists' lobbying resulted in any meaningful federal legislation that actually restricted immigration on the basis of nationality. The Chinese Exclusion Act of 1882 effectively stopped Chinese immigration for ten years and was renewed three times between 1892 and 1902. But the rekindled fear of foreigners around 1900 did serve to exacerbate racial xenophobia among numerous white Protestants and gradually took hold among a larger section of the population during the first decade of the twentieth century.[2]

The debates about the purported menace of immigrants and the proposed strategies to include them in or exclude them from national membership served to conflate US nationalism and Anglo-Saxon whiteness. The Daughters of the American Revolution advocated a form of racial nationalism that reflected these fears as well as the pseudoscientific theories about white racial superiority that undergirded them. Popular books such as Madison Grant's *The Passing of the Great Race*, which was first published in 1910, constructed a hierarchy of white and nonwhite races that placed "Nordic" races at the top. Consequently, the inferiority of African Americans and new immigrants was widely accepted as fact, which bolstered the idea that only white Anglo-Saxon Protestants could become members of the national community.[3]

Given the popularity of such racist theories, it was not surprising that the Daughters and like-minded groups were unperturbed by the dismal plight that black citizens faced around 1900. During the same period that saw the arrival of millions of immigrants, southern African Americans were relegated to the status of second-class citizens and lost most of the civil rights they had gained after the Civil War. The Union's victory over the Confederacy and the subsequent Reconstruction Era had ended slavery, declared African Americans citizens of the United States, and granted suffrage to black men, but white southerners made strenuous efforts to reinstate white supremacy. Through a combination of intimidation, violence, and growing northern indifference, southern states were able to win back political power by the late 1870s, and they consolidated white supremacy by introducing legally sanctioned racial segregation and disfranchisement in the following three decades. They also passed numerous antimiscegenation laws that made any intimate relations between white and black Americans a crime and were designed to ensure the supposed purity of the white race. By the early 1890s, the antiblack violence of the Reconstruction Era gave way to lynching as a final means to cement the region's racial hierarchies and ensure a docile black labor force.[4]

The DAR's nationalist ideology reflected this amalgam of nativism and racism. In the organization's vision of America, citizens of color were at the very bottom. Especially southern Daughters loudly proclaimed their disdain for the descendants of African slaves and fervently supported Jim Crow, a legalized system of racial segregation and disfranchisement that southern legislatures began to implement in the late nineteenth century. When in 1901 President Theodore Roosevelt invited the famous black leader Booker T. Washington to dine with him and his family at the White House, southern members reacted with shock and disbelief. Two years later, many of them skipped the traditional White House reception that was traditionally given to DAR delegates who attended the organization's annual meeting in Washington, DC.[5] But not only members from the former Confederacy felt strongly about "the race question." In 1904, the prominent black intellectual and civil rights activist W. E. B. Du Bois drew the ire of Daughters in Chicago when he asserted in a speech before the city's Woman's Club that one eighth of America's white population had black ancestry. Shocked and indignant, many members publicly vented their anger at Du Bois. "I can trace my ancestry back to the monkeys," said a Daughter named Mrs. Frederick Lee. "I hope the monkey I sprang from had as big a twist in his tail and as many wrinkles in his face as any monkey, but I know there is not a drop of negro blood in my family."[6] Interracial sex had occurred as early as the seventeenth century, when the first African slaves arrived in North America. Similarly unacknowledged by the Daughters, many of these sexual encounters were white men's assaults on women of color during and after slavery.[7]

The DAR's statements on race reflected a deep-seated fear of miscegenation, which troubled many Americans but seemed to be of special concern to southern Daughters who prided themselves on their illustrious Anglo-Saxon lineage. In an article on the organization's goals that was published in the *Atlanta Constitution* in 1905, a DAR officer identified as Mrs. Edgar A. Ross explained how important it would be to teach white children about the accomplishments of their heroic ancestors to protect the white nation. "We wish our children to so well understand their origin, their duty to men and to the God who has prospered us," she wrote, "that they will preserve the nation from decay and their grand old Anglo-Saxon blood from amalgamation with the inferior races within our gates."[8] At the 1906 annual conference of the Georgia DAR, Ross also criticized what she believed was African Americans' goal to attain "social equality." The Daughters, she said in a proposed resolution on compulsory education in Georgia, "have always believed in pure blood, and should do all in their power to keep that of the southern people untainted." Georgia therefore needed to do everything it could to educate its white citizens to prevent interracial marriages.[9] Three years after this debate, the Georgia DAR lobbied the state legislature to pass a compulsory education bill that the organization's members deemed essential to ensure "the 'survival of the fittest' race in America." The proposed legislation targeted primarily white children, and the Daughters were willing to include "the inferior races" only if they were confined to "industrial schools" to prevent them from attaining advanced degrees.[10]

Given their dread of racial amalgamation, especially southern members recoiled from the thought of admitting black women to the DAR. Thousands of female descendants of the approximately 5,000 African American soldiers who had served in the Continental Army during the Revolutionary War would have been eligible to apply for membership, but the Daughters made sure that such applications, should they ever be made, would be unsuccessful. The organization did not officially discriminate against African Americans, and its constitution's section on eligibility did not mention race, but Daughters found subtle ways to ensure the membership's racial homogeneity.

The DAR's strategy was probably best explained by Dr. Francis H. Orme, a Georgian homeopath who was the chairman of the advisory board of the Atlanta DAR Chapter. In 1896 he addressed its members on the topic "Duty of Being Select," explaining the difference between "eligibility" and "acceptability." While the national DAR determined women's eligibility, he said, acceptability was "something to be settled by the choice of each chapter, as indicated by its secret ballot, the result of which no one has a right to challenge." Elaborating on this significant distinction, which was also part of the DAR's constitution, Orme freely admitted that African Americans had fought for American independence and that their descendants would be eligible for membership. Yet, he surmised, "they would not be acceptable." He cloaked this form of racial discrimination in explications about "unsuitable and objectionable members" who would destroy the "harmony" and "efficiency" of the DAR, but his audience clearly understood that such methods would be applied only to black citizens.[11]

Nine years after Orme's speech, DAR leader Ross was more blunt, unequivocally stating in the *Atlanta Constitution*, "It is a self-evident fact that eligibility to our ranks is not attainable by any Afro-American whatsoever, and the northern and southern branches of this order can meet without a clash, as to the admission of colored delegates to their conventions." Referencing Roosevelt's dinner invitation to Booker T. Washington in 1901, she concluded by defiantly asserting that even the US president "could not place a black face in our continental congress."[12] To the Daughters, then, African Americans could be neither members of the DAR nor fully accepted members of the nation.

Since the Daughters saw no room for black citizens in the nation, it followed that African Americans were almost completely absent from the DAR's heroic tales about America's past. There were only a few exceptions. In 1909 the Colonel Henshaw Chapter of Leicester, Massachusetts, marked the site of the home of Peter Salem, a black soldier who had fought for the United States at the Battle of Bunker Hill.[13] But such efforts to keep alive the largely forgotten memory of black patriotism were rare and had no impact on the national DAR and its interpretations of US history. If black Americans appeared at all, DAR authors mentioned only slavery and did so primarily within the context of the American Revolution. In doing so they suggested not only that England had forced slavery upon its colonies but also that the United States had actually shown more enthusiasm than its mother country for ending the slave trade and slavery itself.[14] Such examples of historical distortion echoed the general thrust of Civil War memory, which in the name of national reconciliation made little mention of the reasons for which the bloody conflict was fought or the suffering of the almost four million enslaved black men, children, and women who had toiled on southern plantations until the Union's victory.[15] In the Daughters' view, African Americans were of no relevance to the nation's past except that their presence had led white southerners and northerners to fight a tragic war that endangered the Union.

The striking disparity between the DAR's fascination with America's Indigenous population and its contempt for African Americans raises the question of why the organization imagined and treated the two groups so differently. Historians of settler colonialism and the memory of Indian removal suggest answers to this seeming paradox. Patrick Wolfe has cogently argued that the process of settling colonial America and the United States centered on dispossessing Natives of their territory but went hand in hand with their social and cultural elimination. Various forms of removal and confinement to remote reservations largely eliminated Indians as a presence in white communities, while federal assimilation policies served similar purposes, since integrating smaller numbers of Indians into white society offered a less disruptive way of undermining tribal claims to ancestral homelands. Consequently, in the nineteenth century, white settlers were able to fundamentally curtail Indians' ability to challenge the social and political status quo. Final military defeat in the 1880s cemented their status as a nonthreatening and largely invisible element in US society.[16]

A comparable dynamic was at work in America's cultural memory, Andrew Denson's study on southern remembrance of Cherokee removal indicates. White citizens could memorialize and even lament Indians' forced displacement because they conceptualized it as a story of disappearance, which reaffirmed rather than challenged white ownership of Indian territories. Congruent with the logic of elimination, southerners interpreted Natives in terms of their invisibility, a perspective that allowed them to view themselves as rightful inheritors of the land that was seemingly devoid of any Indigenous presence.[17] Thus, even though Indians continued to be seen as an inferior race, their actual and imagined absence reassured the Daughters and other white citizens that this group no longer posed a threat to their dominant position in US society and their claims to tribal territories. This particular interpretation, combined with the DAR's belief in Indian national loyalty in the past and the present, also explains why the organization tolerated the prospect of Native American DAR membership and marriage between white and Indigenous citizens. In the eyes of the Daughters, limited miscegenation, if accompanied by complete assimilation, neither imperiled national stability nor undermined white supremacy.

By contrast, the role of African Americans in US society was defined by their labor and their permanent presence, which is why the Daughters and like-minded citizens believed them to be a dire threat to the nation and white privilege. Especially in the South, black workers were an essential part of the region's economy. Unlike Indians, they could not be displaced; economic necessity thus led to a process of race-based exclusion rather than one of elimination. Wolfe contends that race and racism intensify when different groups share social space, as is reflected in the emergence of Jim Crow segregation and scientific racism after the demise of slavery. Marital unions between black and white Americans were seen as undermining white social, political, and cultural power.

This logic of exclusion also extended to the realm of memory. If the seeming invisibility of the Indigenous population allowed whites to incorporate them into commemorative rituals, the permanent presence of a comparably large number of citizens of color required almost complete erasure of their history from white interpretations of the nation's past or sanitized versions of it that confirmed black inferiority. Paying homage to or mourning the disappearance of Native Americans while deliberately forgetting black contributions to US nation-building were complementary strategies that served to strengthen exclusionary notions of ethnic nationalism. Denson has made this argument with regard to the American South, and the example of the Daughters of the American Revolution suggests that the same dynamic was a nationwide phenomenon, attesting to the activist zeal and cultural authority of white nationalist women around 1900.[18]

Since African Americans were perceived as such an existential threat, the memory of the Civil War did present formidable challenges to the Daughters' emphasis on national unity, notwithstanding their efforts to erase black citizens from most accounts of the past. Especially the frequent overlap of membership between the DAR and the United Daughters of the Confederacy (UDC) was fraught with much potential for sectional strife. Founded in 1894, the UDC was a women's organization that proved enormously popular among white middle-class Protestants in the South, including many DAR members, and boasted a membership of 100,000 by the end of World War I. DAR co-founder Mary Desha, the Kentuckian who had served as a nurse in the Confederate Army, was probably the most prominent Daughter with a UDC membership card. During the first two decades of the twentieth century, the organization spearheaded a tremendously influential movement to cope with the South's traumatic military defeat by idealizing antebellum society and the notions of white racial superiority it was based on as well as by praising the heroic valor of the Confederate soldiers who had defended it. Through such means as monuments and textbooks, its members sought to controvert what they regarded as northern historical falsehoods, primary among them the idea that southern secession was an act of rebellion and that Confederate soldiers had been disloyal to the United States. Although DAR members who belonged to the UDC repeatedly contended that they were loyal citizens of the United States, the Confederate organization's goals clearly contradicted the vision of national unity that the DAR stressed in its commemorative campaigns.[19]

Meanwhile, DAR members who belonged to the UDC's northern counterpart, the Woman's Relief Corps, challenged the South's Confederate nostalgia by celebrating Abraham Lincoln's birthday, for example, to maintain citizens' "true allegiance" to the United States.[20] Given these conflicting interpretations of the Civil War and its legacy within the DAR, sectional tensions occasionally erupted into verbal vitriol. In 1912, DAR President General Julia Green Scott's decision to decorate Memorial Continental Hall with the Confederate flag next to the Stars and Stripes for the opening of a UDC convention in the building drew strong protest from a number of northern Daughters, including the organization's co-founder Mary Lockwood.[21]

Although such tensions flared up infrequently, they became a concern to DAR leaders, who came up with two major strategies to calm sectional passions. The first strategy, introduced in 1914, was simply to ban any discussions on the subject. That year, a concert of hisses and catcalls interrupted the DAR's Continental Congress after President General Daisy Allen Story read a letter in which a member of the Sons of the American Revolution denounced the custom of wearing UDC badges during the Daughters' Continental Congress. To prevent similar disruptions in the future, the delegates unanimously passed a resolution that prohibited "the mentioning of any subject thought likely to cause angry feeling among the Daughters," including sectional issues as well as any other "subjects not directly in sympathy with the patriotic principles of the organization."[22]

The second strategy had been utilized since the DAR's founding and was probably the more successful one because it stressed commonalities rather than differences. It revolved around the common heroism of southern and northern soldiers, especially during the wars in which the two sections stood shoulder by shoulder to defend the United States, and the patriotic lineages their female descendants shared. From the Daughters' perspective, bloodlines were a key indicator of patriotism in the present. Shawn Michelle Smith has pointed out that the DAR and other "genealogical organizations enabled the consolidation of a seemingly stable, embodied, and racialized national identity" that "conflated American borders with Anglo-Saxon bloodlines."[23] During the 1890s DAR members vehemently debated whether the organization should accept applicants who were unable to document their descent from brothers or sisters of known patriots. Initially, these so-called collaterals were eligible to join the DAR as descendants of the "mother of a patriot." Since this mother had raised a known patriot, it was assumed that she and her other children had also been genuine supporters of American independence. By 1895, however, the Daughters decided to discontinue this practice, accepting as members only the lineal descendants of known American patriots. Insisting on ostensibly pure bloodlines among the organization's members highlighted the importance of male ancestors and contributed to the vision of a racialized genealogy of patriotic continuity that even the Civil War could not disrupt.[24]

Especially southern members frequently evoked the Continental Army's valor as proof of shared "revolutionary blood," and US soldiers' exploits during the Spanish-American War convinced members from all regions that national unity had finally been reestablished. In 1899 the idea of common valor prompted the attendees of that year's annual meeting to unanimously adopt a resolution that expressed the DAR's ambition to establish "War between the States" as the official designation of the military conflict between North and South, thus soothing southern members who disdained the idea that their ancestors were traitors, as was suggested by the term "civil war." The organization's careful handling of this sensitive topic thus reflected and contributed to the general discourse of sectional reconciliation, stressing white warriors' heroism and the common racial interests of northerners and southerners.[25]

These efforts to rein in sectional tensions contributed to fairly cordial relations between the two organizations, together with the shared gender ideologies of the DAR and the UDC; both organizations stressed women's patriotic contributions to US nation-building but refrained from directly challenging existing gender hierarchies.[26] Georgia is a case in point. There, the state's revolutionary past made the DAR an attractive organization in the eyes of many white middle-class women. The UDC, however, was more popular, and the overlap of membership and leadership forced the two organizations to cooperate on many occasions. In the early twentieth century, local chapters as well as the state DAR's leadership frequently participated in UDC events that commemorated Confederate heroes such as General Robert E. Lee, whose daughter Mary Custis Lee became a DAR member in 1901. The Daughters also frequently participated in Confederate Memorial Day exercises, supported the UDC's campaign against textbooks that purportedly disparaged the South, and allowed the UDC to use DAR buildings for meetings and social events.[27] In other parts of the South, the two organizations did not collaborate as closely, but their members mingled frequently at official meetings and expressed mutual respect.[28] The Daughters also cooperated with the UDC at the national level. The southern organization was allowed to hold several of its annual meetings at the DAR's Memorial Continental Hall in Washington, DC, and the conveners of the 1906 Continental Congress had no qualms about letting the audience sing "The Star-Spangled Banner" along with "Dixie," the famous southern battle song that became the Confederacy's unofficial anthem.[29] Although the UDC appeared to challenge the DAR's efforts to strengthen patriotism and national unity, then, the shared belief in white masculine valor and the need to preserve white supremacy helped forge strong bonds of sisterhood.

"Qualify the Coming Hordes for Assimilation into the American Type": New Immigrants, Americanization, and the White Mountaineers

If the DAR feared racial miscegenation and suggested that African Americans were an alien element in what its members believed was a white nation, the organization was as disturbed by the deluge of new immigrants who arrived in the United States around 1900. Echoing nativist organiza-

tions' warnings, DAR leaders regarded these newcomers as racially suspect and potentially dangerous to America's stability. At a DAR meeting
that took place in Washington, DC, in 1891, Ella Loraine Dorsey argued
that the "weekly outpouring of the old world into the new threatens to
overwhelm the native Americans and reduce them to a minimum in their
own land." She was therefore "peculiarly grateful" for her organization's
efforts "to maintain our integrity as a people and our individuality as a nation."[30] Two years later, during the DAR's second Continental Congress, co-
founder Mary Lockwood voiced similar concerns, warning that the United
States was "denationalized by Hungarians, Poles, and Italians who have
never read the first letter of the spirit of Americanism."[31] In the eyes of the
Daughters who witnessed violent protests by foreign workers in the 1890s
and the assassination of William McKinley in 1901, it was this seeming
lack of Americanism among the foreign population that made immigrant
communities dangerous "hot beds of anarchy."[32] As millions of immigrants
continued to arrive on America's shores, Daughters across the country were
convinced that it was their patriotic duty to defend the nation against this
un-American menace.

Despite these fears and in stark contrast to their disdain for African
Americans, the Daughters did believe that Syrians, Greeks, and other
"races" could become patriotic US citizens if properly guided. Unlike black
Americans, these European and Middle Eastern men, women, and children
were deemed white enough to be assimilated into the nation. Even Jewish
immigrants appeared to be acceptable as members of the nation. During
a period when anti-Semitism was widespread and rarely condemned, the
Daughters had some Jewish members and did not object to government
officials' favorable statements about this ethnic minority.[33]

Although the new immigrants could not match the Daughters' pedigrees
and lacked Anglo-Saxon blood, the organization suggested that adopting
American culture and accepting the country's civic creed would be sufficient
to transform them into patriotic and productive citizens. During the Progressive Era, Daughters often contended that white old-stock Protestants like
themselves could help immigrants master this transformation. Mrs. Stephen
Chadwick, who in 1913 wrote about the menacing influx of immigrants in
the organization's monthly, said the Daughters needed "to prepare to educate
and qualify the coming hordes for assimilation into the American type."[34]
Despite fears of "denationalization," DAR leaders tended to be sympathetic
toward those hordes. In 1907, one vice regent from Ohio called immigrants

"ignorant and suspicious" but also asked for sympathy for these "men and women who have fled from persecution, civic, religious, or political, in their own land, and whose souls seem embittered against all mankind."[35] Thus, although the Daughters advocated ethnic nationalism, which hinged on preserving a white nation, they repeatedly supported a form of civic nationalism that regarded alien newcomers as potential citizens if they adopted white Protestant values and political beliefs.

Beginning in the late 1890s, Daughters across the nation made strenuous efforts to implement their plans to Americanize the growing immigrant population, although they rarely used the term "Americanize" prior to the Great War. In this endeavor, they became part of a heterogeneous movement of scholars, educators, business people, and government officials who were as concerned about the surge in immigration as the DAR and created a multitude of programs to prepare foreigners for US citizenship.[36] The contributions of the Daughters to this movement initially remained confined to the local or state level before becoming national projects.

The DAR's Americanization campaigns pursued three major strategies. The first strategy was to familiarize newcomers with America's government, laws, and history through illustrated lectures and night classes, most of which were given in immigrants' native languages.[37] By 1906 these local programs had led to the founding of a national DAR Committee on Patriotic Education, which coordinated lectures and similar educational projects such as night classes on American civics on the state and chapter levels. Seeking above all to inculcate patriotism among foreign residents, the committee soon began to offer prepared sets of slides for illustrated lectures on various topics that chapters could order. Lecture topics included "About America," "Our Flag," and "Landmarks in History," and such presentations were given in all areas with sizeable immigrant communities. It is conceivable that many of these talks reached tens of thousands of people. In 1910 the Ohio DAR reported that more than 8,000 immigrants had attended the twenty-one lectures its speakers had given that year. By the time Ohio Daughters reported about their progress, patriotic education committees had been established in almost every state, and they introduced additional initiatives, among them libraries with foreign-language books on the United States in immigrant communities.[38]

The organization's second strategy was an outgrowth of the first, a guidebook that contained the same information the Daughters disseminated in lectures; it was published in simple English as well as in several foreign languages. The Connecticut DAR spearheaded this attempt to educate immigrant communities; it collaborated with the writer John Foster Carr, an ardent advocate of Americanization who authored the first version of the guidebook in English and Italian. Carr's *Guide to the United States,* first published in 1910, contained information on numerous topics that were believed to be of use to immigrants, including sections on how to obtain work, how to learn English, and how to become an American citizen, as well as chapters on the US political system and practical advice ranging from traveling to health care. By late 1913 the Connecticut DAR's *Little Green Book,* as it came to be known, was in its seventh edition and had been translated into Polish and Yiddish. Connecticut Daughters used it in their night classes, made it available in their libraries, distributed it in immigrant communities as well as at ports of entry, and even mailed copies abroad to be distributed by foreign governments at ports of embarkation.[39]

The DAR's third strategy revolved around the Americanization of immigrant children through patriotic clubs for boys and girls. As with lectures for foreigners and the immigrant guidebook, these clubs began as local projects. In 1900 a DAR chapter in Cincinnati, Ohio, formed the first chapter of the Children of the Republic, a club that was open to foreign and American boys who were not eligible to join the DAR's youth auxiliary Children of the American Revolution. The focus, however, was on immigrant boys who in the words of the Ohio DAR needed to be taught "a high standard of civic honor and patriotic citizenship." The long-term goal of these clubs was to instill in immigrant children an abiding faith in the American nation. In 1902 the Daughters officially established Children of the Republic in Ohio and founded numerous chapters, a line of Americanization work that was adopted by the national DAR four years later. Subsequently, hundreds of chapters of Children of the Republic were established across the nation.[40]

Almost a decade after the Children of the Republic's inception, it was once again a chapter in Ohio that introduced a special club for immigrant girls, an idea that reflected the organization's gendered interpretations of nationalism. Daughters in Cleveland explained in the *American Monthly Magazine* in early 1912 that such a club was necessary to protect the American home from the millions of newcomers who arrived in the United States each year. "No wall, however solid," DAR member Elizabeth Neff wrote, "can withstand a tidal wave; no national ideal is strong enough to brave an onslaught of nine to one when the nine have gained a foothold, and the national ideal most seriously threatened is our dearest institution, our most sacred legacy from those remarkable women, our Revolutionary mothers, the American home."[41] To prevent its gradual destruction, Cleveland's Western Reserve Chapter embarked on a campaign to educate immigrant girls on "practical home-making in all its varied activities," establishing the Girl Home-Makers of America in 1911. As with Children of the Republic, this local initiative eventually became a national DAR project.[42] In the eyes of the Daughters, inculcating white middle-class notions of masculinity and femininity in young immigrants was as important to transforming them into patriotic citizens as was teaching America's political system and its history.

These ardent efforts to Americanize immigrant children and their parents also reflected the Daughters' belief in the interrelationship of memory, race, and patriotism. From their perspective, Americanization was essential because national allegiance was no longer reproduced through ancestry and communicative memory during a time that saw the numbers of old-stock Americans dwindle. Already in 1904, DAR chapter historian Angeline Scott explained to readers of the *New York Times* that in light of the diminishing "original American blood," one could not "expect heredity and family tradition to perpetuate American ideals." These ideals, she suggested, were transmitted through one's genes as well as through family memories.[43] Nine years later, Mrs. Stephen Chadwick reiterated the idea that race was an important repository for patriotism. Discussing the changes that the influx of immigrants had wrought in the United States, she claimed that previous newcomers from northern Europe and Britain "were active, intelligent, frugal, industrious, and possessed an inherent democracy of spirit, and hence were readily assimilated." Chadwick said these men and women "became Americans in the truest sense, not in one generation or two, but from the date of their landing. This was but natural, they were blood of our blood, and bone of our bone."[44] Since immigrant men, women, and children were believed to lack old-stock Americans' seemingly inborn sense of patriotism, they needed to be educated about America's past to understand the cultural memory that would transform them into loyal citizens.[45] Like the remembrances of western pioneers and Native Americans, the DAR's Americanization campaigns reaffirmed entrenched notions of white superiority in suggesting that white citizens had something people of color and alien newcomers supposedly lacked: an inborn capacity for patriotism.

Racialized notions of patriotic memory and the belief that the DAR needed to initiate countermeasures to preserve old-stock citizens' nationalist ideals were even more conspicuous in the organization's growing interest in the white mountaineers of the southern Appalachians. This group of white Southerners who lived in a mountainous area that stretched from the southern border of Pennsylvania to the northern rim of Georgia and Alabama had long been part of white America's imagination. During the last third of the nineteenth century, a growing number of scholars and pundits discussed the seeming backwardness of this ill-defined group of several million white citizens who had lived in largely isolated highland areas of the South for many generations. Beginning in the 1880s, Protestant missionaries flocked to the region to proselytize among and educate the people who were described as living in a premodern state of society. From 1885 to 1905, these missionaries established dozens of schools in Appalachia, where illiteracy and poverty were rampant, to help the mountaineers become productive US citizens. During the same period, the growing interest in the region and its people became part of a more general debate about America's past, present, and future. Depending on whether commentators approved or disapproved of the country's trajectory toward modernity, they called either for educational uplift for mountain communities or for more contemplation of their simple life against the backdrop of the downsides of modern civilization.[46]

Joining this debate, the Daughters agreed that the mountaineers needed educational uplift. More importantly, Daughters regarded them as a crucial reservoir of untainted Anglo-Saxon patriotism that would help white America survive the onslaught of the new immigrants. During the first decade of the twentieth century, especially southern DAR leaders began to voice concerns about ignorance and degradation in Appalachia's population. Advocating the founding of new schools and calling for financially supporting existing ones, Daughters repeatedly stressed that the region's white inhabitants were true Americans of good Anglo-Saxon and the best Revolutionary stock who, despite their primitive ways of life, had always loved their country and were ready to defend it. Daughters said it was this combination of racial traits and undiluted traditions of national loyalty that made southern mountaineers a vital storehouse of patriotism.[47] As a result of their concerns and confidence in the potential of educational work in Appalachia, southern DAR state organizations established several schools in the region and lobbied the national leadership for financial assistance.[48]

The DAR's attempts to educate white mountaineers testify to the ambiguities of the organization's Americanization campaign prior to World War I. Although the Daughters' nationalism veered between ethnic and civic nationalism, many Daughters seemed to agree that the nation's well-being depended on white Anglo-Saxon Protestants. DAR President General Julia Green Scott said as much when she addressed the Second National Conservation Congress in 1911. Many Daughters were in favor of what would later be called environmentalism; they joined a movement to conserve the nation's resources and to preserve America's wildlife as well as its flora. The National Conservation Congress offered a forum to activists, scholars, and politicians to discuss ways that resources could be used more efficiently. But to Julia Green Scott, conservation encompassed more than the environment; she declared that the new wave of immigration made it even more important to "conserve the sources of our race in the Anglo-Saxon line." Eliciting thunderous applause, she argued that the Daughters had "a right to insist upon the conserving not only of soil, forest, bird, minerals, fishes, waterways, in the interest of our future home-makers, but also upon the conservation of the supremacy of the Caucasian race in our land."[49] In the DAR's nationalist ideology, immigrants from southern and eastern Europe could become members of the nation but remained racially suspect. World War I would only reinforce these suspicions.

"Foreign Inundation" and "the Purest Anglo Saxons": The DAR's Americanization Campaign after World War I

The Great War marked a major turning point in American ethnic and race relations because it accelerated and amplified prewar ideological currents that would leave a lasting legacy for decades to come. The DAR's perspectives on immigration were fundamentally shaped by these developments and melded with the organization's postwar antiradicalism. Most importantly, America's entry into the war and the growing apprehensions about the Russian Revolution's impact led to an upsurge in antiforeign sentiment and colored debates about immigration and Americanization. Initially, this sentiment was directed primarily toward German immigrants, but as fears of the influence of Bolshevism grew while the temporary halt to immigration was lifted, it extended to virtually all newcomers. Most foreigners were increasingly associated with the un-American radicalism that the DAR and other organizations believed threatened the nation from within. These concerns gave a major boost to the Americanization movement, which had become a mass phenomenon by the time the United States entered the war. Support from state legislatures and the federal government through such agencies as the Bureau of Naturalization and the Bureau of Education gave the movement an aura of legitimacy. In the Northeast and the Midwest, these efforts focused on immigrants from southern and eastern Europe, while Americanization campaigns in the West concentrated on Chinese, Japanese, and Mexican newcomers. Although Americanization continued to be a heterogeneous movement with different agendas, most activists, agencies, and educators expected foreigners to develop a sense of allegiance toward the United States and its political system and laws, speak English, and adopt white middle-class values. The movement's ultimate goal was to prepare immigrants for US citizenship.[50]

As a result of its transformation into the vanguard of antiradicalism after World War I, the DAR had a considerable impact on the invigorated Americanization movement and eagerly cooperated with its various factions. Like other antiradical organizations, it promoted the idea that foreigners might become dangerous Trojan horses of Bolshevism. The Daughters doubled their efforts to reach all foreigners deemed worthy of Americanization and stop those who might endanger the nation. Addressing the DAR's Continental Congress in 1920, President General Sarah Elizabeth Guernsey likened the latter group to "cancerous growths" and "foreign leeches" that jeopardized the body politic and needed to be "cut and cast out."[51] The DAR's decision to institutionalize this aspect of its work after 1918 testifies to the urgency the Daughters believed the situation required. In the summer of 1919, a request by US Secretary of the Interior Franklin K. Lane prompted the DAR to establish a National Americanization Committee to support and advise state and chapter committees in their efforts to educate the foreign-born at the regional and local levels. Although Daughters' fears of radical immigrants grew, the organization still suggested that a sympathetic approach would be more successful in producing loyal new citizens than callous coercion.[52]

In the 1920s the Daughters pursued several strategies to make immigrants more receptive to the Americanization message. One was to greet new citizens after their naturalization ceremonies, a custom the US Bureau of Naturalization had begun during World War I. Many chapters organized festive receptions to honor new citizens. Others invited immigrants to their chapter homes, where they were asked to tell DAR members more about their respective home countries.[53] But the Daughters' most conspicuous means to Americanize the country's foreign-born in the 1920s was a widely distributed immigrant manual that was an outgrowth of the Connecticut DAR's *Little Green Book*. As with many other projects that had begun locally, the organization's national leaders considered the Connecticut campaign a valuable addition to its nationwide Americanization effort. The newly elected President General Anne Rogers Minor explained in 1920 in a letter to state regents that such a booklet would not only help the organization win immigrants' trust but might also speed up the process of assimilation.[54] Less than a year later, the first copies of *Manual of the United States: For the Information of Immigrants and Foreigners* arrived at the DAR's headquarters in Washington, DC, and were subsequently distributed free of charge among immigrants at America's ports of entry. It also was given to new citizens and sent to educators, the Salvation Army, the US Employment Bureau, courthouses, and wherever else the Daughters suspected it might reach the foreign-born. To enhance its effectiveness, the manual was translated into numerous foreign languages including Armenian, Finnish, and Japanese. Eventually the book was available in seventeen languages. By the late 1920s the Daughters had distributed more than two million copies of the *Manual of the United States*.[55]

It is unclear how many immigrants read the manual or how they interpreted its contents, but the publication's intent was unambiguous. In the words of President General Anne Rogers Minor, who wrote the first edition's foreword, the Daughters wanted the book's readers "to become *true Americans* in heart and soul." Minor wrote that attaining that status as well as US citizenship required studying America's history as well as its traditions and laws. The slender volume contained a wealth of practical information on learning English and becoming a citizen, but its sections on American history are most telling with regard to the ways the Daughters sought to influence readers' stance toward the United States. In these parts of the manual, the Daughters dismissed Indian claims to North America, telling readers that "No one" had lived there prior to the arrival of the first white settlers "but savage Indians and wild beasts." The writers also took pains to emphasize that the American Revolution was merely a "war for independence." Clearly trying to undermine comparisons between the Russian Revolution and the American Revolution, the *Manual of the United States* emphasized that colonists fought Britain only to maintain the liberties they already enjoyed. "Americans," readers learned, "abhor the kind of revolution which destroys and overturns, which murders, loots and burns."

To the Daughters, the lesson for present-day immigrants was obvious: the US government would not welcome those who sought to "overthrow that government and the liberties, happiness, and prosperity, which it seeks to insure."[56]

While the manual invoked prejudice against America's Indigenous population and sought to nip in the bud any revolutionary sentiment among immigrant readers, it was silent on the role of women in US history. In contrast to the DAR's various efforts to commemorate the heroines of the American Revolution, the organization taught immigrants primarily about the greatness of male leaders such as George Washington. As in the DAR's clubs for immigrant boys and girls, the foreign-born were expected to pledge allegiance to the American nation and the gender binaries the Daughters believed would ensure its stability.

The DAR's special interest in female immigrants reflected the same gendered interpretations of nationalism. Although the *Manual of the United States* was silent on women in general and immigrant women in particular, the organization regarded women as a crucial element of Americanization. Echoing their commemorative campaigns as well as their concerns about un-American radicalism and the welfare of Native Americans, the Daughters wanted to instill in immigrant women the idea that the home and related notions of femininity were vital to raising patriotic citizens. Even before the founding of the DAR's National Americanization Committee, members entrusted with reaching immigrants spread this message within the organization. "As women and patriots," the head of the Michigan committee of Americanization of Foreign-Born Men and Women wrote in a 1916 report, "I think our greatest care should be our foreign-born sisters to help them in their care of children, to realize our standards of living, and to know and love the best in America. For the women, of course, in their homes determine the ideals of our (potential) citizens."[57] After World War I, Daughters constantly reiterated such appeals in hundreds of immigrant communities across the nation. They visited immigrant mothers in their homes and sent specially trained teachers into immigrant communities to help foreign-born women learn English and the basics of child welfare and housekeeping.[58] The home and the mother remained essential elements of the Daughters' nationalist ideology and were upheld as ideals without which America's society would fracture.

By 1923, however, the DAR's leaders had become frustrated with what they felt was the limited impact of their Americanization campaigns in the face of a continuing stream of arrivals from abroad. They joined in the lamentations of politicians and other patriotic organizations' leaders who not only advocated "100 per cent Americanism" but also called for restrictive immigration legislation. As early as 1922, the DAR's Continental Congress supported more stringent immigration laws, and when members of the US Congress debated an immigration bill in early 1924, numerous DAR members endorsed it. President General Lora Haines Cook voiced the fears of many when she warned of "the disintegration of our justly, far-framed national morale," insisting that the proposed bill "would prove a mighty bulwark to stem the flood of foreign inundation."[59] Given these anxieties, the DAR rejoiced when the US Congress finally passed the National Origins Act of 1924, which reduced immigration from southern and eastern Europe to a mere trickle. It made permanent specific quotas that had been introduced on a temporary basis by the Emergency Quota Act of 1921, which restricted the number of newcomers from each nation to 2 percent of its share in the US population in 1890. Since immigrants from eastern and southern Europe began to arrive in large numbers only in the late nineteenth century, the new law almost completely stopped immigration from that region as well as from Asia. The National Origins Act thus served to consolidate the idea of a white American nation, while it relegated suspect Europeans and nonwhite people of Asian, African, and Mexican descent to the bottom of the national hierarchy.[60]

The Daughters continued their Americanization work after 1924 and were still determined to assimilate the foreign-born, but the passage of the law marked the gradual decline of the Americanization movement and highlighted the organization's ethnic nationalism. During what Eric Kaufmann has described as "a phase of stable, Anglo-Saxon hegemony," the Daughters voiced more openly their disdain for foreign races and explicitly linked whiteness and patriotism.[61] Nonwhite immigrants in particular, even if light-skinned, were anathema to many members. The DAR's Americanization staff worked with Mexican and Asian immigrants before and after 1924, but many members shared the sentiments of a Maryland DAR state regent who during that year's annual meeting proposed rejecting "unassimilable immigrants, particularly orientals," at America's borders. A DAR Continental Congress resolution that was passed two years later called for additional patrols at the US-Mexican border to stop immigration from America's southern neighbor and reflected Daughters' disdain for non-Anglo newcomers.[62] The Daughters deemed it their patriotic duty to help the foreign-born assimilate, but like other white Protestants, they frequently insinuated that people of color generally lacked the ability to become patriotic citizens. Consequently, the organization welcomed the virtual stop to immigration from Asia and became increasingly concerned about Latin American newcomers, who faced no restrictions.

Since the Daughters doubted most immigrants' ability or willingness to become true Americans, they became more convinced than ever that the South's white mountaineers could help them win the war against disloyalty and subversion. Throughout the first half of the 1920s, DAR officers went into raptures about Appalachians' patriotic potential. In 1923, hinting at members' growing doubts about the effectiveness of Americanization, New York state regent Frances Tupper suggested in the *DAR Magazine* that the organization could not rely on naturalized citizens to preserve the nation's ideals. "True patriotism," she claimed, went deeper than mere Americanization. She said "racial ideas and traits" were "difficult to eradicate." The southern mountaineers, by contrast, were "the purest of Anglo Saxons . . . who may yet be the means of preserving our American ideals and principles as set forth and battled for by their forefathers and ours."[63] If the Daughters were afraid the new immigrants might be America's doom, they considered white mountaineers its potential salvation. Like other white middle-class Americans during the 1920s and 1930s, the Daughters continued to romanticize the Appalachian region as a seemingly classless and homogeneous America they believed to have existed in the past.[64] Unlike most fellow Appalachia enthusiasts, however, the Daughters took concrete steps to make patriotic use of what one Daughter referred to as "the unworked gold mines of America"; they spent large sums of money to support schools in the region.[65] In 1920–1921 alone, Daughters donated almost $160,000 to educate southern mountaineers. By 1925 the DAR supported ten schools in Appalachia and founded two new ones. Ten years later, the organization subsidized a total of fifteen schools in the region.[66]

Given the DAR's emphasis on "100 per cent Americanism" and praise for the "Anglo-Saxon strain in American civilization,"[67] the organization echoed tenets that were voiced most loudly by the most notorious right-wing organization of the 1920s, the Ku Klux Klan. The Klan was founded shortly after the Civil War by Confederate veterans who sought to reestablish white supremacy in the South by intimidating and murdering newly freed African American slaves and their white allies; it was revived in 1915 and attracted millions of members across the nation in the early

1920s. Its advocacy of nativism, racism, antisocialism, anti-Catholicism, and anti-Semitism became a widely hailed credo that also reverberated in local, state, and national politics.[68] Because of the considerable ideological commonalities between the Ku Klux Klan and the DAR, liberal critics of the Daughters frequently likened the women's organization to the hooded order. Especially during the controversy over the Daughters' efforts to blacklist liberal speakers, detractors variously called the organization the "Daughters of the Ku Klux Klan" or the "Ku Klux Klan of women."[69] A number of members of the Klan women's auxiliary were also Daughters, but the DAR neither cooperated with the hooded order nor officially endorsed its program. Most members considered the Klan and its female auxiliary to be a lower-class phenomenon whose aggressive methods were deemed unrespectable. When the Klan imploded in the later 1920s as a consequence of internal corruption and the inability to deliver on its political promises, the Daughters did not bemoan the organization's demise.[70]

As the Roaring 1920s came to a crushing end after the stock market crash of 1929, the subsequent economic depression and Franklin D. Roosevelt's New Deal affected the Americanization movement as well as US nationalism. In general, the idea that immigrants needed to be Americanized seemed less urgent since those foreigners who arrived before 1924 gradually adopted an American way of life and the number of new arrivals remained minuscule. Moreover, the US government's New Deal programs put much emphasis on civic rather than ethnic nationalism and encouraged citizens to ponder their own place in a nation faced with unprecedented economic hardship. This less militant approach toward inculcating national loyalty also affected the nationalist rhetoric of the DAR, whose members began to use the term "Americanism" rather than "Americanization" when discussing ways to assimilate immigrants in the 1930s. "Americanism," Mary C. Welch, the chairperson of the DAR's newly established Americanism Committee, wrote in 1934, "endeavors to establish contacts with the foreign-born." She explained that the Americanism Committee sought "to give them a better understanding of our American ideals, to offer more adequate training for citizenship, to help these people to orient in a new land, so that it may become home to them."[71] Continuing their efforts to reach out to immigrants, in some instances including Mexicans and Asians, the Daughters seemed to move closer to the idea of a more inclusive civic nationalism.[72]

"White Artists Only": The Marian Anderson Controversy

With regard to African Americans, the DAR's nationalist ideology showed little of the ambiguity that characterized its efforts to Americanize the country's immigrant population in the 1920s and 1930s. Black citizens were almost entirely absent from the Daughters' remembrance of the past and played virtually no role in its patriotic campaigns. Before World War II, in stark contrast to the organization's commemoration of Indian warriors, the DAR failed to acknowledge black soldiers' military service during America's wars. If people of color appeared at all in the Daughters' interpretations of the past, they continued to be mentioned only in the context of slavery. In 1917 the *DAR Magazine* featured an article on an enslaved man in Virginia named James, whose master permitted him in 1781 to join the Continental Army and become the servant of the famous French officer Marquis de Lafayette. The story is emblematic of the DAR's racialized amnesia, as the Daughters applauded James's faithful service but turned a blind eye to black valor on the battlefield, erasing this group from their vision of a united nation in the past and the present.[73] But such references to men and women of color remained rare, likely because of the Daughters' efforts to foster sectional harmony between northern and southern members of the organization. Given this racial consensus, the Daughters of the American Revolution and the United Daughters of the Confederacy had overlapping memberships and cooperated closely on numerous occasions. The occasional financial support that a few northern DAR chapters provided for African Americans or the small number of black students who were allowed to participate in DAR essay contests remained exceptions and did not undermine the organization's stance on race.[74]

Only the widely publicized controversy over the request of black opera singer Marian Anderson to perform in the DAR's concert hall in Washington, DC, in 1939 finally forced the organization to confront its racial amnesia and the question of whether citizens of color should be regarded as full members of the nation. That year, the organization barred the famous contralto from performing at its Constitution Hall, which had been completed ten years earlier. Anderson was the main attraction of a concert series that the city's African American Howard University organized annually to raise funds for its school of music. Unlike other major cities in the United States, America's capital had no municipal concert hall that was large enough to accommodate the enormous crowds that famous performers such as Anderson usually attracted. For that reason, orchestras, singers, and theater companies regularly booked Constitution Hall, which could seat almost 4,000 people. When Anderson's manager, Sol Hurok, sought to reserve the auditorium in early January 1939, the DAR refused, enforcing a "white artists only" policy that had been requested by a major donor before construction of the auditorium was completed.[75]

In the early 1930s the organization briefly allowed black artists to perform before integrated audiences, which was not uncommon in the nation's capital, where racial segregation existed but remained more flexible than in the American South. But more and more white concertgoers began to complain about these integrated audiences, and when black tenor Roland Hayes clashed with the auditorium's manager over segregated seating during a concert he gave in 1931, the DAR resolved to strictly enforce the ban on black artists. The organization's refusal to let Marian Anderson perform in its concert hall would have caused little controversy if the District of Columbia's Board of Education had approved Howard University's request to use a white high school auditorium as an alternative to the DAR's building. But when the board refused, Anderson's manager, the quickly established Marian Anderson Citizens Committee, and the civil rights organization National Association for the Advancement of Colored People (NAACP) launched a highly publicized campaign to integrate Constitution Hall. This campaign culminated in the free concert that Marian Anderson gave on Easter Sunday 1939 on the steps of the Lincoln Memorial.[76]

Although the controversy over racial segregation in Constitution Hall failed to convince DAR leaders to end its policy allowing white artists only, it did force the organization's members to ponder its nationalist ideology and almost completely destroyed what was left of the DAR's public reputation, which had already been severely tarnished by its zealous anticommunism. Especially liberal pundits denounced the DAR for what they perceived as its narrow ethnic nationalism during a decade that saw the rise of fascist dictators who preached white supremacy. In fact, the Daughters faced an unexpected firestorm of protest from black and white critics alike. Famous musicians, actors, politicians, and activists as well as ordinary citizens inundated the organization with telegrams, letters, and resolutions that condemned the DAR's discriminatory policies. From the critics' perspective, the Daughters espoused a form of un-American ethnic nationalism that maliciously misinterpreted the Founding Fathers' civic creed.[77] These accusations testify to the fundamental differences that characterized

Figure 4.1. African American opera singer Marian Anderson at the Lincoln Memorial, 1939. Anderson performed on the Lincoln Memorial steps on Easter Sunday that year, after the DAR barred her from its Constitution Hall in Washington, DC. Courtesy of Library of Congress Prints and Photographs Division, Harris & Ewing Collection, LC-H22-D-6302.

conservative and liberal interpretations of nationalism during the interwar period. The Daughters and other groups tended to espouse an exclusionary ethnic nationalism that barred or discriminated against nonwhite people, while more liberal voices envisioned an inclusionary nationalism that allowed for critical intellectual exchange and pluralistic understandings of America's civic creed.

DAR leaders were taken aback by liberals' vitriolic criticism, but they argued throughout the controversy that barring Marian Anderson from Constitution Hall had nothing to do with racial prejudice. During the organization's annual meeting in April 1939, the Daughters listened patiently to Republican Congresswoman Edith Nourse Rogers, who called upon the Daughters to replace "race hatred" with "racial cooperation."[78] But President General Sarah Corbin Robert vehemently denied in her speech that the DAR's board of management had acted with any prejudicial or discriminatory intent. Instead, she reiterated arguments that had been put forward since the beginning of the controversy, namely that the organization had simply followed the same discriminatory customs that most public establishments practiced in the capital and that the concert hall had been booked for the requested date, a claim that activists found to be untrue. Yet Robert also hinted at additional reasons for her uncompromising attitude, as she stated that an exception to the clause allowing white artists only would have meant retreating "under fire of widely scattered groups and organizations many of whom knew nothing of the facts and whose interests had nothing to do with the real question." Apparently, the DAR's leaders did not want to appear weak during a conflict in which they felt unjustly attacked, as is suggested by Robert's assertion that the DAR had been a friend of "and worked for many minority groups."[79] Given the Daughters' claim of cordial relations with minorities, which probably referred to their support for Indians and the organization's Americanization campaigns, they felt that neither the DAR's nationalist ideology nor its treatment of minorities required any adjustments.

The enthusiastic applause Robert received from the 4,500 delegates who attended that year's Continental Congress exposes the probability that the organization's members generally supported their leaders' handling of the Anderson affair.[80] The available evidence suggests that a majority of members either approved of or were largely indifferent to racial segregation. A small minority of detractors existed but chose not to voice their disapproval publicly. According to a report prepared by a member of the Michigan delegation to the 1939 Continental Congress, Robert's explanation "satisfied not only the membership of the D.A.R., but those as well who had no particular interest either one way or the other."[81] A number of DAR chapters discussed the Marian Anderson affair and the organization's discriminatory policies at their meetings, but hardly any of their discussions translated into expressions of official protest.[82] It is conceivable that most internal conversations on the topic ended the way a debate was concluded among the members of the Sarah Caswell Angell Chapter of Ann Arbor, Michigan. It began when one member introduced a motion to "send a vigorous protest to national headquarters in Washington against the stand taken in prohibiting Marian Anderson from appearing in Constitution Hall." But since a majority of members refused to support it, the motion did not result in official notes of protest.[83] The public statement of a former chapter regent from Newark, New Jersey, was a rare instance of publicly voiced dissent. She told the *New York Times* that the "action of the national society was definitely not Americanism and absolutely against the principles for which the D.A.R. stands."[84] Those members who objected to the DAR's discriminatory behavior appear to have been silenced by fellow Daughters, while others might have refrained from protesting out of fear of being expelled like the organization's internal critics during the 1920s.

Only one DAR member's criticism was widely noticed, namely that of President Franklin D. Roosevelt's wife, Eleanor. Although she had dutifully accepted the Daughters' invitation to join the organization when the Roosevelts moved into the White House, Eleanor Roosevelt's liberal politics had drawn the ire of the organization long before reports of Anderson's treatment surfaced. As an outspoken champion of pacifism, civil rights, and the welfare of society's lower rungs, she quickly learned that the Daughters were unreceptive to her liberal convictions. Eleanor Roosevelt granted the DAR the traditional privileges it had enjoyed in its long relations with US presidents and first ladies such as the traditional White House receptions, but she grew weary of the organization's elitist exclusionism. Having invited African American organizations to the presidential residence and publicly denounced racial segregation, the president's wife became even more incensed after learning about Marian Anderson's ban. In late February 1939 she wrote a letter to President General Robert in which she severely criticized the DAR's actions and announced her resignation. A few days later, when she alluded to her decision in a syndicated newspaper column she regularly wrote, Roosevelt contributed to the nationwide outcry that the treatment of Anderson had triggered and communicated with black civil rights activists about the best strategy to protest the ban.[85]

If most members of the DAR remained silent about or indifferent to racism, African American civil rights activists and white liberals who sympathized with their cause loudly denounced the organization's discriminatory behavior toward Marian Anderson and condemned its prejudiced remembrance of the American past. Detractors reminded the Daughters of the many sacrifices black soldiers had made for the United States during the American Revolution and in subsequent military conflicts. In a letter to President General Robert in April 1939, the black NAACP activist Charles

H. Houston explicitly addressed the Daughters' amnesia: "We hope that in these days of tension, a great organization like yours dedicated to the ideal of patriotism and democracy will show the way toward greater tolerance and good will. The patriotism of the Negro cannot be challenged. The first martyr to fall in the Revolution was a negro, Crispus Attucks. Negro soldiers fought valiantly with the Continental Army from Bunker Hill to Yorktown. They have fought in all our wars. There has never been a Negro traitor to this country."[86] Other critics likewise cited Attucks, whom black intellectuals and activists repeatedly invoked as a symbol of African American patriotism since the Civil War era. In meetings with DAR leaders after Marian Anderson's Easter Sunday concert, civil rights activists made similar arguments, hoping repeated allusions to the unacknowledged patriotic valor of soldiers of color would sway the organization.[87]

But thousands of editorials and letters of protest, Eleanor Roosevelt's resignation, and references to black soldiers' patriotism failed to persuade the DAR to change its policy of allowing white artists only to perform in its concert hall or to acknowledge that black citizens were legitimate members of the nation. In April 1940, after months of unsuccessful negotiations with the organization's leadership, NAACP activists and members of the Marian Anderson Citizens Committee wired yet another appeal to President General Robert and the delegates of Continental Congress. "Your Congress can make a fine contribution toward cementing the bond between black and white citizens by removing the ban on Negro artists appearing in Constitution Hall," committee chairman Charles Houston wrote. "This will be both a recognition to art and a significant demonstration that America today is in fact a democracy."[88]

The Daughters still refused to budge, only confirming through their actions what many activists had long suspected, that the DAR saw no place for African American citizens in the nation. Black journalists such as the editor of the *Chicago Defender* once more reminded the Daughters of the patriotic service of Crispus Attucks and other black soldiers in the past and the present, deploring that the Daughters mentioned "every race but the Negro in their meeting."[89] Black children faced similar forms of discrimination, as could be seen in the DAR's Good Citizenship pilgrimage, the organization's patriotic contest for female high school students. The Daughters deliberately restricted the contest to white schools, bringing white winners to visit Washington, DC, while victorious girls of color who attended predominantly white schools would be given awards but received no tickets to the capital. In late 1941, one African American member of the District of Columbia's school board bitterly complained about this discriminatory policy and called upon the Daughters to open the contest to black schools.[90] However, nothing indicated that the Daughters were willing to yield.

DAR leaders' unexpected decision in 1942 to invite Marian Anderson to sing at Constitution Hall as part of a series of fundraising concerts for war relief therefore surprised civil rights activists, and they doubted that the invitation reflected a genuine change of mind. Their skepticism was fully justified, as the organization stated in a press release that it had simply honored an earlier request by Anderson's manager, Sol Hurok, and more importantly, that it would not alter its policy of exclusion.[91] Confronted with this half-hearted attempt at reconciliation, Anderson's manager and the Marian Anderson Citizens Committee engaged in a three-month debate with the DAR over the conditions under which the concert would take place and whether Anderson's performance would be a precedent for appearances of other artists of color. NAACP activists pleaded with the black contralto not to accept the invitation if the DAR refused to change its discriminatory policies, but the singer eventually agreed to perform, although she had won only one concession: that the auditorium's seating would not be segregated on the night of the concert. On January 7, 1943, Anderson appeared on the stage of Constitution Hall, singing in front of a capacity audience of almost 4,000 that included many government officials as well as Eleanor Roosevelt.[92]

For Mrs. Roosevelt and her husband, Marian Anderson's concerts were a welcome opportunity to affirm America's commitment to racial egalitarianism during America's fight against racist Nazi Germany abroad and simmering racial tensions at home. From 1941 to 1943, hundreds of racial clashes occurred between white and black citizens in the United States, either on segregated army bases in the American South or in northern and midwestern cities where the percentage of black residents had grown exponentially in the interwar period and the early years of World War II. In 1943 alone, 242 racial clashes erupted in forty-seven cities across the United States. After the bloodiest conflict of the year, in Detroit, twenty-five blacks and nine whites lay dead.[93]

In January that year, during an official presentation of a mural painting that depicted Anderson's Easter Sunday concert, the Roosevelt administration once more used the contralto to counter accusations that its vows to defend democracy were a sham. Civil rights activists had convinced the federal government to have the mural painted in the auditorium of the Department of the Interior building, and a national competition was organized to find the best design. Thousands of schoolchildren and other citizens who had been touched by the black singer's story helped finance the mural by sending in small sums of money to the Marian Anderson Mural Committee established shortly after her 1939 Lincoln Memorial concert to commemorate that event. African Americans were the most visible protagonists of the mural presentation ceremony, reflecting both the event organizers' attempt to symbolically call into question the DAR's discriminatory stance and the US government's efforts to counter criticism over racial discrimination at home and abroad. Not only Marian Anderson performed during the ceremony, but also a double quartet of African American seamen, while black high school cadets served as ushers.[94] From the perspective of Secretary of the Interior Harold Ickes, who helped make Anderson's 1939 Easter Sunday recital possible, the mural symbolized America's ideal of civic nationalism. "At that time," he said when accepting the mural for the federal government, "instead of giving mere lip service to our democratic ideals we gave active allegiance to the greatest of all those ideals—tolerance."[95] For the Roosevelts, the Daughters belied the idea of inclusiveness that FDR's administration claimed to be the cornerstone of America's national creed.

The president scored political points among black citizens and sympathetic white liberals because of his support for Anderson, while the Daughters were certainly right when they complained about being widely denounced for a form of discrimination that was practiced and condoned throughout the United States, including the country's capital. In late April 1939, the editors of the African American newspaper *Pittsburgh Courier* called readers' attention to the discrepancy between the US government's inclusive rhetoric and the reality of racial discrimination. "On one point, however," the *Courier* editors opined, DAR President General Robert was correct that "other individuals and organizations can with ill grace condemn the acts of the D.A.R. while condoning color discrimination by other private and public agencies in Washington, D.C., and elsewhere. If it is wrong for the D.A.R. to deny Negro artists the use of its Constitution Hall, it is equally wrong for Secretary Ickes and the other cabinet officers to permit color discrimination and segregation in their departments, or to remain silent about the wholesale barring of Negroes from hotels, restaurants

Figure 4.2. Marian Anderson, Department of the Interior auditorium, 1943. The occasion for this performance was the dedication of a mural painted in the auditorium to commemorate her famous 1939 recital in front of the Lincoln Memorial. Courtesy of Library of Congress Prints and Photographs Division, FSA/OWI Collection, LC-USE6-D-007911.

and certain residential districts in Washington."[96] Indeed, the Roosevelt administration's lofty ideals notwithstanding, neither the president nor US Congress took the Anderson concert as an opportunity to strike down the most blatant forms of racial discrimination in the United States.

World War II did see important changes for African Americans, but they were primarily the consequence of black activists' efforts to pressure local, state, and federal authorities into living up to the democratic ideals that Secretary Ickes evoked during the formal presentation of the Marian Anderson mural. In early 1941, longtime labor and civil rights leader A. Philip Randolph organized an all-black March on Washington Movement to bring 100,000 African Americans to the capital to protest blatant discrimination in the defense industry. Since the international implications of the looming march would have embarrassed the United States in its avowed struggle to defend democracy against racist Nazi Germany, President Roosevelt yielded to Randolph's demands in issuing an executive order to end discrimination in the defense industry.[97] In 1942 and 1943, moreover, members of the newly founded Congress of Racial Equality launched a series of nonviolent sit-ins in Chicago, Detroit, and other cities outside the South to challenge the custom of racial segregation in restaurants, movie theaters, and other public places. Meanwhile, the *Pittsburgh Courier* launched a "Double-V" campaign for victory over Adolf Hitler abroad and Jim Crow at home.[98]

Despite these promising victories and African Americans' growing determination to confront Jim Crow, World War II ultimately strengthened American ethnic nationalism. Neither black activism nor scientists' growing doubts about the validity of racist theories of the alleged inferiority of nonwhite people fundamentally disrupted the racial foundation of US nationalism.[99] During the war, black soldiers fought in segregated units, received blood from segregated blood banks, and tended to serve in noncombat units because white superiors continued to have doubts about their courage on the battlefield. Those few servicemen of color who did see combat and distinguished themselves on European battlefields received only scant attention in the white press. Other groups that were defined as the racial "other" fared similar fates, chief among them Japanese Americans. Almost 120,000 US citizens and residents of Japanese descent were forced to sell and leave their homes on the West Coast to live in internment camps in remote western regions because they were deemed a security threat. American war propaganda frequently depicted Japanese soldiers as racially inferior rapists or vermin that needed to be wiped out. The white warrior was seen as the icon of the American nation, and others could never be considered true citizens.[100]

In light of these developments in US society during World War II, the Daughters of the American Revolution probably felt confirmed in their nationalist ideology, which largely ignored nonwhite people and opposed any relaxation of America's strict 1924 immigration law. During the Great Depression, their fear of communist radicals, coupled with concerns about seemingly unassimilable immigrants, led them to applaud politicians who advocated even more restrictive legislation. One of these men, Texas Congressman Martin Dies, a staunch anticommunist who later helped establish the US House Un-American Activities Committee, was even invited to write an article on the topic for the *DAR Magazine*. In the 1934 article Dies argued, "The immigration laws should be strengthened instead of weakened, and the quota reduced instead of enlarged." In his eyes, America should permanently "close, lock, and bar" the country's gates "and then throw the key away."[101] The same month that Marian Anderson sang on the steps of the Lincoln Memorial, the DAR's Continental Congress voiced staunch support for Dies's position in unanimously passing a resolution that opposed any liberalization of the National Origins Act.[102]

In early 1945 Mrs. Charles E. Head, the chairwoman of the organization's Americanism Committee, made clear her conviction that the war years had only strengthened the Daughters' determination to keep out "undesirable" foreigners. Claiming in an article in the organization's magazine that immigrants were generally poor, ignorant, and easily influenced by communist radicals, Head concluded that they could "never really be Americans." Only those white Anglo-Saxon Protestants whose ancestors had "tamed the wilderness, cultivated the country" and "built there a civilization and established a government" deserved "to be known by the same name as that country itself."[103] It remained to be seen whether and how the fundamental political and social changes that jolted the United States during the two decades following World War II would affect the DAR's exclusionary ethnic nationalism and its prejudiced interpretations of the American past.

5

"I Wanted It to Change and to Make Up for Its Past"

The Daughters between 1945 and 2000

For many Americans, Marian Anderson's 1939 Easter Sunday concert on the steps of the Lincoln Memorial was a distant memory when the black soprano Leontyne Price opened the DAR's ninety-first Continental Congress in 1982. Yet Price's performance in front of more than three thousand delegates was indelibly intertwined with the famous 1939 recital, serendipitously setting in motion events that finally forced the Daughters to reconsider their ethnic nationalism and racist amnesia. Already their decision to invite Price to sing at the annual meeting reflected gradual changes within the organization, which five years earlier had admitted its first black member. The two-hour concert was explicitly billed as a tribute to Anderson, who had been invited by Price to be her personal guest but could not attend due to illness, and Price sang several songs from the black contralto's legendary concert. But the impact of Price's recital went beyond what the DAR originally intended. In its wake, an African American woman named Lena Ferguson, who had been rejected by several of the organization's Washington, DC, chapters, felt inspired to renew her quest for full membership. By the mid-1980s she had not only managed to join one of the capital's local chapters but also forced the Daughters to finally acknowledge African American soldiers' patriotism.[1]

Before Lena Ferguson's activism, the DAR had shown no intention of acknowledging black citizens' role in US nation-building, and it remained a lukewarm supporter of civic nationalism even after Ferguson had joined the organization. In fact, the Daughters' nationalist ideology and patriotic interpretations of US history throughout the twentieth century were characterized by remarkable continuity. Between 1945 and 2000, its views on communism, race, immigration, gender, and the nation's past remained virtually unchanged, demonstrating the tenacity of a particular strand of nationalism that revolved around white supremacy and entrenched gender binaries.

Race in particular became a recurring public relations problem for the Daughters, who remained squarely in the camp of ethnic nationalism, their claims to the contrary notwithstanding. Although the Daughters briefly regained some political clout as a result of their staunch Cold War anticommunism, the legacies of the Marian Anderson controversy continued to haunt the organization, which upheld its policy of allowing white artists only in Constitution Hall throughout the late 1940s and the 1950s. In 1945 its refusal to let black jazz pianist Hazel Scott perform in the auditorium triggered a storm of protest that echoed the 1939 scandal, but it did not sway the national DAR's leadership to end its discriminatory stance. Although the organization paid lip service to the ideal of an inclusive nation, its vocal opposition to the civil rights movement of the 1950s revealed that the snubs against black singers were part of an entrenched belief in white supremacy. As did other conservatives at the time, the Daughters insisted that the United States was a white nation whose strength and unity would be diluted by the influence of black citizens. The organization's stance on immigration during the 1950s echoed such affirmations of exclusionism, although its rhetoric about immigrants remained more ambivalent than it espoused toward African Americans. As the Cold War rekindled fears of communist infiltration, the Daughters agreed with commentators who contended that restrictive immigration laws were necessary to protect the nation from subversive forces. Although the Daughters continued their efforts to prepare foreigners for citizenship, they spoke with disdain about certain newcomers, especially Mexicans, whom they regarded as unassimilable.

As the DAR cemented its public image as a group of racist and xenophobic jingoists, its remembrance of the nation's past was increasingly confined to the organization's own ranks but showed as much continuity as its nationalist ideology. Indian history and culture remained immensely popular among the Daughters, who still praised Indians' patriotic loyalty and studied their supposedly primitive culture while also continuing paternalistic efforts to help this minority attain education and full citizenship rights. The remembrance of the American Revolution and western pioneers paled in comparison to the flurry of activities pertaining to Native Americans, and it almost completely ignored the accomplishments of women. Their commemorative campaigns no longer reached as many people, generally declined in number, and neglected female patriots, yet the Daughters upheld the very same ideals of femininity and masculinity they had emphasized prior to 1945. The DAR's waning visibility in America's commemorative landscape was due to a number of factors, including the large number of memorials the Daughters had already erected, the growing role of state and federal authorities in the inculcation of patriotic memory, and the DAR's expenditure of most of its energy on battling the United Nations, which the organization and some other groups viewed as part of a communist conspiracy that would undermine America's sovereignty.

Still popular among white middle-class women in the late 1950s, the DAR found itself more often on the defensive since the various social movements that jolted America in the 1960s and 1970s fundamentally challenged the DAR's worldview and vision of the nation. The African American freedom movement's stunning victories were certainly the most shocking events during this period because black activists forced the United States to acknowledge what the Daughters had denied for so long, that citizens of color were true members of the nation. The Daughters were as disturbed by the student movement of the 1960s and its opposition to the Vietnam War that questioned the idea of patriotism itself as well as the masculine heroic valor to which the Daughters had paid tribute since 1890. Second Wave feminism, moreover, challenged the gender dichotomies that Daughters held to be crucial to national unity and stability.

By the time the United States celebrated its bicentennial, especially liberal Americans ridiculed or simply ignored the Daughters. It was ironic that the organization underwent its greatest transformation at a time when so few people paid attention to its activities. In 1977 the DAR accepted its first black member, and by the mid-1980s its leadership actively encouraged women of color to join, praised African American soldiers' contributions to American independence, researched their stories, and lobbied for the erection of a memorial to honor them. But this transformation would have been impossible without Lena Ferguson's activism, and it was a hard-won concession. Even after Ferguson's victory, the legacies of the Daughters' conservative interpretations of American patriotism lingered within the organization and frequently clashed with its public rhetoric of civic tolerance.

"God Created All the Races of Mankind, Each Separate, Distinctive and Individual": The DAR and Race during the Early Cold War

After World War II, the DAR unexpectedly regained some of the respectability it had lost as a consequence of its militant anticommunism and the Marian Anderson controversy. The main reason for this change of fortune was the Cold War. In particular it renewed general fears of communist subversion in US society. Politicians and anticommunist organizations once more warned of the threat of sedition and called for a federal loyalty review program, which was authorized in 1947. But not only federal employees were suspected of being communists. By the early 1950s the FBI and the US House Un-American Activities Committee had begun investigating tens of thousands of citizens suspected of spying for the Soviet Union or being sympathetic to its cause. The exposure of several American spies who had disclosed information on the atomic bomb to Soviet authorities contributed to a rising hysteria about domestic subversion. A number of politicians readily exploited this anxiety, chief among them US Senator Joseph McCarthy, whose false claims in 1950 that hundreds of communists had infiltrated the federal government led to a surge of investigations by the House Un-American Activities Committee. While McCarthy's conspiracy theories were widely discredited by the mid-1950s, a grassroots movement of anticommunists continued clandestine probes into the influence of communism in the United States, mirroring similar post–World War I campaigns.[2] Another commonality between the 1920s and the 1950s was the involvement of a number of white middle-class women's organizations in this movement, chief among them the Daughters of the American Revolution. In communities across the nation, the DAR cooperated with federal agencies and launched local campaigns to eradicate communist influences in schools and churches as well as in local and state governments.[3]

With the new Cold War consensus, the Daughters unexpectedly reentered the political mainstream and felt vindicated by the anticommunist hysteria that gripped US society in the late 1940s. In 1949 one DAR officer gleefully asserted that the Daughters had been right all along. "We were scoffed at, ridiculed, accused of inventing goblins," she wrote. "Today, since Communism has been exposed, the D.A.R. takes its rightful place as the advance guard in detecting, disclaiming and destroying this menace to our Republic."[4] Once more, numerous conservative politicians and government officials praised the organization for its fight against the communist menace and seconded the DAR's demands to outlaw the Communist Party, strip communists of their US citizenship, and institute loyalty oaths for teachers and government employees. In turn, the Daughters praised prominent government anticommunists such as Joseph McCarthy and FBI Director J. Edgar Hoover for their vigilance. Hoover in particular was one of the Daughters' heroes. He spoke frequently at the DAR's annual meetings and published numerous articles in the organization's monthly magazine.[5] Even after the communist hysteria subsided, the organization upheld the banner of anticommunism and warned of the devastating impact that this un-American ideology would have on the United States.[6]

Although the Cold War appeared to boost the DAR's status, the organization's refusal to allow African American artists to perform in Constitution Hall cemented its racist reputation and drew another barrage of criticism that overshadowed members' elation over the emerging anticommunist consensus. In October 1945, pianist Hazel Scott revealed to the national press that the DAR had declined her request to use its auditorium for a commercial concert. Scott's charges received much publicity, not least because she was married to Adam C. Powell Jr., a member of the US House of Representatives. Powell was outraged and sought to punish the DAR by revoking the tax exemption privileges Congress had granted the Daughters for its concert hall. His plan set off a rancorous debate on the House floor, during which the DAR's supporters and critics faced off. While a number of liberal representatives advocated legislation that would terminate the organization's tax privileges if Constitution Hall remained closed to black artists, Mississippi Congressman John E. Rankin dismissed the charges that he said were of "communistic origins." After the debate, several House members introduced bills that would have put Powell's plan into action. Meanwhile, the NAACP urged the Senate Committee on Printing to repeal legislation that had allowed the DAR to print its annual report at government expense since its founding in 1890.[7]

Besides members of Congress who were critical of the DAR's stance, other politicians as well as numerous activists, journalists, and ordinary citizens deplored the organization's racist policies and suggested that its ethnic nationalism misrepresented America's inclusive civic creed. Thousands of protest letters flooded the DAR's mailroom, and NAACP activists in Kansas City picketed the hotel in which President General May Erwin Talmadge stayed during her nationwide tour to visit local chapters. A number of high school students also let the DAR know that they disagreed with

Figure 5.1. African American jazz pianist and singer Hazel Scott, 1945. Scott was interviewed by an Associated Press reporter in October 1945 after the DAR refused to let her perform in Constitution Hall. © Associated Press.

its positions. On George Washington's birthday in 1946, the senior class of a school in Wilmington, Delaware, informed the Daughters in a letter that it would not participate in the organization's Good Citizenship Pilgrimage contest because the DAR's prejudice toward Hazel Scott discredited the competition. In late 1945 a federal district court judge from Trenton, New Jersey, went so far as to ask the town's DAR chapter to stop its participation in naturalization ceremonies for new citizens because he considered it "embarrassing" for these men and women to be welcomed by an organization that practiced racial discrimination.[8] Even President Harry Truman voiced his disapproval, sending Powell a telegram in which he criticized the DAR and called for colorblind respect for American artists. In a curious reversal of roles when compared with the Anderson controversy, however, Truman's wife Bess, who was a DAR member, pretended to agree with her husband but neither considered leaving the organization nor deemed it necessary to cancel her appointment for tea at the DAR's headquarters less than two weeks after Hazel Scott's accusations had become public.[9]

But as in 1939, the DAR's leadership was not swayed by the accusations of being un-American and reminders from the black press that African Americans had fought valiantly for the United States during the American Revolution.[10] In a meeting of the organization's Board of Management, its members unanimously voted to retain the DAR's whites-only policy for performers, justifying the decision by citing the custom of racial segregation in the District of Columbia. To President General Talmadge and her officers, neither Marian Anderson nor Hazel Scott constituted a reason to reconsider its racial politics or its nationalist ideology.[11]

What distinguished the Hazel Scott controversy from the reactions to the spurning of Anderson was the unprecedented turmoil it sparked within the DAR. Six years after the famous 1939 Easter Sunday concert, DAR member and Republican Congresswoman Clare Boothe Luce launched a highly visible campaign to challenge the Daughters' racial politics. After winning a seat in the US House of Representatives for a Connecticut district in 1942, the writer-turned-politician frequently voiced her opposition to racial discrimination and voted for bills that aimed to punish lynch mobs and eliminate the discriminatory poll tax in the American South. The same year that she entered politics, Luce called for racial cooperation on the home front and criticized racial segregation in the US military.[12] She had joined the DAR only in 1941 and remained an inconspicuous member until hearing of the organization's prejudiced behavior toward Hazel Scott. Initially, her protest was confined to her Putnam Hill Chapter in Fairfield, Connecticut. In October 1945 she sent a telegram to the chapter's regent urging that its members draft a resolution in opposition to the DAR's discriminatory actions. But even her threat to resign could not prevent the defeat of the proposed resolution, which was voted down 48–2. Another Connecticut chapter that Luce transferred to after this defeat also rejected her proposal, indicating that many Daughters either approved of racial discrimination or deemed it not important enough to challenge the organization's powerful Board of Management.[13]

Luce then approached the DAR's leadership directly, exchanging several letters with former President General Grace Brosseau, who headed the organization's Resolutions Committee and had crushed a similar internal

Figure 5.2. Eleanor Roosevelt and Clare Boothe Luce in Rome, 1955. Former First Lady Roosevelt and writer-turned-politician Luce became the most prominent DAR members to criticize the organization's discriminatory behavior toward African American artists in the late 1930s to mid-1940s. In 1939 Roosevelt resigned from the DAR when it refused to let Marian Anderson perform in its auditorium in Washington, DC. Courtesy of US National Archives and Records Administration, Collection FDR-PHOCO: Franklin D. Roosevelt Library Public Domain Photographs, 1882–1962, NLR-PHOCO-A-63260(1).

challenge by the liberal DAR member Helen Tufts Bailie in the late 1920s. In their correspondence, Luce elaborated on her motivation to challenge the DAR's racist policy and explained why the organization should terminate it, but Brosseau was adamant in her opposition to such changes. The former president general reiterated Mississippi Congressman John Rankin's argument, asserting that communists and their allies had used Marian Anderson to introduce "the colored angle . . . into the picture," which had forced the DAR to deal with this issue ever since.[14] In her reply, Luce argued that lifting the ban on black artists would actually strengthen the United States in the struggle against communism, as the DAR's racist actions provided "the Communists with a splendid, and I believe, justifiable target for attack."[15] In one final attempt to sway the DAR officer, she reminded Brosseau that the Daughters had been "founded as a gesture against discrimination shown by the S.A.R. when it refused to let women take part in its activities," likening their situation to that of black citizens. But Brousseau would not budge, retorting bluntly that the DAR's critics unjustly pointed fingers at the Daughters while ignoring the widespread practice of racial segregation in the capital.[16]

By February 1946 it had become clear to Luce that her appeals would continue to fall on deaf ears, and the congresswoman decided to make her criticism public. That month she spoke on the issue on the floor of Congress and gave a radio address in which she addressed fellow DAR members and directly criticized President General Talmadge. In her radio talk, which was aired on George Washington's birthday, Luce reiterated her belief that the nationalist ideology the Founding Fathers enunciated during the American Revolution was more inclusive than the Daughters were willing to acknowledge. To her, banning Hazel Scott and other black artists was plainly "Un-American prejudice," which was why she asked DAR members to urge the organization's leadership to terminate the discriminatory policy.[17] In addition to these widely publicized appeals, Luce tried to contact DAR chapters directly, an effort the organization's leaders tried to prevent by denying her request for a complete list of chapters and their postal addresses. The congresswoman's grassroots efforts did prompt discussions within many chapters, and she ultimately convinced more than two dozen of them as well as the Connecticut DAR to send resolutions of protest to the national DAR headquarters. However, almost as many chapters, most of them in the South, publicly supported the organization's stance, casting doubt on Luce's claim that a majority of chapters would have protested the ban if they had been given enough information on the Scott case.[18] Luce experienced another setback when the commissioners of the District of Columbia ruled that Constitution Hall fell into the same category as other places of amusement in the capital, which allowed the owners of these venues to admit "only those persons they desired."[19]

Notwithstanding these challenges, Clare Boothe Luce labored on. In early April 1946 she established the DAR Committee against Racial Discrimination in Constitution Hall to change the organization from within. The new committee's explicit purpose was to persuade DAR members to protest the contract stipulation barring performers of color; Luce hoped such a protest would force the organization's leaders to put the issue to a vote at the organization's approaching Continental Congress. In her appeal to fellow Daughters, the congresswoman once more explained that the DAR's racism ran counter to the inclusive nation that she believed the Founding Fathers had envisioned when fighting for American independence.[20] Again, the results were disappointing. When Lucile F. Goff, a Minnesotan ally of Luce and head of the state's Americanism Committee, sent this appeal to every chapter in her state, only eleven out of fifty chapters agreed to pass a resolution of protest. Goff estimated that about a quarter of the state's members approved of deleting the controversial clause, but a majority of the state's chapters never responded to her appeal. While many members seemed indifferent to Luce's efforts, the DAR's leadership was greatly concerned about her activities and publicly denounced the congresswoman's campaign to integrate Constitution Hall. From President General Talmadge's point of view, the Committee against Racial Discrimination was illegal, and Luce's efforts would only hinder black artists' efforts to perform at Constitution Hall.[21]

That year's Continental Congress, which took place in May 1946, became the ultimate test for Luce's claim that a majority of Daughters would approve of racial integration in Constitution Hall if they were given all the facts. Even before the beginning of the annual meeting, which the *New York Times* expected "to be one of the stormiest" in the organization's history, DAR leaders indicated their intention to derail her crusade. President General Talmadge derided the Committee against Racial Discrimination as unconstitutional and informed the press that the Resolutions Committee would not consider the proposed resolution it had received from Luce's committee.[22] Luce and her allies, some of whom attended the meeting as delegates, intended to circumvent the Resolutions Committee by request-

ing a motion from the floor to force a vote on their proposal, but they underestimated the leadership's craftiness and fellow members' animosity. In
her opening address, Talmadge lambasted the new committee's disloyalty
and announced the creation of a special group that would thoroughly examine the "white artists only" clause, leaving open the question of whether
she was receptive to any changes.[23]

What followed was yet another blow to the congresswoman's ambitions.
Before any action on the white artists clause could be taken, a resolution
was introduced that called for the "immediate dissolution" of the Committee against Racial Discrimination. When the vote was called on the
resolution, a roaring "aye" could be heard from the almost four thousand
delegates. Only one courageous woman dared to vote no. Acknowledging
defeat, a member of the Luce committee then announced the withdrawal of
its resolution, which drew jubilant cheers and mocking laughter from the
large audience.[24] While a few Daughters seem to have supported the committee's notion of civic inclusiveness, a majority of members approved of
the ethnic nationalism that Talmadge so forcefully defended. The controversy over Hazel Scott also did not adversely affect the DAR's membership,
which grew from almost 145,000 members in February 1944 to more than
158,000 members in August 1947.[25]

For the remainder of the 1940s and the following decade, the Daughters
repeatedly purported to stand for an ideal of national belonging that knew
no racial difference, but its actions revealed glaring ideological inconsistencies. Less than two weeks after Luce's defeat, the African American Tuskegee Choir was allowed to give a concert at Constitution Hall as part of a
fundraising effort for the United Negro College Fund. Five years later, black
soprano Dorothy Maynor's performance was the first commercial concert
of a black artist in the auditorium since the mid-1930s. And in 1953 Marian
Anderson was finally given permission to perform at Constitution Hall
in a noncharity capacity. Yet, despite what appeared to be path-breaking
precedents, the DAR clung to its white artists policy and stressed that it had
no intention of changing it. Other black performers, moreover, continued
to be barred, including Hazel Scott, who had probably drawn DAR leaders'
ire when announcing in 1945 that she would be touring the United States to
fight "DAR-ism." There were occasional protests against the DAR, including an open letter to the organization in 1947 by former Secretary of the
Interior Harold Ickes calling attention to the organization's contradictory

stance. But these expressions of dissent had no impact on the DAR's racial politics.[26]

When reminded of their nationalist ideology's inconsistencies, the Daughters responded defensively and flatly dismissed the charges. In 1953 the DAR reacted swiftly to an interview Eleanor Roosevelt had given to *McCall's* magazine in which she commented critically on the organization. Asked about her opinion of the Daughters, Roosevelt stated that she continued to have a negative one. The former first lady said the DAR had been and still was "an extremely narrow and conservative group of people, with a great fear of anything new." She lauded their "excellent patriotic service in the preservation of historical landmarks" but did not consider the organization to be "one of the forces for moving forward in the world today."[27] Deeply hurt by Roosevelt's slight, the new President General Gertrude S. Carraway penned a reply to these charges and sent it to state regents, news agencies, and a number of newspapers. In that letter, which was reprinted in the *DAR Magazine* in November 1953, the president general asserted that the Daughters held Anderson "in the highest esteem as a great singer and patriot," adding that she had been allowed to sing twice in Constitution Hall since 1939 and was about to appear again on the auditorium's stage in 1954. Carraway likewise rejected the accusation that the DAR was narrow, conservative, or afraid of change. From her perspective, Roosevelt's charges were unfair and without foundation.[28]

The Daughters also prided themselves on aiding African American children, claiming in a 1954 brochure on its Good Citizenship Pilgrimage contest that the winners represented "all races and creeds."[29] After 1945, black students were occasionally honored as Good Citizens or won essay contests that local DAR chapters sponsored in the West, Midwest, and parts of the South. The Daughters also awarded nursing scholarships to a number of black girls. It is difficult to ascertain, however, how many of the three thousand students who received Good Citizenship awards during the 1950s were African American, and these awards remained local affairs that had no equivalents at the national level.[30] Neither did the organization's national leadership change its stance on the admission of potential black members, its claims to the contrary notwithstanding. When a black journalist asked President General Talmadge in 1947 whether African American women would be eligible for membership, she answered in the affirmative but stressed that applicants needed to prove their "authentic lineage," would have to be "desirable" and were required to secure endorsements from two

DAR members. Thus, the DAR indicated that "desirability" would still be used to bar black women from membership, although it remained unclear whether women of color had actually tried to join the organization in the early Cold War period.[31]

If the DAR's comments on race were defensive but relatively restrained during the 1940s, the organization's reactions to the civil rights movement's first major victories in the 1950s revealed just how much the Daughters feared the prospect of racial change. Although domestic anticommunism had impeded black civil rights activism, the NAACP won one of its most important legal battles in 1954. That year, the organization's lawyers convinced the US Supreme Court in *Brown v. Board of Education of Topeka* to declare school segregation unconstitutional. The decision rescinded the court's 1896 *Plessy v. Ferguson* ruling, which had allowed segregation as long as it was "separate but equal," yet change was slow to come. White southerners in particular devised various strategies to prevent racial integration, including economic pressure and threats of violence. Meanwhile, black civil rights activists in Montgomery, Alabama, led by the Baptist minister Martin Luther King Jr., staged a successful boycott to end segregation on the city's bus lines. The Montgomery bus boycott's success inspired a number of similar campaigns across the South, but southern resistance to desegregation continued. The civil rights movement's attempts to increase the number of southern black voters in the second half of the 1950s had a similarly negligible impact on the racial status quo. New federal civil rights legislation also did little to help African American activists overcome the enormous obstacles they confronted. Neither the Civil Rights Act of 1957 nor the Civil Rights Act of 1960 provided federal authorities with sufficient power to enforce school integration or prosecute cases of voter discrimination and racist violence.[32]

Although the black freedom movement's successes did not fundamentally change America's racial status quo during the 1950s, the mere prospect of change led the Daughters to voice their deep-seated fear of white supremacy's demise. The 1954 Supreme Court decision on segregated schools especially rankled the DAR. Southern members were most explicit in their statements on the verdict. Shortly after *Brown* was announced, the Mississippi DAR adopted a resolution that affirmed the organization's "firm belief in the segregation of the races, particularly in the schools," and warned of miscegenation if "outside organizations" were allowed to "dictate to the people of Mississippi" how to organize their society.[33] Members in all regions shared this disdain for the prospect of racial integration, as revealed in several resolutions that the organization's Continental Congress passed in 1957 and 1958. Shortly before the passage of the Civil Rights Act of 1957, DAR delegates passed a resolution that called the bill "the gravest peril" to civil liberties because it encouraged federal encroachment on states' rights.

A year later, delegates became even more explicit in their criticism of racial change in passing a resolution on "Racial Integrity" that unequivocally stated, "We believe that God created all the races of mankind, each separate, distinctive and individual—and that the destruction of such distinctions constitutes the maximum degree of race hatred and prejudice." Like Mississippi Daughters had done in 1954, the delegates condemned "the Communist objective of miscegenation" and declared "racial integrity to be a fundamental Christian principle."[34] By linking civil rights activism and civil rights legislation to communist conspiracies, the Daughters echoed claims about pacifism and feminism in the 1920s; they were also in good company with southern and western conservatives, including many women's organizations that wanted to preserve racial segregation in public life. These groups were staunch defenders of what they called "states' rights" and cited the danger of communism in their efforts to halt racial change. In many ways, anticommunism became a shared language of protest among American conservatives who feared the disintegration of what they interpreted as a white Anglo-Saxon nation, and the DAR constantly used that language to justify its defense of ethnic nationalism.[35]

"I Wouldn't Let a Mexican Carry Old Glory—Would You?": The DAR and Immigration after 1945

The DAR's ideological mix of anticommunism and ethnic nationalism also influenced its stance on immigration in the 1950s. America's Cold War struggle against the Soviet Union colored virtually every political debate on the issue, and fears of communist subversion were seen as a justification for retaining the stringent quotas that had been introduced by the National Origins Act of 1924. There were a number of liberal members of Congress who wanted to abolish the quota system, but the controversial Immigration and Nationality Act of 1952, commonly known as the McCarran-Walter Act, upheld the restrictions that had been introduced in the 1920s. The growing number of Mexican immigrants who entered the United States was of particular concern to restrictionists. Politicians' warnings contained fewer references to the purported racial inferiority of Hispanics, but they did depict this group as outsiders whose different culture and language would make it difficult to integrate them into US society.[36] Although the Daughters continued to distribute their manual for immigrants and welcomed new foreign-born citizens, the organization remained squarely in the restrictionist camp and seconded the appeals of conservative politicians and other patriotic organizations to uphold the quota system. As early as 1947, DAR delegates passed a resolution that called on Congress to retain and strictly enforce the National Origins Act. They also lauded the passage of the McCarran-Walter Act, regarding it as a crucial means to preserve a white nation.[37] The new law, the chairwoman of the National Defense Committee wrote in the *DAR Magazine* in 1956, sought "to preserve the cultural integrity of our country" and would "continue the stream of Anglo-Saxon culture and tradition." Such a strategy, she added, was an essential "bulwark of defense of our Republic" in the face of the communist threat. In the eyes of the National Defense Committee's leaders, ending "the National Origins formula would be disastrous to America."[38]

A widely publicized incident in 1957 in Denver attested to the Daughters' growing concerns about Mexican immigrants and Hispanic US citizens. The controversy began in February of that year when Charlotte C. Rush, the chairwoman of the Denver Chapter's Committee on Patriotic Education, told the *Denver Post* in an interview about her work with Mexican American children at the State Industrial School for Boys at Golden, Colorado. The Daughters had long sponsored patriotic events at the school, which was a state correctional institution for juvenile offenders that housed many Mexican American boys, and they planned to do so again in 1957. In the interview Rush related an incident that had taken place in 1950, when she was responsible for selecting one of the school's students to carry the Stars and Stripes during a patriotic ceremony. During the rehearsal for the ceremony, a white boy whom she had selected to carry the flag showed little enthusiasm, while a twelve-year old Mexican American named Dave Lane eagerly volunteered and displayed the patriotic fervor the Daughters sought to instill in students. When advised by her chapter's Committee on Patriotic Education to let the Mexican American boy carry the flag during the ceremony, Rush refused. "I wouldn't let a Mexican carry Old Glory— would you?" she asked the reporter of the *Denver Post*, which published her remarks on February 10, 1957.[39]

Although Rush stressed that her views were her own and assured journalists that she was "not prejudiced against Mexicans," the interview triggered a firestorm of protest across the country, and it once more put pressure on the national DAR to explain its nationalist ideology.[40] A day after the publication of Rush's remarks, the State Industrial School's superintendent, Gunnar F. Soelberg, canceled a planned DAR event to celebrate Abraham Lincoln's birthday. On the same day, the Colorado House of Representatives asked Governor Stephen McNichols to prohibit the DAR and any other group that championed racial discrimination from sponsoring patriotic programs in Colorado state institutions. The House voted unanimously in favor of the strongly worded resolution, as did the state Senate. McNichols told the press that he "deplored" the statement made by Rush. In a letter to the Denver Chapter's regent, Mrs. James McDowell, he voiced his concerns that Rush's statements appeared to reflect the official policy of the DAR toward Hispanics. Many citizens were enraged by Rush's language. White and Hispanic Americans inundated the *Denver Post* and the national DAR with letters of protest, and Rush had her phone service cut off because of the numerous angry calls she received. Liberal organizations joined the critics' chorus. Even in Washington, DC, government officials were worried because they feared the incident might have harmful consequences for US-Mexican relations. As in 1939, the DAR's ethnic nationalism faced national as well as international protest and clashed with the more inclusive civic nationalism espoused by many citizens.[41]

If such criticism echoed reactions to the controversies over Marian Anderson and Hazel Scott, the organization's response in 1957 differed markedly from its previous defensiveness. At the local and national levels, the Daughters quickly apologized and declared that they were committed to civic nationalism; Charlotte Rush was dismissed as chairwoman of the Denver Chapter's Committee on Patriotic Education. According to an official statement the organization released one day after Rush's remarks became public, the organization did "not discriminate in any way on account of color, nationality or religion."[42] The DAR immediately tried to mend fences with Colorado state officials including Governor McNichols, who met with DAR representatives a few days after the controversy erupted. In that meeting, DAR First Vice President General Mrs. E. Thomas Boyd assured the governor that the DAR was not prejudiced and cited as proof the organization's Junior American Citizens program that was meant to train boys of all races to become better citizens. Apparently convinced by the Daughters' assurances, Governor McNichols lifted the ban on DAR-sponsored events at Colorado's state institutions. On February 22, the State Industrial School for Boys finally held the long-planned patriotic event to honor Abraham Lincoln and George Washington without the DAR; a Colorado-born boy of Mexican descent was the designated flag bearer.[43]

It is not entirely clear whether the national DAR's swift apologies in the wake of the Denver controversy simply reflected the organization's ambiguous stance on immigration, which continuously veered between inclusion and exclusion, or whether it sought to avoid the type of public relations disaster that had been triggered by its discrimination against black artists. Within the DAR, officers did reiterate the organization's official position on race, but they tended to downplay the issue, arguing that Charlotte Rush only wanted to prod the reluctant white student into displaying more patriotism and respect for the flag.[44]

Regardless of their motivations and the question of whether their apologies were genuine, the Denver incident indicated that many Daughters continued to regard nonwhite people, including Mexican Americans, as ineligible for inclusion in the nation. Their continuing opposition to civil rights for African Americans gives credence to such a conclusion, and the DAR's unabated admiration for the Appalachian mountaineers and members' demeaning statements about people of Mexican ancestry point in a similar direction. In 1950, DAR officer Grace Ward Calhoun echoed "100 percent Americanism" tenets when praising the pupils of a DAR school for mountaineer children in Tamassee, South Carolina. "They are of the purest Anglo-Saxon stock," she wrote in the organization's monthly, calling them "good-citizenship material." To Calhoun, the school was "a monument to real Americans, by real Americans, for real Americans."[45] In the eyes of the Daughters, then, real Americans were white Anglo-Saxon Protestants, who they believed should be vigilant to protect their nation from nonwhite intruders. In the 1950s Mexicans appeared to pose the greatest threat. Three years after Calhoun's article appeared, the *DAR Magazine* featured an article on "Americanism" warning readers to beware the growing number of Mexicans entering the United States illegally to find work.[46] Race was always on the Daughters' minds in the post–World War II period, and their nationalist ideology reflected notions of racial exclusionism that had changed little since its founding.

This exclusionism was far from exceptional in the 1950s and reflected widespread ideas about national belonging among white Americans such as the white middle-class women who predominated DAR membership.

Memorializing America's Past between 1945 and 1960

The DAR's commemorative activities from the end of World War II through the late 1950s were characterized by ideological continuities, but the Daughters' remembrances were largely confined to their own ranks. Only occasionally did they collaborate with local communities to erect memorials or organize commemorative events. Curiously, the Daughters continued to spend a considerable amount of time studying and memorializing the Indian past. While they recoiled from the thought of making African Americans full members of the nation and virtually erased them from their accounts of US history, the organization's interest in Indigenous America's past and present continued unabated during a period that saw a gradually declining interest in this ethnic group among white citizens.[47]

Throughout the period 1945–1960, numerous DAR chapters devoted entire meetings to Indian history and culture, and the *DAR Magazine* featured scores of articles on this minority. In their interpretations of Indigenous America, the Daughters shifted back and forth between praise for Indians' patriotism and a paternalistic fascination with the perceived primitivism of their culture. The memory of violent confrontations between white settlers and Native American tribes was largely absent in the organization's magazine or in chapters' Indian programs. Instead, the Daughters tended to concentrate on Indian culture, including music, dance, art, handicraft, and relics, which constituted a less controversial way of indulging in their fascination with Native exoticism. In their interest in the exotic other, chapters still engaged in playing Indian by organizing historical pageants, fashion shows, and dances to vicariously experience Indigenous peoples' cultures. Some chapters carried on the tradition of inviting Indians to their meetings to speak on their history and culture.[48] During such meetings and in the organization's publications, the Daughters frequently acknowledged the Indigenous population's contributions to the progress of white civilization and American nation-building, but they also highlighted what they regarded as its low position in civilization. One author stressed that "the knowledge and culture of the early American Indians helped our ancestors to survive disease, famine, and shelter," and another called Native Americans "a distinct and separate race" whose members all had "the same simple and primitive habits," including their "love of . . . painted faces and bodies, feathers, plumes, feats and dances."[49]

This fascination with Indian primitivism, combined with the DAR's continuing admiration for Native Americans' allegiance to the United States and occasional expressions of remorse over their unjust treatment, led the organization to continue its campaign for Indians' social uplift and full citizenship rights.[50] The Daughters regarded America's Indigenous population, in the words of DAR officer Mrs. Earl Foster, "a very integral part of our civilization" and implored the federal government to help impoverished tribes and recognize Indians as full-fledged citizens. From 1947 to 1959, the DAR's Continental Congress passed several resolutions urging Washington as well as state governments to support Native Americans.[51] During the 1950s, however, the US Congress was generally opposed to such ideas, instead discussing ways to decrease or even terminate federal financial assistance to many tribes, a trend to which the DAR responded with renewed efforts to help Indigenous communities. Supported by the organization's American Indians Committee, numerous DAR chapters funded scholarships for Indian students, created community centers on some reservations to aid unemployed youth, and continued to sponsor Indian schools.[52]

The DAR's commemorations of the American Revolution and western pioneers during the period 1945–1960 paled in comparison to the flurry of activities pertaining to the Indian past and present. The organization's endeavors to honor Revolutionary patriots and pioneer settlers had decreased in number and visibility during the 1930s, and the post–World War II period saw even fewer major campaigns. The most visible effort to commemorate the American Revolution came to fruition in 1953 when the national DAR erected the 114-foot Memorial Bell Tower at Valley Forge, Pennsylvania, to honor the veterans of the War of Independence, World War I, and World War II.[53] A number of chapters as well as some state organizations in the Northeast, South, and Midwest celebrated the accomplishments of members of the Continental Army by adorning their graves with bronze plaques or small monuments. Occasionally, Daughters invited descendants of these soldiers to attend the ceremonies that accompanied the dedications of the memorials.[54] In the 1950s, mentions of women were scarce in the Daughters' remembrances. The women of the Revolution received virtually no public acknowledgments in those years, and even the *DAR Magazine* was largely silent on their heroic exploits.[55]

If authors mentioned the heroines of the American Revolution, they did so primarily within the context of women's military service in the present. Female members of the US armed forces were occasionally asked to write articles for the organization's publication, and they tended to make brief references to their Revolutionary predecessors. Motherhood was rarely mentioned in these articles, but the writers did occasionally invoke the idea that it was a wife's responsibility to support her husband. In 1959, Adelaide Bledsoe Cormack Kingman, the vice chairwoman of the Defense Advisory Committee on Women in the Services, not only stressed women's patriotism as a motivation to serve in the military but also stated that women had "accepted the time-honored law of life, that women stand beside their men, to help whenever possible."[56]

Commemorative activities and publications that honored western pioneers declined in number, as did efforts to highlight women's contributions to American nation-building in the West. Only a few chapters in the Midwest erected stone markers on the graves of their communities' first white settlers or marked historic sites related to territorial expansion. The national DAR no longer pursued projects that focused on the western past and largely ignored the pioneer mothers it had so lavishly praised in the late 1920s. Despite this waning interest in the history of the West, Daughters appeared to uphold the same racial and gender hierarchies they had affirmed before World War II. At a commemorative ceremony that the DAR chapter of Kalamazoo County, Michigan, organized in 1957, members paid tribute to the "Parents of the First White Child in the County," and the event's keynote speaker, Willis Dunbar, president of the Michigan State Historical Society, echoed the DAR's gendered rhetoric of the interwar period.[57] It is not entirely clear why the DAR lost interest in highlighting the accomplishments of women in its interpretations of the past during the 1950s; it might have been a reaction to American Cold War culture in the 1950s, which tended to stress traditional notions of femininity as a bulwark against Soviet communism.

The waning visibility of the Daughters in America's commemorative landscape can be attributed to a number of factors. The increasing remoteness of the past made it difficult to create meaningful connections between members' communicative memories and the cultural memory of the nation.

Also, the DAR and other organizations had marked thousands of historical spots before World War II, and additional memorials seemed less urgent; by the mid-1950s more than a thousand historic sites had been marked in the United States. And probably just as important a factor was that state and federal authorities assumed ever more active roles in preserving and celebrating the nation's cultural memory. In 1949, Congress established a National Trust for the United States to strengthen cooperation between the federal government, particularly the National Park Service, and private organizations that sought to preserve America's cultural heritage. By 1956 the trust consisted of 182 organizations including the DAR and actively selected buildings and sites that were deemed important enough to preserve for posterity. Although the Daughters remained sought-after advisers, the federal government displayed a new determination to shape national cultural memory.[58] At the same time, many Daughters no longer seemed willing to engage in the tedious work of researching and fundraising that commemorative projects required. By the early 1950s, many chapters tended to focus primarily on celebrating themselves and their accomplishments, as could be seen on the pages of the *DAR Magazine*. The magazine featured hundreds of reports on chapter anniversaries and Revolutionary teas and luncheons but very few articles on members' historical research or efforts to shape America's cultural memory.[59]

A final reason for the Daughters' waning commemorative activities in the 1950s was that its anticommunist activism and related opposition to the United Nations consumed much of their energy. The organization's vociferous opposition to the UN was closely connected to its nationalist ideology that tolerated no supranational authorities that rivaled the US government's authority. In the post–World War II era, the DAR repeatedly voiced hostility toward "world government" and legislation that would bring "any form of international control."[60] At first, the Daughters distinguished between world government, which they detested, and the UN, which they supported. After 1949 they began to conflate the two. While denouncing Soviet communism, the Daughters also warned of the catastrophic consequences of UN campaigns for world peace and human rights. In 1953 the DAR's Continental Congress passed a resolution that reiterated its "opposition to the Genocide Convention, Covenant on Human Rights and all other United Nations agencies or treaties which would have the effect of superseding our Constitution or limiting our national and state liberties or freedoms."[61]

Three years later, another resolution called on the UN to "desist from participation in any plan, project, agency or principles which would intervene in our internal affairs, interfere with our domestic legislation, or spread doctrines contrary to our American philosophies and way of life."[62] All UN agencies were suspected of undermining America's sovereignty as a nation, and the Daughters imagined conspiracies that echoed pre–World War II fears of communist subversion. In the late 1950s the Daughters claimed that a "very substantial part of the funds" of the United Nation's Children's Fund (UNICEF) went "to Communist and Communist-controlled countries." Worse, they said, UNICEF tried "to remove the Christ from Christmas," since the Christmas cards that UNICEF sold were devoid of the holy day's "Spirit."[63]

The Daughters were not alone in their anticommunist-inspired opposition to the United Nations. They were part of a growing right-wing movement that consisted of male and female intellectuals, diverse citizens, and various national and regional organizations. Although the DAR might have been among the most prominent proponents of this conspiracy-prone anti-internationalism, a number of conservative groups, including smaller anticommunist women's organizations such as the Minute Women of the U.S.A., also warned of any international entanglements and conjured the specter of Soviet collectivism.[64] The DAR's importance could also be seen in the praise of some prominent conservatives for the Daughters and their vigilant activism; among them were FBI Director J. Edgar Hoover and a handful of members of Congress.[65] The editors of the conservative magazine *American Mercury* likewise lauded the DAR, opining in 1958 that the organization deserved recognition for its unwavering support "for the preservation of American ideals."[66] As suggested by such praise, the Daughters were part of a large network of right-wing organizations that championed anticommunism and other conservative causes. While denounced by liberal commentators, the Daughters were far from being isolated in conservative circles.[67]

Although the Daughters were part of the conservative mainstream, their Cassandra-like warnings increasingly marginalized their presence in public discourse. Particularly their uncompromising attitude toward communism and the UN cost them much political legitimacy. Probably the most conspicuous reflection of their marginalization was the organization's deteriorating relations with the White House. In 1955 President Dwight D. Eisenhower, whose policies the Daughters had frequently criticized, broke with the tradition of addressing the DAR's annual meeting, instead sending written statements in which he suggested that it was time for the Daughters to move on. Continuing his subtle critique throughout the 1950s, Eisenhower explicitly told the Daughters in his final message that one could not rest on traditions alone.[68] Other critics were less tactful. In 1957, liberal activist E. V. Dunklee, a Denver-based attorney and president of the Colorado Committee for the United Nations, publicly called the DAR's stance on UNESCO "crackpot super-patriotism." Two years later a reporter covering the DAR's Continental Congress for a Michigan newspaper opined that the DAR's opposition to the UN was "an unrealistic, ostrich-like attitude" that would contribute "little to world peace."[69] Liberal columnists voiced similar opinions, while a growing number of newspapers simply stopped reporting on the organization's diatribes.[70]

While many Americans belittled the Daughters as racist, xenophobic, and jingoistic conspiracists by the end of the 1950s, the organization's leaders actually had reason to be delighted. For one thing, the DAR had never been more popular among middle-class white women. Its membership grew from 162,000 in 1949 to almost 186,000 in late 1959. During the same period it had gained more than 200 chapters across the country, boasting 2,847 by early 1960.[71] Apparently, neither the controversies over the organization's racism nor its enmity toward communism and the United Nations had deterred women from joining the Daughters. In addition, the Cold War boosted citizens' patriotism and their interest in the American past. The Department of Justice and the National Archives convinced the American Heritage Foundation to finance a traveling exhibit of historical documents. It crisscrossed America in a red and blue "Freedom Train" in 1947–1949, and almost four million people came to see the exhibit's 127 documents. Among a considerable number of Americans the Cold War also strengthened traditional notions of gender and the family. Some politicians and social scientists considered the nuclear family a bulwark against the Soviet Union's expansionism and put new emphasis on motherhood while denouncing any behavior that smacked of feminism.[72] Thus, although Daughters might have felt unjustly disparaged, the 1950s probably came closest to the social and political ideals that the organization so fervently upheld. When these ideals came under heavy attack only a few years later, the Daughters feared for the worst and were shocked to see their vision of the nation turned upside down.

The DAR's Vision of the Nation Upended, 1960–1976

After the relatively tranquil 1950s, the 1960s and the first half of the 1970s were probably the most traumatic period for the DAR since its founding. The various social movements that emerged during this period as well as the fundamental legislative changes they brought about challenged almost everything the organization stood for. African American activism in particular upended the Daughters' vision of what they regarded as a white Anglo-Saxon nation. The sit-ins of 1960 revived the flagging black freedom struggle and were followed by various nonviolent protest campaigns that ultimately led to the passage of the Civil Rights Act of 1964 and the Voting Rights Act of 1965. Long rejected by the DAR as members of the nation, black citizens were subsequently able to take on roles in American politics in unprecedented numbers.[73]

White college students likewise challenged the social and political status quo, especially criticizing America's growing involvement in the Vietnam War. By 1968 the student-led antiwar movement called for an end to the military conflict in Southeast Asia and questioned the notions of patriotism and military heroism that had been voiced to justify it. Meanwhile, white women began to protest against America's traditional gender order, calling for an end to sexual discrimination and male privilege. Native American activists launched several widely publicized protest campaigns in the late 1960s and early 1970s denouncing centuries of white oppression as well as the stereotypical portrayals of Indians that the DAR and other white commentators had helped to perpetuate. In addition to such grassroots attacks on racism, nationalism, and sexism, President Lyndon B. Johnson managed to usher through US Congress path-breaking legislation that liberalized America's immigration laws and created medical aid programs for its citizens. Many commentators hailed the subsequent increase in nonwhite immigration and the growing involvement of the federal government in people's lives as a fulfillment of the promise of America's civic creed, but to the Daughters and other conservatives, the long 1960s seemed to set in motion a downward spiral toward Armageddon.[74]

The civil rights movement certainly constituted the most shocking disruption of the Daughters' vision of the nation during the 1960s, but compared to its very explicit resolutions on racial integration and the perceived danger of miscegenation in the 1950s, the DAR's official response to the civil rights revolution was quite subdued. In 1961 it passed a resolution that called on Congress to "reject all pending civil rights legislation and recognize the rights of the states to protect all citizens as provided in the Bill of Rights of the Constitution of the United States of America."[75] But in 1963 DAR President General Marion Moncure Duncan agreed to attend a meeting with President John F. Kennedy and other leaders of American women's organizations at the White House. Duncan also claimed in a letter to Kennedy that the DAR had no official position on the issue of racial integration but did strongly support states' rights. Replying to Kennedy's appeal to "aid in the great struggle to close the remaining gaps in the American dream of equality and brotherhood," Duncan repeated the arguments of southern segregationists but stopped short of explicitly endorsing white supremacy.[76]

Behind closed doors, however, some Daughters appear to have regarded the black freedom struggle as the harbinger of America's doom. Sara Roddis Jones, a high-ranking DAR officer who would become the organization's president general in 1974, was far from subdued in a frank exchange of letters with conservative journalist Elizabeth Churchill Brown in 1963 and 1964. In Jones's view, the black freedom struggle's goal was "not civil rights but revolution" that reinforced her suspicion that America had "already lost control of its destiny as a nation." Like many fellow Daughters, Jones contended that the movement for racial equality was connected to communism and would contribute to the victory of communism in America. Feeling that she and like-minded citizens were "being closed in on," it was all the more frustrating for Jones that she had been asked by DAR leaders not to publish any critical comments on the Civil Rights Act of 1964.[77]

The organization's invitations to segregationist politicians to attend its annual meetings indicated that at least some of Jones's fellow officers shared her apprehensions. One of the invitees was South Carolina Senator Strom Thurmond, a staunch defender of white supremacy who had waged marathon filibusters to derail civil rights legislation. Thurmond was an occasional guest at the DAR's Continental Congress and considered the organization an important ally in the South's fight against the black freedom struggle. After one visit in 1961, he profusely lauded the Daughters on the Senate floor, telling his fellow senators that he knew "of no more patriotic, liberty-loving organization in this country than the National Society, Daughters of the American Revolution."[78] Like Thurmond, many Daughters appear to have been convinced that the civil rights legislation of the 1960s, in the words of one member who assessed the nation's state of affairs in the *DAR Magazine* in 1968, had "led the people away from their traditional liberties toward a totalitarian state."[79]

But the Daughters were just as disturbed by the student movement of the 1960s, particularly by its opposition to the Vietnam War. Organizations such as the Students for a Democratic Society questioned not only traditional values and authorities; they also took issue with long-cherished notions of patriotism and heroic valor on the battlefield in the wake of what they viewed as an unjust war in Southeast Asia.[80] For the Daughters, who had always implored the American public to stand behind America's troops and whose nationalist ideology revolved around the memory of heroic warriors, such behavior was unacceptable, and they loudly railed against it. As it had during its fight against pacifism after World War I, the DAR denounced antiwar activists and sought to prevent them from recruiting more followers. In August 1967 the organization denied the famous folk singer Joan Baez the use of its Constitution Hall because Baez refused to pay part of her income tax to protest US military involvement in Vietnam. While DAR President General Adele Erb Sullivan lamented that Baez's antiwar "agitation" would in effect aid and abet "the cause of the enemy," the singer ultimately gave a free concert at the Washington Monument in front of an audience of almost thirty thousand and wryly thanked the Daughters for the free publicity. Prior to Baez's performance, the DAR had unsuccessfully lobbied Interior Secretary Stewart L. Udall to deny the folk singer permission to give her concert on federal property.[81]

Disgusted by such forms of antiwar activism, the Daughters considered Baez and student antiwar activists unpatriotic "Destroyers of Freedom" who seemed "dedicated to the overthrow of duly constituted government, and destruction of the rights of all as defined in our United States Constitution."[82] But it was especially students' "downgrading of patriotism" that the Daughters identified as "one of the most serious of the dangers" facing America in the late 1960s, voicing concerns that were widespread among conservatives at the time. The DAR regarded such behavior as a form of assistance to communism and as the beginning of the end of the American way of life.[83] To demonstrate the organization's continuing commitment to the United States and its war effort, President General Sullivan undertook a journey to Vietnam in January 1968 to present Americanism medals to several servicemen who had distinguished themselves in combat.[84]

If the disruption of America's racial order and students' assault on entrenched traditions of US nationalism were not enough, the Second Wave feminism of the 1970s fundamentally challenged the country's gender hierarchies, prompting the DAR to view it as yet another front on which the nation required protection. In an echo of the 1920s, the Daughters opposed the legislative goals of the women's liberation movement because they were deemed pernicious to women, the family, and the nation. The Equal Rights Amendment (ERA) in particular rankled the DAR, and the organization waged a nationwide battle to prevent its ratification. First proposed in 1923 by feminist activists who demanded more than political equality for women, the constitutional amendment stated that equal rights under the law would "not be abridged or denied . . . on account of sex." The amendment's surprisingly quick congressional approval in 1972 mobilized a vocal opposition movement that received considerable support from the Daughters.[85] Throughout the remainder of the 1970s the organization warned that women would lose many of the sex-specific privileges they enjoyed and might have to engage in tasks they were physically incapable of performing; ERA critics singled out compulsory military service and military combat as particularly detestable. Especially mothers, the Daughters claimed, would lose the support of their husbands and the protections they had traditionally been entitled to.[86]

The Daughters actively tried to prevent the ERA's ratification by supporting a nationwide campaign waged by DAR officer Phyllis Schlafly. A member since 1954, Schlafly had made a name for herself as an ardent anticommunist writer and quickly ascended in the DAR hierarchy. After the ERA's congressional passage, she almost single-handedly launched a STOP ERA movement, which lobbied state legislators and citizens to reconsider their support for the new amendment. The campaign could count on faithful DAR officers such as Kathryn Fink Dunaway, the chairwoman of Georgia's STOP ERA Committee who tirelessly sent out appeals to politicians and "Concerned Americans." In her letters to thousands of citizens, Dunaway called the ERA "a fraudulent amendment to force women to be treated the same as men." The amendment, she wrote, was "a ripoff of the rights of homemakers, and a big grab for power by the Federal bureaucrats."[87] As in the past, the small minority of liberal Daughters who disagreed with such assessments occasionally voiced their dissent but found themselves isolated and ignored.[88]

Underneath the warnings about the ERA's dreadful consequences and the federal government's related usurpation of power lay deep beliefs in gender difference and the fear that any attempt to ignore these differences

Figure 5.3. Phyllis Schlafly at a STOP ERA protest in Washington, DC, in front of the White House in 1977. Schlafly was an anticommunist writer who joined the DAR in the 1950s and became a high-ranking officer. After the congressional passage of the Equal Rights Amendment in 1972, she launched the STOP ERA campaign, which was supported by the DAR and many of its members and contributed to preventing enough states from ratifying the amendment. Courtesy of Library of Congress Prints and Photographs Division, U.S. News & World Report Magazine Photograph Collection, LC-U9-33891-33.

would jeopardize the nation. "The good Lord made us male and female," Sara Roddis Jones wrote in the *DAR Magazine* in 1972, "and no constitutional amendment can alter that."[89] In the following years, numerous DAR officers and rank-and-file members seconded Jones's analysis, demonstrating that the organization's thinking on gender and the nation had changed little since the late nineteenth century. In a 1978 letter to the editor of the *DAR Magazine,* an Alabama Daughter made clear her conviction that the country's future depended on strict lines of gender demarcation. "I am for what is best for us, our families, and our nation," she wrote, "and I think that a recognition of the differences between the sexes is essential for the continuation of our society."[90]

Yet, it was especially the specter of female combat soldiers that prompted members' most explicit statements on why they believed America's gender binaries were so crucial to safeguarding the nation. Notwithstanding decades of praise for Margaret Corbin and other female patriots who took up arms during the American Revolution, the DAR was adamant that allowing female soldiers to engage in combat would endanger the nation's security as well as its social and moral cohesion. "Women are not physically, emotionally or psychologically suited for the rigors of combat," a DAR resolution on "Women in Combat" stated in 1979, "and if quotas of men and women serving in the military in combat were enforced it would be disruptive to military operations, jeopardizing national security." Reflecting nineteenth-century notions of femininity and masculinity, the resolution continued, "civilization . . . has evolved with male's physical strength and aggressiveness toward protecting the female; the demand for equality on the battlefield, overcoming natural civilizing impulses, is a move toward barbarism."[91] While the Daughters still praised the patriotic women of the Revolution and applauded those who joined the US military in the present, the Daughters insisted that women's femininity could not be compromised.[92] The DAR's anti-ERA campaign, which helped derail the amendment's ratification by three-fourths of all state legislatures, demonstrated the Daughters' unbending commitment to a conservative vision of the nation as doomed if traditional notions of femininity, masculinity, and the family were challenged.

The DAR's entangled ideas about communism, the United Nations, and the role of the US government in American society also remained unchanged. The Daughters staunchly opposed communism and highlighted their opposition to the "atheist" Soviet Union in 1972 by changing the organization's motto from "Home and Country" to "God, Home, and Country."[93] They deplored every policy that appeared to compromise America's national sovereignty. In particular, US involvement in the United Nations rankled the DAR, which repeatedly called for an immediate withdrawal by the United States and the removal of UN headquarters from American soil.[94] At the same time, the Daughters feared any government intervention in US society, regarding it as a violation of citizens' constitutional rights as well as a dangerous trend toward socialist collectivism. They opposed the federal government's New Deal programs, and the Daughters viewed President Lyndon B. Johnson's Great Society programs, especially Medicare, as further dangerous steps toward totalitarian communism.[95]

Finally, the Daughters were still convinced that immigration needed to be highly restricted to protect the nation against subversive elements and detrimental foreign influences. In 1964 DAR President General Marion Duncan explicitly voiced such apprehensions when speaking before the US Congressional Subcommittee on Immigration and Nationality. In Duncan's view, any liberalization of the McCarran-Walter Act would aggravate existing problems and lead to "unfavorable repercussions on all facets of our economy . . . and national security, offering additional threat to the American heritage—cultural, social and ethnic traditions." Restating previous racial arguments, Duncan stressed that the earliest colonial settlers "shared common Anglo-Saxon bonds and arrived with the full knowledge and intent of founders or pioneers who knew there was a wilderness to conquer and a nation to build."[96] In the twentieth century, by contrast, newcomers not only would be much more difficult to assimilate but also posed health problems and might turn out to be communist spies. When the Immigration Act of 1965 brought the very liberalization that the Daughters had sought to prevent since 1924, allowing millions of new immigrants to make America their home, the Daughters and fellow conservatives were appalled and braced for the worst.[97]

Confronted with such fundamental changes, memory remained the Daughters' only means to preserve their particular ideal of a white nation. While the federal government and textbook publishers reacted to women's and minorities' social activism by creating more inclusionary histories of US nation-building, the DAR's tales of the past were still populated primarily by manly white soldiers and pioneers whose patriotic wives and daughters readily supported them in their quest to build and defend the United States. Stories about black citizens' contributions to the nation's progress, or rather, the continuing absence of such stories, also followed a familiar pattern. The Daughters ignored not only the role of citizens of color in the nation's wars but also African American history in general. If they did occasionally address that history, they focused on the antebellum South and reiterated tales that revolved around happy slaves and benevolent masters. Native Americans, too, were still remembered for being allies of the United States in the American Revolution or in wars with hostile tribes, for ceding their land to the US government, or for ostensibly giving gifts to white settlers and white civilization. The Daughters still organized and financed campaigns to improve Indians' opportunities for advancement through education and economic aid, which they viewed as the only paths for them to become civilized members of the nation.[98]

Predictably, the Daughters condemned any textbook that challenged their particular version of America's cultural memory because they contended that the United States could be saved only if young citizens learned the right history, that is, their variation. Especially the country's youth, the Daughters asserted, were in dire need of the patriotic lessons they believed post–World War II textbooks no longer taught. Children also needed to be shielded from what the Daughters regarded as communist ideas as well as the interpretations of "guilt-ridden historians" whom a DAR writer accused in 1963 of being "unable to ascribe a single unselfish motive to any action in our foreign or domestic policies."[99] Just as they had done in the 1920s, the national DAR and its state organizations, together with like-minded conservatives, deemed dozens of textbooks unsatisfactory and sought to ban them from public schools in the 1950s and 1960s. Their campaigns were rarely successful.[100]

Change at Last? The Daughters in the Post–Civil Rights Era

By the time the DAR celebrated the bicentennial of America's founding, the organization's membership had grown to more than 200,000, but its confidence in the nation's future was severely shaken.[101] DAR leaders grew bitter as many liberal Americans either mocked or simply ignored their efforts to strengthen citizens' patriotism. From the perspective of liberal commentators, the organization's unyielding support for racial segregation as well as its rabid anticommunism and conspiracy-prone isolationism had reduced the DAR to a ridiculed remnant of an era that seemed utterly anachronistic in a more globalized world. The organization's deteriorating relations with the White House were particularly hard to swallow. Neither President Eisenhower nor President John F. Kennedy had accepted invitations to address the Daughters. In 1963 First Lady Jacqueline Kennedy added insult to injury when calling the Daughters "lonely old women" who seemed to have little else to do.[102] In general the 1960s cemented the Daughters' comical image in much of the mainstream media. In 1968 the men's magazine *True* published a scathing persiflage by the writer John Keats, who mockingly stated that it would be a tragedy if the Daughters changed their traditional image because they so often brought "a shout of laughter to our lives." He wrote, "By doing all the silly stuff they do and say, the Daughters try to make themselves appear ridiculous. They do this gaily, gladly, hoping to amuse us, to make us laugh with them, in order that, refreshed, we can get on with the good work that began in 1776."[103]

Shortly before the US bicentennial, the DAR seemed to be a shadow of its former patriotic self in the eyes of liberal pundits. The journalist Elaine Kendall wrote in the *New York Times Book Review* in August 1974, "Though some of the resolutions issued at the annual D.A.R. Congress in Washington are laughably reactionary, no one really pays much attention to them. The D.A.R. doesn't make headlines or influence policy."[104] If the Daughters did make headlines in the first half of the 1970s, their publicity only reflected the organization's marginalized status in public discourse. Such was the case a few months before Kendall's article appeared when President Richard Nixon ended a seventeen-year period of Continental Congresses without an address by a US President. Being under immense political pressure because of the Watergate scandal, Nixon welcomed the DAR's support, and the Daughters relished the publicity that his visit brought for the organization. Nixon resigned less than four months after his appearance in Constitution Hall, which symbolized the Daughters' waning social, cultural, and political influence.[105]

Ironically, at a time when America paid the least attention to the DAR, it underwent its greatest transformation. In the 1970s, a few initial signs indicated that the Daughters sought to shed the organization's racist image. More and more African American students received Good Citizenship awards as well as prizes in DAR essay contests. A closer look at the organization's activities in North Carolina, for instance, reveals numerous black honorees between the late 1960s and 1980. The Daughters also began to welcome black Americans who seemed ideologically in line with them as guest speakers in Washington, DC. In 1973, Air Force Major General Daniel James Jr. became the first African American to deliver a keynote address at the DAR's annual meeting. James defended embattled President Richard Nixon and condemned student radicals as well as militant black nationalists, indicating that his appearance marked no major change in the Daughters' thinking.[106] Yet, two years later, DAR leaders even began to voice support for "a large influx of black members," noting approvingly that a growing number of citizens of color had conducted genealogical research at the organization's library.[107]

In 1977, eighty-seven years after it was established, the DAR finally admitted its first black member. While some African Americans interested in genealogy had begun to frequent the Daughters' library in Washington, DC, black Detroit real estate agent Karen B. Farmer also traced her ancestry to find in 1976 that she was the descendant of a white man named William Hood who had served in the Continental Army. In the summer of 1977, after finding a chapter in Michigan that agreed to sponsor her application, she applied for membership in the DAR. A few months later she was accepted into the organization with little fanfare. Farmer's application caused no controversy probably in large part because of her rather unremarkable reasons for becoming a Daughter. When asked by journalists about her motivation for joining an organization that had discriminated against African Americans for so long, she replied that DAR membership would enhance her reputation as a genealogist, a line of work she planned to pursue professionally. She had grown up reading the works of NAACP co-founder W. E. B. Du Bois, who in the early twentieth century had enraged some Daughters when claiming that they had black blood in their veins. Farmer described herself as "slightly radical" during her college years in the early 1970s. Yet, she did not view her membership as a form of political protest. In the spring of 1978 she attended her first DAR Continental Congress and claimed that she experienced no hostility from fellow Daughters, not even for being married to a white man.[108] From an outsider's perspective, it seemed that the DAR had quietly discarded its opposition to racial integration and was ready to accept African Americans as full members of the nation.

But the case of Lena Santos Ferguson, a black administrative secretary who sought to become a member in the early 1980s, revealed that the organization was still not fully prepared for fundamental change. It was only due to Ferguson's determined perseverance that she eventually became a full member while simultaneously forcing the Daughters to end almost a century of racist amnesia. As happened with Karen Farmer, Ferguson's decision to join the DAR began with a personal search for her family's roots and was influenced by a general interest in black genealogy. "I wanted my ancestor recognized for serving during the American Revolution," she told a *Washington Post* reporter in 1983, adding that she also wanted to assist other African Americans in learning more about their patriotic forebears.[109]

Encouraged by her nephew Maurice Barboza, a black lawyer and congressional lobbyist who had joined the Sons of the American Revolution without any opposition, Ferguson first applied for membership in 1980, choosing the Mary Washington Chapter, one of the capital's thirty-nine

DAR chapters. After being rejected by this and several other chapters, she reluctantly accepted the national DAR's offer to become a member at large in April 1983.[110] At-large members could not vote in DAR elections, hold office, or participate in social activities, and Ferguson was still hopeful of finding a local chapter that would accept her, but these hopes were repeatedly dashed. She was confronted with a familiar pattern that reflected the Daughters' time-honored differentiation between "eligibility" and "acceptability" that allowed them to reject any applicant they deemed undesirable. In an interview, one of the two white women who had sponsored her application confirmed Ferguson's suspicions that the unsuccessful bids for membership were a result of racial animosity. The Daughters simultaneously planned to establish more rigid eligibility requirements that would have forced applicants to prove they were "legitimately descended" from Revolutionary patriots through official marriage certificates. That requirement appeared to furnish more evidence that women of color were unwelcome, since many of their ancestors had been slaves whose marriages were rarely officially sanctioned.[111]

It was this experience of prejudice that transformed Ferguson's personal search for her roots into a widely publicized political campaign that challenged the DAR's exclusionary membership policies and ethnic nationalism. In this campaign, 1984 became a watershed year. In March the *Washington Post* published a front-page article on Ferguson and her unsuccessful bid for membership in a local DAR chapter. The genealogist-turned-activist had deliberately sought out the prestigious *Post* to publicize the discriminatory behavior to which she had been subjected, and the article had the desired effect. Compared to past controversies over the DAR's racist policies, the speed of the changes that Ferguson's public charges triggered was remarkable. Only one day after the article was published, David A. Clarke, the white chairman of the District of Columbia's City Council, called a press conference during which he threatened to revoke the DAR's real estate tax exemption in the district. This threat had been unsuccessfully used before, most notably in 1946 when politicians and pundits denounced the DAR's ban against Hazel Scott. But in the 1980s the chances for passing a bill that would strip the Daughters of their tax privileges appeared to be much higher. If passed, such a law would have cost the Daughters $900,000 of additional taxes each year. Also important, the civil rights legislation of the 1960s provided the legal basis for taking the Daughters to court.[112]

Figure 5.4. Activist and eventual DAR member Lena Santos Ferguson, with a photograph of her great-grandfather, 1985. John Curtis Gay, in the photo, was a descendant of Ferguson's white ancestor Jonah Gay, who had fought for the United States in the American Revolution. Ferguson's activism forced the Daughters to allow more African American women to join the organization and pressured the DAR to finally acknowledge black soldiers' patriotism in the American Revolution. Photo © Associated Press. Photographer: Scott Stewart.

Ferguson was fully aware of these options but decided to pursue a course of action that she hoped would accomplish what had eluded the supporters of Marian Anderson and Hazel Scott. "I could have sued the organization and tried to destroy it," she wrote two years later. "But I wanted it to change and to make up for its past."[113] And this the DAR did within a matter of days. Confronted with the prospect of heavy financial losses and costly lawsuits, the DAR immediately tried to mend fences and ultimately consented to Ferguson's demands. Only two days after the publication of the *Washington Post* article, DAR President General Sarah M. King promised to assist Ferguson in finding a local chapter in the nation's capital and pledged "to work toward greater minority membership and participation in the DAR during my administration."[114] Meanwhile, behind closed doors, DAR leaders and Ferguson, who was represented by the law firm Hogan and Hartson, negotiated a revolutionary agreement that upended the vision of the nation the DAR had defended for almost a century. In this agreement, the DAR consented to issue a written apology to Ferguson, to adopt a new by-law that would prevent racial discrimination in local chapters, to support a pending federal bill that was intended to honor black soldiers' service during the American Revolution, to issue a pamphlet that would assist prospective members of color, and to research and publish the names of the Continental Army's African American members.[115]

Also astoundingly, within a two-year period the DAR implemented almost all of these promises. In April 1984 the Daughters adopted a historic resolution on "Black Patriots in the American Revolution," which officially honored "the heroic contributions made by black soldiers and patriots, who served their country with valor, helping to bring to a successful conclusion the American Revolution and to secure the sovereignty of this great Republic."[116] Meanwhile, President General King announced that the organization had appropriated $90,000 to hire black genealogist James Dent Walker to research the names of African Americans, Native Americans, and women who had made important contributions to the cause of independence during the Revolutionary Era. Walker subsequently penned the demanded pamphlet for prospective members that provided advice as well as resources for African Americans and members of other minorities who intended to join the DAR.[117] Even before Walker delved into his research, in November 1984 the DAR published *Black Courage, 1775–1783: Documentation of Black Participation in the American Revolution*, a 140-page book the organization had commissioned military historian Robert Ewell

Greene to write. By December, Lena Ferguson had become a member of the capital's Elizabeth Jackson Chapter and began to recruit other women of color. Two months later, Walker's article "Minorities in the American Revolution" became the first essay in the long history of the *DAR Magazine* that detailed African American soldiers' military service during the War of Independence. It was also the first time the publication featured the image of an African American who was not enslaved; it was a watercolor of a determined-looking black soldier with his rifle that challenged centuries of racist stereotyping. And in April 1985 the organization's Continental Congress passed a bylaw amendment that banned discrimination on the basis of race or creed in DAR chapters, the final demand to which the Daughters had consented in their negotiations with Ferguson.[118]

But the impact of Ferguson's quest did not stop there; her actions also affected the memory of black patriotism more generally. A resolution that urged patriotic organizations and historical societies to honor the 5,000 soldiers of color who had fought for the United States during the American Revolution was a direct outgrowth of Ferguson's campaign. Signed by President Ronald Reagan in March 1984 in an official White House ceremony, it had begun as a lobbying initiative that Ferguson's nephew Maurice Barboza launched after the capital's DAR chapters had rejected his aunt. In September 1983, Barboza had been able to convince Connecticut Congresswoman Nancy L. Johnson to introduce a resolution in the US House of Representatives that praised the heroic contributions of black soldiers to American independence. Members of the Congressional Black Caucus co-sponsored Johnson's resolution and convinced more than 250 representatives to vote for it. In the Senate the proposal likewise found broad bipartisan support. It was this resolution that Ferguson forced the DAR to support in her negotiations with Sarah King.[119]

A little more than a year after President Reagan signed the legislation, the national DAR, again spurred by Barboza and Ferguson, spearheaded a campaign for a memorial to the black men and women who had fought in the American Revolution. On July 4, 1985, DAR President General Sarah King went beyond the 1984 agreement, joining hands with Ferguson, Barboza, and members of a host of other patriotic organizations on the steps of Constitution Hall before marching to the proposed site on the National Mall. At a press conference she held prior to the march, King told reporters that the monument was "needed to raise public awareness of Black Participation in the Revolutionary War" and to honor "America's invisible patriots."[120] When the crowd of several hundred marchers arrived at the site, some of them stepped forward to read aloud the names of 200 of the 5,000 black soldiers who had participated in the American Revolution. To Ferguson, the sight of this scene was truly astounding. "I looked around in amazement at a scene I had never thought I would see in my life-time," she wrote later. "A smiling and flag waving crowd of both blacks and whites, including members of the DAR, was honoring the courage and heroism of forgotten black Revolutionary soldiers—just around the corner from the building where the most accomplished black opera singer of her time could not perform 46 years before."[121]

As unprecedented as this moment must have seemed to African Americans, however, it did not necessarily reflect a complete break with the DAR's racist past. Commenting on the changes the organization had initiated by 1985, a DÁR member surmised in a letter to former Congresswoman Clare Boothe Luce, who had challenged the organization's segregationist policy in 1946, "I have reason to believe that there is a lack of sincerity in these actions."[122] The organization's official resolutions as well as its actions in the 1980s suggest that there was some truth to this assessment. Any internal criticism of the organization's racial politics still led to swift punishment. In April 1984 DAR members Joyce K. Finley and Faith K. Tiberio had called for the impeachment of President General King for supporting the controversial amendment to the organization's bylaws that they said was intended to exclude black members; they were quickly reprimanded for disturbing "the harmony" of the organization. The DAR honored former Congresswoman Luce in 1984 with the organization's exclusive History Award for promoting the study of the American past, seemingly ignoring her challenge to the DAR's policy of white artists only almost forty years earlier, yet Finley and Tiberio were subjected to the same retributions that previous dissenters like Luce had suffered.[123]

Nor did the organization's acknowledgment of black heroism during the American Revolution prompt its leaders to reconsider the DAR's support for South Africa's racist regime. In 1985, the same year that the DAR called for a Black Revolutionary Patriots War Memorial, it passed a resolution that called for stable and friendly relations with the African country's government. Two years later, reacting to the Anti-Apartheid Act that Congress passed in 1986, the DAR protested efforts to "undermine" South Africa's regime and to legitimize the black African National Congress, which it denounced as a "Soviet-backed terrorist organization" that would "mean much less freedom for all peoples of South Africa."[124] Finally, although the Daughters expressed concern about the dire situation of many Indians, they said nothing about the economic problems that urban black communities faced across the country. While the Daughters readily acknowledged black citizens' contributions to American nation-building in the past, they did not consider supporting them in their quest for full equality in the present.

Some observers may have doubted the DAR's sincerity, but its leaders probably regarded the 1980s as a decade of victories and vindications. The Ferguson controversy gave the Daughters documented ammunition in their efforts to counter long-standing charges of racism, and a few commentators did acknowledge the Daughters' efforts. Even *Jet* magazine in 1985 praised the DAR's "courageous move" to publish Robert Ewell Greene's book *Black Courage* on African American participation in the Revolution.[125] At the same time, the presidency of Ronald Reagan gave the Daughters hope that their conservative vision of America might become a reality after all. The Reagan administration's staunch Cold War anticommunism, the president's opposition to government intervention, and his support for the traditional family as well as his efforts to roll back the civil rights movement's victories received much applause from the DAR. Reagan's focus on strong leadership and unwavering patriotism similarly lifted the Daughters' spirits. Unlike most of his predecessors after the 1940s, Reagan cherished the organization's support and addressed its members on several occasions. Nancy Reagan, moreover, strengthened the bonds between the White House and the DAR by becoming the eighth First Lady to join the organization since its founding year. The 1980s were also a time of continuing growth for the Daughters. By 1984, the organization had 212,000 members in 3,160 chapters across the country and abroad.[126] The end of the Cold War in 1989, which was widely hailed as an American victory, undoubtedly marked the high point of a decade that the Daughters and many fellow conservatives would remember fondly for years to come. Celebrating its centennial in 1990, the organization's members looked back with pride and no doubt felt that their organization continued to be vital to American patriotism.[127]

After the end of the Cold War, the Daughters remained dedicated to the DAR's goals, but contrary to their self-perception, the organization's impact on patriotism and the memory of the American past remained limited. In an increasingly diverse and democratized world of commemoration characterized by federal projects as well as by hundreds of regional and local initiatives, hereditary organizations such as the DAR were one voice among many and lost much of their influence. If America's cultural memory was diversified geographically, it was also democratized in terms of which social and ethnic groups were presented as being part of the American nation. Already during the 1980s, civil rights activists had established a number of museums and historic sites that shed light on the experiences of Indians and African Americans, a trend that continued through the last decade of the twentieth century. School textbooks also gave more room to ethnic minorities and women and tended to present them not just as victims but as active agents of historical change and patriotic contributors to US nation-building.[128]

Despite this radically altered patriotic and commemorative environment, the Daughters' long-standing ideological pillars proved resilient. Despite the concessions they had made in the 1980s, their nationalist ideology and interpretations of America's past had changed little, although some of their official resolutions were no longer passed unanimously and frequently became subject to heated debates during annual meetings. Yet, the Daughters remained staunchly opposed to immigration. Throughout the 1980s and 1990s, as the number of new immigrants surged to heights unseen since the early twentieth century, the DAR warned that unrestricted immigration would jeopardize the nation. Undocumented immigrants especially from Mexico, DAR leaders asserted, would contribute to higher crime and unemployment rates and strain the country's welfare system. From the Daughters' perspective, the wave of immigrants was also difficult to assimilate into US society because, they contended, these newcomers would refuse to learn English or familiarize themselves with US history and culture. Given such renewed fears that foreigners would erode American patriotism, the DAR denounced more liberal approaches to immigration, among them bilingualism and multiculturalism, as perilous experiments that would only exacerbate existing problems.[129]

Their views on women and the family also remained virtually the same. The stability of the nation, they said, depended not only on the traditional, heterosexual family but also on notions of femininity that did not challenge traditional gender hierarchies. In 1980 the DAR passed a resolution that called the nuclear family "the cornerstone of our entire Judeo-Christian social structure" and "the foundation for a strong American society." It warned of tendencies to redefine families in a way that would extend "family benefits" to homosexual or unmarried couples.[130] That same year, former Vice President General Isabel R. Ward insisted in the *DAR Magazine* that women were "most powerful and most influential" when they were "fulfilling their role as women—and that role is the nurture of the young, the formation of our cultural ideals and patterns and when necessary, the fierce defense of their young."[131] As in the early twentieth century, colonial women and pioneer mothers were seen as the epitome of this supposed truism, stoically enduring hardships and veering away from female respectability only temporarily to support their husbands to build the nation. The Daughters drew parallels between Revolutionary women who had taken up arms to defend the United States and women who had made careers for themselves in the US military in the late twentieth century, but they remained utterly opposed to women who sought to emulate Margaret Corbin's example on a permanent, professional basis. In an ironic twist, in 2000 the national DAR created the Margaret Cochran Corbin Award to honor servicewomen who had distinguished themselves through extraordinary military service. However, during a time when women constituted almost 15 percent of the US armed forces and frequently found themselves in combat situations, the prospect of women in combat remained anathema to the Daughters, who held to the argument that such forms of compromised femininity would jeopardize the nation's security.[132]

Race, too, remained a contentious issue, even in the face of the fundamental changes that Ferguson's quest for membership forced upon the DAR. The Daughters prided themselves on the Minority Military Service Project they initiated in 1985. African American students gained more visibility in DAR publications as more of them won DAR essay contests and were then featured in the organization's magazine. As for Native Americans, the Daughters also appeared to be intent on correcting some of the stereotypes they had helped to perpetuate. In 1991 the organization's leaders politely applauded a speech by W. Richard West Jr., the Cheyenne director of the newly built National Museum of the American Indian, when he reminded them that "the representation and interpretation of Indian culture" needed to be approached "without paternalism and without condescension."[133]

Even with the greater visibility of African Americans in DAR publications and hints of remorse over previous expressions of prejudice, the Daughters remained unwilling to discuss their racist past and seemed just as reluctant to fully embrace the idea of inclusionary civic nationalism in their interpretations of the nation's history. With regard to Marian Anderson, the organization still dismissed suggestions that it had practiced racial discrimination by banning her from Constitution Hall in 1939. After Anderson's death in 1993, as newspapers once more reported about her famous recital on the steps of the Lincoln Memorial, DAR President General Wayne Garrison Blair insisted that "race had nothing to do with the decision" to ban her from performing in Constitution Hall.[134] Several weeks after Blair's statement, the historian Scott A. Sandage, who had published an article on the DAR's role in the Anderson controversy in the *Journal of American History,* countered her claims in a letter to the *New York Times,* expressing his frustration with the organization's evasiveness. "Even 50 years later," Sandage commented, "the D.A.R. persists in denying its documented actions, proving itself again the guardian not of our history, but of its own."[135]

In the face of such unflattering assessments, the Daughters clung to their notions that they were indeed the guardians of America's history and that history should not dwell on race. Consequently, they repeatedly denounced the growing racial inclusiveness of high school and college textbooks about the nation's past. By the early 1990s such publications gave much more room to the history of racial and ethnic minorities, documenting the violent oppression they had faced and asking students to make sense of that violence in the context of US nation-building.[136] Like other conservative groups, the Daughters were appalled by what they regarded as poison for patriotism. In a 1992 resolution the DAR claimed that American history was "severely distorted by the theory of multiculturalism, which teaches ethnic identity to enhance self-esteem instead of knowledge and skills." Such diversity, the resolution warned, would weaken the idea of a united nation and a unique American identity.[137]

In the following years, former STOP ERA leader Phyllis Schlafly, still a high-ranking DAR officer, minced no words when elaborating on the dangers of inclusiveness in current academic interpretations of US history. Writing in the *DAR Magazine* in 1993, Schlafly asserted that college students were "burdened with the current academic fads called diversity, multiculturalism, Political Correctness (P.C.), and deconstructionism." Earlier history books had inspired and encouraged students because of their stories of "grandeur, heroism and achievement." More recent publications, she wrote, were tainted by a left-wing bias and would only dampen patriotic sentiments with their "broad-scale attack on Western civilization and historically DWEMs (Dead White European Males)."[138] In 1995, shortly after the National Center for History in the Schools released its National Standards for United States History, which asked teachers to familiarize students with the nation's diverse past, the Daughters joined the public outcry among traditionalists.[139] Like conservative critics such as talk-radio celebrity Rush Limbaugh, Phyllis Schlafly reiterated her attack on political correctness and claimed it was "historically false" to write accounts of the past "in which all ethnic groups except white males are portrayed as victims." Only if schools would "return to the teaching of American history as it really happened" could the United States survive "as a free nation."[140]

The Daughters lamented what they perceived as the declining cultural power of the white warrior hero whom they had praised since the 1890s as the icon of US nationalism. On the eve of the twenty-first century, the DAR proved that conservative notions of gender and exclusionist nationalism were slow to wane in a society that had long prided itself on the nation's civic creed.

Conclusion

In the twenty-first century, the DAR no longer grabs headlines or dominates discussions about patriotism, but the history of its commemorative activism raises important questions about the complex entanglements between conservatism and feminism in the past and the present. First, probing the organization's ideology and activism adds depth to scholarly accounts of conservatism in US history because doing so points toward conspicuous historical continuities. As historians have come to acknowledge the impossibility of understanding twentieth-century America without a thorough analysis of this influential if heterogeneous political movement, a deluge of studies has explored its evolution. In general, historians have defined modern conservatism as a post–World War II phenomenon whose ideological commonalities revolved around anticommunism, laissez-faire capitalism, limited authority of the federal government, opposition to racial equality, and strong support for traditional interpretations of gender and sexuality.[1] Shedding light on additional facets of this movement, the present study confirms that women's grassroots activism played a key role in conservatism's ascent and suggests that many of the movement's defining ideological features, albeit in different forms, were already in place during or possibly even before World War I.[2] The DAR might have adjusted its activism to changing historical circumstances, but its underlying ideas about race, gender, and the nation changed little over the course of the twentieth century. Although World War II marked a turning point in the history of US conservatism, the Daughters' memorial campaigns suggest significant continuities across the twentieth century while also indicating that white middle-class women were crucial bridge figures who connected the prewar and postwar periods.

The analysis of DAR activism adds another layer of complexity to the question of whether conservative women can justifiably be called feminists.

As with conservatism, the heterogeneity of feminist ideologies in the twentieth-century United States makes precise definitions difficult. Nancy Cott has argued that feminism in the interwar period revolved around a general opposition to sex hierarchy, the conviction that women's circumstances are not predestined but socially constructed, and consequently the idea that women need to identify themselves as a social group to address their grievances.[3] Radical feminists of the 1970s went beyond such initial attempts to understand women's oppression. They dismissed liberal feminists' efforts to work within the electoral system to reform society and regarded men as enemies, advocated separation, and called for the overthrow of patriarchy. So-called politicos, by contrast, interpreted women's subjugation from a Marxist perspective and stressed that race, class, and gender oppression were inseparably entwined. Like radical feminists, they considered moderates' reform agenda futile but believed that men could become important allies in the struggle for revolutionary change.[4]

Regardless of feminists' factional and ideological differences, the Daughters of the American Revolution consistently vilified activists who claimed that label and argued that their challenge to the social and political status quo would only hasten America's demise. The DAR generally deemed patriarchy essential to the nation's survival, dismissed the idea that gender was a social construct, and viewed separation and revolution as foolish fantasies. By paying tribute to heroic female helpmates while lauding men as the true agents of nation-building, the organization reinforced gender difference and affirmed male privilege. Yet, the DAR did engage in activism that demonstrated women's social, cultural, and political agency, and its assertive challenge to the male-centeredness of US nationalism allowed its members to push the boundaries of what women could do in the public sphere. While gender scholars might take exception to calling the Daughters feminists, the organization's history does beg the question of whether historians need to consider a broader definition of feminism to make sense of conservative women's activism.[5] In her work on female right-wing populism in post–World War II California, the historian Michelle Nickerson contends that "the process of creating a conservative feminist consciousness is . . . a project of cognitive dissonance, selective memory, and mythmaking."[6] The DAR's history affirms many of Nickerson's findings and reveals that historical memory was crucial to the emergence of a particular form of conservative feminism that abounded with such dissonances.

Another important question that the organization's history raises is why the Daughters were and remain so popular. As the United States enters the third decade of the twenty-first century, more than 185,000 members continue the organization's educational, patriotic, and commemorative work in 3,000 chapters across the country and abroad, which makes it the country's largest hereditary patriotic organization. In 2013 the DAR actually reported its largest gain in membership since 1921.[7] In part, these impressive numbers may be explained by the growing popularity and democratization of genealogy. While searching for and documenting one's roots has long been popular, millions of Americans have taken up this hobby since the 1970s. Boosted by the popular television series *Roots*, which first aired in 1977 and tells the history of a black family from slavery to the Jim Crow era, the efforts of citizens of color to trace their ancestry have participated in a process to make sense of their families' roles in US nation-building and the brutal attempts to exclude them from national membership.[8]

Spearheaded by women like Karen Farmer and Lena Ferguson, this movement convinced many black women to use the DAR's genealogical resources to trace their ancestry and to join the organization to honor their forebears. In the twenty-first century, black members remain a small minority, but their visibility in the DAR has increased exponentially since the 1980s. In New York City in 2012, Wilhelmena Rhodes Kelly became the first black founding regent of a DAR chapter. African American members and their contributions to genealogical research and DAR activities have been regularly featured in the organization's magazine *American Spirit* and on its website.[9] African American Daughters even began to hold an annual luncheon during the DAR's Continental Congress in Washington, DC. These "Daughters of Color," as they call themselves, most likely agree with Wilhelmena Kelly's reasons for becoming involved in an organization that had discriminated against black citizens for so many years. "They are welcoming," Kelly told the *New York Times*. "They are committed to remembering these people, and as a woman of color, why not join the D.A.R.? Why not make our presence felt?"[10]

The presence of Farmer, Ferguson, Kelly, and other African American Daughters did indeed leave a lasting imprint on both the organization's membership and its memorialization of black America. In 2002 the DAR's museum in Washington, DC, opened the exhibit "Forgotten Patriots: African American and American Indian Service in the Revolutionary War, 1775–1783," which followed the publication of a book by the same title. In

2008 the Daughters published a second edition of this volume, which documents the contributions of almost 6,600 black, Indian, and mixed-race soldiers to American independence. In the following decade, the organization's monthly magazine published more articles on African Americans than it had in the entire twentieth century. The articles laud the bravery of African American soldiers who served in the Continental Army as well as the patriotism of other people of color who contributed to the cause of the American Revolution.[11]

Black women also have received unprecedented attention in the DAR's magazine. The African American colonial-era poet Phillis Wheatley as well as black modern-day writers and politicians such as Toni Morrison, Shirley Chisholm, and Condoleezza Rice have been featured and acknowledged in *American Spirit* as women who also "shaped our country's history."[12] And the Daughters finally tried to make amends for barring Marian Anderson from its auditorium on the eve of World War II; in 2009 the DAR joined with the Abraham Lincoln Bicentennial Commission to pay tribute to Anderson's famous recital at the Lincoln Memorial. "The DAR deeply regrets that Marian Anderson was not given the opportunity to perform her 1939 Easter concert in Constitution Hall because of her race," the organization stated in a press release, calling it "a pivotal event in the struggle for racial equality."[13] Such public expressions of remorse, together with the DAR's continuing efforts to memorialize the patriotic contributions of white women and Native Americans to US nation-building, add weight to the Daughters' argument that the organization is "one of the most inclusive genealogical societies in the country."[14]

If the DAR's popularity in the twenty-first century stems in part from a more democratic membership policy and egalitarian perspective on America's cultural memory, many members continue to be drawn to its conservative nationalism. In fact, despite the organization's new commitment to diversity, the conservative continuities that characterized its ideology in the twentieth century are still discernible in the new millennium. Before and after 9/11, its members unanimously passed resolutions that called for lower immigration quotas "to preserve social and civil cohesion" and reaffirmed declarations from the 1980s and 1990s in which they had demanded to make English the official language of the United States, rejected bilingual education, and denounced "the use of hyphenated nationalistic terms."[15] Other resolutions restated their resistance to the civil rights movement, castigating "special interest groups" that claimed "rights above and beyond those set forth in the Constitution," and reiterated the organization's hostility toward the United Nations. The DAR's steadfast support for the US military and adamant opposition to gun control likewise reflect the continuing appeal of conservative core beliefs among its members.[16] These ideological continuities suggest that the DAR was much more mainstream than its liberal critics were willing to admit, and it is conceivable that numerous members applauded the election of President Donald Trump, who has advocated the type of exclusionary ethnic nationalism the Daughters embraced for much of the twentieth century.

Against the backdrop of these ideological continuities with the organization's constant wavering between civic and ethnic nationalism, one wonders how the DAR's more diverse membership reconciles competing visions of patriotism in the age of Donald Trump. Barbara Truesdell's research on the Daughters' patriotic rituals that she conducted in the 1990s provides answers that are also applicable in the twenty-first century. By invoking a quasireligious model for civic loyalty, Truesdell argues, the DAR evokes "a sense of mission larger than individuals' lives, deeper than the present moment's trials, calling upon loyalty and communal efforts to realize a vision of a shared, better future, justifying that vision by invoking the lessons of the past." It is this multivocal abstraction, Truesdell notes, that "allows disparate groups and dissenting beliefs to exist within a single institutional entity by maintaining membership without necessarily adopting every article of dogma and tradition endorsed by the group's leaders or the group's official stance."[17] Consequently, even African American and white southern Daughters can coexist within the DAR because its members share notions of patriotism that allow for individualized ways of honoring and interpreting their ancestors' contributions to the nation's founding. The organization's decision in 2013 to cease passing official—and often controversial—resolutions to lobby for major policy changes probably facilitates harmony among the organization's members by depoliticizing their activism.[18]

While it remains to be seen how these recent developments will affect the DAR's commemorative, educational, and patriotic activism in the years to come, its history reminds us that the Daughters played a vital role in shaping and disseminating conservative notions of nationalism that continue to reverberate in the new millennium. Memory was of crucial importance in this endeavor because it helped make the abstract idea of the nation and accompanying notions of gender and race seem real and meaningful. Studying the Daughters of the American Revolution thus helps us better understand the persistence of a particular strand of US nationalism that regards national, racial, and gender identities not only as natural and unchanging but as part and parcel of a patriotic equilibrium that must be protected and preserved.

Notes

Introduction

1. Grace D. Johnson, "A Plea for the Heroines of the American Revolution in History," *DAR Magazine*, April 1914, 269.

2. For a southern perspective, see Brundage, "White Women and the Politics of Historical Memory"; Cox, *Dixie's Daughters*; Faust, "Altars of Sacrifice"; Gulley, "Women and the Lost Cause"; Janney, *Burying the Dead but Not the Past*; McMichael, "Memories Are Short but Monuments Lengthen Remembrances"; Gardner, *Blood and Irony*; Mills and Simpson, *Monuments to the Lost Cause*; Parrott, "Love Makes Memory Eternal"; Talley, *Southern Women Novelists and the Civil War*. An exception is Julie Des Jardins's study on women and historical writing in the United States, but the Daughters of the American Revolution play only a marginal role in her study (*Women and the Historical Enterprise in America*).

3. Benowitz, *Challenge and Change*; Benowitz, *Days of Discontent*; K. Blee, *Women of the Klan*; Brennan, *Wives, Mothers, and the Red Menace*; Critchlow, *Phyllis Schlafly and Grassroots Conservatism*; Erickson, "I Have Not Had One Fact Disproven"; Erickson, "We Want No Teachers Who Say There Are Two Sides to Every Question"; Jeansonne, *Women of the Far Right*; Marshall, *Splintered Sisterhood*; Morgan, *Women and Patriotism in Jim Crow America*; Nickerson, *Mothers of Conservatism*; Rymph, *Republican Women*.

4. Although the organization has received increasing scholarly attention in recent decades, historians have primarily focused on its racism and antiradicalism in the interwar period. Among those studies are Delegard, *Battling Miss Bolsheviki*; Medlicott, "Constructing Territory, Constructing Citizenship"; Medlicott, "One Social Milieu, Paradoxical Responses"; Morgan, "Regions Remote from Revolutionary Scenes"; Morgan, *Women and Patriotism in Jim Crow America*; Nielsen, *Un-American Womanhood*; Strange, "Sisterhood of Blood."

5. Medlicott and Heffernan, "Autograph of a Nation"; Teachout, "Forging Memory."

6. Anderson, *Imagined Communities*.

7. Given the DAR's elite membership, I pay attention to class because of the intersectional nature of gender and race, but since a number of fine studies have already examined this particular aspect, it will not be the study's focus. See, for example, Marshall, *Splintered Sisterhood*; Morgan, "Regions Remote from Revolutionary Scenes"; Nielsen, *Un-American Womanhood*.

8. DAR, *Constitution and By-Laws of the National Society of the Daughters of the American Revolution* (Washington, DC: DAR, 1890), Article II; US Senate, "Report of the Daughters of

the American Revolution: 1890 to 1897," 55th Congress, 3d Session, Document no. 164, February 23, 1899 (Washington, DC: Government Printing Office, 1899), 11–13.

9. "By Patriotic Women," *Washington Post,* August 10, 1891, 8; "Address of the State Regent, Mrs. John McClure, First State Conference of the Arkansas Daughters of the American Revolution, Little Rock, Arkansas, February 22, 1909," Western Reserve Historical Society (hereafter cited as WRHS), 22; "Women as Patriots," *American Monthly Magazine,* November 1897, 583, 586.

10. "Patriotism Necessary to Good Citizenship," *DAR Magazine,* June 1914, 355–356; Mrs. Benjamin A. Fessenden, "Woman, Teacher of Patriotism," *American Monthly Magazine,* July 1905, 11.

11. On Republican Motherhood, see Kerber, "Republican Mother and the Woman Citizen"; Norton, *Liberty's Daughters.* On true womanhood, see Roberts, "True Womanhood Revisited"; Welter, "Cult of True Womanhood, 1820–1860."

12. US Senate, "Report of the Daughters of the American Revolution: 1890 to 1897," 17–19.

13. Weil, *Family Trees,* 112–179; Morgan, "Noble Pursuit," 135–151; Morgan, "'Home and Country,'" 38, 44, 56–57; St. Paul, *History of the National Society SAR,* 25, 67; Cox, *Dixie's Daughters,* 50; Davies, *Patriotism on Parade,* 63, 77, 95–98, 135.

14. Truesdell, "God, Home, and Country," 21–23; Gibbs, *The DAR,* 19, 59; Morgan, "'Home and Country,'" 37–60.

15. On the Daughters' antiradicalism, see Nielsen, *Un-American Womanhood;* Wendt, "Defenders of Patriotism."

16. Breuilly, *Nationalism and the State,* 2; Calhoun, *Nationalism,* 4–5; Yuval-Davis, *Gender and Nation,* 21; Billig, *Banal Nationalism;* Anderson, *Imagined Communities;* D. Brown, "Are There Good and Bad Nationalisms?"; Fahrmeir, *Citizenship,* 2–4.

17. Yuval-Davis, *Gender and Nation,* 21; Nieguth, "Beyond Dichotomy"; Gerstle, *American Crucible.*

18. Butler, *Bodies That Matter;* Butler, *Gender Trouble;* Butler, *Undoing Gender.*

19. Pettegrew, "The Soldier's Faith"; Linenthal, *Changing Images of the Warrior Hero in America,* 27; Goldstein, *War and Gender,* 265–272, 274–279.

20. Yuval-Davis, *Gender and Nation,* 22–24; Mayer, "Gender Ironies of Nationalism"; McClintock, "Family Feuds"; McClintock, "No Longer in a Future Heaven."

21. Morgan, *Women and Patriotism in Jim Crow America,* 3.

22. Zerubavel, "From 'Social Memories: Steps towards a Sociology of the Past,'" 223; Confino, "Collective Memory and Cultural History: Problems of Method," 1398–1400; Wood, "Memory's Remains," 144; Schwartz, *Abraham Lincoln and the Forge of National Memory,* 18; Brundage, "Introduction: No Deed but Memory," 3–5.

23. Smith and Gellner, "The Nation: Real or Imagined?," 362; Confino, "Collective Memory and Cultural History," 1402.

24. Assmann, "Collective Memory and Cultural Identity." See also Assmann, *Cultural Memory and Early Civilization.* Assmann's conceptual differentiation is similar to arguments made by John Bodnar (*Remaking America*) and David Glassberg (*Sense of History*), who distinguish between "official" or "public" memories (Bodnar) and unofficial or "vernacular" memories (Glassberg). Assmann's distinction, however, allows for a more precise analysis of the tensions and dynamic interrelationships between elites' and non-elites' communicative and cultural memories.

Chapter 1. "Woman Proved Herself Man's Helpmate": Nationalism, Gender, and the Memory of the American Revolution

1. St. Paul, *History of the National Society SAR*, 10; Mary S. Lockwood, "Women Worthy of Honor," *Washington Post*, July 12, 1890, 8.

2. St. Paul, *History of the National Society SAR*, 16–18; "Building Up History," *Washington Post*, July 10, 1904, E8; "Honor Mrs. Lockwood," *Washington Post*, July 11, 1915, E10; William O. McDowell, "Hannah Arnett's Life," *Washington Post*, July 21, 1890; Eugenia Washington, "Daughters of the American Revolution," *Washington Post*, August 17, 1890, 7; William O. McDowell, to Every Member of the National Society of the Daughters of the American Revolution, April 13, 1904, William Osborne McDowell Papers, vertical file, WRHS; Lockwood and Sherwood, *Story of the Records D.A.R.*, 20–25. In the following years, the founders of the DAR vehemently argued over who had actually founded the organization and which date should be regarded as the actual founding day. Flora Adams Darling in particular believed that she had been slighted in the official accounts of the DAR's founding, claiming that it was she who founded and organized the patriotic association. Eventually, these disputes led Darling to create a rival organization, which she named the Daughters of the Revolution. See "A Question of Origin," *Washington Post*, August 2, 1891, 4; "Mrs. Darling Answers," *Washington Post*, August 5, 1891, 3; "Mrs. Darling's Compromise," *Washington Post*, November 22, 1891, 16; "Mrs. Darling Snubbed," *Washington Post*, November 30, 1891, 8; Desha, *The True Story of the Origins of the National Society of the DAR;* "Reply to Mrs. Darling," *Washington Post*, April 23, 1901, 4. For more information on the founding period of the Daughters of the Revolution, see Davies, *Patriotism on Parade*, 67–69.

3. Kammen, *Mystic Chords of Memory*, 52.

4. Kammen, *Mystic Chords of Memory*, 42–80.

5. Lowenthal, *The Past is a Foreign Country*, 105–116; Brundage, *The Southern Past*, 17–18; McConnell, "Reading the Flag," 102–103; O'Leary, *To Die For*, 4.

6. O'Leary, *To Die For*, 29, 32; Pettegrew, "The Soldier's Faith," 49–73; Blight, *Race and Reunion*, 72.

7. Lowenthal, *The Past Is a Foreign Country*, 116–121; West, *Domesticating History*, 42; Davies, *Patriotism on Parade*, 49–50; St. Paul, *History of the National Society SAR*, 1; Kammen, *Mystic Chords of Memory*, 88–160.

8. Even before the Civil War, some white middle-class women had engaged in historic preservation campaigns to keep alive the memory of the American past and to strengthen national unity. The Mount Vernon Ladies' Association was the most prominent example. Founded in 1854, it raised funds to buy the home of America's first president, George Washington, in Virginia and transform it into a museum (West, *Domesticating History*, 1–37).

9. Janney, *Burying the Dead but Not the Past*, 2–8; Janney, "Right to Love and to Mourn"; Davies, *Patriotism on Parade*, 38, 76; Mills, introduction; Brundage, "White Women and the Politics of Historical Memory"; Cox, *Dixie's Daughters*, 1–6; Morgan, *Women and Patriotism in Jim Crow America*, 37–39.

10. P. Baker, "The Domestication of Politics," 631–633; A. Scott, *Natural Allies*, 1–73; Cott, *The Grounding of Modern Feminism*, 16–19. On true womanhood, see Roberts, "True Womanhood Revisited"; Welter, "Cult of True Womanhood."

11. A. Scott, *Natural Allies*, 80–120, 135–139; P. Baker, "Domestication of Politics," 632–638; Gere, *Intimate Practices*, 2–5; Chafe, *Paradox of Change*, 9–11.

12. Davies, *Patriotism on Parade,* 57–61; Hunter, *Century of Service,* 27–38; "Last D.A.R. Founder," *Washington Post,* April 7, 1913, 3; "Mary Desha Is Dead," *Washington Post,* January 30, 1911, 2.

13. Davies, *Patriotism on Parade,* 63.

14. Weil, *Family Trees,* 112–179; Morgan, "Noble Pursuit?," 135–151; Morgan, "'Home and Country,'" 38, 44, 56–57; St. Paul, *History of the National Society SAR,* 25, 67; Davies, *Patriotism on Parade,* 63, 77, 95–98, 135.

15. Mrs. J. H. Robbins, "Address," *American Monthly Magazine,* August 1894, 148; "Daughters of the Revolution," *Chicago Daily Tribune,* May 20, 1893, 2; Angeline Scott, "A Defense of Genealogical Literature and Research," *New York Times,* September 17, 1904, 26; "Patriotism," *American Monthly Magazine,* March 1894, 302–304; Johnston, *Iowa Daughters of the American Revolution,* 191.

16. "Address of the President General, Mrs. Matthew T. Scott," *American Monthly Magazine,* May 1912, 205; "Michigan Women Perpetuate Historic Spots," *Detroit Free Press,* January 9, 1916, 3.

17. Thomas Forsythe Nelson, "How Ancestry Figures," *Washington Post,* June 3, 1906, E8; Mrs. William Conyers Clark, "Work of Georgia D.A.R. Disproves the Charges of Bishop C.D. Williams," *Atlanta Constitution,* July 11, 1909, C6; "Reminiscence," in Record Book Presented by the First Historian, Charity Cook Chapter (Homer, MI), Records of the Daughters of the American Revolution of Michigan (hereafter cited as Michigan DAR Records), Michigan Historical Collections, Bentley Library, University of Michigan, Ann Arbor, (hereafter cited as MHC); Anne Rogers Minor, "The Deeper Meaning of Our Daughters of the American Revolution," *DAR Magazine,* June 1918, 345 (quotes).

18. "By Patriotic Women," *Washington Post,* August 10, 1891, 8; "Address of the State Regent, Mrs. John McClure, First State Conference of the Arkansas Daughters of the American Revolution, Little Rock, Arkansas, February 22, 1909," WRHS, 22; Bryant quoted in "Women as Patriots," *American Monthly Magazine,* November 1897, 583, 586.

19. "Patriotism Necessary to Good Citizenship," *DAR Magazine,* June 1914, 355–356; Mrs. Benjamin A. Fessenden, "Woman, Teacher of Patriotism," *American Monthly Magazine,* July 1905, 11. On Republican Motherhood, see Kerber, "Republican Mother and the Woman Citizen"; M. Nash, "Rethinking Republican Motherhood"; Norton, *Liberty's Daughters.*

20. On the New Woman, see Patterson, *American New Woman Revisited;* Patterson, *Beyond the Gibson Girl;* Richardson and Willis, *New Woman in Fiction and Fact.*

21. Quoted in "Daughters of Patriots," *Boston Daily Globe,* September 26, 1895, 3.

22. Foster quoted in "Daughters of the Revolution," *New York Times,* February 23, 1896, 12.

23. See, for example, "Daughters of the Revolution," *Washington Post,* February 15, 1898, 6; "All the Woman's Club News of Georgia," *Atlanta Constitution,* July 16, 1905, D6.

24. Smith quoted in "D.A.R. at Lowell," *Boston Daily Globe,* October 17, 1900, 4.

25. Small quoted in "Craigie House Scene of Gathering of Many Patriotic Georgia Women," *Atlanta Constitution,* November 6, 1903, 3. See also "Dr. Steele on Womanhood," *New York Times,* May 22, 1899, 5; "Patriotism of Women," *Washington Post,* February 23, 1904, 9; "Honor is Paid to 'Old Glory,'" *Atlanta Constitution,* June 1912, 4.

26. "The D.A.R.'s Great Work," *Washington Post,* April 19, 1910, 6.

27. Berkin, *Revolutionary Mothers,* xi–xiv; Des Jardins, *Women and the Historical Enterprise in America,* 17–25.

28. Janet Elizabeth Richards, "Heroic Women of the American Revolution," *American Monthly Magazine,* September 1892, 278.

29. "The Dolly Madison Chapter's Meeting," *Washington Post,* April 19, 1894, 5; Jennie J. B. Goodwin, "The Women of the Revolution," *American Monthly Magazine,* October 1897, 350–357; "Quaint Costumes Worn in Pageant," *Boston Daily Globe,* May 23, 1915, 4; "Daughters to Confer," *Washington Post,* February 23, 1897, 2.

30. The DAR's magazine underwent several name changes between 1892, when it was first published, and the twenty-first century. From July 1892 to June 1913, it was published as the *American Monthly Magazine;* in July 1913 it became the *Daughters of the American Revolution Magazine* until November 1937; from December 1937 to June 1946, it was published as the *National Historical Magazine;* thereafter, it became once again the *Daughters of the American Revolution Magazine;* beginning with the July–August 2001 issue, it was published as *American Spirit.* All issues of the DAR's magazine are accessible on the organization's website, at services.dar.org/members/magazine_archive/default.cfm.

31. "The Inspiration of Revolutionary Memories," *American Monthly Magazine,* May 1902, 573–578; "The Women of 1776," *Lexington Herald,* May 6, 1906, 6; Annie Morehead Whitfield, "Heroines of the American Revolution," *American Monthly Magazine,* February 1893, 205; Mrs. John F. Develin, "Pennsylvania's Patriotic Women during the Revolution," *DAR Magazine,* April 1915, 252–257; Emily Hendree Park, "Sarah McIntosh: A Heroine of the Revolution," *American Monthly Magazine,* October 1908, 878; "Monitions from Our Mothers of the American Revolution," *American Monthly Magazine,* October 1893, 389–392; Mrs. Charles C. Abbott, "Molly Aiken," *American Monthly Magazine,* September 1910, 213–215.

32. Mary Merrill Mann, "A Revolutionary Heroine," *DAR Magazine,* September 1916, 161.

33. Mary Elizabeth Springer, "Men and Women of the Revolution," *American Monthly Magazine,* February 1896, 137–140; Camille Benson Bird, "Women of Revolutionary Times in New England," *American Monthly Magazine,* June 1913, 303–306; Claudine Rhett, "Emily Geiger: A Heroine of the Revolution," *American Monthly Magazine,* March 1896, 302–304; Sarah Upson, "A Woman's Courage," *American Monthly Magazine,* November 1895, 405; "Women of 1776," *Lexington Herald,* May 6, 1906, 6.

34. Mary Virginia Ellet Cabell, "A Daughter of the American Revolution—Betsey Zane, of Virginia," *American Monthly Magazine,* March 1901, 229–233; "A Woman Patriot," *American Monthly Magazine,* February 1893, 225–226; "A New Jersey Heroine," *DAR Magazine,* December 1914, 339.

35. Butterfield, "Lie There My Darling, while I Avenge Ye!"; Berkin, *Revolutionary Mothers,* 138–139; Alice Burke, "Molly Pitcher," *American Monthly Magazine,* July–December, 1898, 418–426; Reginald Pelham Bolton, "Margaret Corbin," *New York Times,* April 27, 1902, SM4; "Tablets Marking Historic Sites and Other Memorials," *American Monthly Magazine,* January 1909, 12–18.

36. See Young, *Masquerade,* 3–11, 284–292; J. Richards, "Heroic Women of the American Revolution," *American Monthly Magazine,* September 1892, 286–287; Grace M. Pierce, "Three American Women Pensioned for Military Service," *DAR Magazine,* September 1917, 140–145; Mrs. John Gates Jr., "Contributions of Women to the American Revolution," *DAR Magazine,* September 1931, 544–545.

37. Hume, "Press, Published History, and Regional Lore," 200–209; "Southern Battles," *Atlanta Constitution,* February 23, 1895, 2; "The Grave of Nancy Hart," *Atlanta Constitution,* October 8, 1901, 5; Wallace Putnam Reed, "Search for Nancy Hart's Grave Raises a Question as to Whether or Not There Ever Was a Nancy Hart," *Atlanta Constitution,* October 14, 1901, 3; Mrs. Julius L. Brown, "Nancy Hart," *American Monthly Magazine,* January 1902, 4–10; James Waddy Austin, "Ladies-Daughters of the American Revolution," October 16, 1905, folder 1,

box 1, Daughters of the American Revolution, Atlanta Chapter Records (hereafter cited as DAR Atlanta Chapter Records), Atlanta History Center Archive (hereafter cited as AHCA), Atlanta, GA; "Session Was Interesting," *Atlanta Constitution,* November 22, 1906, 4; "Splendid Record Made by Georgia D.A.R. in 1909," *Atlanta Constitution,* January 9, 1910, E2; "Habersham Chapter Shows Tableaux for Georgia Day," *Atlanta Constitution,* February 14, 1910, 4; "The Historical Pageant," *Atlanta Constitution,* June 19, 1914, 8.

38. "Piedmont Chapter Presents Picture to Georgia Today," *Atlanta Constitution,* November 25, 1916, 7; Acts and Resolutions of the General Assembly of the State of Georgia, 1916, Part IV.—Resolutions, 1916, vol. 1, 1049 (sequential number 344).

39. "D.A.R. November 13th '95," folder 1, box 1, DAR Western Reserve Chapter Records, WRHS; "Recollections of Revolutionary Times," *American Monthly Magazine,* January 1896, 1–8; Goodwin "The Women of the Revolution," *American Monthly Magazine,* October 1897, 350; "Historical Research Work for the Public Schools," *Atlanta Constitution,* December 17, 1911, 13.

40. Florence Hague Becker, "Hidden History in Chapter Names," *DAR Magazine,* April 1932, 203–207; Ward, *State History of the New Jersey DAR,* 65, 71, 156; DAR Georgia State Society, *Chapter Histories,* 74; Lester, *Ohio State History of the DAR,* 193, 115; Clarkson, *Historical Records of the Michigan DAR,* 95.

41. "What We Are Doing and Chapter Work," *American Monthly Magazine,* July–December 1898, 139; Marion Howard Brazier, "'Real Daughters' of the American Revolution," reprint from *Patriotic Review,* n.d., folder Daughters of the American Revolution 1905, box 825, Breckinridge Family Papers, Library of Congress, Washington, DC (hereafter cited as LOC); "Another Real Daughter Dies," *DAR Magazine,* August 1913, 467; Mrs. Henry C. Lytton to Dear Sir, January 16, 1905, folder 2, box 5, Orlando John Hodge Papers, WRHS; DAR, *Proceedings of the Twenty-First Continental Congress of the National Society DAR* (1912), 744–746, DAR Archives of the National Society DAR, Washington, DC; "Real Daughters," *American Monthly Magazine,*" July 1909, 19–20; Mary S. Andrews, "A Real Daughter," *DAR Magazine,* April 1914, 246; "Death of a Real Daughter," *DAR Magazine,* July 1915, 36.

42. "Acceptance of Bust of Mrs. Mary Hammond Washington," *American Monthly Magazine,* May 1912, 264; "Stories of the American Revolution," *DAR Magazine,* August 1916, 105–106; "A 'Real Daughter,'" *Philadelphia Inquirer,* December 17, 1898, 13.

43. Nellie V. Mark, "The Effect of the War of the Revolution on the Character of the Women," *American Monthly Magazine,* June 1899, 1209.

44. Goodwin, "The Women of the Revolution," *American Monthly Magazine,* October 1897, 356.

45. Hagemann, "Of 'Manly Valor' and 'German Honor,'" 219; Pettegrew, "Soldier's Faith."

46. Mrs. John McClure, "Address of the State Regent," First State Conference of the Arkansas DAR, Little Rock, February 22, 1909, 23.

47. "Athens Chapter," *American Monthly Magazine,* December 1892, 633–646; Mrs. F. G. De Fontaine, "Neglected Graves of Revolutionary Heroes," *American Monthly Magazine,* October 1892, 315–321; Mary J. Seymour, "The Minute Man of the American Revolution," *American Monthly Magazine,* February 1893, 172–181; Henry S. Curtis, "The Valley Forge of To-Day," *American Monthly Magazine,* March 1912, 97–100; "Our Sea Forces of the Revolution," *DAR Magazine,* September 1916, 149–161; Edward Hale Brush, "Memorial to Nathan Hale, Hero and Martyr," *DAR Magazine,* October 1917, 195–201; "Report of the Daughters of the American Revolution, 1890–1897," 59, 63–64, 67–78; Mrs. F. G. De Fontaine, "Neglected Graves of Revolutionary Heroes," *American Monthly Magazine,* October 1892; "Decorate Heroes' Graves,"

New York Times, April 26, 1897, 3; "Memorial Exercises for the Men Who Fought for Independence of the Colonies," *Worcester Spy*, May 31, 1901, 1; Ida T. Spencer, "Decoration of Revolutionary Graves on Friday, July 11th," *Atlanta Constitution*, July 6, 1913, B8; "D.A.R. to Mark 27 Graves," *Washington Post*, May 30, 1915, 8; Massachusetts DAR, *History of the Massachusetts Daughters of the American Revolution*, 46, 80–81; "Outline History of the Sarah Caswell Angell Chapter," Historian's Book, Started May 1913, box 5, Sarah Caswell Angell Chapter, Ann Arbor, box 5, Michigan DAR Records; Clarkson, *Historical Records of the Michigan DAR*, 142.

48. "A Memorial Day for Revolutionary Soldiers," *Atlanta Constitution*, October 30, 1910, E8.

49. Schwartz, "Social Change and Collective Memory," 232 (quote); Lengel, *Inventing George Washington*, x, 65.

50. Elizabeth Gadsby, "Washington's Wedding Day," *American Monthly Magazine*, March 1909, 262–263; "Celebration of Washington's Birthday at Memorial Continental Hall," *DAR Magazine*, March 1914, 131–132; McLean quoted in "Ten-Year Marriage? Absurd,—D.A.R.-Ters," *New York Times*, January 7, 1905, 7.

51. "Tablets Marking Historic Sites and Other Memorials," *American Monthly Magazine*, January 1909, 12–18; Edith Marden Ridout, "Marking the Spot Where Washington Resigned," *DAR Magazine*, July 1916, 7–11; Elson, *Guardians of Tradition*, 194 (quote).

52. On this movement, see Lindgren, *Preserving Historic New England*; West, *Domesticating History*.

53. "To Restore Old Fort Cralo," *New York Times*, November 13, 1899, 4; "Gives Historic Edifice," *Chicago Daily Tribune*, February 26, 1899, 5; Barrington, *Historic Restorations of the DAR*; "Gov. Clinton's House Rescued," *New York Times*, January 21, 1898, 1; "General George Clinton," *American Monthly Magazine*, August 1908, 428–435.

54. "A Patriotic Lawn Party," *New York Times*, May 23, 1897, 5; "White Plains Gay on 225th Birthday," *New York Times*, November 22, 1908, 16; Lindgren, "Constant Incentive to Patriotic Citizenship"; Lindgren, *Preserving Historic New England*, 5–10; "Session Was Interesting," *Atlanta Constitution*, November 22, 1906, 4; "Tenth Meeting of the D.A.R., February 8th 1893," folder 1, box 1, DAR Western Reserve Chapter Records, WRHS; "Memorial Hall Fund," *Washington Post*, February 22, 1902, 3.

55. "To Stimulate the Study of History," *New York Times*, September 28, 1895, 1; "Seventh State Regency of Michigan: Miss Alice Louise McDuffee, 1919–1922," folder Reports to Congress & Conference, box 12, Michigan DAR Records; "History of the Elizabeth Benton Chapter of Kansas City," DAR, Missouri Collection, box 6, Western Historical Manuscript Collection, State Historical Society of Missouri, Columbia, MO (hereafter cited as WHMC-Columbia) (Note: The archival collections of the Western Historical Manuscript Collection are housed at various institutions in Missouri. The WHMC has branches on the Kansas City, Rolla, St. Louis, and Columbia campuses of the University of Missouri. Each branch concentrates on the history of its particular area. For this study I consulted DAR collections that are housed at the State Historical Society of Missouri in Columbia on the campus of the University of Missouri–Columbia and at the Kansas City Archives at the University of Missouri–Kansas City; in note citations those archives are abbreviated as WHMC-Columbia and WHMC–Kansas City.); "Patriotic Women Give Medal," *Atlanta Constitution*, January 17, 1904, B2; *Report of the Thirty-Second Annual State Conference, Texas Daughters of the American Revolution* (1931), 180, 182–183, DAR, Texas Society Collection, Woman's Collection, Texas Woman's University, Denton (hereafter cited as Texas DAR Collection); "The D.A.R. Will Repeat Offer," November 1903, and "School Pupils Given Prizes," 1906, both from unidentified newspapers, Scrapbook 1902–1910, Sarah Caswell Angell Chapter, box 5, Michigan DAR Records.

56. "New Jersey Battles Celebrated," *New York Times*, January 4, 1894, 9; "Wiltwyck Chapter," *American Monthly Magazine*, November 1893, 551–554; "Burning of Kingston Commemorated," *New York Times*, October 17, 1894, 1; "Harrisburg Chapter Celebrates 'Bunker Hill Day,'" *American Monthly Magazine*, August 1895, 145–149; "Honor to Brave Men," *Atlanta Constitution*, October 8, 1895, 4; "Social Event on Battle Anniversary," *Baltimore American*, June 18, 1905, 20; "First Battle of Revolution," *Springfield (MA) Daily Republican*, October 13, 1909, 3; "Kettle Creek Battle Celebration Today," *Macon (GA) Daily Telegraph*, February 14, 1912, 2; "Unveil Memorial on Battlefield," *The State* (Columbia, SC), September 25, 1912, 1.

57. Linenthal, *Sacred Ground*, 3.

58. Lockwood, "Women Worthy of Honor," *Washington Post*, July 12, 1890.

59. Janet Elizabeth Richards, "Heroic Women of the American Revolution," *American Monthly Magazine*, September 1892, 289. See also "Women as Patriots," *American Monthly Magazine*, November 1897, 586; Mrs. Donald McLean, "What Some Women Did," *DAR Magazine*, July 1916, 3–6.

60. Bryant quoted in "Women as Patriots," *American Monthly Magazine*, November 1897, 586. See also Mrs. Donald McLean, "What Some Women Did," *DAR Magazine*, July 1916, 3–6.

61. Curtis, "Valley Forge of To-Day," *American Monthly Magazine*, March 1912, 100.

62. Kimmel, *Manhood in America*, 83–112; Connell, *Masculinities*, 37–38, 77.

63. Kate Woolsey, "No Longer a 'Daughter,'" *Los Angeles Times*, April 12, 1903, 2.

64. "Response of Mrs. John R. Walker," *American Monthly Magazine*, September 1910, 197.

65. "She Calls for Nurses," *Chicago Daily Tribune*, April 2, 1898, 16; "Patriotic Women Will Aid," *Washington Post*, May 1, 1889, 11; Ella Loraine Dorsey, "For Home and Country," *Washington Post*, May 6, 1898, 6; "Aid for Hospital Corps," *Washington Post*, May 12, 1898, 4; "Gulls War Nurses," *Chicago Daily Tribune*, May 28, 1898, 9; "Women Plan for Relief," *Chicago Daily Tribune*, June 21, 1898, 8; "D.A.R. Feeding Wounded Soldiers," *Atlanta Constitution*, August 10, 1898, 5; "Nurses Being Provided," *Washington Post*, August 25, 1898, 2; Hoganson, *Fighting for American Manhood*, 6–13, 125–126.

66. Akers quoted in "Daughters in Session," *Washington Post*, February 21, 1899, 2.

67. "Propose a Continental Hall," *Boston Daily Globe*, February 24, 1898, 12; "Site for Memorial Hall," *Washington Post*, February 10, 1900, 12; Mary Desha, "Site for Memorial Hall," *Atlanta Constitution*, June 29, 1902, 26; "Memorial Continental Hall," *New York Times*, October 12, 1902, 10; "Memorial Hall Begun," *Washington Post*, April 20, 1904, 2.

68. Fairbanks quoted in "Memorial Hall Begun," *Washington Post*, April 20, 1904, 2.

69. "Daughters about to Build," *Washington Post*, February 7, 1904, E8; Margaret B. Downing, "Our National 'Valhalla' Built by American Women," *Los Angeles Times*, March 13, 1910, III16; "A Splendid Mausoleum of Memory," *American Monthly Magazine*, May 1910, 505–510.

70. P. Baker, "Domestication of Politics," 642; Rosenberg, *Divided Lives*, 57–58.

71. "Guarded by the D.A.R.," *Washington Post*, February 24, 1900, 2; "Pointed Views on Equal Suffrage by Prominent Washington Women," *Washington Post*, January 16, 1910, MT1; "How to Be Happy at Ninety," *Washington Post*, October 24, 1920, 62; Margaret B. Downing, "Mrs. Julius Caesar Burrows," *Washington Post*, December 15, 1907, F7; "Mrs. C. W. Fairbanks Dead," *Boston Daily Globe*, October 25, 1913, 3.

72. Rosenberg, *Divided Lives*, 55; Camhi, *Women against Women*, 2–3; Marshall, "In Defense of Separate Spheres," 333–335; Thurner, "Better Citizens Without the Ballot," 33–60; Marshall, *Splintered Sisterhood*, 4–5. For a case study of antisuffrage activism, see Goodier, *No Votes for Women*.

73. Mary Anderson Orton, "The Work of the Ohio Daughters of the American Revolu-

tion," *American Monthly Magazine*, February 1906, 100; "Husband's Hour Idea Approved," *Los Angeles Times*, July 30, 1907, II3; "Calls D.A.R. Politics Hot Enough for Her," *New York Times*, January 7, 1910, 4; Margaret B. Downing, "Women Should Not Be Idle," *Boston Daily Globe*, May 8, 1910, 63 (quote).

74. Marshall, *Splintered Sisterhood*, 48–51; "Suffrage Scare in D.A.R. Ranks," *Boston Daily Globe*, December 26, 1910, 8; "Stirs D.A.R. Anger," *Washington Post*, April 21, 1914, 12 (quote); Morgan, *Women and Patriotism in Jim Crow America*, 87; Morgan, "'Home and Country,'" 301.

75. Farrell, *Beloved Lady*, 194; Scott, *Natural Allies*, 141–165; Rosenberg, *Divided Lives*, 36–54; Morgan, "'Home and Country,'" 289–290, 304–311, 317–321; "Favor Pension for Mothers," *Boston Daily Globe*, November 24, 1912, 8; "The Law and the Child," *American Monthly Magazine*, May 1912, 242–244; Ellen Spencer Mussey, "Legal Protection of Motherhood," *American Monthly Magazine*, December 1912–January 1913, 3–4; Morgan, *Women and Patriotism in Jim Crow America*, 84–85.

76. Johnson, "Determining and Defining 'Wife'"; Phipps, "Marriage and Redemption," 447–451, 453; Ostling and Ostling, *Mormon America*, 70–93. See also Gordon, *Mormon Question*; Talbot, *Foreign Kingdom*.

77. "Against Mormon Senator," *Washington Post*, April 20, 1904, 2.

78. "D.A.R. Smite Roberts," Washington Post, February 26, 1899, 5; "Polygamy and D.A.R.," *Washington Post*, February 23, 1902, 9; "D.A.R. Strikes Mormons," *Chicago Daily Tribune*, April 23, 1905, 5; "D.A.R. Bar Mormons," *Washington Post*, April 23, 1911, 1; "D.A.R. Attacks Mormons," *New York Times*, April 20, 1912, 24; "Outlines D.A.R. Work," *Washington Post*, April 24, 1915, 2; Morgan, *Women and Patriotism in Jim Crow America*, 87–88.

79. Erickson, "So Much for Men," 86; Powers, *Not without Honor*, 10–11; Lemons, *Woman Citizen*, 210–211; Nielsen, *Un-American Womanhood*, 2.

80. "National Preparedness," *Boston Daily Globe*, November 16, 1915, 5; Morgan, *Women and Patriotism in Jim Crow America*, 104–110; George L. Darte (Adjutant-General Military Order of the World War), "Address on Subversive Influences before the Daughters of the American Revolution Congress, Washington, D.C., April 21, 1927," folder "Printed Materials–Attack on Florence Kelley, 1927," box 12, Florence Kelley Papers, New York Public Library, Manuscripts and Archives Division, New York (hereafter cited as NYPL-Archives); Mrs. William Sherman Walker, "Why Patriotic Organizations Should Protect our American Institutions from the Menace of Radicalism," reprint from *DAR Magazine*, April 1929, folder "D.A.R. National Defense Committee Materials," box 17, Henry Joy Bourne Scrapbooks, MHC (hereafter cited as Bourne Scrapbooks); Nellie N. Somerville, "Americanism: What It Was, Is, and Should Be," address to Belvidere Chapter DAR, Greenville, January 22, 1944, folder 45, Nellie Nugent Somerville Papers (Somerville-Howorth Family Papers), Arthur and Elizabeth Schlesinger Library, Radcliffe Institute for Advanced Study, Cambridge, MA (hereafter cited as Schlesinger Library).

81. Morgan, *Women and Patriotism in Jim Crow America*, 135–139; Morgan, "'Home and Country,'" 428; Erickson, "So Much for Men," 86, 88–89; Nielsen, *Un-American Womanhood*, 57, 61; Delegard, "Women Patriots," 6.

82. Nielsen, *Un-American Womanhood*, 2; Erickson, "So Much for Men," 93; Morgan, "'Home and Country,'" 292–298.

83. "Reminiscence," in Record Book Presented by the First Historian, Charity Cook Chapter, Michigan DAR Records; "Report of War Work of the National Society of the Daughters of the American Revolution during the Great World War from August 14, 1914–November 11, 1918," 5–6, box 33, Michigan DAR Records; Mary S. Lockwood, "League of White Feather

Leads Youth to Disloyalty," *Washington Post,* July 19, 1915, 5; Mrs. William Sherman Walker, "Adequate National Defense versus a National Peace Department," folder D.A.R. National Defense Committee Materials, box 17, Bourne Scrapbooks.

84. "Report of War Work of the National Society of the Daughters of the American Revolution during the Great World War from August 14, 1914–November 11, 1918," 5–6, box 33, Michigan DAR Records.

85. Mary S. Lockwood, "League of White Feather Leads Youth to Disloyalty," *Washington Post,* July 19, 1915 (first and second quotes); "D.A.R. Call to Colors," *Washington Post,* April 2, 1917, 5 (third quote). See also Mrs. William Sherman Walker, "Adequate National Defense versus a National Peace Department," folder D.A.R. National Defense Committee Materials, box 17, Bourne Scrapbooks.

86. Morgan, "'Home and Country,'" 353, 360, 405.

87. For examples of praise for the DAR, see "Patriotic Work Praised by James J. Davies," *Washington Post,* April 19, 1928, 1; Speech of Hon. Guy Despard Goff of West Virginia in the Senate of the United States, Monday, April 19, 1926, Daughters of the American Revolution, reel 1, scrapbook 2, Denver Chapter Scrapbooks 1898–1962, Denver Public Library, Denver, Colorado; Bessie Shaw Stafford, "D.A.R. Is Given Rousing Welcome at Opening Session," *Atlanta Constitution,* April 4, 1923, 16; "The D.A.R.'s Great Work," *Washington Post,* April 19, 1910, 6; "Daughters of the American Revolution," *Washington Post,* April 17, 1923, 6; "The D.A.R. and Pacifists," *Washington Post,* June 30, 1924, 6; "Daughters of the Revolution," *Washington Post,* April 20, 1925, 6; "Patriotism of Women," *Washington Post,* April 19, 1927, 6; "Pacifists in the D.A.R.," *Washington Post,* April 15, 1928, S1; "Americanism," *Washington Post,* April 17, 1928, 6; "Welcome to the D.A.R.," *Washington Post,* April 15, 1929, 6.

88. "D.A.R. Policy on 'Blacklist' Draws Censure," *Christian Science Monitor,* April 2, 1928, 1; "Says Bay State D.A.R. Blacklists Liberals," *New York Times,* April 2, 1928, 1; "Pamphlet Attacks D.A.R. Leadership," *New York Times,* April 9, 1928, 1; "D.A.R. Head Replies to Critics of Order," *New York Times,* April 15, 1928, 18; "Attacks on D.A.R. Leadership Meet Crushing Defeat," *Chicago Daily Tribune,* April 21, 1928, 17; "D.A.R. Punishes Insurgent and Then Adjourns," *Chicago Daily Tribune,* April 22, 1928, 22; "D.A.R. Drops Mrs. Bailie, Accused of Injuring Good Name of Body in Blacklist Charges," *New York Times,* June 23, 1928, 1. For a more thorough discussion of the DAR and "un-Americanism" during the interwar period, see Wendt, "Defenders of Patriotism or Mothers of Fascism?," 943–969.

89. Elaine Goodale Eastman, "Are D.A.R. Women Exploited?," reprint from *Christian Century,* September 11, 1929, folder 1, box 1, DAR "Blacklist" Controversy Collection, Stanford University, Department of Special Collections, Stanford, CA (hereafter cited as DAR Blacklist Collection); "Minutes of Regular and Special Meetings of the Denver Chapter, Daughters of the American Revolution," (1927–1930), entry "May 11–1928," folder 16, box 1, Daughters of the American Revolution, Denver Chapter Collection, Denver Public Library; Elaine Goodale Eastman to Dear Member, August 10, 1928, folder 2, box 1, DAR Blacklist Collection; Valeria H. Parker to President General and Members of the National Board of Management, February 8, 1930, reel 139, National Republic Records, Hoover Institution Archives, Stanford, CA (hereafter cited as HIA); "We, The Undersigned," May 15, 1930, folder 4, box 1, DAR Blacklist Collection.

90. Morgan, *Women and Patriotism in Jim Crow America,* 139–140; "Women Eagerly Seek D.A.R. Memberships," *Washington Post,* December 26, 1923, 4; "D.A.R. Cheers as Curtis Talk Hits Pacifists," *Washington Post,* April 21, 1931, 1.

91. Kammen, *Mystic Chords of Memory,* 299–305, 337, 384, 488; Moreau, *School Book Na-*

tion, 176–177, 196–197; Jones, "Search for a Usable American Past," 713–714; R. Nash, *Nervous Generation,* 127–131.

92. Lockwood quoted in "Stark Book Not Original," *Washington Post,* February 16, 1910, 2.

93. Moreau, *School Book Nation,* 176–177, 196–197.

94. DAR, *Proceedings of the Thirty-Second Continental Congress of the National Society DAR* (1924), 274–275. The proceedings of the Continental Congress were frequently published a year after it took place. The proceedings of the 1923 meeting were published in 1924.

95. "D.A.R. Takes Up Textbooks," *New York Times,* April 22, 1922, 23; "American History," *Washington Post,* April 22, 1922, 6; "Text Books Committee," *Atlanta Constitution,* February 1, 1925, D2; Kammen, *Mystic Chords of Memory,* 484–485; Erickson, "So Much for Men," 94–95; Zimmerman, "Storm of the Schoolhouse," 604–605; Elisabeth Ellicott Poe, "Pacifist Poison," *Washington Post,* August 19, 1924, 6; "The Woman's Patriotic Conference on National Defense," *DAR Magazine,* April 1927, 270–273.

96. "Address of Mrs. Alfred J. Brosseau," box 33, Michigan DAR Records.

97. Zimmerman, "Storm of the Schoolhouse," 608; Moreau, *School Book Nation,* 212–215; Kammen, *Mystic Chords of Memory,* 488.

98. Minor quoted in "Calls D.A.R. Host to War on Radicals," *Washington Post,* June 11, 1922, 33.

99. Mrs. Anthony Wayne Cook, "Service to Home and Country," *National Republic,* August 1925, 29, 64.

100. John Spencer Bassett, "The Men Who Thought Out the Revolution," *DAR Magazine,* April 1924, 217–222, and May 1924, 289–294; Florence Seville Berryman, "January's Heroes of the Revolution," *DAR Magazine,* January 1928, 7–15; "Tablet to Signers Unveiled in Albany," *New York Times,* August 3, 1926, 12; Kate Milner Rabb, "D.A.R. Chapter Honors General Clark," *DAR Magazine,* February 1928, 104–105; "D.A.R. Chapter Collects $10,000 to Rebuild General Knox Home," *Christian Science Monitor,* March 17, 1923, 4; Edgar Stanton Maclay, "A Neglected Hero of the Revolution," *DAR Magazine,* March 1918, 119–123; Grace M. Pier, "The True Story of Enoch Crosby—Revolutionary Spy," *DAR Magazine,* February 1918, 73–80; Dolores Boisfeuillet Colquitt, "Burkhalter Family of Georgia Pioneers and Patriots," *DAR Magazine,* March 1922, 148–152; John C. Fitzpatrick, "The Continental Express Rider," *DAR Magazine,* November 1923, 650–662. On the various buildings that the Daughters preserved, see Barrington, *Historic Restorations of the DAR.*

101. Minor quoted in Amelia Day Campbell, "The Pilgrim Tercentenary at Provincetown, Mass., 1620–1920," *DAR Magazine,* December 1920, 705.

102. Cook quoted in "Dedication of Pilgrim Memorial Fountain at Plymouth, Massachusetts, June 24, 1925," *DAR Magazine,* September 1925, 535, 536, 537.

103. "Tablet for Women of Revolution," *Los Angeles Times,* February 23, 1923, II20; "D.A.R. of Kingfield Builds Memorial to Tea Party Heroine," *Christian Science Monitor,* July 14, 1924, 4A; "To Rebury Captain Mollie," *New York Times,* January 28, 1926, 9; "Honors Molly Corbin by two Ceremonies," *New York Times,* April 15, 1926, 27; Amelia Campbell Parker, "Revolutionary Heroine Interred in West Point Cemetery," *DAR Magazine,* June 1926, 347–352.

104. See Associated Press, "Not Capt. Molly: 1776 War Hero Not in Her West Point Grave," reprinted in *Army Times,* December 5, 2017, https://www.armytimes.com/news/your-army/2017/12/05/not-capt-molly-1776-war-hero-not-in-her-west-point-grave/.

105. "D.A.R. Sponsors Naming of Highway for Nancy Hart," *Atlanta Constitution,* January 29, 1928, D3; "The Nancy Hart Highway," unidentified newspaper, n.d., Georgia scrapbook, 1929–1932, DAR, Georgia State Society, Georgia Archives, Morrow, GA; Clare Boifeuil-

let Jones, "Highway Named Nancy Hart," unidentified newspaper, n.d., Georgia scrapbook, 1929–1932; Mrs. Herbert Fay Gaffney (Blanche McFarlin Gaffney) to My Dear Madam Chapter Regents and State Chairmen, July 1929, Grant and Slaton Inman Family Papers, box 22, folder 46, AHCA; "Markers to Be Unveiled on Nancy Hart Highway," unidentified newspaper, February 16, 1930, Georgia scrapbook, 1929–1932; "Two Route Markers Honor Nancy Hart," *Atlanta Constitution,* September 20, 1931, 13A; "Home Site of Nancy Hart Presented to State D.A.R.," *Atlanta Constitution,* March 31, 1932, 5; "Georgia," in Barrington, *Historic Restorations of the DAR* (no pagination); "Program: Unveiling Exercises Nancy Hart Memorial," Georgia scrapbook, 1929–1932; T. J. Hamilton Jr., "Nancy Hart's Brave Feat Is Recalled at Exercises; Gov. Russel is Speaker," unidentified newspaper, n.d., Georgia scrapbook, 1929–1932; "State D.A.R. Regent Makes Address at Nancy Hart Marker Unveiling," unidentified newspaper, n.d., Georgia scrapbook, 1929–1932; Edna Arnold Copeland, "Nancy Hart Homesite Tendered State D.A.R. as Memorial Park," unidentified newspaper, 1931, Georgia scrapbook, 1929–1932.

106. Elizabeth C. Barney Buel, "A Mother of the American Revolution," *DAR Magazine,* September 1924, 361.

107. Powers, *Not Without Honor,* 114–117; Snider, "Patriots and Pacifists," 59; Foster, *The Women and the Warriors,* 110; "Mrs. Magna in New Deal for D.A.R.," *Los Angeles Times,* June 26, 1934, A6.

108. Erickson, "So Much for Men," 89; "Mrs. Becker Wins in D.A.R. Election," *New York Times,* April 19, 1935, 23; "'Red' Charge against Mrs. Roosevelt Now Issue in D.A.R. Race," *Chicago Daily Tribune,* February 25, 1935, 5; Florence H. Becker to Dear Members, September 1, 1932, reel 139, National Republic Records, HIA.

109. "The National Society of the Children of the American Revolution," *American Monthly Magazine,* December 1895, 530–536; "Twigs of Patriotism," *Washington Post,* February 18, 1896, 9; "Children of the Flag," *Washington Post,* February 23, 1896. For a more thorough analysis of the Children of the American Revolution from the perspective of its young members, see Miller, "Assent as Agency."

110. JAC underwent several name changes. It was founded as Children of the Republic and was renamed Sons and Daughters of the U.S.A. in 1933. Shortly thereafter, the DAR named it Junior American Citizens. See Mrs. Robert Bagnell, "Sons and Daughters of the U.S.A.," *DAR Magazine,* January 1934, 41–42; Elizabeth Malott Barnes, "Junior American Citizens," *DAR Magazine,* January 1937, 56–58.

111. "Good Citizenship Medal," n.d., reel 139, National Republic Records, HIA.

112. Buell, *Ohio Society History,* 70, 98; Michigan DAR, *Historical and Genealogical Records of the Michigan DAR,* 30; "16 D.A.R. 'Pilgrims' Tour Washington," *New York Times,* April 14, 1935, 24.

113. Marling, "Of Cherry Trees and Ladies' Teas"; "Husbands See Painting: Twit D.A.R. Wives," *Chicago Daily Tribune,* August 8, 1934, 1; "Need Sense of Humor," unidentified newspaper, n.d., DAR, Kansas City, Scrapbook, 1934–1936, WHMC–Kansas City; "D.A.R. Resents Artist's Slam on Canvas," newspaper clipping, n.d., reel 139, National Republic Records, HIA; "D.A.R. Schools' Worst Enemy, Teachers Told," *Chicago Daily Tribune,* August 19, 1936, 19; "D.A.R. Red Fight Scored," *Los Angeles Times,* April 23, 1937, 3; Crete Cage, "D.A.R. Vital to Dies Group," *Los Angeles Times,* January 19, 1939, A8.

114. Jones, "Search for a Usable American Past"; Kammen, *Mystic Chords of Memory,* 450–455, 465–480.

115. Kammen, *Mystic Chords of Memory,* 375, 417–418, 455–456, 472; Nelson M. Shepard, "The Washington Bicentennial," *DAR Magazine,* May 1925, 303–307; "Report of the Historian

General, Incorporating the Report of Historical Research to Continental Congress, April 19, 1932," Michigan DAR, scrapbook, box 12, Michigan DAR Records; DAR Missouri Chapters, "Radio Program," 1932, George Washington Bi-Centennial, Missouri Chapters, Scrapbook, 1931–1932, Western Historical Manuscript Collection, State Historical Society of Missouri, Columbia, MO (hereafter cited as WHMC-Columbia).

116. Mrs. John Gates Jr., "Contributions of Women to the American Revolution," *DAR Magazine*, September 1931, 545; Mrs. W. B. Cravens, "Contributions of Women to American Revolution," January 19, 1933, scrapbook, vol. 17, 1932–1933, DAR, Missouri Collection, WHMC-Columbia; Mary E. Seymour, "Revolutionary Heroines," *DAR Magazine*, September 1936, 933–934; Louise Hartley, "Through the Year with Feminine Revolutionists," *DAR Magazine*, November 1940, 30–32; Louise Hartley, "Through the Year with Feminine Revolutionists," *DAR Magazine*, April 1941, 32–33; Mrs. John Jacob Repp, "Woman of the Century," *DAR Magazine*, July 1943, 434–437; Messenger, *Ohio State History of the DAR*, 118; Mollie Somerville, "Service to the Nation," *DAR Magazine*, October 1965, 820. See also "Our Real Granddaughters and Their Ancestry," *DAR Magazine*, July 1934, 391–392.

Chapter 2. "A Long and Mighty Race of Heroic Men": Remembering the Pioneers and American Nation-Building

1. Julia H. Platt, "Report of the Committee of Prizes," DAR Denver Chapter, scrapbooks 1898–1962, reel 1, scrapbook 1 (1898–1905), Denver Public Library.

2. Julia H. Platt, "To the Public High Schools of the State of Colorado," 1901; Alice Polk Hill, "To the Public High Schools of the State of Colorado," 1902, both in DAR Denver Chapter, scrapbooks 1898–1962, reel 1, scrapbook 1 (1898–1905). DAR chapters in other western and midwestern states created similar essay prize contests that focused on the early history of the West. See Leach, *Missouri State History of the DAR*, 420; "D.A.R. Feb. 10th, 1897," folder 1, box 1, Western Reserve Chapter DAR Records; "History of Ann Gridley Chapter D.A.R.," Hillsdale, Michigan," box 33, Michigan DAR Records.

3. Morgan, "'Home and Country,'" 56–58, 167–170; Morgan, "Regions Remote from Revolutionary Scenes," 50–54, 58, 60, 76, 78.

4. In June 1925 the Daughters had 151,297 members, 61,780 of whom resided in the West and Midwest. Of the DAR's 2,071 chapters, 848 were in that region ("DAR State Membership," *DAR Magazine*, August 1925, 509). When talking about the West and Midwest in this chapter, I follow the regional divisions devised by the US Census Bureau ("Census Regions and Divisions of the United States," https://www2.census.gov/geo/pdfs/maps-data/maps/reference/us_regdiv.pdf).

5. See Faragher, *Rereading Frederick Jackson Turner*; Wrobel, *End of American Exceptionalism*.

6. See Bederman, *Manliness and Civilization*, 170–215; Testi, "Gender of Reform Politics."

7. Wrobel, *Promised Lands*, 2–12, 98–105, 121–123; Bodnar, *Remaking America*, 121–123; Kammen, *Mystic Chords of Memory*, 275; Glassberg, *Sense of History*, 173–181.

8. Spencer, "We Are Not Dealing Entirely with the Past," 164–170. See also Lewis, *In the Footsteps of Lewis and Clark*.

9. The 1899 dedication of a memorial fountain in honor of a female pioneer named Narcissa Whitman in Tacoma, Washington, was a rare exception. See "In Life a Heroine—In Death, a Martyr," *American Monthly Magazine*, January 1900, 12.

10. See Bagley, *So Rugged and Mountainous*; Dary, *Santa Fe Trail*; Lavender, *Westward Vision*; McLynn, *Wagons West*.

11. Mrs. Charles Oliver Norton, "The Old Oregon Trail," *American Monthly Magazine,* March 1909, 256–257.

12. "Santa Fe Trail Report," November 10, 1909, DAR, Kansas City Chapter, Scrapbook (May 14, 1917, to November 26, 1919), WHMC–Kansas City; Hope Casey Van Brunt, "Kansas City Chapter, D.A.R. Santa Fe Trail Committee," August 2, 1911, folder 13, Van Brunt Collection, WHMC-Columbia.

13. Norton, "Old Oregon Trail," *American Monthly Magazine,* March 1909, 256–257. For a similar interpretation, see Mrs. Overton Gentry Ellis, "Marking the Old Oregon Trail in the State of Washington by the Sons and Daughters of the American Revolution," *DAR Magazine,* November 1916, 306–307.

14. Mrs. W. E. Stanley, "Marking the Santa Fe Trail through Kansas," *American Monthly Magazine,* February 1907, 139.

15. "The Old Oregon Trail," *American Monthly Magazine,* August 1910, 89.

16. Hope Casey Van Brunt, "Report of the Santa Fe Trail Committee," January 13, 1913, folder 13, Van Brunt Collection; Norton, "Old Oregon Trail," *American Monthly Magazine,* March 1909, 255, 256–257; Glassberg, *Sense of History,* 128.

17. Stanley, "Marking the Santa Fe Trail through Kansas," *American Monthly Magazine,* February 1907, 139; Hope Casey Van Brunt, "Report of Santa Fe Trail Committee," October 14, 1908, folder 12, Van Brunt Collection; Hope Casey Van Brunt to Mrs. Samuel McKnight Green, February 17, 1909, folder 8, Van Brunt Collection.

18. "D.A.R. Saw Danger of Forgotten Trail and Marked Famous Route," *Kansas City Journal Post,* September 6, 1925, 6F; Mrs. Charles O. Norton, "The Old Oregon Trail," *American Monthly Magazine,* November 1911, 254–259; "Report of Old Oregon Trail Committee," April 1, 1914, Daughters of the American Revolution: Minutes of the Oregon Trail Committee (hereafter cited as DAR-OTC), DAR State of Washington Collection, Seattle Public Library, Seattle, WA; Lindly, *Nebraska State History of the DAR,* 346; Cordry, *Story of the Marking of the Santa Fe Trail,* 15, 29, 47–49.

19. "The Santa Fe Trail," *American Monthly Magazine,* January 1908, 14–15; Hope Casey Van Brunt to Mrs. Samuel McKnight Green, February 17, 1909, folder 8, Van Brunt Collection; Mrs. John Campbell, "Santa Fe Trail in Colorado," *American Monthly Magazine,* June 1909, 597–599; Tarbell, *History of the DAR of Colorado,* 23–29; "D.A.R. Saw Danger of Forgotten Trail and Marked Famous Route"; "Markers for Santa Fe Trail," *Kansas City Star,* May 11, 1909; "The Approved Design for Santa Fe Trail Markers," unidentified newspaper, Kansas City Chapter DAR scrapbook (May 14, 1917 to November 26, 1919); Norton, "The Old Oregon Trail," *American Monthly Magazine,* November 1911, 254–259; Lindly, *Nebraska State History of the Daughters of the American Revolution,* 346; Mrs. H. B. Patten to Dear Mrs. McCleary, September 27, 1913, DAR-OTC; Mrs. H. B. Patten to Dear Mrs. Ellis, March 21, 1914, DAR-OTC; "Report of Old Oregon Trail Committee," April 1, 1914, DAR-OTC; G. E. Tilton to George A. Virtue, March 4, 1915, DAR-OTC; Cordry, *The Story of the Marking of the Santa Fe Trail,* 85–87, 139; Stanley, "The Marking of the Santa Fe Trail through Kansas," 138.

20. Cordry, *Story of the Marking of the Santa Fe Trail,* 11–61; Tarbell, *History of the Daughters of the DAR,* 23–29; Norton, "Old Oregon Trail," *American Monthly Magazine,* November 1911, 254–259; Lindly, *Nebraska State History of the DAR,* 346; George H. Himes to Mrs. Jennie W. Ellis, January 7, 1915, DAR-OTC.

21. "The Santa Fe Trail," *American Monthly Magazine,* January 1908, 14–15; Hope Casey Van Brunt, "Madam State Regent and Other Members of the Ninth State Conference," October 1908, folder 12, Van Brunt Collection; Hope Casey Van Brunt, "Report of Santa Fe Trail

Committee," October 14, 1908, folder 12, Van Brunt Collection; Cordry, *Story of the Marking of the Santa Fe Trail*, 39, 47, 55, 98.

22. Cordry, *Story of the Marking of the Santa Fe Trail*, 98.

23. "Report of Oregon Trail Committee, Washington State Society, Daughters of the American Revolution," 1916, 1–5, 6, DAR-OTC.

24. "Marks the Old Trail," *Washington Post*, July 11, 1909, TP4; "Report of Oregon Trail Committee, Washington State Society, Daughters of the American Revolution," 1916, 7, DAR-OTC; Ellis, "Marking the Old Oregon Trail," *DAR Magazine*, November 1916, 304–307; Stanley, "Marking the Santa Fe Trail through Kansas," *American Monthly Magazine*, February 1907, 138; "Markers for Santa Fe Trail," *Kansas City Star*, May 11, 1909; "The Approved Design for Santa Fe Trail Markers," unidentified newspaper, Kansas City Chapter DAR scrapbook (May 14, 1917, to November 26, 1919); Norton, "Old Oregon Trail," *American Monthly Magazine*, November 1911, 254–259; Hope Casey Van Brunt, "Report of the Santa Fe Trail Committee," January 13, 1913, folder 13, Van Brunt Collection; Kansas DAR, *History of the Kansas DAR*, 36.

25. Cordry, *Story of the Marking of the Santa Fe Trail*, 85–87; Stanley, "Marking the Santa Fe Trail through Kansas," *American Monthly Magazine*, February 1907, 138; "Place Last Marker of Old Santa Fe Trail," *Christian Science Monitor*, September 9, 1912, 2; Mrs. H. B. Patten to Dear Mrs. Ellis, March 21, 1914, DAR-OTC; "Oregon Trail Monument Dedicated," *DAR Magazine*, September 1915, 177–178; Lindly, *Nebraska State History of the DAR*, 351.

26. Norton, "Old Oregon Trail," *American Monthly Magazine*, November 1911, 258–259; Mrs. H. B. Patten, "Oregon Trail Monument," *DAR Magazine*, August 1913, 465–467; Mrs. H. B. Patten to Dear Mrs. McCleary, September 27, 1913, DAR-OTC; "Accept Lewis Model for Fine Fountain on Old Oregon Trail," unidentified newspaper, n.d., DAR-OTC; "Spirit of the Trail," *Olympia Daily Recorder*, January 15, 1917, 4; "Report of the Oregon Trail Committee of the Washington State Society, Daughters of the American Revolution, Annual Assembly, March 30, 1917," 25, DAR-OTC; "Pioneers Are Honored," *Oregonian*, April 1, 1918, 7. On John Gast's painting, see Rawlinson, *American Visual Culture*, 32–35.

27. Helen Campbell, "The Santa Fe Trail," *American Monthly Magazine*, November 1910, 382.

28. Ward quoted in Delight E. R. Keller, "Report of National Chairman Committee on Preservation of Historic Spots," in *Proceedings of the Twentieth Continental Congress of the National Society DAR* (1912), 740.

29. See, for example, Hope Casey Van Brunt, "Madam Regent, Officers, and Daughters of the American Revolution," October 29, 1912, folder 13, Van Brunt Collection; "Marking the Old Trail," April 21, 1913, unidentified newspaper, folder 10, Van Brunt Collection; "D.A.R. Old Trails Boosters on Way to Dedicate Monument at New Franklin," *Kansas City Post*, May 15, 1913, folder 10, Van Brunt Collection; "The Old Oregon Trail," *American Monthly Magazine*, August 1910, 92; "Oregon Trail Monument Dedicated," *DAR Magazine*, September 1915, 177–178; "Ten Monuments Mark Old Trail," unidentified newspaper, n.d., DAR-OTC; "Boundary Marker to be Placed at Vancouver," unidentified newspaper, n.d., DAR-OTC.

30. Cordry, *Story of the Marking of the Santa Fe Trail*, 82, 106; "Report of the Oregon Trail Committee of the Washington State Society, Daughters of the American Revolution, Annual Assembly, March 30, 1917," 6–10, DAR-OTC; "Place Last Marker of Old Santa Fe Trail," *Christian Science Monitor*, September 9, 1912, 2; "Unveiling of the Marker on the Old Oregon Trail at Kelso," DAR-OTC; "Trail's End Now Marked," unidentified newspaper, n.d., DAR-OTC; "Marking the Old Trail," April 21, 1913, Van Brunt Collection; "D.A.R. Old Trails

Boosters," *Kansas City Post,* May 15, 1913; Van Brunt, "Madam Regent, Officers, and Daughters of the American Revolution," October 29, 1912; Marie Rowe, "Patriotic Order Unveils Oregon Trail Marker," unidentified newspaper, n.d., DAR-OTC; "Report of the Oregon Trail Committee of the Washington State Society, Daughters of the American Revolution, Annual Assembly, March 30, 1917," 3, DAR-OTC; Wrobel, *Promised Lands,* 2, 4.

31. One rare exception was the unveiling of a marker at Grand Mound Prairie, Washington, in October 1916 ("On Anniversary of the Discovery of America by Columbus, Thursday, October 12, 1916," DAR-OTC). For more information on women's roles in the "pioneer reminiscences genre" and in pioneer societies more generally, see Wrobel, *Promised Lands,* 115, 130–131.

32. "Old Oregon Trail," *American Monthly Magazine,* August 1910, 90. See also Hope Casey Van Brunt, "Marking the Santa Fe Trail in Missouri," *DAR Magazine,* November 1913, 643.

33. Slotkin, *Gunfighter Nation,* 10–13; Cordry, *The Story of the Marking of the Santa Fe Trail,* 111; Stanley, "Marking the Santa Fe Trail Through Kansas," *American Monthly Magazine,* February 1907, 358; Wrobel, *Promised Lands,* 177.

34. Cordry, *Story of the Marking of the Santa Fe Trail,* 111.

35. Stanley, "Marking the Santa Fe Trail through Kansas," *American Monthly Magazine,* February 1907, 139, 358.

36. Wrobel, *Promised Lands,* 177.

37. Cordry, *Story of the Marking of the Santa Fe Trail,* 111.

38. Van Brunt, "Marking the Santa Fe Trail in Missouri," *DAR Magazine,* November 1913, 644; "Marks the Old Trail," *Washington Post,* July 11, 1909, TP4.

39. "Unveiling of the Marker on the Old Oregon Trail at Kelso," DAR-OTC; "Ten Monuments Mark Old Trail," unidentified newspaper, n.d., DAR-OTC.

40. Norton, "Old Oregon Trail," *American Monthly Magazine,* November 1911, 258; "Oregon Trail Monument Dedicated," *DAR Magazine,* September 1915, 177–178; Patten, "Oregon Trail Monument," *DAR Magazine,* August 1913, 465–467; Lindly, *Nebraska State History of the DAR,* 351; Ellis, "Marking the Old Oregon Trail," *DAR Magazine,* November 1916, 304–307; "Work of Chapters," *DAR Magazine,* January 1917, 35–36; "Ten Monuments Mark Old Trail," n.d., DAR-OTC.

41. Van Brunt, "Marking the Santa Fe Trail in Missouri," *DAR Magazine,* November 1913, 647.

42. "Report of the Oregon Trail Committee of the Washington State Society, Daughters of the American Revolution, Annual Assembly, March 30, 1917," 7, DAR-OTC.

43. "The Oregon Trail," *Atlanta Constitution,* October 9, 1910, C11; Louise Mac Nair Crawford, "Marking the Oregon Trail," *American Monthly Magazine,* January 1911, 19–20; Patten, "Oregon Trail Monument," *DAR Magazine,* August 1913, 465–467.

44. Front-page article, no title, *The Chronicle* (Woodland, OR), n.d., DAR-OTC.

45. Beauford, *History of the Louisiana Society DAR,* 29; Mrs. Lipscomb Norwell, "'King's Highway' across Texas," *DAR Magazine,* March 1916, 157–160; Ford, *Markers Placed by the Texas DAR,* 8–12; Mrs. A. S. C. Forbes, "El Camino Real," *DAR Magazine,* May 1915, 338–341.

46. On Boone's life and legacy, see M. Brown, *Daniel Boone and the Making of America;* Faragher, *Daniel Boone.*

47. "First Marker for Trail of Daniel Boone, Pioneer," *Nashville Banner,* August 22, 1914, folder 11, Van Brunt Collection; Mrs. William Lawson Peel, "The Old Trail Roads," *Atlanta Constitution,* June 21, 1915, A4; "Daniel Boone's Trail through North Carolina Marked by the

D.A.R. of That State," 1–4, folder DAR Mar.–Apr. 1916, William Blout Rodman Papers, North Carolina State Archives, Raleigh (hereafter cited as NCSA).

48. See Johnston, *Iowa Daughters of the American Revolution*, 112, 162; Ethel Massie Withers, "Pioneering in Missouri," 1916, folder 1, Ethel Massie Withers Collection, WHMC-Columbia.

49. "Daniel Boone's Trail through North Carolina," 2, Rodman Papers, NCSA.

50. Leach, *Missouri State History of the DAR*, 420; Elizabeth Butler Gentry, "Report of Good Roads Committee, D.A.R.," November 1911, folder 13, Van Brunt Collection; Elizabeth Butler Gentry, "National Old Trails Road Department," *DAR Magazine*, August–September 1914, 132–135. On the good roads movement, see Hugill, "Good Roads and the Automobile in the United States."

51. Gentry, "Report of Good Roads Committee, D.A.R.," November 1911.

52. Gentry, "Report of Missouri Good Roads Committee," April 17, 1912, 814–816; "Report, National Old Trails Road Committee," *Proceedings of the Twenty-Second Continental Congress of the National Society DAR* (1913), 892; Hobsbawm, introduction.

53. Gentry, "Report of Missouri Good Roads Committee," April 17, 1912, 813; Elizabeth Butler Gentry, "National Old Trails Road Department," *DAR Magazine*, November 1913, 663–664; "D.A.R. Urging 'Post Road' for National Way," *Christian Science Monitor*, December 5, 1914, 13; "Report of Old Trails Road in Georgia," folder 9, box 6, Lucy Cook Peel Papers, AHCA.

54. "Report, National Old Trails Road Committee," *Proceedings of the Twenty-Second Continental Congress of the National Society DAR* (1913), 889; Medlicott and Heffernan, "Autograph of a Nation," 247; Harper, "Preserving the National Road Landscape," 385; Gentry, "The Old Trails Road," *American Monthly Magazine*, March 1913, 161; Elizabeth Butler Gentry, "National Old Trails Road Association," *DAR Magazine*, October 1914, 205.

55. "Report, National Old Trails Road Committee," *Proceedings of the Twenty-Second Continental Congress of the National Society DAR* (1913), 889; Gentry, "National Old Trails Road Department," *DAR Magazine*, August–September 1914, 132–135; Gentry, "The Old Trails Road," *American Monthly Magazine*, March 1913, 161.

56. On these developments, see Shaffer, *See America First*; Kammen, *Mystic Chords of Memory*, 275, 305, 338–340; Glassberg, *Sense of History*, 189–191.

57. US Congress, National Old Trails Road: Hearing before the Committee on Agriculture, House of Representatives on H.R. 17919, April 19, 1912 (Washington, DC: Government Printing Office, 1912), 13; H.R. 2864, 63d Congress, 1st Session, House of Representatives, April 14, 1913; "National Old Trails Highway from Ocean to Ocean: Speech of Hon. William P. Borland of Missouri in the House of Representatives, September 3, 1913" (Washington, DC: Government Printing Office, 1913); "Plan to Preserve and Mark Famous Old Trails," *New York Times*, August 26, 1917, 54; H.R. 8011, 65th Congress 2nd session, House of Representatives, January 3, 1918.

58. Marder, "Pleasing the Eye," 60.

59. "An Ocean-to-Ocean Highway," *Woman's National Weekly*, January 4, 1913, folder 10, Van Brunt Collection; "Report, National Old Trails Road Committee," *Proceedings of the Twenty-Second Continental Congress of the National Society DAR* (1913), 891; "D.A.R. Saw Danger of Forgotten Trail," *Kansas City Journal Post*, September 6, 1925; R. Scott, *Illinois State History*, 293; Gentry, "National Old Trails Road Department," *DAR Magazine*, August–September 1914, 133; Elizabeth Butler Gentry, "National Old Trails Road Department," *DAR Magazine*, October 1914, 202; "The Madonna of the Trail," *DAR Magazine*, July 1929, 399; Mrs. H. E. Candace Cornell Engell, "Romance of the Road," *DAR Magazine*, December 1914, 335.

60. "Report, National Old Trails Road Committee," *Proceedings of the Twenty-Second*

Continental Congress of the National Society DAR (1913), 891; Gentry, "National Old Trails Road Department," *DAR Magazine,* August–September 1914, 132; "Old Trails Gumbo Goes," unidentified newspaper, n.d., Kansas City Chapter DAR scrapbook (May 14, 1917, to November 26, 1919); Hunter, *Century of Service,* 142; Elizabeth Butler Gentry, "Report of National Old Trails Road Committee," *Proceedings of the Twenty-Fourth Continental Congress of the National Society DAR* (1915), 1355.

61. Elizabeth Butler Gentry, "Report of the National Old Trails Road Committee to the 24th Annual D.A.R. Congress, Washington, D.C., April 19, 1915," folder 16, Van Brunt Collection.

62. Gentry, "Report of the National Old Trails Road Committee," April 19, 1915, Van Brunt Collection. See also Elizabeth Butler Gentry, "National Old Trails Road Department," *DAR Magazine,* May 1915, 338.

63. Engell, "Romance of the Road," *DAR Magazine,* December 1914, 335.

64. Mrs. Henry McCleary, "National Old Trails Road Committee," *Proceedings of the Twenty-Sixth Continental Congress of the National Society DAR* (1917), 1057; Bertha H. Talbott to Dear Madam State Regent, n.d., folder Letters to State Chairmen and State Regents–National Old Trails Road Committee, ca. 1923–1924, box 1, series 1, Madonna of the Trail Collection (hereafter cited as MOTC), Archives of the National Society Daughters of the American Revolution, Washington, DC (hereafter cited as DAR Archives).

65. Arlene B. N. Moss, "Foreword to State Regent," n.d., folder Letters to State Chairmen and State Regents–National Old Trails Road Committee, ca. 1923–1924, box 1, series 1, MOTC.

66. DAR National Old Trails Committee, "Resolution," 1924, folder Resolutions–National Old Trails Road Committee, 1924, box 1, series 1, MOTC; "Invitation," DAR, Missouri State Society Scrapbooks, vol. 8, 1928, WHMC-Columbia; "Bethesda Old Trails Shaft to Mark Route," *Washington Post,* July 22, 1928, 24.

67. Elizabeth Butler Gentry (Missouri Good Roads Committee, DAR), "The Old Trails Road, the National Highway: A Memorial to the Pioneer Men and Women," 1911, 9, folder The Old Trails Road, the National Highway: A Memorial to the Pioneer Men and Women, box 1, series 1, MOTC.

68. "The Madonna of the Trail," *Kansas City Star,* August 8, 1915, 1; "A Madonna of the Prairies," *Century Illustrated Magazine,* December 1909, 287; Gentry, "National Old Trails Road Department," *DAR Magazine,* August–September 1914, 133; "Notable Meeting," *Democrat News* (Marshall, MO), August 13, 1914, unidentified newspaper, folder 11, Van Brunt Collection.

69. "Madonna of the Trail Statuette," folder Reference File, Madonna of the Trail, *DAR Magazine,* 1914–1993, HG Papers, series 2.6 administrative, MOTC; Amelia M. McFig, "Pioneer Mothers' Memorial Monument," June 22, 1929, folder Dedication and Unveiling of the New Mexico Madonna, 1928–1929, box 3, series 2, MOTC.

70. "The Pioneer Mothers of the Covered Wagon Days," DAR, Missouri State Society Scrapbooks, vol. 8, 1928, WHMC-Columbia; "A Community Remembers Its Debt to Pathfinders," September 18, 1928, unidentified newspaper, DAR, Missouri State Society Scrapbooks, vol. 8, 1928; "Springerville, Arizona," "Vandalia, Illinois," "Upland, California," all in folder Cornerstone Items–Maryland Madonna Statue, c. 1929, box 4, series 5, MOTC.

71. "Springerville, Arizona," MOTC.

72. Burton L. Smith, "Upland Relives Early Era," *Los Angeles Times,* February 2, 1929, 1.

73. See "Dedication and Unveiling: September 24th, 1928, Lamar, Colorado," folder Program—Unveiling and Dedication, Madonna of the Trail, Colorado, 1928, box 1, series 2, MOTC; "Washington, Pennsylvania," folder Cornerstone Items—Maryland Madonna Statue, ca. 1929, box 4, series 5, MOTC.

74. "Vandalia, Illinois," MOTC; R. Scott, *Illinois State History*, 111; Bodnar, *Remaking America*, 35, 119.

75. "Dedication and Unveiling: September 24th, 1928, Lamar, Colorado," MOTC; "Albuquerque, New Mexico," folder Cornerstone Items–Maryland Madonna Statue, c. 1929, box 4, series 5, MOTC; "Statue Is Unveiled to Pioneer Mother," *Washington Post*, April 20, 1929, 20; "Vandalia, Illinois," MOTC; "The Madonna of the Trail," *DAR Magazine*, July 1929, 403.

76. Smith, "Upland Relives Early Era," *Los Angeles Times*, February 2, 1929, 1; "Vandalia, Illinois," MOTC; R. Scott, *Illinois State History*, 111; "Upland, California," MOTC; "Springerville, Arizona," MOTC.

77. Arlene Moss quoted in "Old Trails Road Marker Unveiled," April 1929, unidentified newspaper, DAR in Georgia Scrapbook, 1929–1932. See also "Statue Is Unveiled to Pioneer Mother," *Washington Post*, April 20, 1929, 20.

78. Arlene Moss quoted in B. Moss, "Statue of the Madonna of the Trail," 539. The invitations to the dedication ceremony in Missouri contained similar language ("Invitation," DAR, Missouri State Society Scrapbooks, vol. 8, 1928).

79. "Albuquerque, New Mexico," MOTC. See also J. Baker, *West Virginia State History of the DAR*, 149.

80. Quoted in J. Baker, *West Virginia State History of the DAR*, 149.

81. "Springerville, Arizona," MOTC; "A Community Remembers Its Debt to Pathfinders," September 18, 1928, unidentified newspaper, DAR, Missouri State Society Scrapbooks, vol. 8, 1928; Smith, "Upland Relives Early Era," *Los Angeles Times*, February 2, 1929, 1.

82. "Upland, California," MOTC. A similar example is found in folder Cornerstone Items—Maryland Madonna Statue, ca. 1929, box 4, series, 5, MOTC.

83. In 1915 the Pioneer Mother Monument Association of San Francisco managed to raise almost $30,000 for *The Pioneer Mother*, a bronze statue that adorned the front of San Francisco's Palace of Fine Arts (Prescott, *Gender and Generation*, 145).

84. Mrs. Carl Christol, "South Dakota D.A.R. Markers," *DAR Magazine*, May 1937, 381–384; Mrs. C. A. Rasmusson, "Montana History Revealed by Its Markers," *DAR Magazine*, January 1936, 38. On earlier Lewis and Clark markers in Montana, see Mrs. C. A. Rasmusson, "D.A.R. Activities in Montana," *DAR Magazine*, July 1927, 515; Mrs. Lewis D. Smith, *State History: Daughters of the American Revolution in Montana*, no pagination, MOTC; Kansas DAR, *History of the Kansas DAR*, 54; J. Baker, *West Virginia State History of the DAR*, 138; Louise Hartley, "Around the Calendar with Famous Americans: VI. Daniel Boone," *National Historical Magazine*, February 1940, 20–21; Morley, *History of California State Society DAR*, 116; Lindly, *Nebraska State History of the DAR*, 365; Somerville, *Historic and Memorial Buildings of the DAR*, 248.

85. Christol, "South Dakota D.A.R. Markers," *DAR Magazine*, May 1937, 381; Speulda, "Unveiling of the Kelley Cabin Marker," 242–252. For similar forms of commemoration, see "D.A.R. To Mark Historic Site," *Los Angeles Times*, November 29, 1925, 15; "History of the Sarah Ann Cochrane Chapter," box 22, Michigan DAR Records; "Patriots Pay Honor to Illinois Pioneer," *Christian Science Monitor*, December 12, 1927, 4; Lindly, *Nebraska State History of the DAR*, 373; Somerville, *Historic and Memorial Buildings of the DAR*, 262, 266, 278, 304, 314.

86. Morley, *History of California State Society DAR*, 116. For a similar example, see Mrs. Carl Christol, "South Dakota D.A.R. Markers," *DAR Magazine*, May 1937, 383.

87. Mrs. James E. Babb, "Marker Erected by Idaho Daughters," *DAR Magazine*, January 1925, 34.

88. Morley, *History of California State Society DAR*, 112, 115–116; Rensch and Rensch, *Historic Spots in California*, ix, 38; Glassberg, *Sense of History*, 193.

89. Jacobson, "Becoming Caucasian," 90.

90. Grace A. Cooper, "Utah Spots Marked," *DAR Magazine,* September 1937, 811–812.

91. Rensch and Rensch, *Historic Spots in California,* 213.

92. Glassberg, *Sense of History,* 193.

93. "State Historian's Annual Report. Kalamazoo, Mich., October 8, 1929," Minutes of the Michigan State Executive Board D.A.R. from June 1928 to 1931, box 1, Michigan DAR Records; 1931 Folder, box 17, Michigan DAR Records. For similar forms of commemoration in Missouri, see "First Settlement Marked," June 24, 1928, unidentified newspaper, DAR, Missouri State Scrapbooks, vol. 8, 1928.

94. Catherine Cate Coblentz, "The Cradle of the States: III. The First Babies of the Midwest," *National Historical Magazine,* January 1941, 6–15; Catherine Cate Coblentz, "The Cradle of the States: IV. The First Far Western Babies," *National Historical Magazine,* February 1941, 37–38, 42 (quote), 47.

95. Morgan, "'Home and Country,'" 176; DAR Eunice Sterling Chapter, *Illustrated History of Early Wichita;* Lucy Wilder Morris, "Old Trails in Minnesota," *DAR Magazine,* August 1913, 512 (quote).

96. "Pioneers of Michigan," box 17, Michigan DAR Records; "Seventh State Regency of Michigan: Miss Alice Louise McDuffee, 1919–1922," folder Reports to Congress & Conference, box 12, Michigan DAR Records; Farrar McFarland, "Report of State Historian, Oct. 9, 1923," folder Annual Reports, box 12, Michigan DAR Records. See also "Glimpses of Pioneer Life," box 17, Michigan DAR Records; Mary A. Goodhue to My Dear Madam Historian, May 21, 1936, Michigan DAR scrapbook, box 12, Michigan DAR Records. See also Sarah R. Hadenworth Staffler, "Pioneer Stories," 1935, box 17, Michigan DAR Records; State Historian to Dear Chapter Historian, August 2, 1937, folder Letter to Chapters, box 12, Michigan DAR Records; review of *Men of Champoeg: A Record of the Lives of the Pioneers Who Founded the Oregon Government,* by Caroline C. Dobbs, Metropolitan Press, Portland, Oregon, 1932, *DAR Magazine,* August 1933, 509–510; DAR Sarah Platt Decker Chapter, *Pioneers of San Juan Country,* vols. 1 and 2.

97. Lou Wheeler, "Historical Report of Coldwater Chapter D.A.R., 1925–1926," box 33, Michigan DAR Records. See also "Priscilla Mullens Chapter (Galena, Ill.)," *DAR Magazine,* January 1928, 30–31; Mrs. Charles H. Smith, "Pioneer Women of Deerfield, Portage County, 1799–1850," n.d., folder 6, box 1, Western Reserve Chapter DAR Records; Mrs. Leah Beach Garner, "Pioneer Women of Genesee County," 1935, Michigan DAR Records. For a similar view on women in Michigan, see "History of the Sarah Ann Cochrane Chapter," box 22, Michigan DAR Records.

98. Margaret Ward, "Sarah Wood Ward," folder Sarah Wood Ward, DAR Yankton, SD, Chapter Papers, LOC.

99. See Lerna Diez Veling, "In Early Days," folder In Early Days, DAR Yankton Chapter Papers; Mrs. Lee Cope, "Pioneering in Clay County," folder Pioneering in Clay County, DAR Yankton Chapter Papers; Jessie M. Bartholomew, "Reminiscences of Early Life in Yankton," folder "Reminiscences of Early Life in Yankton," DAR Yankton Chapter Papers.

100. Bodnar, *Remaking America,* 114–119; O'Leary, *To Die For,* 3–6; Gladys Stowe Minahan, "Wisconsin Tercentennial," *DAR Magazine,* July 1934, 413; Mrs. Charles D. Beagle to Dear Chapter Historians, September 25, 1935, folder Letter to Chapters, box 12, Michigan DAR Records; Edna Gay Laity, "Dakota Territorial Diamond Jubilee," folder Dakota Territory Diamond Jubilee, 4, 8, DAR Yankton Chapter Papers.

101. Wrobel, *Promised Lands,* 112; Kammen, *Mystic Chords of Memory,* 398–399; Bodnar, *Remaking America,* 134–135.

Chapter 3. "Let Us Clasp Hands, Red Man and White Man": The DAR and the American Indian

1. "Uplift of Indians Is Urged on D.A.R.," *Washington Post*, April 21, 1921, 1; "D.A.R. Notes," *Washington Post*, April 18, 1921, 3; Deloria, *Indians in Unexpected Places*, 206; Levy, *Frontier Figures*, 107–108; Troutman, *Indian Blues*, 201, 233–238.

2. "Uplift of Indians Is Urged on D.A.R.," *Washington Post*, April 21, 1921, 1; DAR, *Proceedings of the Thirtieth Continental Congress of the National Society DAR* (1921), 158, 162.

3. DAR, *Proceedings of the Thirtieth Continental Congress of the National Society DAR* (1921), 214.

4. See Dippie, *Vanishing American*, 200; Ostler, *Lakotas and the Black Hills*; Richardson, *Wounded Knee*.

5. See Adams, *Education for Extinction*; Bolt, *American Indian Policy and American Reform*; Genetin-Pilawa, *Crooked Paths to Allotment*; Hoxie, *Final Promise*; Stremlau, *Sustaining the Cherokee Family*.

6. Dippie, *Vanishing American*, 241–257; Basson, *White Enough to Be American?*, 1–5; Horsman, *Race and Manifest Destiny*, 190–191; Berkhofer, *White Man's Indian*, 155; Wolfe, "Land, Labor, and Difference," 867, 892.

7. On these developments, see Dilworth, *Imagining Indians in the Southwest*; Huhndorf, *Going Native*; Berkhofer, *White Man's Indian*; Deloria, *Playing Indian*; Moses, *Wild West Shows and the Images of American Indians*; Trachtenberg, *Shades of Hiawatha*.

8. See Huhndorf, *Going Native*, 15; Pearce, *Savagism and Civilization*; Rosaldo, "Imperialist Nostalgia"; S. L. Smith, *Reimagining Indians*; Trachtenberg, *Shades of Hiawatha*.

9. "Indian Markers Set Up by D.A.R.," *Christian Science Monitor*, May 9, 1913, 10; J. Baker, *West Virginia State History of the DAR*, 139; Edith W. Wallace and Sarah Parker Dunlap, "Conference of the National Society, Daughters of the American Revolution, August 15–21, 1916," *DAR Magazine*, November 1916, 299; "Olla-Podrida," *Morning Herald* (Lexington, KY), June 1, 1896, 6; "Monument Reminder of Indian Campaign," *Philadelphia Inquirer*, October 30, 1902, 3; "Pascommuck Massacre of 1704," *Boston Journal*, May 25, 1904, 6; Mary Crawford Hornady, "Growing Service of Federation," *Atlanta Constitution*, November 24, 1912, D7; "The Captain Jessen Leavenworth Chapter," *DAR Magazine*, March 1919, 173–174.

10. Berkhofer, *White Man's Indian*, 171.

11. Cross quoted in "Captain Christopher Robinson Chapter," *DAR Magazine*, February 1918, 103–104. For similar examples of DAR monuments and publications that honored American Indians for ceding their lands by signing treaties with the US government and lauded them for their friendship with white settlers, see "History of the Saginaw Chapter Daughters of the American Revolution," 1924, 15–17, box 22, Michigan DAR Records; Lindly, *Nebraska State History DAR*, 355–357; Lila Young Franklin, "Historic Spots in Mississippi," *American Monthly Magazine*, November 1911, 261–262; "Daughters of the American Revolution: Treaty Oak," *The State* (Columbia, SC), November 1, 1911, 15; "Monument to Creek Indians Is Finished," *Macon (GA) Daily Telegraph*, January 1, 1912, 2; "Captain Richard Somers Chapter," *DAR Magazine*, March 1915, 147–148; "To Place Granite Boulder in Commemoration of Treaty," *Atlanta Constitution*, July 30, 1911, B12; "Treaty of Peace to Be Observed in Coleraine Monument to Be Unveiled in Commemoration," *Macon Daily Telegraph*, June 17, 1912, 6.

12. Dippie, *Vanishing American*, 262.

13. Blanche M. Haines, "Historic Work along the St. Joseph," *American Monthly Magazine*, May 1912, 262–264; "Markers Placed by Abiel Fellows Chapter 1905 to 1940," box 33, Michi-

gan DAR Records. On Sauganash, whose Christian name was Billy Caldwell, see Edmunds, *Potawatomis.*

14. "Historic M'Intosh Rock Marked by Bronze Tablet," *Atlanta Constitution,* July 3, 1911, 11; "Society," *Macon Daily Telegraph,* July 4, 1911, 5; M. Green, "William McIntosh."

15. Alfriend quoted in "Famous M'Intosh House, Indian Spring, Where D.A.R. Recently Unveiled Tablet," *Atlanta Constitution,* July 21, 1912, C7. On McIntosh and the Creek, see Griffith, *McIntosh and Weatherford;* Wright, *Creeks and Seminoles.*

16. On Logan Fontenelle and the Omaha, see Boughter, *Betraying the Omaha Nation;* Wishart, *Unspeakable Sadness.* On the controversy over whether Fontenelle was a legitimate chief, see O'Shea and Ludwickson, "Omaha Chieftainship in the Nineteenth Century," 347n6.

17. Lindly, *Nebraska State History of the DAR,* 353. For similar examples of the DAR's praise for "loyal" Native American chiefs prior to the end of World War I, see "Boston Notes," *New York Times,* May 13, 1905, 31; "Chief Keokuk in Bronze," *New York Times,* October 23, 1913, 12; "Bronze Indian Marks Early Trail," *Popular Mechanics,* January 1914, 24; "Keokuk Chapter," *DAR Magazine,* July 1914, 13–14.

18. "Marking an Indian's Grave," *Chicago Daily Tribune,* December 4, 1908, 8; "Junaluska," *American Monthly Magazine,* July 1911, 64 (first quote); M. Hall, *Brief History of the Maine DAR,* 14 (second quote).

19. "Captain Christopher Robinson Chapter," 104.

20. "Junaluska," *American Monthly Magazine,* July 1911, 65; Lunsford, *God's Messengers from the Mountains,* 75; "Historic M'Intosh Rock Marked by Bronze Tablet," *Atlanta Constitution,* July 3, 1911, 11.

21. Cornsilk quoted in Duncan and Riggs, *Cherokee Heritage Trails Guidebook,* 122.

22. M. Hall, *Brief History of the Maine DAR,* 14, 18; Mrs. S. L. Boardman, "Work of Maine Daughters," *American Monthly Magazine,* December 1912–January 1913, 65 (quote).

23. "Dedication of the Indian Memorial Monument at Pleasant Point Reservation, Maine, June 14, 1916," *DAR Magazine,* September 1916, 163–164; M. Hall, *Brief History of the Maine DAR,* 20–21. On Louis Mitchell, see Murphree, *Native America,* 480; Prins and McBride, *Asticou's Island Domain,* 315–316.

24. Flora Clarke Huntington, "An Outline of the Six Nations or the League of the 'Iroquois,'" *American Monthly Magazine,* October 1897, 389.

25. Deloria, *Indians in Unexpected Places,* 20.

26. See Feest, "Pride and Prejudice"; R. Green, "Pocahontas Perplex," 203–211.

27. Jane S. Owen, "Pocahontas, Mother of an Empire," *American Monthly Magazine,* November 1907, 702.

28. Lelia Cavins Baughman, "Colonial Women," *American Monthly Magazine,* October 1909, 987.

29. Bratton, *History of the South Carolina DAR,* 53–55, 56. For a similar story on an Indian "princess," see Eunice Strickland, "Captain Samuel Brady," *American Monthly Magazine,* November 1909, 1066–1068, 1069.

30. Ella Cox Cromer, "Abbeville in Colonial Times," *The State* (Columbia, SC), August 8, 1915, 18.

31. Hefernan and Medlicot, "Feminine Atlas?," 114.

32. Brooks, "Sacajawea, Meet *Cogewa*," 184. On the memory of Sacagawea and the Portland exhibition, see L. Blee, "Completing Lewis and Clark's Westward March"; Kessler, *Making of Sacagawea.*

33. Richards, "Inventing Sacagawea."

34. "In Sacajawea's Honor," *Anaconda (MT) Standard,* October 1, 1914, 28; "Honor Indian Heroine," *Washington Post,* November 9, 1914, 5; Bertha Taft Keith, "Montana Daughters Unveil a Tablet," *DAR Magazine,* December 1914, 306. Similar memorials were erected in Wyoming and Idaho.

35. "What Became of Sacajawea?," *Sunday Oregonian* (Portland), April 9, 1916, 4; Lewis, *In the Footsteps of Lewis and Clark,* 26.

36. "Indian Princess and American Composer Will Give Concert Here for Local D.A.R. Chapter," unidentified newspaper, n.d., in "The Ideal Scrapbook," box 21, Michigan DAR Records.

37. Troutman, "Indian Blues," 298, 304–306; Troutman, *Indian Blues,* 233, 238.

38. Morgan, "'Home and Country,'" 49–50; "Of Indian Descent," *Washington Post,* April 20, 1905, 2.

39. "The Indian and We," *Atlanta Constitution,* October 13, 1912, C6.

40. "Chapter of D.A.R. Here," *Morning Olympian,* November 23, 1905, 1; Lester, *Ohio State History of the DAR,* 295.

41. Ward, *State History of the New Jersey DAR,* 98, 171, 174. See also DAR Georgia State Society, *Chapter Histories,* 78; White, *Tennessee State History of the DAR,* 123; Clarkson, *Historical Records of the Michigan DAR,* 222, 254, 359; "History of Coldwater Chapter D.A.R.," box 33, Michigan DAR Records; Florence Hague Becker, "Hidden Histories in Chapter Names," *DAR Magazine,* April 1932, 205; "Georgia Indian Names and What They Mean," *Atlanta Constitution,* June 14, 1914, C2.

42. "State Meeting of D.A.R. Closes with Memorial," unidentified newspaper, 1916, Sarah Caswell Angell Chapter, box 5, Michigan DAR Records; "Indian Basketry Will Be Revived," unidentified newspaper, October 18, 1916, scrapbook, DAR Charity Cook Chapter, Michigan DAR Records; "D.A.R. Observes Annual Indian Day," unidentified newspaper, May 26, 1917, DAR Charity Cook Chapter, Michigan DAR Records.

43. "Historical Pageant by Dalton Chapter," *Atlanta Constitution,* June 14, 1914, C2. That same year, a similar pageant was performed by a DAR chapter in Michigan (Sue I. Silliman, "History of the Abiel Fellows Chapter, Daughters of the American Revolution, Three Rivers, Mich., 1915–1916," box 33, Michigan DAR Records).

44. Silliman, "History of the Abiel Fellows Chapter," Michigan DAR Records.

45. Britten, *American Indians in World War I,* 71, 84, 186–187; Carroll, *Medicine Bags and Dog Tags,* 102–103, 112; Holm, *Strong Hearts, Wounded Souls,* 89, 99–101; Rosier, *Serving Their Country,* 9 (quote), 46–48.

46. DAR, *Proceedings of Thirtieth Continental Congress of the National Society DAR* (1921), 158, 214. See also Anne Rogers Minor, "Message from President General," *Atlanta Constitution,* July 31, 1921, C3.

47. Berkhofer, *White Man's Indian,* 176.

48. Rosier, *Serving Their Country,* 60; Bernstein, *American Indians and World War II,* 19.

49. Morley, *History of California State Society DAR,* 145.

50. Burke in "Menace in Aliens He Tells D.A.R.," *Washington Post,* April 20, 1922, 4.

51. "Americanization and Law Enforcement Stressed," *Washington Post,* April 18, 1924, 8; "Veterans' Bureau Change Demanded," *Christian Science Monitor,* March 15, 1924, 2.

52. Berkhofer, *White Man's Indian,* 178–182; Bernstein, *American Indians and World War II,* 3–4.

53. DAR, *Proceedings of the Twenty-Eighth Continental Congress of the National Society DAR* (1919), 165 (quotes); DAR, *Proceedings of the Twenty-Ninth Continental Congress of the National Society DAR* (1920), 125–126.

54. Mrs. John Trigg Moss, "Conservation and Thrift," *Washington Post,* April 17, 1922, 8.

55. Myra H. Patch, "Prize Winning Paper on Indian Life, History and Ideals," *DAR Magazine,* July 1922, 402–403.

56. "Tragedy Scene to be Marked," *Los Angeles Times,* February 4, 1921, I10; Mrs. Robert N. Whiteford, "Ohio Honors Anthony Wayne: Revolutionary War Hero," *DAR Magazine,* December 1929, 721–722; Zella Armstrong, "Women and Children in Indian Massacres," *DAR Magazine,* September 1931, 551–556; Esther Virgin, "Historical Markers in Wyoming," *National Historical Magazine,* July 1938, 28–30; Lester, *Ohio State History of the DAR,* 76; "Mrs. Carl Christol, "South Dakota D.A.R. Markers," *DAR Magazine,* May 1937, 381–384; Barrington, *Historic Restorations of the DAR* (entries "California: Fort Humboldt," "Kansas: Fort Leavenworth," "Nevada: Fort Churchill").

57. Mrs. C. A. Rasmusson, "Montana History Revealed by Its Markers," *DAR Magazine,* January 1936, 38 (quote). See also Mrs. C. A. Rasmusson, "The Trail of the Markers," July 1940, in Mrs. Lewis D. Smith, *State History: Daughters of the American Revolution in Montana,* ed. Mrs. Lewis D. Smith (n.p., n.d.), no pagination, DAR Archives.

58. "Marker Placed in Honor of Famed Cherokee Chief," *Atlanta Constitution,* July 13, 1922, 2; "Ross Homestead Marked," *Atlanta Constitution,* August 6, 1922, D8.

59. White, *Tennessee State History of the DAR,* 124.

60. Garrison, *Legal Ideology of Removal,* 199–202.

61. "History of Abiel Fellows Chapter, 1921–1922"; Annette Cowling, "Thirty-Five Candles and Their Highlights," 8 (quote), box 33, Michigan DAR Records. For similar commemorations in Mississippi and Washington State, see "Marker Will Be Dedicated," *Morning Oregonian,* June 14, 1922, 11; Porter, *History of the Mississippi State Society DAR,* 135.

62. Photograph of the bronze marker, in the author's possession.

63. Sleeper-Smith, *Indian Women and French Men,* 107; "Tried to Live as Whites," *Kansas City Star,* May 18, 1922, 8; "Tablet Marks Indian Exodus," unidentified newspaper, 1926, folder Historical, box 17, Michigan DAR Records. For a comprehensive history of the commemoration of Indian removal in the South, see Denson, *Monuments to Absence.*

64. Jones and Reynolds, *Coweta County Chronicles,* 2.

65. DAR, Kansas City Chapter, "George Washington Bicentennial Musical Pageant," June 3, 1932, box 6, Missouri DAR Collection, WHMC–Kansas City.

66. Viola Warren Hively, "Princess Aracoma," *National Historical Magazine,* April 1938, 43. On what is known about Aracoma, see "Aracoma (ca. 1740s-1780)," in Murphree, *Native America,* 1239–1240.

67. "Creek Council Tree at Tulsa Recalls City's Early History," *Christian Science Monitor,* October 4, 1924, 17. For similar examples from Idaho, Georgia, and Michigan, see "Old Fort Hall Chapter (Blackfoot, Idaho)," *DAR Magazine,* February 1929, 109; "Hightower Path Marker Unveiled," unidentified newspaper, October 20, 1931, DAR in Georgia, scrapbook 1929–1932, Georgia Archives; Michigan DAR, *Historical and Genealogical Records,* 81, 83; "D.A.R. Tablet to Mark Site of Old Indian Village," unidentified newspaper, July 1927, folder "1931," box 17, Michigan DAR Records; "D.A.R. Unveils Tablet," *New York Times,* November 17, 1929, N4.

68. "Pueblo Chapter," *DAR Magazine,* June 1930, 371.

69. "Roanoke D.A.R. Has Meeting Devoted to Study of Indians," unidentified newspaper, n.d., DAR in Georgia, scrapbook 1929–1932, Georgia Archives.

70. For additional examples of the DAR's focus on Indian arts and crafts, Indian Days, and playing Indian in the Midwest, West, and South, see "Southern California D.A.R. Chap-

ters Have Indian Day Program and Luncheon," *Los Angeles Times*, November 26, 1933, B6; Lena Creswell, "The Spirit of the Hand-Made," *National Historical Magazine*, July 1938, 16–20; "D.A.R. to Give Pageant," unidentified newspaper, scrapbook, DAR Colorado Society, 1939–1940, OV folio 1, DAR Colorado State Society Collection, Denver Public Library; Beagle, *Michigan Society DAR Presents "The Fairy Isle"*; "Report on Indian Work in Michigan 1938–1939," box 15, Michigan DAR Records; "D.A.R. Chapter in Indian Program," unidentified newspaper, September 20, 1935, scrapbook, Benjamin Lyon Chapter DAR, Texas DAR Collection.

71. Berkhofer, *White Man's Indian*, 182–186; Bernstein, *American Indians and World War II*, 5–10. On the Indian Reorganization Act, see Philip, *John Collier's Crusade for Indian Reform*; Taylor, *New Deal and American Indian Tribalism*.

72. Berkhofer, *White Man's Indian*, 185. On missionaries' opposition to the IRA, see Daily, *Battle for the BIA*.

73. DAR, *Proceedings of the Forty-Third Continental Congress of the National Society DAR* (1934), 625.

74. "The American Indian and Present-Day Education," *DAR Magazine*, August 1932, 496; Medlicott, "One Social Milieu, Paradoxical Responses," 44n51.

75. "Daughters of the American Revolution Seek Citizenship for Indians in Ambitious Program," *Washington Post*, February 14, 1937, S6; Sarah Corbin Robert, "If I Could Talk to You," *National Historical Magazine*, September 1940, 3; Mrs. William H. Schlosser to Mrs. Loren E. Rex, October 29, 1941, scrapbook, Daughters of the American Revolution (hereafter cited as DAR Scrapbook), American Indian Committee Papers (hereafter cited as AIC Papers), Carl A. Kroch Library, Division of Rare and Manuscript Collections, Cornell University, Ithaca, NY.

76. National Society DAR, "What the Daughters Do" (Washington, DC: DAR, 1941), 4, DAR Scrapbook, AIC Papers.

77. Leda Ferrell Rex to My Dear State Chairman, August 1941; "Fifty-First Continental Congress—Second Day, Afternoon," 1942, 129, both in DAR Scrapbook, AIC Papers; "Committee Reports: The American Indians Committee," *National Historical Magazine*, February 1942, 115.

78. National Society Daughters of the American Revolution, "What the Daughters Do," 4, DAR Scrapbook, AIC Papers.

79. Since the bureau did not include in its count Indians of mixed racial heritage, who were not officially registered on tribal rolls or in Indian agencies' files, the actual number was probably much higher (Bernstein, *American Indians and World War II*, 11; Trachtenberg, *Shades of Hiawatha*, 211).

80. Ramona Kaiser, "American Indians Committee," *National Historical Magazine*, November 1945, 592.

81. Leda Rex to My Dear State Chairman, August 1942, AIC Papers; "Committee Reports: American Indians Committee," *National Historical Magazine*, June 1942, 457–468; "Chicago Report–1942," DAR Scrapbook, AIC Papers.

82. Kaiser, "American Indians Committee," November 1945, 592.

83. See, for example, Messenger, *Ohio State History of the DAR*, 81–82.

84. "Fifty-First Continental Congress—Second Day, Afternoon," 1942, 129; Leda Rex to My Dear State Chairman, August 1942, AIC Papers; "Committee Reports: American Indians Committee," *National Historical Magazine*, February 1943, AIC Papers.

85. Leda Ferrell Rex to My Dear State Chairman, December 1941 (quote), DAR Scrapbook, AIC Papers. See also Leda Ferrell Rex to My Dear State Chairman, July 1943, AIC Papers;

"Fifty-First Continental Congress—Second Day, Afternoon," 1942, 129; Leda Ferrell Rex, "1943," AIC Papers; "Committee Reports: American Indians Committee," *National Historical Magazine*, June 1942, 457–468; "Chicago Report–1942," DAR Scrapbook, AIC Papers; Leda Ferrell Rex to My Dear State Chairman, July 1943.

86. Leda Ferrell Rex to My Dear State Chairman, July 1943.

87. Carroll, *Medicine Bags and Dog Tags*, 40–42, 55, 87, 115–120; Holm, *Strong Hearts, Wounded Souls*, 104–107; Leda Rex to My Dear State Chairman, December 7, 1943 (quote), AIC Papers.

88. Mrs. Loren Edgar Rex, "The American Indian and National Defense," *National Defense News*, September–October 1942, 15–17, AIC Papers.

89. Vylla Poe Wilson, "D.A.R. Plans Party for Indians Here on War Activities," *Times-Herald* (Washington, DC), July 13, 1942, 10; "Young Indians D.A.R. Guests at Program," unidentified newspaper, DAR Scrapbook, AIC Papers; "American Indians Committee," *National Historical Magazine*, August 1942, 645. Pouch's remarks were paraphrased in this report on the event.

90. Leda Rex to My Dear State Chairman, August 1942, AIC Papers.

91. "Committee Reports: American Indians Committee," February 1943; Rex, "1943," AIC Papers; Messenger, *Ohio State History of the DAR*, 81; Leda Ferrell Rex to My Dear State Chairman, July 1943; "Committee Reports: American Indians Committee," *National Historical Magazine*, July 1943 (quotes), AIC Papers.

92. Hattie Starcher, "Our American Indians," *National Historical Magazine*, September 1945, 490–491.

93. Bernstein, *American Indians and World War II*, 112–130.

94. Leda Rex, "American Indians," *National Historical Magazine*, December 1945, 638.

95. Rex, in "Committee Reports: The American Indian Committee," February 1942, 114.

Chapter 4. "Conserve the Sources of Our Race in the Anglo-Saxon Line": African Americans, New Immigrants, and Ethnic Nationalism

1. "Throng Honors Marian Anderson in Concert at Lincoln Memorial," *New York Times*, April 10, 1939, 15; "Constitution Hall, D.A.R. Auditorium, Is Dedicated," *Washington Post*, October 24, 1929, 1; Edward T. Folliard, "Ickes Introduces Contralto at Lincoln Memorial; Many Officials Attend Concert," *Washington Post*, April 10, 1939, 1.

2. Bennett, *Party of Fear*, 160–180; Higham, *Strangers in the Land*, 4–172; Mirel, *Patriotic Pluralism*, 6.

3. Roediger, *Colored White*; Jacobson, *Whiteness of a Different Color*; Hale, *Making Whiteness*, 4–9; Fredrickson, *Racism*, 100; Blum, *Reforging the White Republic*, 3–16.

4. On these historical developments, see Berg, *Popular Justice*; Foner, *Reconstruction*; Hahn, *Nation under Our Feet*; McMillen, *Dark Journey*.

5. "Daughters Mad at Roosevelt," *Atlanta Constitution*, March 1, 1903, 5; "D.A.R. in East Room," *Washington Post*, February 28, 1903, 2. On this controversy and the American public's reactions to it, see Davis, *Guest of Honor*.

6. Lee quoted in "Women Angry at Negro," *Chicago Daily Tribune*, December 16, 1904, 7.

7. See S. Green, *Remember Me to Miss Louisa*; Hodes, *White Women, Black Men*; Smithers, *Slave Breeding*; Sommerville, *Rape and Race in the Nineteenth-Century South*.

8. Mrs. Edgar A. Ross, "Objects of D.A.R.," *Atlanta Constitution*, April 23, 1905, E2.

9. Ross quoted in "Session Was Interesting," *Atlanta Constitution*, November 22, 1906,

4. See also "Georgia D.A.R. to Urge Important Legislation," *Atlanta Constitution*, March 14, 1909, D8.

10. "Georgia D.A.R. to Urge Important Legislation," *Atlanta Constitution*, March 14, 1909, D8.

11. "Dr. Orme Speaks," *Atlanta Constitution*, February 17, 1896, 7. The DAR's constitution stated that "any woman" could join the organization if she was at least eighteen years old and descended from a patriot, "provided that the applicant shall be acceptable to the Society" (*Constitution and By-Laws of the Daughters of the American Revolution*), 4.

12. Ross, "Objects of D.A.R.," *Atlanta Constitution*, April 23, 1905.

13. "Honor Colonial War Negro Hero," *Christian Science Monitor*, July 17, 1909, 13.

14. William L. Scruggs, "Slavery in Colonial Days," *American Monthly Magazine*, November 1894, 429–435; Mary Shelley Pechin, "The Bond Slaves; Or, the White Indentured," *American Monthly Magazine*, October 1900, 323–332.

15. See Blight, *Race and Reunion*; Gallagher and Nolan, *Myth of the Lost Cause*.

16. Wolfe, "Land, Labor, and Difference"; Wolfe, "Settler Colonialism and the Elimination of the Native."

17. Denson, *Monuments to Absence*, 2–7.

18. Wolfe, "Land, Labor, and Difference," 880–883, 887; Denson, *Monuments to Absence*.

19. "Organized New Chapter," *Washington Post*, May 20, 1905, 4; "Funeral of Miss Desha," *Washington Post*, January 31, 1911, 2; Cox, *Dixie's Daughters*, 1–9, 94–96; Stott, "From Lost Cause to Female Empowerment," 5–6, 162–163; "D.A.R. Delegates Are Welcomed to Capital," *Washington Post*, April 17, 1906, 3; "All the Woman's Clubs News of Georgia," *Atlanta Constitution*, July 16, 1905, D6; "Echoes of Flag Day," *Atlanta Constitution*, June 30, 1912, C7; "Flag Day Observed," *Washington Post*, June 13, 1913, 3; "Power of the South," *Washington Post*, November 13, 1912, 1.

20. Silber, *Romance of Reunion*, 163; Morgan, *Women and Patriotism in Jim Crow America*, 12; "Lincoln Program Arranged by D.A.R.," *Chicago Daily Tribune*, February 11, 1912, 16; "Report of the Committee on Promotion of Patriotism in the Public Schools," folder 2, box 1, Western Reserve Chapter DAR Records; "Auxiliary to the Veterans," *Washington Post*, October 6, 1902, G8; "Aids of the Soldiers," *Washington Post*, February 25, 1896, 2 (quote).

21. "Flags Cause Controversy," *Washington Post*, November 24, 1912, E1.

22. "Stirs D.A.R. Anger," *Washington Post*, April 21, 1914, 12.

23. S. M. Smith, *American Archives*, 136. See also McConnell, "Reading the Flag," 113–114.

24. S. M. Smith, *American Archives*, 137–143. Historian Carolyn Strange has rightly pointed out that mere descent from an American patriot did not necessarily guarantee DAR membership, since members' active patriotism in the present was another crucial requirement, but the controversy over the constitution's "mother of a patriot" clause clearly testifies to the inextricable interrelationship that the Daughters saw between genealogy, whiteness, and patriotism ("Sisterhood of Blood," 115).

25. Silber, *Romance of Reunion*, 11–12, 164, 168–169; "The Daughters in Congress," *Atlanta Constitution*, October 19, 1895, 2; "Daughters of Revolution Celebrate Anniversary," *Atlanta Constitution*, July 5, 1902, 8; "Substitutes for 'Dixie,'" *Atlanta Constitution*, July 16, 1905, D6; Susie Derry Parker, "Greeting to Ga. Daughters from the New State Regent," *Atlanta Constitution*, May 10, 1914, B6; Mrs. Dunbar Rowland, "Outline of Historical Study, 1916–1917," pamphlet, Mississippi Daughters of the American Revolution, vertical file, Mississippi Department of Archives and History, Archives and Records Services Division, Jackson (hereafter cited as MDAH); Eloise C. Pittman, "Woman and Society," *Atlanta Constitution*, March 2,

1899, 9; "Daughters in Session," *Washington Post,* February 21, 1899, 2; Kate Mason Rowland, "War between the States," *Washington Post,* April 30, 1899, 17.

26. Like the DAR, the UDC disputed male-centered accounts of the past and countered men's efforts to confine them to the sphere of the home but refrained from demanding woman suffrage or other political rights for women. Rather, like the Daughters, the UDC regarded motherhood and women's seemingly sex-specific sentiments as the driving force behind their efforts to enlarge female citizens' cultural and political influence in US society. See Cox, *Dixie's Daughters,* 110–111, 120–127; Stott, "From Lost Cause to Female Empowerment," 5–6, 162–163.

27. Mary Custis Lee's application for DAR membership, *American Monthly Magazine,* February 1902, 125–128; "Lee Exercises at High School Today," *Atlanta Constitution,* January 18, 1901, 7; "Patriotic Women Meet to Honor Hero's Memory," *Atlanta Constitution,* January 13, 1904, A3; "Plans for Memorial Day," *Atlanta Constitution,* April 23, 1902, 7; "D.A.R. Conference Opens at Augusta," *Atlanta Constitution,* March 27, 1913, 16; "State Convention Daughters of Confederacy," *Atlanta Constitution,* October 4, 1904, 8; "Atlanta Chapter U.D.C.," *Atlanta Constitution,* February 23, 1906, 8; Mrs. W. D. Lamar, "State D.A.R. Convention Greeted by U.D.C. President," *Atlanta Constitution,* February 22, 1914, B2.

28. See, for example, "Report of the Historian of the Texas Division U.D.C.," *Dallas Morning News,* November 30, 1899, 6; "United Daughters of the Confederacy," *Montgomery Advertiser,* December 22, 1907, 1; "Daughters of the American Revolution," *The State* (Columbia, SC), January 12, 1908, 15; "D.A.R. to Meet in Orangeburg," *The State,* November 3, 1910, 15; "Appointed Sponsor for the South to U.C.V. Reunion, Chattanooga," *Dallas Morning News,* March 21, 1913, 5; "Daughters Here for State Meeting," *Charlotte Daily Observer,* November 4, 1913, 7; "U.D.C. Convention Meets Tonight," *Charlotte Daily Observer,* October 5, 1915, 7.

29. Cox, *Dixie's Daughters,* 147; "Taft to Welcome Southern Women to Capital of Union Next," *Washington Post,* November 3, 1912, ES10; "Power for the South," *Washington Post,* November 13, 1912, 1; "D.A.R. Will Send Relief to Earthquake Victims," *Washington Post,* April 20, 1906, 8.

30. Dorsey quoted in "Honoring the Fathers," *Washington Post,* April 21, 1891, 6.

31. Lockwood quoted in "Women and Patriotism," *Washington Post,* February 23, 1893, 7.

32. Grace M. H. Wakeman, "An Antidote to Anarchy," letter to the editor, *New York Times,* September 16, 1901, 6; Mrs. L. A. Scott, "Patriotism," *American Monthly Magazine,* March 1910, 246 (quote). See also "Women's Club News of Georgia," *Atlanta Constitution,* February 10, 1907, C8.

33. Mrs. Stephen Chadwick, "The Little Green Book," *American Monthly Magazine,* June 1913, 321–323; Higham, *Strangers in the Land,* 160; Morgan, *Women and Patriotism in Jim Crow America,* 46; "Would Educate Our Immigrants," *New York Times,* October 27, 1911, 8.

34. Chadwick, "Little Green Book," *American Monthly Magazine,* June 1913, 323.

35. "Mrs. Joseph Benson Foraker," interview, *Washington Post,* June 9, 1907, E8.

36. For more information on this movement, see Mirel, *Patriotic Pluralism.*

37. Wakeman, "An Antidote to Anarchy," *New York Times,* September 16, 1901, 6; "Horace Porter Honored by the D.A.R. Congress," *Washington Post,* April 22, 1906, 11; "Women's Club News of Georgia," *Atlanta Constitution,* December 23, 1906, D3; "Patriotism Permeates the Reports of the Regents," *Washington Post,* April 18, 1906, 8; "Russian Is Prize Winner," *Washington Post,* March 7, 1907, 5; DAR, Columbus Chapter, *History of the Columbus Chapter National Society, DAR,* 7; "Head of Revolution Daughters Coming," *Los Angeles Times,* January 3, 1909, II2; "Progress, Prosperity," *Boston Daily Globe,* March 25, 1910, 14; Scott, "Patriotism," 295–297.

38. Ellen Mecum, "Committee on Patriotic Education," *American Monthly Magazine,*

January 1906, 22–23; "Moving Picture Shows Run by D.A.R. Chapters," *Atlanta Constitution*, January 15, 1911, D13; "Report of Work Done on Patriotic Education in Connection with the Board of Education, May 1910," folder 8, box 1, Western Reserve Chapter DAR Records; "The Committee on Patriotic Education," *American Monthly Magazine*, November 1910, 384–386.

39. "List of Speeches Delivered by Mr. Carr in Connection with Immigration"; "Chapter and Conn. D.A.R."; "Speech Before D.A.R. Congress, Washington, D.C., 19 April, 1912," all in folder Speeches, box 3, John Foster Carr Papers, Manuscripts and Archives Division, New York Public Library, New York; Chadwick, "The Little Green Book," *American Monthly Magazine*, June 1913, 321–323; "D.A.R. Quarter Century Work to Be Marked," *Christian Science Monitor*, July 15, 1915, 4; Clara Lee Bowman, "A National Program for 'The Little Green Book,'" *DAR Magazine*, October 1913, 614–617.

40. Caroline M. Murphy, "The Children of the Republic," *American Monthly Magazine*, December 1903, 433; Anne P. Burkham, "The Children of the Republic," *American Monthly Magazine*, October 1906, 637–644; "Committee of the Children of the Republic," *American Monthly Magazine*, November 1910, 386–387.

41. Elizabeth Neff, "The Girl Home-Makers of America," *American Monthly Magazine*, February 1912, 63–64.

42. Carrie Peables Cushman, "The Girl Home-Makers," *DAR Magazine*, February 1927, 130–131.

43. Angeline Scott, "From Readers," letter to the editor, *New York Times*, September 17, 1904, 26.

44. Chadwick, "The Little Green Book," *American Monthly Magazine*, June 1913, 321.

45. During the Children of the Republic's weekly meetings, boys studied the lives of famous statesmen as part of the DAR's goal to "cherish the memory of those forefathers and emulate them to make our country just what they intended it to be" ("Committee of the Children of the Republic," *American Monthly Magazine*, November 1910, 386 [quote]).

46. Henry Shapiro, *Appalachia on Our Mind*, ix–66.

47. "Horace Porter Honored by the D.A.R. Congress," *Washington Post*, April 22, 1906, 11; "Educational Association Makes Stirring Appeal," *Atlanta Constitution*, October 3, 1909, A4; "Philanthropy and Educational Work of D.A.R. More Important Than Their 'Ancestry Activity,'" *Washington Post*, April 14, 1912, M5; "Educational Work of the D.A.R.," *Atlanta Constitution*, April 5, 1914, D3. On the scholarly debate about Appalachia, see Henry Shapiro, *Appalachia on Our Mind*, 80–86.

48. Louise McCrory Spencer, "The Mountain School at Devil's Fork," *DAR Magazine*, July 1913, 382–386; Katherine Braddock Barrow, "The Helen Dunlap School for Mountain Girls at Winslow, Arkansas," *DAR Magazine*, August–September 1914, 80–82; "D.A.R. Will Establish School in the South," *Atlanta Constitution*, January 18, 1915, 2.

49. Scott quoted in Lovett, *Conceiving the Future*, 124.

50. Bennett, *Party of Fear*, 183–196; McClymer, "Federal Government and the Americanization Movement"; Higham, *Strangers in the Land*, 244–248, 255–256, 259; Van Nuys, *Americanizing the West*, 5–6; Ziegler-McPherson, *Americanization in the States*, 3–17; Mirel, *Patriotic Pluralism*, 5–11; Schneider, *Crossing Borders*, 151–163.

51. Guernsey quoted in "D.A.R. Chief for Ruthless Knife on Alien Cancer," *Chicago Daily Tribune*, April 20, 1920, 5. See also "At the Turning Point," *Atlanta Constitution*, January 5, 1919, C11.

52. "D.A.R. War Work Told," *Washington Post*, April 16, 1919, 4; "D.A.R. Rules Contest," *Washington Post*, April 18, 1919, 2; Franklin K. Lane, "Making Americans," *DAR Magazine*, July 1919, 399–401; "D.A.R. Americanization Committee," *DAR Magazine*, July 1919, 401;

"Comments by the President General," *DAR Magazine*, July 1919 402; Elizabeth Ellicott Poe, "America's Greatest Problem," *DAR Magazine*, January 1920, 29, 31, 32; "Urges Daughters to Assist in Americanizing Foreign Population," *Atlanta Constitution*, July 6, 1919, C3.

53. Higham, *Strangers in the Land*, 242–243; "Philip Schuyler Chapter," *DAR Magazine*, September 1917, 158; "Urges Daughters to Assist in Americanizing Foreign Population," *Atlanta Constitution*, July 6, 1919, C3; "New Citizens to Be Guests of the D.A.R.," *Christian Science Monitor*, June 13, 1918, 6; "Report of Chapter Regents to State Regents," vertical file, DAR Americanization Committee Collection (hereafter cited as DAR-ACC), WRHS; "Report of Chapter Regents to State Regents," Canton Chapter, Ohio, 1919–1920, DAR-ACC; Lester, *Ohio State History of the DAR*, 151; "Joyous Welcome for New Citizens," *Washington Post*, February 6, 1921, 20; "New Citizens to Be Guests," *Washington Post*, November 20, 1921, 9; "Report of Historian Nova Caesarea Chapter–May 5, 1922 to May 4, 1923," folder 6, box 4, DAR Nova Caesarea Chapter Collection, New Jersey Historical Society, Newark; Charlotte Prior Shelton, report, box 6, DAR, Missouri Collection, WHMC-Columbia; "History of Abiel Fellows Chapter," box 33, Michigan DAR Records; Mrs. Charles A. Davis, "Annual Report of Atlanta Chapter D.A.R., April 1921–22," folder 1, box 1, DAR Atlanta Chapter Records; "Chicago Exhibits Art of Alien Lands," *Christian Science Monitor*, September 25, 1919, 3.

54. "D.A.R. to Publish Immigrant Guide," *Washington Post*, August 8, 1920, 45.

55. DAR, National Society, *Manual of the United States*; "History of Abiel Fellows Chapter, 1923–1924, Con. 1," box 33, Michigan DAR Records; "Annual Report of Historian Nova Caesarea Chapter–1923–1924," folder 6, box 4, DAR Nova Caesarea Chapter Collection; "District D.A.R. Reports on Patriotic Activities," *Washington Post*, March 6, 1924, 5; "Speakers at D.A.R. Meet Urge Nation to Watch Ideals," *Washington Post*, April 17, 1924, 8; "D.A.R. Gives Manuals to Intended Citizens," *Washington Post*, November 25, 1924, 18; Grace H. Brosseau, "D.A.R.: Home and Country," *North American Review*, January–June 1928, 595.

56. DAR, National Society, *Manual of the United States*, 12, 29, 33, 38.

57. McClymer, "Gender and the 'American Way of Life'"; "Report of Chairman of Americanization of Foreign-Born Men and Women," 1916 (quote); Report of State Chairmen, 1927, Michigan DAR, vol. 1, A-G, box 8, Michigan DAR Records.

58. "Urges Daughters to Assist in Americanizing Foreign Population," *Atlanta Constitution*, July 6, 1919, C3; "Urges Women Work for Americanism," *Boston Daily Globe*, December 4, 1919, 5; "Minutes of the Nineteenth Annual State Conference Daughters of the American Revolution," Lansing, MI, October 7–9, 1919, box 3, Michigan DAR Records; Van Nuys, *Americanizing the West*, 122–124; Gullett, "Women Progressives," 71–94; Barrett, "Americanization from the Bottom Up," 1012; "D.A.R. of Oregon," *Atlanta Constitution*, December 11, 1921, B2; Charlotte Prior Shelton, Report, box 6, DAR, Missouri Collection, WHMC-Columbia; "Seventh State Regency of Michigan: Miss Alice Louise McDuffee, 1919–1922," folder "Reports to Congress and Conference," box 12, Michigan DAR Records; "Report of Chapter Regents to State Regents," Canton Chapter, Ohio, 1919–1920, DAR-ACC; "Annual Report of Historian Nova Caesarea Chapter–1923–1924," 2, folder 6, box 4, DAR Nova Caesarea Chapter Collection.

59. Lora Haines Cook, "A Message from the President General," *DAR Magazine*, March 1924, 140, 141; "Nation Needs Faith of Early Fathers, Mrs. Cook Declares," *Washington Post*, April 15, 1924, 8.

60. Ngai, "Architecture of Race," 67–92.

61. "History of Abiel Fellows Chapter, 1924–1925, Con. 1," Michigan DAR Records; *Proceedings of the Michigan State Conferences D.A.R.*, box 3, Michigan DAR Records; "Report of State

Chairman of Committee on Manual," Report of State Chairmen, 1927, Michigan D.A.R., vol. 1, A-G, box 8, Michigan DAR Records; "Address of Mrs. Alfred J. Brosseau," box 33, Michigan DAR Records; "Patriots Plan Season's Work," *Los Angeles Times*, September 2, 1928, C14; "D.A.R. Entertain Aliens' Children," *Christian Science Monitor*, December 20, 1928, 6; "State Conferences," *DAR Magazine*, May 1929, 289–290; Kaufmann, *Rise and Fall of Anglo-America*, 34.

62. Gullett, "Women Progressives," 71–94; Margaret Hart Strong, "Angel Island—Keeper of the Western Door," *DAR Magazine*, May 1929, 351–356; "Speakers at D.A.R. Meet Urge Nation to Watch Ideals," 8; *Proceedings of the Thirty-Fifth Continental Congress of the National Society DAR* (1926), 519.

63. Frances Tupper Nash, "Tamassee: New York's Contribution and a Look into the Future," *DAR Magazine*, October 1923, 601. See also "The 34th Continental Congress of the Daughters of the American Revolution," *DAR Magazine*, May 1925, 280; Anne Rogers Minor, "A Message from the President General," *DAR Magazine*, January 1923, 17; "Educational Work in Southern Mountains," *Atlanta Constitution*, December 13, 1925, D2; Lora Haines Cook, "'Home and Country' Slogan of D.A.R. Proud Heritage, President General States," *Washington Post*, April 19, 1926, DE1.

64. Kaufmann, *Rise and Fall of Anglo-America*, 34.

65. "Uplift of Indians Is Urged on D.A.R.," *Washington Post*, April 21, 1921, 1.

66. "Uplift of Indians Is Urged on D.A.R.," *Washington Post*, April 21, 1921, 1; "Aiding Hill Whites," *Washington Post*, April 17, 1922, 7; Grace Ward Calhoun, "The Industrial School for Mountain Girls at Tamassee, S.C.," *DAR Magazine*, January 1923, 31–33; "Alabama Has New Mountain School," *Christian Science Monitor*, October 22, 1924, 1. See also "Mountain Schools," *Atlanta Constitution*, January 11, 1925, D5; "Educational Work in Southern Mountains," *Atlanta Constitution*, December 13, 1925, D2; Lucile E. Earle, "The Kate Duncan Smith D.A.R. School," *DAR Magazine*, December 1931, 719; Helen Pouch, "Approved Schools of the D.A.R.," *DAR Magazine*, February 1934, 78.

67. "Uplift of Indians Is Urged on D.A.R.," *Washington Post*, April 21, 1921, 1.

68. On the Ku Klux Klan of the 1920s, see Harcourt, *Ku Klux Culture*; MacLean, *Behind the Mask of Chivalry*.

69. "D.A.R. Pained by Charges of Klan Leanings," *Chicago Daily Tribune*, March 29, 1928, 25; "Mrs. Bailie Takes Case to Delegates," *New York Times*, April 15, 1928, 28; "White Sees Klan Nightie under D.A.R. Petticoat," *Chicago Daily Tribune*, April 6, 1928, 37; "Urges New Society to Offset D.A.R.," *New York Times*, April 23, 1928, 30.

70. Blee, *Women of the Klan*, 121; Nielsen, *Un-American Womanhood*, 54; Medlicott, "One Social Milieu, Paradoxical Responses," 21–47.

71. Schneider, *Crossing Borders*, 167; Mary C. Welch, "Daughters Dine with Ukrainians," *DAR Magazine*, February 1934, 99 (quote).

72. Michigan DAR, *Historical and Genealogical Records*, 44, 47, 64; Alice F. Moore to My Dear Madam Regent, September 20, 1932, folder 2, box 6, DAR Nova Caesarea Chapter Collection; "March, 1933 Report of State Chairman of Americanism for Michigan," Report of State Chairmen, 1927, Michigan DAR, vol. 1, A-G, box 8, Michigan DAR Records; "State Plans for 1933–34," *DAR Magazine*, November 1933, 671; Welch, "Daughters Dine with Ukrainians," *DAR Magazine*, February 1934, 98–99; "D.A.R. Speeds Campaign to Educate Foreigners," *Washington Post*, November 15, 1936, F6; "State Conference: Daughters of the American Revolution of Michigan, 1939," box 15, Michigan DAR Records.

73. Elizabeth Henry Lyons, "A Soldier of the Revolution," *DAR Magazine*, November 1917, 280–283. See also Jones and Reynolds, *Coweta County Chronicles*, 124; Mrs. H. H. McCluer,

"Social Life of George Washington," September 15, 1932, scrapbook vol. 17, 1932–1933, DAR, Missouri Collection, WHMC-Columbia.

74. See, for example, "Splendid Patriotic Work of Georgia D.A.R. Told in Report of State Regent," *Atlanta Constitution*, April 7, 1918, B10; "U.D.C. To Raise Fund for Hospital Ward," *Dallas Morning News*, September 7, 1918, 12; "U.D.C. Meeting to Begin Today," *Miami Herald* (Miami, FL), November 9, 1920, 1; "Women Make Pilgrimage to Gibralter [*sic*] of Confederacy," *Charlotte Observer*, October 12, 1922, 1; "U.D.C. Convene at Birmingham," *Charlotte Observer*, November 15, 1922, 17; "Atlanta Chapter U.D.C. Honors D.A.R. Regents and Delegates," *Atlanta Constitution*, April 7, 1923, 15; "U.D.C. Leader 'Cannot Desert Party That Stood by the South,'" *Atlanta Constitution*, October 7, 1928, 9M; "Report of Chapter Regents to State Regents," Mary Chesney Chapter DAR Collection, vertical file, WRHS; unidentified newspaper, n.d. (ca. 1921), scrapbook, DAR Nova Caesarea Chapter Collection; "Wins Highest Honor," *Chicago Defender*, June 21, 1919, 1; "State Conference: Daughters of the American Revolution of Michigan, 1939," box 15, Michigan DAR Records.

75. Fred E. Hand, "Facts Concerning the Management of Constitution Hall Dating from 1929 to 1940," folder 5, box 596, Clare Boothe Luce Papers (hereafter cited as Luce Papers), LOC; Arsenault, *Sound of Freedom*, 90–93, 113–128; Weiss, *Farewell to the Party of Lincoln*, 257–262.

76. Fred E. Hand, "Facts Concerning the Management of Constitution Hall Dating from 1929 to 1940," folder 5, box 596, Luce Papers, LOC; Arsenault, *Sound of Freedom*, 90–93, 113–128; Weiss, *Farewell to the Party of Lincoln*, 257–262.

77. "Stars Protest D.A.R. Ban on Miss Anderson," *Chicago Daily Tribune*, January 31, 1939, 6; "D.A.R. Bar on Negroes in Hall Stirs Protest," *Christian Science Monitor*, February 2, 1939, 17; "Anderson Ban Protested," *New York Times*, February 23, 1939, 24; "Artists Assail D.A.R.'s Ban on Miss Anderson," *State Gazette* (Trenton, NJ), February 23, 1939, folder 1, box L2, series II, NAACP Papers, LOC; "Protests on D.A.R. Ban against Singer Grow," *New York Times*, March 2, 1939, 17; "Protests Anderson Ban," *New York Times*, March 27, 1939, 10; "Mrs. Roosevelt Indicates She Has Resigned from D.A.R. over Refusal of Hall to Negro," *New York Times*, February 28, 1939, 1; American Society for Race Tolerance Inc., press release, February 25, 1939, folder 1, box L2, series II, NAACP Papers; Dr. S. P. Rosenthal to Mrs. Henry M. Robert Jr., March 14, 1939, folder 1, box L2, series II, NAACP Papers; Joseph F. Guffey to Mrs. Henry M. Robert, May 9, 1939, folder 2, box 1, Marian Anderson DAR Controversy Collection, Moorland-Spingarn Research Center, Howard University, Washington, DC (hereafter cited as Anderson-DAR Collection).

78. Edith Nourse Rogers, "Present Day Conditions a Challenge to the D.A.R.," April 20, 1939, Edith Nourse Rogers Papers, folder 152, box 10, Schlesinger Library. See also Christine Sadler, "D.A.R. Urged to Lead Way to Racial Co-Operation," *Washington Post*, April 21, 1939, 1.

79. "Excerpt from the Report of the President General Mrs. Henry M. Robert, Jr., 48th Continental Congress April 1939," folder 39, box 2, Anderson-DAR Collection; "D.A.R. Ban Explained," *Los Angeles Times*, April 19, 1939, 2; "D.A.R. Says Its Anderson Ban Obeyed D.C. Customs," *Washington Post*, April 19, 1939, 1; "Asks D.A.R. to Reconsider," *New York Times*, April 20, 1939, 21.

80. "The D.A.R. Alibi," *Pittsburgh Courier*, April 29, 1939, 10.

81. "Forty-Eighth Continental Congress, D.A.R., Washington, D.C., April 16–21, 1939," 2–3, DAR Sarah Angell Chapter, folder DAR National Congress, box 5, Michigan DAR Records.

82. "Record Book of the Board of Management of the Columbian Chapter of the Daughters of the American Revolution at Columbia, Missouri," 1939–1939, box 2, DAR, Columbia,

MO, Chapter Records, 1902–1995, WHMC-Columbia; Minutes of Regular and Board and Special Meetings of the Denver Chapter, 1938–1942, entry "March 10th 1939," folder 1, box 2, DAR Denver Chapter Collection; Minutes of Chapter Meetings, entry March 10, 1939, 39, folder 2, box 1, DAR Nova Caesarea Chapter Collection.

83. "Minute Book, 1932–1940," entry on March 16, 1939, Sarah Caswell Angell Chapter, box 1, Michigan DAR Records.

84. "Shuns Anderson Protest," *New York Times*, March 20, 1939, 17.

85. Mrs. Franklin Delano Roosevelt, "The Education of Our Mountain People," 43d Continental Congress, N.S.D.A.R., 1934, reel 140, National Republic Records; "Mrs. Roosevelt Calls for Peace in D.A.R. Talk," newspaper clipping, scrapbook, Ann Arbor Chapter DAR, 1932–1937, Sara Caswell Angell Chapter, box 5, Michigan DAR Records; "We Should 'Live for Our Country,' Mrs. Roosevelt Tells the D.A.R.," *New York Times*, April 21, 1934, 17; "'Red' Charge against Mrs. Roosevelt Now Issue in D.A.R. Race," *Chicago Daily Tribune*, February 25, 1935, 5; "Mrs. Roosevelt's Refusal to Speak Intrigues D.A.R.," *Los Angeles Times*, April 15, 1935, 1; "D.A.R. Greeted by First Lady at White House," *Washington Post*, April 22, 1937, 12; Black, "Championing a Champion," 719–720, 725–726; "Capital Hears Mrs. Roosevelt Has Quit D.A.R.," *Christian Science Monitor*, February 27, 1939, 2; "Mrs. Roosevelt Quits D.A.R. in Anderson Row," *Washington Post*, February 28, 1939, 1; Walter White to Charles H. Houston, telegram, April 14, 1939, folder 19, box L1, series II, NAACP Papers; Eleanor Roosevelt to Walter White, April 12, 1939, folder 2, box L2, series II, NAACP Papers.

86. Charles H. Houston to the Daughters of the American Revolution, April 17, 1939, folder 5, box 1, Anderson-DAR Collection.

87. Joseph A. Gavagan to Mrs. Henry A. Robert, February 28, 1939, folder 1, box L2, series II, NAACP Papers; "Re Marian Anderson," 11, folder 2, box L2, series II, NAACP Papers; Kachun, *First Martyr of Liberty*, 117; Stokes, *Art and the Color Line*, 21.

88. Charles H. Houston to Mrs. Henry M. Robert Jr., April 15, 1940, telegram, folder 1, box A18, series II, NAACP Papers; "Continue Fight on DAR's Ban," *Pittsburgh Courier*, April 20, 1940, 2.

89. "DAR Has a Hard Time with Race," *Chicago Defender*, April 5, 1941, 6.

90. "D.A.R. Relents, Bends Color Bar in Citizenship Award," *Chicago Defender*, March 8, 1941, 1; "Opposes D.C. Jim Crow in School Test," *Chicago Defender*, December 20, 1941, 9.

91. DAR, National Society, press release, September 29, 1942, folder 3, box A18, series II, NAACP Papers; "D.A.R. Invites Marian Anderson to Sing in Constitution Hall," *Washington Post*, September 30, 1942, 1.

92. Walter White to Marian Anderson, October 1, 1942, telegram; Walter White to S. Hurok, October 1, 1942, telegram, both in folder 3, box A18, series II, NAACP Papers; "D.A.R. Bid Accepted by Miss Anderson," *New York Times*, October 6, 1942, 19; "Miss Anderson Rebukes DAR," *Chicago Defender*, October 10, 1942, 1; "DAR Retains Ban on Hall; Marian to Give Concert," *Pittsburgh Courier*, October 10, 1942, 1; "Marian Anderson Accepts D.A.R. Bid to Sing, Waiving Dispute in Order to Aid Army Fund," *New York Times*, November 7, 1942, 17; "Marian and DAR Agree," *Pittsburgh Courier*, December 19, 1942, 1; "Mrs. Roosevelt Hears Marian Anderson Sing in D.A.R. Hall for China Relief Fund," *New York Times*, January 8, 1943, 24; "Marian Thrills 3,800; Also Adds $7,777 to China Relief," *Pittsburgh Courier*, January 16, 1943, 11.

93. Sitkoff, "Racial Militancy and Interracial Violence"; Herbert Shapiro, *White Violence and Black Response*, 305.

94. Office of War Information, Department of the Interior, press release, December 30, 1942; Office of War Information, Department of the Interior, press release, January 13, 1943,

both in folder 3, box A18, series II, NAACP Papers; "Mural of Marian Anderson Is Presented to the Nation," *Washington Post*, January 7, 1943, B1.

95. "File-Only Copy," January 19, 1943, folder 3, box A18, series II, NAACP Papers.

96. "The D.A.R. Alibi," *Pittsburgh Courier*, April 29, 1939, 10.

97. On Randolph and the MOWM, see Bynum, *A. Philip Randolph*; Lucander, *Winning the War for Democracy*; Pfeffer, *A. Philip Randolph*.

98. See James, *Double V*, 141–143; Meier and Rudwick, *CORE*.

99. Gerstle, *American Crucible*, 211–214, 231; Barkan, *Retreat of Scientific Racism*, 3–4; Jarvis, *Male Body at War*, 122.

100. Jarvis, *Male Body at War*, 120, 146–154.

101. Martin Dies, "Immigration Legislation," *DAR Magazine*, March 1934, 139.

102. "D.A.R. Urges Strict Control of Alien Activities in U.S.," *Times-Herald*, April 22, 1939, Georgia State scrapbook of the DAR, 1938–1939, Georgia Archives, Morrow.

103. Mrs. Charles E. Head, "Americanism," *National Historical Magazine*, February 1945, 86–87.

Chapter 5. "I Wanted It to Change and to Make Up for Its Past": The Daughters between 1945 and 2000

1. Susan Heller Anderson, "Leontyne Price—Still a Diva," *New York Times*, February 7, 1982, D1; "Briefing," *New York Times*, April 20, 1982, A22; Elisabeth Bumiller, "Anthems and Images of the Daughters," *Washington Post*, April 21, 1982, B3.

2. See Fried, *Nightmare in Red*; Powers, *Not without Honor*; Schrecker, *Many Are the Crimes*.

3. See Brennan, *Wives, Mothers, and the Red Menace*; Nickerson, *Mothers of Conservatism*; Walls, "Defending Their Liberties."

4. DAR, *Proceedings of the Sixty-Second Continental Congress of the National Society DAR* (1953), 141; *Proceedings of the Sixty-Third Continental Congress of the National Society DAR* (1954), 352; Eugenie Grover Carothers, "Why Patriots?," *DAR Magazine*, August 1949, 650 (quote).

5. "Outlaw Reds, DAR Board Asks Truman," *Washington Post*, October 18, 1952, 16; Osie Smith Coolbaugh, "Our Most Powerful Weapon of Defense," *DAR Magazine*, July 1953, 395; "Communist Spies Inside U.S. Government," *DAR Magazine*, November 1953, 1213–1216; Katherine G. Reynolds, "National Defense," *DAR Magazine*, April 1953, 539–541; J. Edgar Hoover, "The Challenge," *DAR Magazine*, February 1950, 95.

6. Marguerite C. Patton, "National Defense," *DAR Magazine*, March 1954, 241.

7. "Charges Racial Bias," *New York Times*, October 1, 1945, 25; "Asks Truman Act in Ban of D.A.R. on Hazel Scott," *Chicago Daily Tribune*, October 2, 1945, 7; "Fight Pushed on Tax Exemption of D.A.R.," *Los Angeles Times*, October 14, 1945, 3; "Communistic Origin Seen for Attack on the D.A.R.," *Christian Science Monitor*, October 17, 1945, 3; "Congress Debates D.A.R. Hall Row," *New York Times*, October 17, 1945, 19; "Rankin, Coffee Clash on DAR Controversy," *New York Amsterdam News*, October 27, 1945, 11; Leslie S. Perry to Walter White, October 17, 1945, folder 10, box A373, series II, NAACP Papers; "Tax-Free D.A.R. Hall Object of House Bill," *Christian Science Monitor*, October 18, 1945, 6; "From Washington Bureau, Dictated to E. M. Wasem," October 18, 1945, folder 10, box A373, Series II, NAACP Papers.

8. "Dewey Criticizes D.A.R. in Scott Case," *New York Times*, October 16, 1945, 20; Frances Melrose, "DAR Head Unruffled by Hazel Scott Case," *Rocky Mountain News*, October

24, 1945, DAR Denver Chapter, Scrapbooks 1898–1962, reel 1, scrapbook 9; "Protests Mount against DAR Racist Policy," *Chicago Defender*, October 27, 145, 1; Carl R. Johnson to Walter White, October 18, 1945, folder 10, box A373, series II, NAACP Papers; "Leaders Hit DAR Hall Ban," *Pittsburgh Courier*, October 20, 1945, 1; "Delaware Students Rap DAR as 'Un-American,'" *Chicago Defender*, March 9, 1946, 8; "D.A.R. Head Affirms Stand of Group on Negro Issue," *Christian Science Monitor*, December 3, 1945, 13.

9. "Trumans Hit Discrimination in D.A.R. Issue," *Christian Science Monitor*, October 12, 1945, 7; "Trumans Condemn D.A.R. Negro Ban," *New York Times*, October 13, 1945, 16; "Why Not?," *Crisis*, November 1945, 313.

10. "Alps Asks Inquiry in Capital on D.A.R.," *New York Times*, October 14, 1945, 46; "Catholic Protest Urged," *New York Times*, October 17, 1945, 19; "The D.A.R. Auditorium," *Pittsburgh Courier*, October 20, 1945, 6; "History Lessons for the DAR," *Chicago Defender*, October 27, 1945, 12.

11. "Memo for National Board," October 11, 1945, folder 5, box 596, Luce Papers; "Trumans Condemn D.A.R. Negro Ban," *New York Times*, October 13, 1945, 16; Melrose, "DAR Head Unruffled by Hazel Scott Case."

12. "Clare Boothe Luce Says U.S. Must End Oppression at Home," *Afro-American*, December 5, 1942, 8; "Clare Luce on 92nd Front," *New Journal and Guide*, March 31, 1945, 1; "Clare Luce Takes Her Stand," *Chicago Defender*, December 15, 1945, 11. On the life of Luce, see S. Morris, *Price of Fame*.

13. "Application for Membership to the National Society of the Daughters of the American Revolution," folder 5, box 705, Luce Papers; "Threat to Quit D.A.R. Voiced by Rep. Luce," *Los Angeles Times*, October 14, 1945, 3; "D.A.R. Shift Is Announced by Mrs. Luce," *Christian Science Monitor*, November 2, 1945, 2; "Mrs. Luce Heeds D.A.R. Decision," *Christian Science Monitor*, November 21, 1945, 5; "Mrs. Luce to Change DAR Chapter," *New York Times*, November 29, 1945, 19.

14. Grace L. H. Brosseau to Clare Boothe Luce, October 16, 1945, folder D.A.R., reel 471, National Republic Records.

15. Clare Boothe Luce to Grace L. H. Brosseau, October 29, 1945, folder D.A.R., reel 471, National Republic Records.

16. Grace L. H. Brosseau to Clare Boothe Luce, October 31, 1945; Clare Boothe Luce to Grace L. H. Brosseau, November 9, 1945; Grace L. H. Brosseau to Clare Boothe Luce, November 14, 1945, all in folder D.A.R., reel 471, National Republic Records.

17. "DAR Fears Democratic Vote on Color Ban, Says Rep. Luce," *Chicago Defender*, February 16, 1946, 4; "Extension of Remarks of Hon. Clare Boothe Luce of Connecticut in the House of Representatives," Monday, February 4, 1946, Exclusion of Negro Artists from Constitution Hall, *Congressional Record*, Appendix A, 495, reel 139, National Republic Records; "Mrs. Luce in Plea to DAR," *New York Times*, February 22, 1946, 17; "For Release Upon Delivery," 2, 7, 9, folder 7, box 680, Luce Papers.

18. "DAR Chapter Decries Hazel Scott Action," *New York Times*, October 20, 1945, 7; "Protest Mounts against DAR Racist Policy," *Chicago Defender*, October 27, 1945, 1; "D.A.R. Unit against Race Ban," *New York Times*, November 22, 1945, 22; Records, entries "Nov. 12-45" and "Jan. 14-1946," Lewis Cass Chapter, Escabana, Records, 1909–1972, Michigan DAR Records; "Charles Meseroll Chapter D.A.R.: Record," entry November 5, 1945, Charles Meseroll Chapter Minutes, 1941–1965, Michigan DAR Records; "Stanford D.A.R. Reverses Stand on Racial Issue," *Christian Science Monitor*, January 18, 1946, 4; "Resolutions (protests) passed," January 10, 1946; "Resolutions—Pro," both in folder 5, box 596, Luce Papers; "D.A.R. Unit Attacks Race

Bias," *New York Times*, March 22, 1946, 28; "Copies of Resolutions Adopted by Various Chapters," folder 5, box 596, Luce Papers; "Resolutions—Contra," folder 5, box 596, Luce Papers.

19. "D.C. Commissioners OK Lily-White DAR Policy," *Chicago Defender*, February 23, 1946, 12.

20. "D.A.R. Committee Opens Drive to Delete 'White Artists Only' Clause in Hall Leases," *New York Times*, April 4, 1946, 25; "Substance of What Was Said to the Press April 2, 3, 1946," folder 5, box 596, Luce Papers; Clare Boothe Luce to Dear Mrs. [blank], March 27, 1946, folder "D.A.R.," reel 471, National Republic Records; Clare Boothe Luce to Grace L. H. Brosseau, April 22, 1946, folder 5, box 596, Luce Papers.

21. Lucile F. Goff to Dear Daughters, May 11, 1946, folder 5, box 596, Luce Papers; Clare Boothe Luce to Mrs. Julius Y. Talmadge, April 15, 1946; Mrs. Julius Talmadge to Clare Boothe Luce, April 16, 1946, both in folder D.A.R., reel 471, National Republic Records; "D.A.R. Head Hits 'Interference' by Clare Luce," *Chicago Daily Tribune*, April 18, 1946, 8.

22. Lucy Greenbaum, "D.A.R. Delegates Ready for Clash," *New York Times*, May 20, 1946, 25; "D.A.R. Convention Is Facing Row on Negro Ban at Constitution Hall," *New York Times*, May 17, 1946, 23.

23. Lucy Greenbaum, "D.A.R. Delegates Ready for Clash," *New York Times*, May 20, 1946, 25; Lucy Greenbaum, "D.A.R. Head Assails Critics as Disloyal," *New York Times*, May 21, 1946, 25; "DAR to Study Change in Jim Crow Clause," *Atlanta Journal*, May 21, 1946, 4.

24. Lucy Greenbaum, "D.A.R. Vote Orders Dissolution of the Luce Anti-Bias Committee," *New York Times*, May 22, 1946, 23; "D.A.R. Applauds Canceling of Move for Race Equality," *Christian Science Monitor*, May 23, 1946, 3; *Proceedings of the Fifty-Fifth Continental Congress of the National Society DAR* (1946), 31–32; "DAR Amendment Muzzles Group Fighting Bias," *New York Amsterdam News*, May 25, 1946, 1; "DAR Repeats Historic Bias," *Chicago Defender*, June 1, 1946, 1.

25. "Department of the Treasurer General: D.A.R. Membership," *National Historical Magazine*, April 1944, 205; "Department of the Treasurer General: D.A.R. Membership," *DAR Magazine*, August 1947, 417.

26. "Tuskegee Choir Performs while Pickets Parade," *Chicago Defender*, June 15, 1946, 12; "D.A.R. Renews Policy of Bias," *Chicago Defender*, May 24, 1947, 4; "The Reluctant Daughters," *Chicago Defender*, May 5, 1951, 6; "D.A.R. Hall Open to Negro Singer," *New York Times*, April 22, 1951, 60; "Constitution Hall Books Miss Anderson," *Chicago Defender*, March 14, 1953, 1; "Marian Anderson to Sing in Constitution Hall," *Jet*, March 19, 1953, 32; "Hazel Scott to Tour Nation in Fight against Jim Crow," *Chicago Defender*, December 1, 1945, 6; Harold L. Ickes, "Shame on the DAR!," *Atlanta Constitution*, May 30, 1947, 6.

27. Roosevelt quoted from *McCall's* in "'Attack' on D.A.R. by Mrs. E. Roosevelt Answered by Society," *Press Digest: National Society DAR*, November 1953, in Cherokee Chapter D.A.R. Minutes, December 21, 1948, including May 16, 1952, box 1, Cherokee Chapter DAR Collection, AHCA.

28. "The D.A.R. as a Force for Moving Ahead," *DAR Magazine*, November 1953, 1227–1228.

29. DAR, "Highlights of Program Activity," comp. and ed. by Marguerite Schondau, 4th ed., 1954, folder 14, box 87, Herbert A. Philbrick Papers Philbrick Papers, LOC.

30. "Athens High School Senior Wins DAR Award for Good Citizenship," *Pittsburgh Courier*, January 21, 1956, A15; "DAR Says They Represent Good Citizenship," *Denver Post*, February 15, 1959, press scrapbook, OV folio 10, DAR Colorado State Society Collection, Denver Public Library; "Seven Students to Receive DAR 'Good Citizen Awards,' *Ann Arbor News*, February 14, 1958, folder Press Clippings, box 7, Sarah Caswell Angell Chapter, Michigan DAR

Records; "Centennial Research, Book Immigrants and Work of DAR, Proceedings 3/3," (59th DAR Continental Congress), 135–136, series 11.2 Projects, HG Papers, DAR Archives, Washington, DC; DAR, "Highlights of Program Activity" and "Report for Continental Congress: National Defense Committee, April 17, 1956," both in folder 14, box 87, Philbrick Papers.

31. "DAR Open to Negroes Who Hurdled High Barrier of 'Ifs,'" *Chicago Defender,* October 25, 1947, 2.

32. On the history of the civil rights movement in the 1940s and 1950s, see Berg, *Ticket to Freedom;* Klarman, *Brown v. Board of Education.*

33. "Final Report of the Resolutions Committee Adopted by the 48th State Conference of the Mississippi Society, Daughters of the American Revolution, March 2–4, 1954," DAR 1950–1959, subject file, Mississippi Department of Archives and History, Archives and Records Services Division, Jackson.

34. Frances Lewine, "DAR Demands Cut in Budget," *Los Angeles Times,* April 19, 1957, A5; *Proceedings of the Seventy-Sixth Continental Congress of the National Society DAR* (1958), 303.

35. Nickerson, *Mothers of Conservatism,* xx–xxi. For examples of the DAR's charges that the *Brown* decision and subsequently passed civil rights laws were either communist-inspired or would aid communist agitators, see Mary Barclay Erb, "National Defense," *DAR Magazine,* October 1957, 1153–1157, 1226; *Proceedings of the 54th State Conference, Tennessee Society, DAR,* March 30–April 1, 1959, Chattanooga, 188, 189, DAR Archives.

36. Fleegler, *Ellis Island Nation,* 104–134.

37. "With the Chapters," *DAR Magazine,* October 1951, 807; "D.A.R. Welcomes New Citizens," *DAR Magazine,* November 1954, 1156, 1176; Mary Spargo, "Seventy-Nine Nationalities Learn 'American,'" *DAR Magazine,* June 1955, 681; *Proceedings of the Fifty-Sixth Continental Congress of the National Society DAR* (1947), 113; "National Defense," *DAR Magazine,* June 1956, 569.

38. "National Defense Committee," *DAR Magazine,* July 1956, 630.

39. Barbara Browne, "Ex-Inmate Isn't Bitter about Flag Incident," *Rocky Mountain News,* February 13, 1957, 10; "Denver DAR Bans 'Mexicans'; Stirs Tempers," *Washington Post,* February 12, 1957, B4; Robert Byers, "Mexican Boys Barred as DAR Flag Bearers," *Denver Post,* February 10, 1957, 2A (Rush quote).

40. "DAR Officials Prefer American Flagbearers," *Rocky Mountain News,* February 10, 1957, 66.

41. Barbara Browne, "Flag Controversy Stirs Civic Turmoil," *Rocky Mountain News,* February 11, 1957, 5; "House Demands Ban on DAR," *Denver Post,* February 11, 1957, 3; "Barbara Browne, "Governor McNichols Bans DAR from Colorado Institutions," *Rocky Mountain News,* February 12, 1957, 5; "Steve Demands DAR Explain 'Principles,'" *Denver Post,* February 11, 1957, 3; Barbara Browne, "Governor McNichols Bans DAR from Colorado Institutions," 5; "The Open Forum," *Denver Post,* February 11, 1957, 5; "Elks Rap Stand on Flag Bearer," *Denver Post,* February 11, 1957, 3; Margaret Bourne, "Spirit of America," *Denver Post,* February 13, 1957, 20; "Head of DAR Offers Flag to Latin Vets," *Denver Post,* February 14, 1957, 12; "Denver DAR Member Bans 'Mexicans,'" B4; "Stirs Statewide Storm of Protest," *Denver Post,* February 11, 1957, 3; "Denver's DAR Flag Issue Echoes in Washington, Mexico," *Denver Post,* February 12, 1957, 5.

42. "DAR Ousts Officer in Flag Boy Incident," *Denver Post,* February 11, 1957, 2; "Barrer of Mexican Dismissed by D.A.R.," *New York Times,* February 12, 1957, 9.

43. "Governor Lifts Ban against DAR Activities in State Institutions," *Denver Post,* February 15, 1957, 3; Mrs. Frederick A. Groves to Mrs. Richard Frank Carlson, February 15, 1957,

telegram, scrapbook 1950–1970, OV folio 7, DAR Colorado State Society Collection; "Multi-Racial Color Guard to Carry Flag," *Daily Defender,* February 13, 1957, 17; "Gonzales Carries Flag in Colorado," *New York Times,* February 23, 1957, 19.

44. "Mexican Boy Can Tote Flag, D.A.R. Head Says," *Chicago Daily Tribune,* February 13, 1957, A4; Mary Barclay Erb, "Memorandum Regarding the Recent Denver Incident," March 1957, folder Daughters of the American Revolution 1956/57, box 52, Alfred Kohlberg Collection, HIA.

45. Grace Ward Calhoun, "Tamassee D.A.R. School," *DAR Magazine,* December 1950, 929, 936.

46. Pearl Faulkner Eddy, "Americanism," *DAR Magazine,* November 1953, 1209.

47. Huhndorf, *Going Native,* 127. Between 1945 and 1960 only one article that appeared in the *DAR Magazine* mentioned African American soldiers who fought during the American Revolution (David L. Smiley, "Americanism and the Revolution of 1776," *DAR Magazine,* March 1959, 222–223, 350).

48. DAR, *Proceedings of the Fifty-Seventh Continental Congress of the National Society DAR* (1948), 284–287; Georgia L. O'Marr, "Report of American Indians Committee," 57th Continental Congress, 288, scrapbook, AIC Papers; *Proceedings of the Fifty-Ninth Continental Congress of the National Society DAR* (1950), 143–145; *Proceedings of the Sixtieth Continental Congress of the National Society DAR* (1951), 183–187; "Indian Fashion Show," *Press Digest: Daughters of the American Revolution,* December 1952, Cherokee Chapter D.A.R. Minutes, Dec. 21, 1948, including May 16, 1952, box 1, Cherokee Chapter DAR Collection; "Cherokee Drama Set Friday at Stone Mountain Theater," *Atlanta Journal,* June 3, 1953, 21; "D.A.R. State Convention Held in Lansing," *State Journal* (Lansing, MI), September 25, 1953, 18; "State Activities," *DAR Magazine,* August 1955, 853; "State Activities," *DAR Magazine,* June 1956, 572–574.

49. Twila Daugherty, "Our Indian Wards," *DAR Magazine,* January 1953, 25; Dorothy V. Croft, "Indians of Tennessee," *DAR Magazine,* October 1950, 801, 805. See also Kinney, *Ohio Indian Lore,* 5, 7; Marion R. Todd, "The Gift of the American Indian to the World," *DAR Magazine,* August 1950, 669.

50. Eva V. Park, "Indians in the War: 1945," *DAR Magazine,* August 1947, 397–401; Ramona Kaiser, "American Indians in Action," *DAR Magazine,* August 1951, 652; Mrs. Earl Foster, "Our American Indians," *DAR Magazine,* November 1951, 929; "The American Indian, His Wants and Needs," *DAR Magazine,* November 1952, 1142, 1146.

51. Foster, "Our American Indians," *DAR Magazine,* November 1951, 929; *Proceedings of the Fifty-Sixth Continental Congress of the National Society DAR* (1947), 410; *Proceedings of the Fifty-Ninth Continental Congress of the National Society DAR* (1950), 189; *Proceedings of the Sixty-Eighth Continental Congress of the National Society DAR* (1959), 223.

52. Mrs. Louis J. O'Marr, "American Indians Committee," 174, DAR scrapbook, AIC Papers; *Proceedings of the Fifty-Eighth Continental Congress of the National Society DAR* (1949), 347; Georgia L. O'Marr to My Dear State Chairman, July 1949, DAR scrapbook, AIC Papers; "American Indian Work Is Expanding," *Press Digest: Daughters of the American Revolution,* October 1952, Cherokee Chapter D.A.R. Minutes, Dec. 21, 1948, including May 16, 1952, box 1, Cherokee Chapter DAR Collection; *Proceedings of the Sixty-First Continental Congress of the National Society DAR* (1952), 154; "DAR Aids Indian Girls—3 Given Scholarships," *St. Paul Pioneer Press,* March 15, 1950, DAR scrapbook, AIC Papers; Scrapbook DAR, 1941–1961, 26, DAR Stevens Thomson Mason Chapter (Ionia, MI), box 27, Michigan DAR Records; "With the Chapters," *DAR Magazine,* February 1957, 159; Florence R. Patterson, "Bacone College," *DAR Magazine,* March 1957, 285–287.

53. Marguerite Schondau, ed., "Highlights of Program Activity," 4th ed. (DAR, 1954), 20, folder 14, box 87, Philbrick Papers.

54. "Chapter Activities," *DAR Magazine,* May 1948, 355–356; "With the Chapters," *DAR Magazine,* November 1950, 886; "DAR Marker Is Dedicated," *News and Observer* (Raleigh, NC), September 11, 1951, scrapbook, DAR, 1949–1952, North Carolina State Archives, Raleigh; "State Activities," *DAR Magazine,* March 1955, 289; "With the Chapters," *DAR Magazine,* February 1958, 159–167; Maud Proctor Callis, "Sixteen Revolutionary War Heroes and Patriots Honored by District Daughters," *DAR Magazine,* March 1959, 231–232, 346.

55. Between 1945 and 1960, only a handful of articles focused on women's accomplishments during the Revolution. See "Notable Women of the Revolution," *DAR Magazine,* November 1956, 874–876; Hilda Ellis Schulze, "Betsy Ross; Fact, Not Fiction," *DAR Magazine,* March 1959, 229–230.

56. Adelaide Bledsoe Cormack Kingman, "The Defense Advisory Committee on Women in the Services," *DAR Magazine,* December 1959, 759, 760 (quotes); Ivy Lee Buchanan, "Defense of America," *DAR Magazine,* April 1951, 281–284; Colonel Katherine A. Towel, "Women Marines," *DAR Magazine,* October 1951, 756–758.

57. "With the Chapters," *DAR Magazine,* June 1956, 578; "With the Chapters," *DAR Magazine,* May 1957, 639, 644; Mildred C. Farrell, "Oregon Pioneer History Preserved for Posterity," *DAR Magazine,* March 1958, 265–266; Edna Mingus, "Pioneer Mothers' Memorial Log Cabin," *DAR Magazine,* June 1955, 683, 690; Bertha Rachel Palmer, "Our Pioneer Mother: Eliza Ludlow Palmer," *DAR Magazine,* March 1957, 280–284, 362; Elizabeth Slye, "100 Attend Marking of Grave Site," *Schoolcraft Express,* October 17, 1957, in Chapter Activities, 1931–1950 scrapbook, box 34, Michigan DAR Records.

58. Kammen, *Mystic Chords of Memory,* 539–540, 558–559, 572.

59. "Chapter Activities," *DAR Magazine,* May 1948, 355–373; "With the Chapters," *DAR Magazine,* September 1954, 953–955; "With the Chapters," *DAR Magazine,* November 1954, 1183–1192; "With the Chapters," *DAR Magazine,* March 1955, 279–288.

60. "DAR Opposes World Rule," *Washington Post,* April 21, 1950, 1; "Patriotic Women," *Chicago Daily Tribune,* April 19, 1951, 16; Dera D. Parkinson, "World Organization versus Super Government," *DAR Magazine,* June 1949, 460–468.

61. DAR, *Proceedings of the Sixty-Second Continental Congress of the National Society DAR* (1953), 139.

62. DAR, *Proceedings of the Sixty-Fifth Continental Congress of the National Society DAR* (1956), 167, 168.

63. DAR, *Proceedings of the Sixty-Eighth Continental Congress of the National Society DAR* (1959), 222.

64. Olsen, "One Nation, One World," 2–28; Nickerson, *Mothers of Conservatism,* xx.

65. Marguerite C. Patton, "National Defense," *DAR Magazine,* June 1954, 759; "Extension of the Remarks of Hon. Wint Smith of Kansas," House of Representatives, Tuesday, May 12, 1959, *Congressional Record,* Appendix, 1959, A3993, folder Press Clippings, box 7, Sarah Caswell Angell Chapter, Michigan DAR Records.

66. Quoted in Benowitz, *Challenge and Change,* 39.

67. Benowitz, *Challenge and Change,* 39–40.

68. "Eisenhower Stirs Charge of D.A.R.," *New York Times,* April 23, 1955, 17; Dwight Eisenhower to Mrs. Frederic A. Groves, August 21, 1956, DAR, Missouri State Society, Scrapbook, 1956–1958, WHMC-Columbia; "'We Can't Rest on Tradition,' Ike Tells DAR," *Washington Post,* April 21, 1959, B4.

69. "'Crackpot' Cry Leveled at DAR," *Mountain Empire*, March 15, 1957, 52; Elizabeth Erskine, "Old Battle Cry, Weapons, Highlight DAR Convention," *Michigan Daily*, April 25, 1959, folder Press Clippings, box 7, Sarah Caswell Angell Chapter, Michigan DAR Records.

70. "Patriotic Women," *Chicago Daily Tribune*, April 19, 1951, 16; "D.A.R. Rebellion," *Washington Post*, April 24, 1953, 30; "D.A.R. Is Called 'Destructive' As Official of Unit Here Quits," *New York Times*, July 4, 1958, 21.

71. "Department of the Treasurer General: D.A.R. Membership," *DAR Magazine*, February 1949, 155; "Department of the Treasurer General: D.A.R. Membership," *DAR Magazine*, January 1960, 55. See also "DAR Membership Up," *Washington Post*, December 8, 1955, 39.

72. Kammen, *Mystic Chords of Memory*, 574–578; Chafe, *The Paradox of Change*, 187–188; Rosenberg, *Divided Lives*, 147–156; Storrs, "Attacking the Washington 'Femmocracy,'" 118–152.

73. On the black freedom struggle of the 1960s, see, for example, Tuck, *We Ain't What We Ought to Be.*

74. On these various social movements and the social, cultural, and political consequences of their protest campaigns, see, for example, Chin and Villazor, *Immigration and Nationality Act of 1965*; Cobb, *Native Activism in Cold War America*; Hall, *Peace and Freedom*; Isserman and Kazin, *America Divided*; Gilmore and Evans, *Feminist Coalitions*.

75. DAR, *Proceedings of the Seventieth Continental Congress of the National Society DAR* (1961), 297.

76. Benowitz, *Challenge and Change*, 122; "DAR Ducks Integration, Segregation Issues," *Daily Defender*, April 17, 1963, 3; Marie Smith, "No Policy on Integration, DAR Head Writes JFK," *Washington Post*, April 17, 1963, D3.

77. Sara Roddis Jones to Mrs. Constantine Brown, June 26, 1963; Sara Roddis Jones to Mrs. Constantine Brown, August 5, 1963; Sara Roddis Jones to Mrs. Constantine Brown, February 10, 1964; all in folder 13, box 40, Elizabeth Churchill Brown Papers, HIA.

78. "Patriotic Principles of Americanism," *Congressional Record*, 87th Congress, First Session, Extension of Remarks of Hon. Strom Thurmond of SC, in Senate, Wednesday, April 19, 1961. Thurmond's other documented visits to the DAR's Continental Congress took place in 1962 and 1966 ("Major is Undecided What to Tell DAR," *Palladium-Item* (Richmond, IN), April 18, 1962, 2; Nora W. Blackshear, "75th Continental Congress: Report," May 11, 1966, Minutes: Cherokee Chapter, DAR, 1964–1966, box 3, Cherokee Chapter DAR Collection, AHCA).

79. Enid Hall Griswold, "Where We Stand Today," *DAR Magazine*, May 1968, 556. Two years earlier, Griswold had penned a similar assessment (Griswold, "The Great Illusion," *DAR Magazine*, April 1966, 350–354, 409).

80. On the anti–Vietnam War movement and students' opposition to traditions of military valor, see DeBenedetti, *American Ordeal*; Foley, *Confronting the War Machine.*

81. "Joan Baez Barred from D.A.R.'s Hall," *New York Times*, August 13, 1967, 59; "DAR Loses Bid to Ban Baez Show," *Washington Post*, August 15, 1967, A3; Mrs. William Henry Sullivan Jr. to Stewart L. Udall, August 14, 1967; Mrs. William Henry Sullivan Jr., "Memorandum," both in Minutes: Cherokee Chapter Daughters of the American Revolution, 1966–1968, box 3, Cherokee Chapter DAR Collection, AHCA; "Singer Baez Gives Concert at Monument," *Chicago Tribune*, August 15, 1967, 16; "Joan Baez Triumphs Over DAR Rejection," *Los Angeles Times*, August 15, 1967, 7.

82. Enid Hall Griswold, "Destroyers of Freedom," *DAR Magazine*, January 1968, 10.

83. Betty Newkirk Seimes, "Power of the Franchise and Good Citizenship," *DAR Magazine*, December 1968, 884 (quote); Betty Newkirk Seimes, "America—In Whose Hands," *DAR Magazine*, May 1969, 502–503. See also Adele Erb Sullivan, "The Pursuit of Happiness," *DAR*

Magazine, April 1968, 423–427; Betty Newkirk Seimes, "Treason or Patriotism," *DAR Magazine,* May 1970, 518–520.

84. "Minutes of National Board of Management: Regular Meeting, February 1, 1968," *DAR Magazine,* April 1968, 445; "Service to the Nation," *DAR Magazine,* April 1968, 412–415. On US citizens' continuing support for America's war effort in Vietnam, see Scanlon, *Pro-War Movement.*

85. DAR, *Proceedings of the Eighty-First Continental Congress of the National Society DAR* (1972), 138.

86. Eleanor Washington Spicer, "Courage: Onward in Faith," *DAR Magazine,* January 1973, 4–6; *Proceedings of the Eighty-Second Continental Congress of the National Society DAR* (1973), 157–158; *Proceedings of the Eighty-Third Continental Congress of the National Society DAR* (1974), 138–139; *Proceedings of the Eighty-Sixth Continental Congress of the National Society DAR* (1977), 133; *Proceedings of the Eighty-Seventh Continental Congress of the National Society DAR* (1978), 138–139; Phyllis Schlafly, "Time Extension for ERA?," *DAR Magazine,* November 1978, 864–868.

87. "National Chairmen: 1977–1980," *DAR Magazine,* December 1977, 1004–1005; Critchlow, *Phyllis Schlafly and Grassroots Conservatism,* 71–72, 212–242; Phyllis Schlafly, "Why Stoop to Equality," *DAR Magazine,* June–July 1973, 536–540, 609; Kathryn Fink Dunaway to Dear Candidate, n.d., folder 23, box 1, Kathryn Fink Dunaway Papers (hereafter cited as Dunaway Papers), Emory University Archives, Atlanta, GA; Kathryn Dunaway to Honorable Member of the General Assembly, August 1976; Kathryn Dunaway to Dear Concerned American, December 1976 (quotes), both in folder 31, box 1, Dunaway Papers. For a more detailed analysis of Kathryn Dunaway's activism and its impact in Georgia, see R. Morris, "Organizing Breadmakers," 161–182.

88. Benowitz, *Challenge and Change,* 330n99; *Proceedings of the Eighty-Second Continental Congress of the National Society DAR* (1973), 158–159; Osta Underwood to Mrs. Donald Spicer, October 29, 1973, folder 13, box 11, Marguerite Rawalt Papers, Schlesinger Library (hereafter cited as Rawalt Papers); Marguerite Rawalt to Mrs. Donald Spicer, November 27, 1973, folder 12, box 11, Rawalt Papers; "Resolution for the District of Columbia Daughters of the American Revolution," January 1977, folder 13, box 11, Rawalt Papers.

89. Sara Roddis Jones, "Are We Building for the Future?," *DAR Magazine,* October 1972, 769.

90. Helen Bowling McKnight, letter to the editor, *DAR Magazine,* April 1978, 283. For a similar assessment by Phyllis Schlafly, see Schlafly, "The Equal Rights Amendment," *DAR Magazine,* January 1978, 12.

91. "Women in Combat," resolution, in *Proceedings of the Eighty-Eighth Continental Congress of the National Society DAR* (1979), 171.

92. See Bessie F. Nesmith, "Plympton's Famous Revolutionary Soldier—Deborah Sampson," *DAR Magazine,* October 1961, 586; Hazel E. Pendleton, "Patriotic Women of North Carolina," *DAR Magazine,* November 1962, 683–685; Emily Ross, "The Female Paul Revere," *DAR Magazine,* April 1967, 392–393; Helen E. Whitman, "Molly Stark, Patriot," *DAR Magazine,* January 1969, 24–29, 44, 48; Jean Campbell Acton, "Heroines of the American Revolution," *DAR Magazine,* November 1970, 800–803; Emily Ross, "Captain Molly: Forgotten Heroine of the Revolution," *DAR Magazine,* February 1972, 109–11, 186; Colonel Nellie H. Hill, "Historical Role of Women in the United States Armed Forces," *DAR Magazine,* May 1975, 438–441; Wilma Ratchford Craig, "Women of the American Revolution," *DAR Magazine,* November 1976; Phyllis Schlafly, "Women's Place in the Armed Services," *DAR Magazine,* December 1979, 1114–1118.

93. Hunter, *Century of Service*, 19.

94. DAR, *Proceedings of the Seventy-Second Continental Congress of the National Society DAR* (1963), 107; DAR, *Proceedings of the Eighty-First Continental Congress of the National Society DAR* (1972), 144.

95. Griswold, "The Great Illusion," *DAR Magazine*, April 1966, 353.

96. Mrs. Robert V. H. Duncan, "Importance of Maintaining Walter-McCarran Immigration and Nationality Act," *DAR Magazine*, November 1964, 885–886. See also Elizabeth Chesnut Barnes, "National Defense," *DAR Magazine*, March 1960, 195–198.

97. Griswold, "The Great Illusion," *DAR Magazine*, April 1966, 353.

98. Kammen, *Mystic Chords of Memory*, 616, 630; Moreau, *School Book Nation*, 281–282; Florence Morey, "Women Pioneers of Crawford Notch, New Hampshire," *DAR Magazine*, January 1961, 7–8, 58; Sara Withers Beauchamp, "Pioneer Life Was a Testing Ground for the Nation," *DAR Magazine*, May 1968, 572–573; Helen Bartlett, "The Madonna of the Trail," *DAR Magazine*, October 1969, 693–697, 730, 736; Elizabeth d'Autray Riley, "Life on a Monroe County (Alabama) Plantation before the War Between the States," *DAR Magazine*, June–July 1962, 531–532; Florence Sillers Ogden, "Happy Birthday, Mississippi—1817–1967," *DAR Magazine*, February 1968, 86–88; Aren Akweks (Ray Fadden), "The Oneida Nation—Our Revolutionary Ally," *DAR Magazine*, May 1960, 370–373; Frank E. Klapthor, "PEACE—North American Indians," *DAR Magazine*, March 1961, 175–177; Stella Love Robinson, "American Indians—Yesterday and Today," *DAR Magazine*, January 1962, 12–14, 96; *Proceedings of the Seventy-Third Continental Congress of the National Society DAR* (1964), 100–102; *Proceedings of the Seventy-Fifth Continental Congress of the National Society DAR* (1966), 164; Margaret Rector Johnson, "Innovation in Indian Education," *DAR Magazine*, May 1967, 532–534; Mary Thurmond Brush, "The Indian and His Contribution to the American Way of Life," *DAR Magazine*, May 1968, 562–565; Anna Ruth Kietzman to DAR National Vice Chairmen, State and Chapter Chairmen, July 1972, folder 7, box 1, Dunaway Papers; Anna Ruth Kietzman, "The National Society and the American Indian," *DAR Magazine*, March 1973, 226–228.

99. DAR, *Proceedings of the Sixty-Fourth Continental Congress of the National Society DAR* (1955), 333; Marilyn Dayton Rommel, "Patriotism," *DAR Magazine*, December 1963, 938.

100. "Virginia Textbooks Blacklisted by DAR," *Washington Post*, July 6, 1960, C7; *Proceedings of the Seventy-Fourth Continental Congress of the National Society DAR* (1965), Resolution "American History-Textbooks-Patriotic Education." For a more detailed account of the efforts of the DAR and other conservative organizations to ban certain textbooks from public schools in the 1950s and early 1960s, see Moreau, *School Book Nation*, 253–266; Nelson and Roberts, *Censors and the Schools*.

101. By early 1978 the DAR had 207,000 members in 3,091 chapters across the country and abroad, gaining approximately three thousand members annually between 1973 and 1978 (Katharine R. Stark, "Where Do We Grow from Here?" *DAR Magazine*, August–September 1978, 681).

102. "Remark by Jackie Inspires DAR Hunt for 'New Image,'" *Detroit Free Press*, April 11, 1963, C1.

103. John Keats, "The D.A.R. Must Be Kidding," *True*, April 1968, 8.

104. Elaine Kendall, "The Daughters," book review, *New York Times Book Review*, August 4, 1974, 241.

105. Norman Kempster, "DAR Voices Support for Nixon," *Washington Star-News*, April 18, 1974; John Margolis, "Nixon's Still the One to Loyal D.A.R.," *Chicago Tribune*, April 19, 1974, 3.

106. "Citizenship Awards from D.A.R. Got To Eight Students in Area," *Stanly News and*

Press (Albemarle, NC), June 11, 1968, 1B; "DAR Honors Good Citizens," *Salisbury Evening Post,* June 5, 1969, 6; "DAR Good Citizens Named," *Goldsboro News* (Argus, NC), October 29, 1973, 5; "Good Citizens Awards," *Gastonia Gazette,* June 27, 1975, 9A; "History Essay Winners," *The Sun* (Durham, NC), February 5, 1976, 4A; "Six Students Named DAR 'Good Citizens,'" *Alamance News,* May 29, 1975, 11A; "Yolanda Ellerbe Is Bowman DAR Good Citizen," unidentified newspaper, November 15, 1976, National Society DAR, Press Book, 1976–1977, NCSA; Jeannette Smyth, "Ovations and a First at the DAR's 82nd," *Washington Post,* April 17, 1973, B2.

107. Dorothy McCardle, "A Revolutionary Tolerance," *Washington Post,* April 19, 1975, D3.

108. "Black Woman in Daughters of America," *New York Amsterdam News,* December 31, 1977, B6; "First Black DAR Member Urges Search for Roots," *Jet,* March 9, 1978, 21; "DAR Welcomes Its First Black," *Chicago Tribune,* December 4, 1977, 3; "DAR's 1st Black Quits Jobs, Plans 'Roots' Center," *Jet,* May 25, 1978, 26; "DAR Welcomes Its First Black," 3.

109. Jacqueline Trescot, "National DAR Admits Black," *Washington Post,* May 10, 1983, B3.

110. Jacqueline Trescot, "National DAR Admits Black," *Washington Post,* May 10, 1983, B3; Hass, *Sacrificing Soldiers on the National Mall,* 62; Jill Lawrence, "The DAR: Black Daughters Now Welcome," *Daily-Times News* (Burlington, NC), April 17, 1985, 11A.

111. Ronald Kessler, "Black Unable to Join Local DAR," *Washington Post,* March 12, 1984, A1; Jeff Jacoby, "Revolutionary Daughters in Racial Time Warp," *Wall Street Journal,* January 6, 1986, 1.

112. Kessler, "Black Unable to Join Local DAR," *Washington Post,* March 12, 1984, A1; Marcia A. Slacum, "D.C. City Council's Clark Threatens DAR's Tax Break," *Washington Post,* March 13, 1984, B2; "Woman Accuses DAR of Racism," *New York Amsterdam News,* March 17, 1984, 4; "Woman Banned from DAR Gets Help to Form Chapter," *Jet,* April 9, 1984, 9.

113. Lena Santos Ferguson, "A Memorial to Forgotten Black Patriots," *Wall Street Journal,* March 21, 1986, 28.

114. "DAR Offers Chapter to Snubbed Black Woman," *Los Angeles Times,* March 14, 1984, B8.

115. Glen Elsasser, "DAR Chief Hits Racism, Invites Blacks to Join," *Chicago Tribune,* April 5, 1984, 3; Ronald Kessler, "Embattled Head of National DAR Pledges Action against Any Bias," *Washington Post,* April 5, 1984, C3; Ronald Kessler, "DAR Chief Says Black's Application Handled 'Inappropriately,'" *Washington Post,* April 18, 1984, C1; Lawrence, "The DAR," *Daily-Times News,* April 17, 1985, 11A; Sarah Booth Conroy, "The DAR Marches On," *Washington Post,* April 21, 1984, B3; Lena Santos Ferguson to the editor of the *Wall Street Journal,* January 15, 1986, folder 5, box 705, Luce Papers.

116. DAR, *Proceedings of the Ninety-Third Continental Congress of the National Society DAR* (1984), 135.

117. Kessler, "Embattled Head of National DAR Pledges Action against Any Bias," *Washington Post,* April 5, 1984, C3; *The Forgotten Patriots* (Washington, DC: DAR, 1985), folder 5, box 705, Luce Papers. After the publication of the pamphlet, Walker's research focused on the patriotic contributions of African Americans, Native Americans, and women to the American Revolution. The results of that research were subsequently published by the DAR in Washington, DC, in several installments between 1988 and 1997. They are titled *Minority Military Service, 1775–1783* and cover different states: *Minority Military Service: Connecticut, 1775–1783.* Washington, DC: National Society DAR, 1988; *Minority Military Service: Maine, 1775–1783.* Washington, DC: National Society DAR, 1990; *Minority Military Service: Massachusetts, 1775–1783.* Washington, DC: National Society DAR, 1989; *Minority Military Service: New Hampshire, Vermont, 1775–1783.* Washington, DC: National Society DAR, 1991; *Minority Military Service: Rhode Island, 1775–1783.* Washington, DC: National Society DAR, 1988; *Mi-*

nority Military Service: South Carolina, Georgia, 1775–1783. Washington, DC: National Society DAR, 1997.

118. "White History Group Backs Book on Black Soldiers," *Jet,* March 18, 1985, 11; Greene, *Black Courage;* Sam Zagoria, "Keeping Up with the DAR," *Washington Post,* March 27, 1985, A22; Lena Santos Ferguson to the editor of the *Wall Street Journal,* January 15, 1986; James Walker, "Minorities in the American Revolution," *DAR Magazine,* February 1985, 86; "The DAR: Taking Stock at 95," *Washington Post,* April 22, 1985, A14.

119. Public Law 98–245, March 27, 1984, 98th Congress, Joint Resolution: "Honoring the Contribution of Blacks to American Independence"; "New Law Urges Nation to Honor Black U.S. Patriots," *Jet,* April 30, 1984, 23.

120. Hass, *Sacrificing Soldiers on the National Mall,* 71–72, 75; "The Story of the Efforts to Create a Black Patriots Memorial," *DAR Magazine,* January 1986, 16; "DAR Marches for a New Memorial for Black Heroes," *Jet,* July 29, 1985, 37 (quotes).

121. Ferguson, "Memorial to Forgotten Black Patriots," *Wall Street Journal,* March 21, 1986.

122. Josephine E. Hill to Clare Boothe Luce, December 30, 1985, folder 5, box 705, Luce Papers.

123. Sarah R. Melvin to Mrs. Walter Hughey King, December 5, 1983; Sarah M. King to Clare Boothe Luce, December 6, 1983, both in folder 12, box 14, Luce Papers; "President General's Message," *DAR Magazine,* February 1984, 67; "Remarks of Mrs. Clare Boothe Luce," *DAR Magazine,* May 1984, 308–309.

124. *Proceedings of the Ninety-Fourth Continental Congress of the National Society DAR* (1985), 146; *Proceedings of the Ninety-Sixth Continental Congress of the National Society DAR* (1987), 136.

125. "White History Group Backs Book on Black Soldier," *Jet,* March 18, 1985, 11.

126. Jane Leavy, "DAR, in Step with the Times," *Washington Post,* April 19, 1985, C1, C4; photograph of President Ronald Reagan and DAR President General Mrs. Richard D. Shelby, *DAR Magazine,* May 1983, 522; "DAR Denies Proposal for Impeachment," *News and Observer* (Raleigh, NC), April 18, 1984, 8A.

127. See, for example, Hunter, *Century of Service,* 224.

128. Kammen, *Mystic Chords of Memory,* 571–572, 588, 682–685.

129. DAR, *Proceedings of the One-Hundredth Continental Congress of the National Society DAR* (1991), 155–156; DAR, *Proceedings of the One-Hundredth-and-Sixth Continental Congress of the National Society DAR* (1997), 263; Stacy Palmer and Wyne Lutton, "The Immigration Time Bomb," *DAR Magazine,* April 1986, 308–312; Hunter, *Century of Service,* 225; Phyllis Schlafly, "America Should Address the Immigration Problem," *DAR Magazine,* October 1993, 598; Elizabeth Oglesby Haugh, "Is the United States Still a Melting Pot?," *DAR Magazine,* April 1997, 250–253.

130. DAR, *Proceedings of the Eighty-Ninth Continental Congress of the National Society DAR* (1980), 281.

131. Isabel R. Ward, "The Role of Women in National Defense," *DAR Magazine,* December 1980, 1200.

132. Adelaide M. Cole, "Mary Draper Ingles: Pioneer Heroine," *DAR Magazine,* March 1991, 195–197; Charlotte L. Kovalenko, "Patriotic Female Ancestry of the American Revolution," *DAR Magazine,* January 1992, 16–21, 68; Carol Riling, "A Symbol for American Women," *DAR Magazine,* January 1993, 19–21; Anna-Ruth Moore Kietzman, "Women in Military Nursing," *DAR Magazine,* April 1981, 289–293; Anne Rollins, "Memorials to Women Warriors," *DAR Magazine,* March 1995, 263–267, 336; Kathryn Sheldon, "American

Military Women at War," *DAR Magazine*, March 1997, 180–184; Denise Doring Van Buren, "A Proud Tradition of Service: Women in the United States Military," *DAR Magazine*, November 2000, 620–626; Bailey, *America's Army*, 218–219.

133. Elisabeth Whitman Schmidt, "The NSDAR Minority Military Service Project," *DAR Magazine*, February 1996, 77; "American History Month Essays—1986," *DAR Magazine*, October 1986, 703; "American History Month Essays," *DAR Magazine*, October 1987, 694; Michael Rather, "Our Responsibilities as 'We The People,'" *DAR Magazine*, August–September 1989, 621; W. Richard West Jr., "The National Museum of the American Indian: At the Cultural Interface," *DAR Magazine*, November 1991, 620.

134. William H. Honan, "Fresh Perspectives on the D.A.R.'s Rebuff on Marian Anderson," *New York Times*, May 18, 1993, C13. See also Andi Rierden, "Revolution's Heirs Keep Patriotism High and Profile Low," *New York Times*, June 24, 1990, CN1.

135. Scott A. Sandage, "Apologies for D.A.R. Racism Never End," *New York Times*, June 7, 1993, A16. See also Sandage, "Marble House Divided."

136. Moreau, *School Book Nation*, 265–267.

137. Resolution "Multiculturalism—A Distortion of History," in DAR, *Proceedings of the One-Hundred-and-First Continental Congress of the National Society DAR* (1992). See also Phyllis Schlafly, "Whatever Happened to George Washington," *DAR Magazine*, February 1990, 91; *Proceedings of the One-Hundredth Continental Congress of the National Society DAR* (1991), 156–158.

138. Phyllis Schlafly, "What's Happening on College Campuses Today," *DAR Magazine*, May 1993, 338, 340.

139. Nash, Crabtree, and Dunn, *History on Trial*, 5.

140. Phyllis Schlafly, "What's Happened to the Teaching of American History," *DAR Magazine*, April 1995, 355. See also Elizabeth Oglesby Haugh, "National Standards for United States History—Updated," *DAR Magazine*, February 1996, 82–84; Lynda Williams Closson, "Americanism: Our Responsibility," *DAR Magazine*, March 1996, 156–159.

Conclusion

1. Phillips-Fein, "Conservatism," 726–727; Critchlow, "Rethinking American Conservatism," 753. For additional historiographical discussions of US conservatism, see Brinkley, "Conservatism as a Growing Field of Scholarship"; Brinkley, "Problem of American Conservatism"; McGirr, "Now that Historians Know So Much about the Right."

2. Phillips-Fein, "Conservatism," 728–729, 736–737.

3. Cott, *Grounding of Modern Feminism*, 4.

4. Chafe, *Paradox of Change*, 202–210.

5. On the various analytical attempts to come to terms with the history of conservative women's activism in the United States, see K. Blee, "Troubling Women's History"; Delegard, "Women's Movements, 1880s–1920s"; Spruill, "Gender and America's Right Turn."

6. Nickerson, *Mothers of Conservatism*, 174.

7. DAR National Society, "Who We Are," http://www.dar.org/national-society/who-we-are; "Daughters of the American Revolution Sees Record Growth," *Stewart Houston Times* (Dover, TN), February 4, 2014, A6.

8. See Weil, *Family Trees*, 180–216; Morgan, "My Furthest-Back Person," 63–78.

9. Sarah Maslin Nir, "For Daughters of the Revolution, a New Chapter," *New York Times*, July 4, 2012, A1; Lena Anthony, "Battle Detective," *American Spirit*, January–February 2013, 5;

Lena Anthony, "For the People: Philadelphia Daughter Finds Fulfillment in Serving Others," *American Spirit*, July–August 2017, 5; "Million Members Celebration," DAR, National Society, https://www.dar.org./national-society/million-members-celebration.

10. Kelly quoted in Nir, "For Daughters of the Revolution, a New Chapter," *New York Times*, July 4, 2012.

11. See, for example, Bill Hudgins, "Fighting for British Freedom," *American Spirit*, May–June 2012, 40–44; Bill Hudgins, "They Also Served: African American Patriots Emerge from History's Shadows," *American Spirit*, January–February 2013, 30; "No Longer Forgotten Patriots," *American Spirit*, January–February 2017, 11; Kim Harke, "Searching for African-American Patriots in a Connecticut Town," *American Spirit*, January–February 2017, 38–40.

12. Elisabeth Whitman Schmidt, "Black Patriots: Unsung Heroes of the Revolution," *American Spirit*, January–February 2003, 16–19; Jamie Roberts, "Phillis Wheatley's Journey to Greatness," *American Spirit*, January–February 2011, 46–48; Susan Chapell, "First Ladies," *American Spirit*, March–April 2003, 23 (quote).

13. "DAR Pays Tribute to Marian Anderson on 70th Anniversary of Lincoln Memorial Concert," DAR, National Society, press release, April 9, 2009, https://www.dar.org/national-society/media-center/news-releases/dar-pays-tribute-marian-anderson-70th-anniversary.

14. "Who We Are" (quote), DAR, National Society, https://www.dar.org/national-society/about-dar/who-we-are/who-we-are. Examples of the more recent articles include Stacey Evers, "Defenders of Freedom," *American Spirit*, March–April 2003, 29–34; Courtney Peter, "Pass It On: How Women Inspire a Sense of Patriotism in Each Other," *American Spirit*, July–August 2011, 32–34; Rachel Hartman, "Spy Heroes: Women in Revolutionary Espionage," *American Spirit*, March–April 2011, 31–33; Megan Pacella, "Captain Molly: Establishing the True Identity of an American Military Heroine," *American Spirit*, March–April 2011, 44–48; Hazel Kreinheder, "Brothers in Arms," *American Spirit*, January–February 2004, 33; Pauline Moore and Jamie Roberts, "Nan-ye-hi: Cherokee Beloved Woman and Promoter of Peace," *American Spirit*, March–April 2014, 48; Gin Phillips, "Sacagawea: The Woman Behind the Myth," *American Spirit*, November–December 2004, 35–38; Bill Hudgins, "Clash of Civilizations," *American Spirit*, November–December 2013, 42–46; Bill Hudgins, "New England Burning," *American Spirit*, January–February 2014, 42–48; Megan Hamby, "Sequoyah's Cabin: The Cherokee Statesman's Final Homestead," *American Spirit*, November–December 2017, 44–46.

15. DAR, *Annual Proceedings of the National Society DAR* (2000), resolution "Immigration and America's Future," 204 (first quote); DAR, *Annual Proceedings of the National Society DAR* (2002), 255; DAR, *Annual Proceedings of the National Society DAR* (2009), resolution "English as the Official Language of the United States of America," 287 (second quote).

16. DAR, *Annual Proceedings of the National Society DAR* (2001), resolution "Rights or Entitlements," 205 (quote); *Annual Proceedings of the National Society DAR* (2002), resolution "Serfdom of the World," 71; *Annual Proceedings of the National Society DAR* (2008), resolution "Support our Troops," 263–264; *Annual Proceedings of the National Society DAR* (2001), resolution "Gun Control Precedes Genocide."

17. Truesdell, "Exalting 'U.S.Ness,'" 274, 275.

18. DAR, *Annual Proceedings of the National Society DAR* (2011), 201.

Bibliography

Archives

Anderson, Marian, DAR. Controversy Collection. Moorland-Spingarn Research Center, Howard University, Washington, DC.

Bourne, Henry Joy. Scrapbooks. Michigan Historical Collections, Bentley Library, University of Michigan, Ann Arbor.

Breckinridge Family Papers. Library of Congress, Washington, DC (LOC).

Brown, Elizabeth Churchill. Papers. Hoover Institution Archives, Stanford, CA (HIA).

Carr, John Foster. Papers. New York Public Library, Manuscripts and Archives Division, New York (NYPL).

Daughters of the American Revolution, American Indian Committee. Papers. Carl A. Kroch Library, Division of Rare and Manuscript Collections, Cornell University, Ithaca, NY.

Daughters of the American Revolution, Americanization Committee. Vertical file. Collection. Western Reserve Historical Society, Cleveland, OH (WRHS).

Daughters of the American Revolution, Atlanta Chapter. Records. Atlanta History Center Archive, Atlanta, GA (AHCA).

Daughters of the American Revolution, "Blacklist" Controversy. Collection. Department of Special Collections, Stanford University, Stanford, CA.

Daughters of the American Revolution, Cherokee Chapter. Collection. Atlanta History Center Archive, Atlanta, GA (AHCA).

Daughters of the American Revolution, Colorado State Society. Collection. Denver Public Library, Denver.

Daughters of the American Revolution, Columbia, MO, Chapter. Records, 1902–1995. Western Historical Manuscript Collection, State Historical Society of Missouri, Columbia (WHMC-Columbia).

Daughters of the American Revolution, Denver Chapter. Collection. Denver Public Library, Denver.

———. Scrapbooks, 1898–1962. Denver Public Library, Denver.

Daughters of the American Revolution, Georgia State Society. Georgia Scrapbook, 1929–1932. Georgia Archives, Morrow.

———. Georgia State Scrapbook, 1938–1939. Georgia Archives, Morrow.

Daughters of the American Revolution, Kansas City Chapter. Scrapbook (May 14, 1917, to November 26, 1919). Western Historical Manuscript Collection, University of Missouri–Kansas City Archives, Kansas City, MO (WHMC–Kansas City).

———. Scrapbook, 1934–1936. Western Historical Manuscript Collection, University of Missouri–Kansas City Archives, Kansas City, MO (WHMC–Kansas City).

Daughters of the American Revolution, Mary Chesney Chapter, Warren, OH. Collection. Vertical file. Western Reserve Historical Society, Cleveland, OH (WRHS).

Daughters of the American Revolution, Michigan Society, Records (Michigan DAR Records). Michigan Historical Collections, Bentley Library, University of Michigan, Ann Arbor (MHC).

Daughters of the American Revolution, Mississippi. 1950–1959. Subject file. Mississippi Department of Archives and History, Archives and Records Services Division, Jackson (MDAH).

———. Vertical file. MDAH.

Daughters of the American Revolution, Missouri Chapters. George Washington Bi-Centennial, Scrapbook, 1931–1932. Western Historical Manuscript Collection, State Historical Society of Missouri, Columbia (WHMC-Columbia).

Daughters of the American Revolution, Missouri Collection. Western Historical Manuscript Collection, State Historical Society of Missouri, Columbia (WHMC-Columbia).

Daughters of the American Revolution, Missouri State Society. Scrapbooks. Western Historical Manuscript Collection, State Historical Society of Missouri, Columbia (WHMC-Columbia).

Daughters of the American Revolution, North Carolina. National Society Press Book, 1976–1977. North Carolina State Archives, Raleigh.

Daughters of the American Revolution, North Carolina. Scrapbook, 1949–1952. North Carolina State Archives, Raleigh.

Daughters of the American Revolution, Nova Caesarea Chapter. Collection. New Jersey Historical Society, Newark.

Daughters of the American Revolution, State of Washington. Collection. Seattle Public Library, Seattle.

Daughters of the American Revolution, Texas Society. Collection. Woman's Collection, Texas Woman's University, Denton.

Daughters of the American Revolution, Western Reserve Chapter, Cleveland, OH. Records. Western Reserve Historical Society, Cleveland (WRHS).

Daughters of the American Revolution, Yankton, SD, Chapter. Papers. Library of Congress, Washington, DC (LOC).

Dunaway, Kathryn Fink. Papers. Emory University Archives, Atlanta, GA.

Hodge, Orlando John. Papers. Western Reserve Historical Society, Cleveland, OH (WRHS).

Inman, Grant and Slaton. Family Papers. Atlanta History Center Archive, Atlanta, GA (AHCA).

Kelley, Florence. Papers. New York Public Library, Manuscripts and Archives Division, New York (NYPL).

Kohlberg, Alfred. Collection. Hoover Institution Archives, Stanford, CA (HIA).

Luce, Clare Boothe. Papers. Library of Congress, Washington, DC (LOC).

Madonna of the Trail. Collection. Archives of Daughters of the American Revolution, National Society, Washington, DC.

McDowell, William Osborne. Papers. Vertical file. Western Reserve Historical Society, Cleveland, OH (WRHS).

National Association for the Advancement of Colored People (NAACP). Papers. Library of Congress, Washington, DC (LOC).

National Republic. Records. Hoover Institution Archives, Stanford, CA (HIA).

Peel, Lucy Cook. Papers. Atlanta History Center Archive, Atlanta, GA (AHCA).

Philbrick, Herbert A. Papers. Library of Congress, Washington, DC (LOC).

Rawalt, Marguerite. Papers. Arthur and Elizabeth Schlesinger Library, Radcliffe Institute for Advanced Study, Cambridge, MA.

Rodman, William Blout. Papers. North Carolina State Archives, Raleigh.

Rogers, Edith Nourse. Papers. Arthur and Elizabeth Schlesinger Library, Radcliffe Institute for Advanced Study, Cambridge, MA.

Somerville, Nellie Nugent. Papers. Somerville-Howorth Family Papers, Arthur and Elizabeth Schlesinger Library, Radcliffe Institute for Advanced Study, Cambridge, MA.

Van Brunt, Hope Casey. Collection. Western Historical Manuscript Collection, State Historical Society of Missouri, Columbia (WHMC-Columbia).

Withers, Ethel Massie. Collection. Western Historical Manuscript Collection, State Historical Society of Missouri, Columbia (WHMC-Columbia).

Secondary Sources

Adams, David Wallace. *Education for Extinction: Americans and the Boarding School Experience, 1875–1928*. Lawrence: University Press of Kansas, 1995.

Anderson, Benedict. *Imagined Communities: Reflections on the Origin and Spread of Nationalism*. Rev. ed. New York: Verso, 1991.

Arsenault, Raymond. *The Sound of Freedom: Marian Anderson, the Lincoln Memorial, and the Concert that Awakened America*. New York: Bloomsbury Press, 2009.

Assmann, Jan. "Collective Memory and Cultural Identity." *New German Critique* 65 (Spring–Summer 1995): 125–133.

———. *Cultural Memory and Early Civilization: Writing, Remembrance, and Political Imagination*. Cambridge, England: Cambridge University Press, 2011.

Bagley, Will. *So Rugged and Mountainous: Blazing the Trails to Oregon and California*. Norman: University of Oklahoma Press, 2010.

Bailey, Beth. *America's Army: Making the All-Volunteer Force*. Cambridge, MA: Belknap Press, 2009.

Baker, Juliette Boyer, ed. *West Virginia State History of the Daughters of the American Revolution*. N.p., 1928.

Baker, Paula. "The Domestication of Politics: Women and American Political Society, 1780–1920." *American Historical Review* 89, no. 3 (1984): 620–647.

Barkan, Elazar. *The Retreat of Scientific Racism: Changing Concepts of Race in Britain and the United States between the World Wars*. Cambridge, England: Cambridge University Press, 1992.

Barrett, James R. "Americanization from the Bottom Up: Immigration and the Remaking of the Working Class in the United States, 1880–1930." *Journal of American History* 79, no. 3 (1992): 996–1020.

Barrington, Lewis. *Historic Restorations of the Daughters of the American Revolution*. New York: Richard R. Smith, 1941.

Basson, Lauren L. *White Enough to Be American? Race Mixing, Indigenous People, and the Boundaries of State and Nation*. Chapel Hill: University of North Carolina Press, 2008.

Beagle, Maude Stewart. *The Michigan Society Daughters of the American Revolution Presents "The Fairy Isle."* N.p.: Michigan Society DAR, 1934.

Beauford, Gertrude Marie, ed. *A History of the Louisiana Society DAR and Its Chapters*. New Orleans: Louisiana Society DAR, 1991.

Bederman, Gail. *Manliness and Civilization: A Cultural History of Gender and Race in the United States, 1880–1917*. Chicago: University of Chicago Press, 1995.

Bennett, David H. *The Party of Fear: From Nativist Movements to the New Right in American History*. Chapel Hill: University of North Carolina Pres, 1988.

Benowitz, June Melby. *Challenge and Change: Right-Wing Women, Grassroots Activism, and the Baby Boom Generation.* Gainesville: University Press of Florida, 2015.

———. *Days of Discontent: American Women and Right-Wing Politics, 1933–1945.* De Kalb: Northern Illinois University Press, 2002.

Berg, Manfred. *Popular Justice: A History of Lynching in America.* Lanham, MD: Ivan R. Dee, 2011.

———. *The Ticket to Freedom: The NAACP and the Struggle for Black Political Integration.* Gainesville: University Press of Florida, 2005.

Berkhofer, Robert F. Jr. *The White Man's Indian: Images of the American Indian from Columbus to the Present.* New York: Vintage Books, 1979.

Berkin, Carol. *Revolutionary Mothers: Women in the Struggle for America's Independence.* New York: Vintage, 2005.

Bernstein, Alison. *American Indians and World War II: Toward a New Era in Indian Affairs.* Norman: University of Oklahoma Press, 1991.

Billig, Michael. *Banal Nationalism.* London: Sage, 1995.

Black, Allida. "Championing a Champion: Eleanor Roosevelt and the Marian Anderson 'Freedom Concert.'" *Presidential Studies Quarterly* 20 (Fall 1990): 719–736.

Blee, Kathleen M. "Troubling Women's History: Women in Right-Wing and Colonial Politics." *Journal of Women's History* 15, no. 2 (2003): 214–220.

———. *Women of the Klan: Racism and Gender in the 1920s.* Berkeley: University of California Press, 1991.

Blee, Lisa. "Completing Lewis and Clark's Westward March: Exhibiting a History of Empire at the 1905 Portland World's Fair." *Oregon Historical Quarterly* 16, no. 2 (2005): 232–253.

Blight, David W. *Race and Reunion: The Civil War in American Memory.* Cambridge, MA: Harvard University Press, 2001.

Blum, Edward J. *Reforging the White Republic: Race, Religion, and American Nationalism, 1865–1898.* Baton Rouge: Louisiana State University Press, 2005.

Bodnar, John. *Remaking America: Public Memory, Commemoration, and Patriotism in the Twentieth Century.* Princeton, NJ: Princeton University Press, 1992.

Bolt, Christine. *American Indian Policy and American Reform: Case Studies of the Campaign to Assimilate the American Indians.* London: Allen and Unwin, 1987.

Boughter, Judith A. *Betraying the Omaha Nation, 1790–1916.* Norman: University of Oklahoma Press, 1998.

Bratton, Virginia Mason. *History of the South Carolina Daughters of the American Revolution, 1892–1936.* York, SC: South Carolina DAR, 1937.

Brennan, Mary C. *Wives, Mothers, and the Red Menace: Conservative Women and the Crusade against Communism.* Boulder: University Press of Colorado, 2008.

Breuilly, John. *Nationalism and the State.* Chicago: University of Chicago Press, 1993.

Brinkley, Alan. "Conservatism as a Growing Field of Scholarship." *Journal of American History* 98, no. 3 (2011): 748–751.

———. "The Problem of American Conservatism." *American Historical Review* 99, no. 2 (1994): 409–429.

Britten, Thomas A. *American Indians in World War I: At Home and at War.* Albuquerque: University of New Mexico Press, 1997.

Brooks, Joanna. "Sacajawea, Meet *Cogewa*: A Red Progressive Revision of Frontier Romance." In *Lewis and Clark: Legacies, Memories, and New Perspectives,* edited by Kris Fresonke and Mark Spence, 184–197. Berkeley: University of California Press, 2004.

Brown, David. "Are There Good and Bad Nationalisms?" *Nations and Nationalisms* 5, no. 2 (1999): 281–302.

Brown, Meredith Mason. *Daniel Boone and the Making of America*. Baton Rouge: Louisiana State University Press, 2008.

Brundage, W. Fitzhugh. "Introduction: No Deed but Memory." In *Where These Memories Grow: History, Memory, and Southern Identity,* edited by W. Fitzhugh Brundage, 1–28. Chapel Hill: University of North Carolina Press 2000.

———. *The Southern Past: A Clash of Race and Memory.* Cambridge, MA: Belknap Press, 2005.

———. "White Women and the Politics of Historical Memory in the New South, 1880–1920." In *Jumpin' Jim Crow: Southern Politics from Civil War to Civil Rights,* edited by Jane Dailey, Glenda Elizabeth Gilmore, and Bryant Simon, 115–139. Princeton: Princeton University Press, 2000.

Buell, Gertrude Landphair, ed. *Ohio Society History of the Daughters of the American Revolution.* Vol. 3. Painesville, OH: Painesville, 1945.

Butler, Judith. *Bodies That Matter: On the Discursive Limits of "Sex."* New York: Routledge, 1993.

———. *Gender Trouble: Feminism and the Subversion of Identity.* New York: Routledge, 1990.

———. *Undoing Gender.* New York: Routledge, 2004.

Butterfield, Emily Lewis. "'Lie There My Darling, while I Avenge Ye!': Anecdotes, Collective Memory, and the Legend of Molly Pitcher." In *Remembering the Revolution: Memory, History, and Nation Making from Independence to the Civil War,* edited by Michael A. McDonnell, Clare Corbould, Frances M. Clarke, and W. Fitzhugh Brundage, 198–213. Amherst: University of Massachusetts Press, 2013.

Bynum, Cornelius L. *A. Philip Randolph and the Struggle for Civil Rights.* Champaign: University of Illinois Press, 2010.

Calhoun, Craig. *Nationalism.* Buckingham, England: Open University Press, 1997.

Camhi, Jane Jerome. *Women against Women: American Anti-Suffragism, 1880–1920.* Brooklyn, NY: Carlson, 1994.

Carroll, Al. *Medicine Bags and Dog Tags: American Indian Veterans from Colonial Times to the Second Iraq War.* Lincoln: University of Nebraska Press, 2008.

Chafe, William H. *The Paradox of Change: American Women in the 20th Century.* New York: Oxford University Press, 1991.

Chin, Gabriel J., and Rose Cuison Villazor, eds. *The Immigration and Nationality Act of 1965: Legislating a New America.* Cambridge, MA: Cambridge University Press, 2015.

Clarkson, Emily Sarah Watkins (Mrs. Sidney W. Clarkson), ed. *Historical Records of the Michigan Daughters of the American Revolution, 1893–1930.* Vol. 1. Ann Arbor: Ann Arbor Press, 1930.

Cobb, Daniel M. *Native Activism in Cold War America: The Struggle for Sovereignty.* Lawrence: University Press of Kansas, 2008.

Confino, Alon. "Collective Memory and Cultural History: Problems of Method." *American Historical Review* 102, no. 5 (1997): 1386–1403.

Connell, R. W. *Masculinities.* Cambridge, England: Polity Press, 1995.

Cordry, Mrs. T. A. *The Story of the Marking of the Santa Fe Trail.* Topeka, KS: Crane, 1915.

Cott, Nancy F. *The Grounding of Modern Feminism.* New Haven, CT: Yale University Press, 1987.

Cox, Karen L. *Dixie's Daughters: The United Daughters of the Confederacy and the Preservation of Confederate Culture.* Gainesville: University Press of Florida, 2003.

Critchlow, Donald T. *Phyllis Schlafly and Grassroots Conservatism: A Woman's Crusade.* Princeton, NJ: Princeton University Press, 2005.

———. "Rethinking American Conservatism: Toward a New Narrative." *Journal of American History* 98, no. 3 (2011): 752–755.

Daily, David W. *Battle for the BIA: G.E.E. Lindquist and the Missionary Crusade against John Collier.* Tucson: University of Arizona Press, 2004.

DAR (Daughters of the American Revolution), Columbus Chapter. *History of the Columbus Chapter National Society, Daughters of the American Revolution, 1899–1911.* Columbus, OH: Columbus Chapter NSDAR, 1911.

DAR (Daughters of the American Revolution), Eunice Sterling Chapter. *Illustrated History of Early Wichita: Incidents of Pioneer Days.* Wichita, KS: Daughters of the American Revolution, 1914.

DAR (Daughters of the American Revolution), Georgia State Society. *Chapter Histories: Daughters of the American Revolution in Georgia, 1891–1931.* Augusta, GA: Ridgely-Tidwell, 1932.

DAR (Daughters of the American Revolution), Michigan Society. *Historical and Genealogical Records of the Michigan Daughters of the American Revolution, 1930–1940.* Vol. 3. Adrian, MI: Adrian College Press, 1940.

DAR (Daughters of the American Revolution), National Society. *Manual of the United States: For the Information of Immigrants and Foreigners.* Washington, DC: Judd and Detweiler, 1928.

DAR (Daughters of the American Revolution), Sarah Platt Decker Chapter. *Pioneers of San Juan Country.* Vol. 1. Colorado Springs, CO: Out West, 1942.

———. *Pioneers of San Juan Country.* Vol. 2. Colorado Springs, CO: Out West, 1946.

Dary, David. *The Santa Fe Trail: Its History, Legends, and Lore.* Lawrence: University Press of Kansas, 2000.

Davies, Wallace Evan. *Patriotism on Parade: The Story of Veterans' and Hereditary Organizations in America, 1783–1900.* Cambridge, MA: Harvard University Press, 1955.

Davis, Deborah. *Guest of Honor: Booker T. Washington, Theodore Roosevelt, and the White House Dinner that Shocked the Nation.* New York: Atria, 2012.

DeBenedetti, Charles. *An American Ordeal: The Antiwar Movement of the Vietnam Era.* Syracuse, NY: Syracuse University Press, 1990.

Delegard, Kirsten Marie. *Battling Miss Bolsheviki: The Origins of Female Conservatism in the United States.* Philadelphia: University of Pennsylvania Press, 2011.

———. "Women Patriots: Female Activism and the Politics of American Anti-Radicalism, 1919–1935." PhD diss., Duke University, 1999.

———. "Women's Movements, 1880s–1920s." In *A Companion to American Women's History,* edited by Nancy A. Hewitt, 328–347. Malden, MA: Blackwell, 2002.

Deloria, Philip J. *Indians in Unexpected Places.* Lawrence: University Press of Kansas, 2004.

———. *Playing Indian.* New Haven: Yale University Press, 1998.

Denson, Andrew. *Monuments to Absence: Cherokee Removal and the Contest over Southern Memory.* Chapel Hill: University of North Carolina Press, 2017.

Des Jardins, Julie. *Women and the Historical Enterprise in America: Gender, Race, and the Politics of Memory, 1880–1945.* Chapel Hill: University of North Carolina Press, 2003.

Desha, Mary. *The True Story of the Origins of the National Society of the Daughters of the American Revolution.* Washington, DC, 1892.

Dilworth, Lea. *Imagining Indians in the Southwest: Persistent Visions of a Primitive Past.* Washington, DC: Smithsonian Institution Press, 1996.

Dippie, Brian W. *The Vanishing American: White Attitudes and U.S. Indian Policy.* Middletown, CT: Wesleyan University Press, 1982.

Duncan, Barbara R., and Brett Riggs. *Cherokee Heritage Trails Guidebook*. Chapel Hill: University of North Carolina Press, 2003.

Edmunds, R. David. *Potawatomis: The Keepers of the Fire*. Norman: University of Oklahoma Press, 1978.

Elson, Ruth Miller. *Guardians of Tradition: American Schoolbooks of the Nineteenth Century*. Lincoln: University of Nebraska Press, 1964.

Erickson, Christine K. "'I Have Not Had One Fact Disproven': Elizabeth Dilling's Crusade against Communism in the 1930s." *Journal of American Studies* 36, no. 3 (2002): 473–489.

———. "'So Much for Men': Conservative Women and National Defense in the 1920s and 1930s." *American Studies* 45, no. 1 (2004): 85–102.

———. "'We Want No Teachers Who Say There Are Two Sides to Every Question': Conservative Women and Education in the 1930s." *History of Education Quarterly* 46, no. 4 (2006): 487–502.

Fahrmeir, Andreas. *Citizenship: The Rise and Fall of a Modern Concept*. New Haven, CT: Yale University Press, 2007.

Faragher, John Mack. *Daniel Boone: The Life and Legend of an American Pioneer*. New York: Holt, 1992.

———. *Rereading Frederick Jackson Turner: "The Significance of the Frontier in American History" and Other Essays*. New Haven, CT: Yale University Press, 1999.

Farrell, John C. *Beloved Lady: A History of Jane Addams' Ideas on Reform and Peace*. Baltimore, MD: Johns Hopkins Press, 1967.

Faust, Drew Gilpin. "Altars of Sacrifice: Confederate Women and the Narratives of War." *Journal of American History* 76, no. 4 (1990): 1200–1228.

Feest, Christian F. "Pride and Prejudice: The Pocahontas Myth and the Pamunkey." In *The Invented Indian: Cultural Fictions and Government Policies*, edited by James A. Clifton, 49–61. New York: Transaction, 1990.

Fleegler, Robert L. *Ellis Island Nation: Immigration Policy and American Identity in the Twentieth Century*. Philadelphia: University of Pennsylvania Press, 2013.

Foley, Michael Stewart. *Confronting the War Machine: Draft Resistance during the Vietnam War*. Chapel Hill: University of North Carolina Press, 2003.

Foner, Eric. *Reconstruction: America's Unfinished Journey, 1863–1877*. New York: Harper and Row, 1988.

Ford, Anne Johnston. *Markers Placed by the Texas Daughters of the American Revolution*. Dallas: Clyde C. Cockrell, 1936.

Foster, Carrie A. *The Women and the Warriors: The U.S. Section of the Women's International League for Peace and Freedom, 1915–1946*. Syracuse, NY: Syracuse University Press, 1995.

Fredrickson, George M. *Racism: A Short History*. Princeton, NJ: Princeton University Press, 2002.

Fried, Richard M. *Nightmare in Red: The McCarthy Era in Perspective*. New York: Oxford University Press, 1990.

Gallagher, Gary W., and Alan T. Nolan, eds. *The Myth of the Lost Cause and Civil War History*. Bloomington: Indiana University Press, 2000.

Gardner, Sarah E. *Blood and Irony: Southern White Women's Narratives of the Civil War, 1861–1937*. Chapel Hill: University of North Carolina Press, 2004.

Garrison, Tim Allen. *The Legal Ideology of Removal: The Southern Judiciary and the Sovereignty of Native American Nations*. Athens: University of Georgia Press, 2002.

Genetin-Pilawa, C. Joseph. *Crooked Paths to Allotment: The Fight over Federal Indian Policy after the Civil War.* Chapel Hill: University of North Carolina Press, 2012.

Gere, Anne Ruggles. *Intimate Practices: Literary Cultural Work in U.S. Women's Clubs, 1880–1920.* Champaign: University of Illinois Press, 1997.

Gerstle, Gary. *American Crucible: Race and Nation in the Twentieth Century.* Princeton, NJ: Princeton University Press, 2001.

Gibbs, Margaret. *The DAR.* New York: Holt, Rinehart, and Winston, 1969.

Gilmore, Stephanie, and Sara Evans, eds. *Feminist Coalitions: Historical Perspectives on Second-Wave Feminism in the United States.* Champaign: University of Illinois Press, 2008.

Glassberg, David. *Sense of History: The Place of the Past in American Life.* Amherst: University of Massachusetts Press, 2001.

Goldstein, Joshua S. *War and Gender: How Gender Shapes the War System and Vice Versa.* Cambridge, England: Cambridge University Press, 2001.

Goodier, Susan. *No Votes for Women: The New York State Anti-Suffrage Movement.* Champaign: University of Illinois Press, 2013.

Gordon, Sarah Barrington. *The Mormon Question: Polygamy and Constitutional Conflict in Nineteenth-Century America.* Chapel Hill: University of North Carolina Press, 2004.

Green, Michael D. "William McIntosh: The Evolution of a Creek National Idea." In *The Human Tradition in the Old South,* edited by James C. Klotter, 45–62. Wilmington, DE: Scholarly Resources, 2003.

Green, Rayna. "The Pocahontas Perplex: The Image of Indian Women in American Culture." In *Native American Voices: A Reader,* edited by Susan Lobo, 203–211. New York: Longman, 1998.

Green, Sharony. *Remember Me to Miss Louisa: Hidden Black-White Intimacies in Antebellum America.* DeKalb: Northern Illinois University Press, 2015.

Greene, Robert Ewell. *Black Courage, 1775–1783: Documentation of Black Participation in the American Revolution.* Washington, DC: National Society Daughters of the American Revolution, 1984.

Griffith, Benjamin W. Jr. *McIntosh and Weatherford: Creek Indian Leaders.* Tuscaloosa: University of Alabama Press, 1988.

Gullett, Gayle. "Women Progressives and the Politics of Americanization in California, 1915–1920." *Pacific Historical Review* 64, no. 1 (1995): 71–94.

Gulley, H. E. "Women and the Lost Cause: Preserving a Confederate Identity in the American Deep South." *Journal of Historical Geography* 19, no. 2 (1993): 125–141.

Hagemann, Karen. "Of 'Manly Valor' and 'German Honor': Nation, War, and Masculinity in the Age of the Prussian Uprising against Napoleon." *Central European History* 30, no. 2 (1997): 187–220.

Hahn, Steven. *A Nation under Our Feet: Black Political Struggles in the Rural South from Slavery to the Great Migration.* Cambridge, MA: Belknap, 2003.

Hale, Grace Elizabeth. *Making Whiteness: The Culture of Segregation in the South, 1890–1940.* New York: Vintage, 1998.

Hall, Mabel Goodwin, ed. *A Brief History of the Main Daughters of the American Revolution to March 1, 1925.* N.p., 1925.

Hall, Simon. *Peace and Freedom: The Civil Rights and Antiwar Movements in the 1960s.* Philadelphia: University of Pennsylvania Press, 2004.

Harcourt, Felix. *Ku Klux Kulture: America and the Klan in the 1920s.* Chicago: University of Chicago Press, 2017.

Harper, Glenn A. "Preserving the National Road Landscape." In *The National Road*, edited by Karl Raitz, 376–414. Baltimore, MD: Johns Hopkins University Press, 1996.

Hass, Kristin Ann. *Sacrificing Soldiers on the National Mall*. Berkeley: University of California Press, 2013.

Hefernan, Michael, and Carol Medlicott. "A Feminine Atlas? Sacagawea, the Suffragettes, and the Commemorative Landscape of the American West." *Gender, Place, and Culture* 9, no. 2 (2002): 109–131.

Higham, John. *Strangers in the Land: Patterns of American Nativism*. New Brunswick, NJ: Rutgers University Press, 1955.

Hobsbawm, Eric. "Introduction: Inventing Traditions." In *The Invention of Tradition*, edited by Eric Hobsbawm and Terence Ranger, 1–9. Cambridge, England: Cambridge University Press, 1983.

Hodes, Martha. *White Women, Black Men: Illicit Sex in the Nineteenth-Century South*. New Haven, CT: Yale University Press, 1997.

Hoganson, Kristin L. *Fighting for American Manhood: How Gender Politics Provoked the Spanish-American and Philippine-American Wars*. New Haven, CT: Yale University Press, 1998.

Holm, Tom. *Strong Hearts, Wounded Souls: Native American Veterans of the Vietnam Era*. Austin: University of Texas Press, 1996.

Horsman, Reginald. *Race and Manifest Destiny: The Origins of Racial Anglo-Saxonism*. Cambridge, MA: Harvard University Press, 1981.

Hoxie, Frederick E. *A Final Promise: The Campaign to Assimilate the Indians, 1880–1920*. Lincoln: University of Nebraska Press, 1984.

Hugill, Peter J. "Good Roads and the Automobile in the United States, 1880–1929." *Geographical Review* 72, no. 3 (1982): 327–349.

Huhndorf, Shari M. *Going Native: Indians in the American Cultural Imagination*. Ithaca, NY: Cornell University Press, 2001.

Hume, Janice. "Press, Published History, and Regional Lore: Shaping the Public Memory of a Revolutionary War Heroine." *Journalism History* 30, no. 4 (2005): 200–209.

Hunter, Ann Arnold. *A Century of Service: The Story of the DAR*. Washington, DC: National Society Daughters of the American Revolution, 1991.

Isserman, Maurice, and Michael Kazin. *America Divided: The Civil War of the 1960s*. New York: Oxford University Press, 1999.

Jacobson, Matthew Frye. "Becoming Caucasian: Vicissitudes of Whiteness in American Politics and Culture." *Identities* 8, no. 4 (2001): 83–104.

———. *Whiteness of a Different Color: European Immigrants and the Alchemy of Race*. Cambridge, MA: Harvard University Press, 1998.

James, Rawn, Jr. *The Double V: How Wars, Protest, and Harry Truman Desegregated America's Military*. New York: Bloomsbury, 2013.

Janney, Caroline E. *Burying the Dead but Not the Past: Ladies' Memorial Associations and the Lost Cause*. Chapel Hill: University of North Carolina Press, 2008.

———. "'The Right to Love and to Mourn': The Origins of Virginia's Ladies' Memorial Associations, 1865–1867." In *Crucible of the Civil War: Virginia from Secession to Commemoration*, edited by Edward L. Ayers, Gary W. Gallagher, and Andrew J. Torget, 165–188. Charlottesville: University of Virginia Press, 2006.

Jarvis, Christina S. *The Male Body at War: American Masculinity during World War II*. DeKalb: Northern Illinois University Press, 2004.

Jeansonne, Glen. *Women of the Far Right: The Mothers' Movement and World War II*. Chicago: University of Chicago Press, 1996.

Johnson, Jeffrey Ogden. "Determining and Defining 'Wife': The Brigham Young Households." *Dialogue: A Journal of Mormon Thought* 20, no. 3 (1987): 57–70.

Johnston, Mary. *Iowa Daughters of the American Revolution, 1891–1911*. N.p.: Iowa Daughters of the American Revolution, 1911.

Jones, Alfred Haworth. "The Search for a Usable American Past in the New Deal Era." *American Quarterly* 23, no. 5 (1971): 710–724.

Jones, Mary G., and Lily Reynolds, eds. *Coweta County Chronicles for One Hundred Years*. Atlanta, GA: Stein, 1928.

Kachun, Mitch. *First Martyr of Liberty: Crispus Attucks in American Memory*. New York: Oxford University Press, 2017.

Kammen, Michael. *Mystic Chords of Memory: The Transformation of Tradition in American Culture*. New York: Knopf, 1991.

Kansas Daughters of the American Revolution. *History of the Kansas Daughters of the American Revolution, 1894–1938*. Wichita: Kansas Daughters of the American Revolution, 1938.

Kaufmann, Eric P. *The Rise and Fall of Anglo-America*. Cambridge, MA: Harvard University Press, 2004.

Kerber, Linda K. "The Republican Mother and the Woman Citizen: Contradictions and Choices in Revolutionary America." In *Women's America: Refocusing the Past*, edited by Linda K. Kerber and Jane Sherron De Hart, 119–127. 6th ed. New York: Oxford University Press, 2004.

Kessler, Donna J. *The Making of Sacagawea: A Euro-American Legend*. Tuscaloosa: University of Alabama Press, 1996.

Kimmel, Michael. *Manhood in America: A Cultural History*. New York: Free Press, 1996.

Kinney, Mrs. J. E., ed. *Ohio Indian Lore, 1947*. N.p.: Daughters of the American Revolution, Ohio Society, 1947.

Klarman, Michael J. *Brown v. Board of Education and the Civil Rights Movement*. New York: Oxford University Press, 2007.

Lavender, David. *Westward Vision: The Story of the Oregon Trail*. Lincoln: University of Nebraska Press, 1985.

Leach, Frank Sayre. *Missouri State History of the Daughters of the American Revolution*. Kansas City, MO: Smith-Grieves, 1929.

Lemons, J. Stanley. *The Woman Citizen: Social Feminism in the 1920s*. Champaign: University of Illinois Press, 1973.

Lengel, Edward G. *Inventing George Washington: America's Founder, in Myth and Memory*. New York: HarperCollins, 2011.

Lester, Annie Jopling, ed. *Ohio State History of the Daughters of the American Revolution*. Greenfield, OH: Greenfield, 1928.

Levy, Beth E. *Frontier Figures: American Music and the Mythology of the American West*. Berkeley: University of California Press, 2012.

Lewis, Wallace G. *In the Footsteps of Lewis and Clark: Early Commemoration and the Origins of the National Historic Trail*. Boulder: University Press of Colorado, 2010.

Lindgren, James M. "'A Constant Incentive to Patriotic Citizenship': Historic Preservation in Progressive-Era Massachusetts." *New England Quarterly* 64, no. 4 (1991): 594–608.

———. *Preserving Historic New England: Preservation, Progressivism, and the Remaking of Memory*. New York: Oxford University Press, 1995.

Lindly, Mabel, ed. *Nebraska State History of the Daughters of the American Revolution.* Lincoln: J. North, 1929.

Linenthal, Edward Tabor. *Changing Images of the Warrior Hero in America: A History of Popular Symbolism.* New York: Edwin Mellen, 1982.

———. *Sacred Ground: Americans and their Battlefields.* 2nd ed. Champaign: University of Illinois Press, 1991.

Lockwood, Mary S., and Emily Lee Sherwood. *Story of the Records D.A.R.* Washington, DC: George E. Howard, 1906.

Lovett, Laura L. *Conceiving the Future: Pronatalism, Reproduction, and the Family in the United States, 1890–1939.* Chapel Hill: University of North Carolina Press, 2007.

Lowenthal, David. *The Past Is a Foreign Country.* Cambridge, England: Cambridge University Press, 1985.

Lucander, David. *Winning the War for Democracy: The March on Washington Movement, 1941–1946.* Champaign: University of Illinois Press, 2014.

Lunsford, Fred B. *God's Messengers from the Mountains.* Bloomington, IN: WestBow, 2010.

MacLean, Nancy K. *Behind the Mask of Chivalry: The Making of the Second Ku Klux Klan.* New York: Oxford University Press, 1995.

Marder, Walter S. "Pleasing the Eye: Brick Paving and the Dixie Highway in the Sunshine State." In *Looking Beyond the Highway: Dixie Roads and Culture,* edited by Claudette Stager and Martha Carver, 53–72. Knoxville: University of Tennessee Press, 2006.

Marling, Karal Ann. "Of Cherry Trees and Ladies' Teas: Grant Wood Looks at Colonial America." In *The Colonial Revival in America,* edited by Alan Axelrod, 294–319. New York: W. W. Norton, 1985.

Marshall, Susan E. "In Defense of Separate Spheres: Class and Status Politics in the Antisuffrage Movement." *Social Forces* 65, no. 2 (1986): 327–351.

———. *Splintered Sisterhood: Gender and Class in the Campaign against Woman Suffrage.* Madison: University of Wisconsin Press, 1997.

Massachusetts Daughters of the American Revolution. *History of the Massachusetts Daughters of the American Revolution.* Somerville, MA: Somerville, 1932.

Mayer, Tamar. "Gender Ironies of Nationalism: Setting the Stage." In *Gender Ironies of Nationalism: Sexing the Nation,* edited by Tamar Mayer, 1–22. New York: Routledge, 2000.

McClintock, Anne. "Family Feuds: Gender, Nationalism and the Family." *Feminist Review* 44 (Summer 1993): 61–80.

———. "'No Longer in a Future Heaven': Gender, Race, and Nationalism." In *Dangerous Liaisons: Gender, Nation, and Postcolonial Perspectives,* edited by Anne McClintock, Aamir Mufti, and Ella Shohat, 89–112. Minneapolis: University of Minnesota Press, 1997.

McClymer, John F. "The Federal Government and the Americanization Movement, 1915–24." *Prologue* 10, no. 1 (1978): 23–41.

———. "Gender and the 'American Way of Life': Women in the Americanization Movement." *Journal of American Ethnic History* 10, no. 3 (1991): 3–20.

McConnell, Stuart. "Reading the Flag: A Reconsideration of the Patriotic Cults of the 1890s." In *Bonds of Affection: Americans Define their Patriotism,* edited by John Bodnar, 102–119. Princeton, NJ: Princeton University Press, 1996.

McGirr, Lisa. "Now That Historians Know So Much about the Right, How Should We Best Approach the Study of Conservatism?" *Journal of American History* 98, no. 3 (2011): 765–770.

McLynn, Frank. *Wagons West: The Epic Story of America's Overland Trails.* New York: Grove, 2004.

McMichael, Kelly. "'Memories Are Short but Monuments Lengthen Remembrances': The United Daughters of the Confederacy and the Power of Civil War Memory." In *Lone Star Pasts: Memory and History in Texas,* edited by Gregg Cantrell and Elizabeth Hayes Turner, 95–118. College Station: Texas A&M University Press, 2007.

McMillen, Neil R. *Dark Journey: Black Mississippians in the Age of Jim Crow.* Champaign: University of Illinois Press, 1990.

Medlicott, Carol, and Michael Heffernan. "'Autograph of a Nation': The Daughters of the American Revolution and the National Old Trails Road, 1910–1927." *National Identities* 6, no. 3 (2004): 234–260.

——. "Constructing Territory, Constructing Citizenship: The Daughters of the American Revolution and 'Americanisation' in the 1920s." *Geopolitics* 10 (2005): 99–120.

——. "One Social Milieu, Paradoxical Responses: A Geographical Reexamination of the Ku Klux Klan and the Daughters of the American Revolution in the Early Twentieth Century." In *Spaces of Hate: Geographies of Discrimination and Intolerance in the U.S.A.,* edited by Colin Flint, 21–47. New York: Routledge, 2004.

Meier, August, and Elliott M. Rudwick. *CORE: A Study in the Civil Rights Movement, 1942–1968.* New York: Oxford University Press, 1973.

Messenger, Amanda Long, ed. *Ohio State History of the Daughters of the American Revolution.* Greenfield, OH: Greenfield, 1946.

Miller, Susan E. "Assent as Agency in the Early Years of the Children of the American Revolution." *Journal of the History of Childhood and Youth* 9, no. 1 (2016): 48–65.

Mills, Cynthia. Introduction to *Monuments to the Lost Cause: Women, Art, and the Landscapes of Southern Memory,* edited by Cynthia Mills and Pamela H. Simpson, xv–xxx. Knoxville: University of Tennessee Press, 2003.

Mills, Cynthia, and Pamela H. Simpson, eds. *Monuments to the Lost Cause: Women, Art, and the Landscapes of Southern Memory.* Knoxville: University of Tennessee Press, 2003.

Mirel, Jeffrey E. *Patriotic Pluralism: Americanization Education and European Immigrants.* Cambridge, MA: Harvard University Press, 2010.

Moreau, Joseph. *School Book Nation: Conflicts over American History Textbooks from the Civil War to the Present.* Ann Arbor: University of Michigan Press, 2003.

Morgan, Francesca. "'Home and Country': Women, Nation, and the Daughters of the American Revolution, 1890–1939." PhD diss., Columbia University, 1998.

——. "'My Furthest-Back Person': Black Genealogy before and after *Roots.*" In *Reconsidering* Roots: *Race, Politics, Memory,* edited by Erica L. Ball and Kellie Carter Jackson, 63–78. Athens: University of Georgia Press, 2017.

——. "A Noble Pursuit? Bourgeois America's Uses of Lineage." In *The American Bourgeoisie: Distinction and Identity in the Nineteenth Century,* edited by Sven Beckert and Julia Rosenbaum, 135–151. New York: Palgrave Macmillan, 2010.

——. "'Regions Remote from Revolutionary Scenes': Regionalism, Nationalism, and the Iowa Daughters of the American Revolution, 1890–1930." *Annals of Iowa* 56, no. 1–2 (1997): 46–79.

——. *Women and Patriotism in Jim Crow America.* Chapel Hill: University of North Carolina Press, 2005.

Morley, Mrs. Walter S., comp. *History of California State Society Daughters of the American Revolution, 1891–1938.* Berkeley, CA: Lederer, Street, and Zeus, 1938.

Morris, Robin. "Organizing Breadmakers: Kathryn Dunaway's ERA Battle and the Roots of Georgia's Republican Revolution." In *Entering the Fray: Gender, Politics, and Culture in* the New South, edited by Jonathan Daniel Wells and Sheila R. Phipps, 161–182. Columbia: University of Missouri Press, 2010.

Morris, Sylvia Jukes. *Price of Fame: The Honorable Clare Boothe Luce.* New York: Random House, 2014.

Moses, L. G. *Wild West Shows and the Images of American Indians, 1883–1933.* Albuquerque: University of New Mexico Press, 1996.

Moss, Bess D. "Statue of the Madonna of the Trail Unveiled at Vandalia by Daughters of the American Revolution." *Journal of the Illinois State Historical Society* 21, no. 4 (1929): 534–540.

Murphree, Daniel S., ed. *Native America: A State-by-State Historical Encyclopedia.* Santa Barbara, CA: ABC-CLIO, 2012.

Nash, Gary B., Charlotte Crabtree, and Ross E. Dunn. *History on Trial: Culture Wars and the Teaching of the Past.* New York: Vintage, 2000.

Nash, Margaret A. "Rethinking Republican Motherhood: Benjamin Rush and the Young Ladies' Academy of Philadelphia." *Journal of the Early Republic* 17, no. 2 (1997): 171–191.

Nash, Roderick. *The Nervous Generation: American Thought, 1917–1930.* Chicago: Ivan R. Dee, 1990.

Nelson, Jack, and Gene Roberts Jr. *The Censors and the Schools.* Westport, CT: Greenwood, 1963.

Ngai, Mae M. "The Architecture of Race in American Immigration Law: A Reexamination of the Immigration Act of 1924." *Journal of American History* 86, no. 1 (1999): 67–92.

Nickerson, Michelle M. *Mothers of Conservatism: Women and the Postwar Right.* Princeton: Princeton University Press, 2012.

Nieguth, Tim. "Beyond Dichotomy: Concepts of the Nation and the Distribution of Membership." *Nations and Nationalism* 5, no. 2 (1999): 155–173.

Nielsen, Kim E. *Un-American Womanhood: Antiradicalism, Antifeminism, and the First Red Scare.* Columbus: Ohio State University Press, 2001.

Norton, Mary Beth. *Liberty's Daughters: The Revolutionary Experience of American Women, 1750–1800.* Ithaca, NY: Cornell University Press, 1980.

O'Leary, Cecilia Elizabeth. *To Die For: The Paradox of American Patriotism.* Princeton, NJ: Princeton University Press, 1999.

Olsen, Margaret Nunnelley. "One Nation, One World: American Clubwomen and the Politics of Internationalism, 1945–1961." PhD diss., Rice University, 2008.

O'Shea, John M., and John Ludwickson. "Omaha Chieftainship in the Nineteenth Century." *Ethnohistory* 39, no. 3 (1992): 316–352.

Ostler, Jeffrey. *The Lakotas and the Black Hills: The Struggle for Sacred Ground.* New York: Penguin, 2011.

Ostling, Richard N., and Joan K. Ostling. *Mormon America: The Power and the Promise.* New York: Harper, 1999.

Parrott, Angie. "'Love Makes Memory Eternal': The United Daughters of the Confederacy in Richmond, Virginia, 1897–1920." In *The Edge of the South: Life in Nineteenth-Century Virginia,* edited by Edward L. Ayers and John C. Willis, 219–238. Charlottesville: University Press of Virginia, 1991.

Patterson, Martha H. *Beyond the Gibson Girl: Reimagining the American New Woman, 1895–1915.* Champaign: University of Illinois Press, 2005.

———, ed. *The American New Woman Revisited: A Reader, 1894–1930.* New Brunswick, NJ: Rutgers University Press, 2008.

Pearce, Roy Harvey. *Savagism and Civilization: A Study of the Indian and the American Mind.* Rev. ed. Baltimore, MD: Johns Hopkins University Press, 1965.

Pettegrew, John. "'The Soldier's Faith': Turn-of-the-Century Memory of the Civil War and the Emergence of Modern American Nationalism." *Journal of Contemporary History* 31, no. 1 (1996): 49–73.

Pfeffer, Paula F. *A. Philip Randolph, Pioneer of the Civil Rights Movement.* Baton Rouge: Louisiana State University Press, 1996.

Philip, Kenneth R. *John Collier's Crusade for Indian Reform, 1920–1954.* Tucson: University of Arizona Press, 1977.

Phillips-Fein, Kim. "Conservatism: A State of the Field." *Journal of American History* 98, no. 3 (2011): 723–743.

Phipps, Kelly Elizabeth. "Marriage and Redemption: Mormon Polygamy in the Congressional Imagination, 1862–1887." *Virginia Law Review* 95, no. 2 (2009): 435–487.

Porter, Anne Hughes. *The History of the Mississippi State Society Daughters of the American Revolution.* Kosciusko, MS: Mississippi State Society Daughters of the American Revolution, 1996.

Powers, Richard Gid. *Not without Honor: The History of American Anticommunism.* New Haven, CT: Yale University Press, 1998.

Prescott, Cynthia Culver. *Gender and Generation on the Far Western Frontier.* Tucson: University of Arizona Press, 2007.

Prins, Harald E. L., and Bunny McBride. *Asticou's Island Domain: Wabanaki Peoples at Mount Desert Island, 1500–2000.* Boston: Northeast Region Ethnography Program, 2007.

Rawlinson, Mark. *American Visual Culture.* New York: Berg, 2009.

Rensch, Hero Eugene, and Ethel Grace Rensch. *Historic Spots in California.* Stanford, CA: Stanford University Press, 1932.

Richards, Cindy Koenig. "Inventing Sacagawea: Public Women and the Transformative Potential of Epideictic Rhetoric." *Western Journal of Communication* 73, no. 1 (2009): 1–22.

Richardson, Angelique, and Chris Willis, eds. *The New Woman in Fiction and Fact: Fin-de-Siècle Feminisms.* New York: Palgrave Macmillan, 2001.

Richardson, Heather Cox. *Wounded Knee: Party Politics and the Road to an American Massacre.* New York: Basic, 2010.

Roberts, Mary Louise. "True Womanhood Revisited." *Journal of Women's History* 14, no. 1 (2002): 150–155.

Roediger, David R. *Colored White: Transcending the Racial Past.* Berkeley: University of California Press, 2002.

Rosaldo, Renato. "Imperialist Nostalgia." *Representations* 26 (Spring 1989): 107–122.

Rosenberg, Rosalind. *Divided Lives: American Women in the Twentieth Century.* New York: Hill and Wang, 1992.

Rymph, Catherine E. *Republican Women: Feminism and Conservatism from Suffrage through the Rise of the New Right.* Chapel Hill: University of North Carolina Press, 2006.

Sandage, Scott A. "A Marble House Divided: The Lincoln Memorial, the Civil Rights Movement, and the Politics of Memory, 1939–1963." *Journal of American History* 80, no. 1 (1993): 135–167.

Scanlon, Sandra. *The Pro-War Movement: Domestic Support for the Vietnam War and the Making of Modern American Conservatism.* Amherst: University of Massachusetts Press, 2013.

Schneider, Dorothee. *Crossing Borders: Migration and Citizenship in the Twentieth-Century United States.* Cambridge, MA: Harvard University Press, 2011.

Schrecker, Ellen. *Many Are the Crimes: McCarthyism in America*. New York: Little, Brown, 1998.

Schwartz, Barry. *Abraham Lincoln and the Forge of National Memory*. Chicago: University of Chicago Press, 2000.

———. "Social Change and Collective Memory: The Democratization of George Washington." *American Sociological Review* 56, no. 2 (1991): 221–236.

Scott, Anne Firor. *Natural Allies: Women's Associations in American History*. Urbana: University of Illinois Press, 1991.

Scott, Rose Moss, ed. *Illinois State History: Daughters of the American Revolution*. Danville, IL: Illinois Printing, 1929.

Shaffer, Marguerite. *See America First: Tourism and National Identity, 1880–1940*. Washington: Smithsonian Institution Press, 2001.

Shapiro, Henry D. *Appalachia on Our Mind: The Southern Mountains and Mountaineers in the American Consciousness, 1870–1902*. Chapel Hill: University of North Carolina Press, 1978.

Shapiro, Herbert. *White Violence and Black Response: From Reconstruction to Montgomery*. Amherst: University of Massachusetts Press, 1988.

Silber, Nina. *The Romance of Reunion: Northerners and the South, 1865–1900*. Chapel Hill: University of North Carolina Press, 1993.

Sitkoff, Harvard. "Racial Militancy and Interracial Violence in the Second World War." *Journal of American History* 58, no. 3 (1971): 661–681.

Sleeper-Smith, Susan. *Indian Women and French Men: Rethinking Cultural Encounter in the Western Great Lakes*. Amherst: University of Massachusetts Press, 2001.

Slotkin, Richard. *Gunfighter Nation: The Myth of the Frontier in Twentieth Century America*. Norman: University of Oklahoma Press, 1998.

Smith, Anthony, and Ernest Gellner. "The Nation: Real or Imagined? The Warwick Debates on Nationalism." Transcript. *Nations and Nationalism* 2, no. 3 (1996): 357–370.

Smith, Shawn Michelle. *American Archives: Gender, Race, and Class in Visual Culture*. Princeton, NJ: Princeton University Press, 1999.

Smith, Sherry L. *Reimagining Indians: Native Americans through Anglo Eyes, 1880–1940*. New York: Oxford University Press, 2000.

Smithers, Gregory D. *Slave Breeding: Sex, Violence, and Memory in African American History*. Gainesville: University Press of Florida, 2012.

Snider, Christy Jo. "Patriots and Pacifists: The Rhetorical Debate about Peace, Patriotism, and Internationalism, 1914–1930." *Rhetoric and Public Affairs* 8, no. 1 (2005): 59–84.

Somerville, Mollie. *Historic and Memorial Buildings of the Daughters of the American Revolution*. Washington, DC: National Society Daughters of the American Revolution, 1979.

Sommerville, Diane Miller. *Rape and Race in the Nineteenth-Century South*. Chapel Hill: University of North Carolina Press, 2004.

Spencer, John. "'We Are Not Dealing Entirely with the Past': Americans Remember Lewis and Clark." In *Lewis and Clark: Legacies, Memories, and New Perspectives*, edited by Kris Fresonke and Mark Spence, 159–183. Berkeley: University of California Press, 2004.

Speulda, Alta Mae. "The Unveiling of the Kelley Cabin Marker Dec. 3 1927." *Journal of the Illinois State Historical Society* 21, no. 2 (1928): 242–252.

Spruill, Marjorie J. "Gender and America's Right Turn." In *Rightward Bound: Making America Conservative in the 1970s*, edited by Bruce J. Schulman and Julian E. Zelizer, 71–89. Cambridge, MA: Harvard University Press, 2008.

Stokes, Anson Phelps. *Art and the Color Line*. Washington, DC: Marian Anderson Committee, 1939.

Storrs, Landon R. Y. "Attacking the Washington 'Femmocracy': Antifeminism in the Cold War Campaign against 'Communists in Government.'" *Feminist Studies* 33, no. 1 (2007): 118–152.

Stott, Kelly McMichael. "From Lost Cause to Female Empowerment: The Texas Division of the United Daughters of the Confederacy, 1896–1966." PhD diss., University of North Texas, 2001.

St. Paul, John, Jr. *The History of the National Society of the Sons of the American Revolution.* Gretna, LA: Firebird, 1998.

Strange, Carolyn. "Sisterhood of Blood: The Will to Descend and the Formation of the Daughters of the American Revolution." *Journal of Women's History* 26, no. 3 (2014): 105–128.

Stremlau, Rose. *Sustaining the Cherokee Family: Kinship and the Allotment of an Indigenous Nation.* Chapel Hill: University of North Carolina Press, 2011.

Talbot, Christine. *A Foreign Kingdom: Mormons and Polygamy in American Political Culture, 1852–1890.* Urbana: University of Illinois Press, 2013.

Talley, Sharron. *Southern Women Novelists and the Civil War: Trauma and Collective Memory in the American Literary Tradition since 1861.* Knoxville: University of Tennessee Press, 2014.

Tarbell, Mrs. Winfield Scott (Grace E. Butler Tarbell). *History of the Daughters of the American Revolution of Colorado, 1894–1941.* Denver, 1941.

Taylor, Graham D. *The New Deal and American Indian Tribalism: The Administration of the Indian Reorganization Act, 1934–45.* Lincoln: University of Nebraska Press, 1980.

Teachout, Woden Sorrow. "Forging Memory: Hereditary Societies, Patriotism, and the American Past, 1876–1898." PhD diss., Harvard University, 2003.

Testi, Arnaldo. "The Gender of Reform Politics: Theodore Roosevelt and the Culture of Masculinity." *Journal of American History* 81, no. 4 (1995): 1509–1533.

Thurner, Manuela. "'Better Citizens without the Ballot': American AntiSuffrage Women and Their Rationale during the Progressive Era." *Journal of Women's History* 5, no. 1 (1993): 33–60.

Trachtenberg, Alan. *Shades of Hiawatha: Staging Indians, Making Americans, 1880–1930.* New York: Hill and Wang, 2004.

Troutman, John W. *Indian Blues: American Indians and the Politics of Music, 1879–1934.* Norman: University of Oklahoma Press, 2009.

———. "'Indian Blues': American Indians and the Politics of Music, 1890–1935." PhD diss., University of Texas at Austin, 2004.

Truesdell, Barbara. "Exalting 'U.S.Ness': Patriotic Rituals in the Daughters of the American Revolution." In *Bonds of Affection: Americans Define their Patriotism*, edited by John Bodnar, 273–289. Princeton, NJ: Princeton University Press, 1996.

———. "God, Home, and Country: Folklore, Patriotism, and the Politics of Culture in the Daughters of the American Revolution." PhD diss., Indiana University, 1996.

Tuck, Stephen. *We Ain't What We Ought to Be: The Black Freedom Struggle from Emancipation to Obama.* Cambridge, MA: Belknap, 2010.

Van Nuys, Frank. *Americanizing the West: Race, Immigrants, and Citizenship, 1890–1930.* Lawrence: University Press of Kansas, 2002.

Walls, Patricia Carol. "Defending Their Liberties: Women's Organizations during the McCarthy Era." PhD diss., University of Maryland College Park, 1994.

Ward, Grace Louise Cadmus, ed. *State History of the New Jersey Daughters of the American Revolution.* Sea Isle City, NJ: Atlantic, 1929.

Weil, François. *Family Trees: A History of Genealogy in America.* Cambridge, MA: Harvard University Press, 2013.

Weiss, Nancy J. *Farewell to the Party of Lincoln: Black Politics in the Age of FDR.* Princeton, NJ: Princeton University Press, 1983.

Welter, Barbara. "The Cult of True Womanhood, 1820–1860." *American Quarterly* 18, no. 2 (1966): 151–174.

Wendt, Simon. "Defenders of Patriotism or Mothers of Fascism? The Daughters of the American Revolution, Antiradicalism, and Un-Americanism in the Interwar Period." *Journal of American Studies* 47, no. 4 (2013): 943–969.

West, Patricia. *Domesticating History: The Political Origins of America's House Museums.* Washington, DC: Smithsonian Institution Press, 1999.

White, Kate K., ed. *Tennessee State History of the Daughters of the American Revolution.* Knoxville, TN: S. B. Newman. 1930.

Wishart, David J. *An Unspeakable Sadness: The Dispossession of the Nebraska Indians.* Lincoln: University of Nebraska Press, 1995.

Wolfe, Patrick. "Land, Labor, and Difference: Elementary Structures of Race." *American Historical Review* 106, no. 3 (2001): 866–905.

———. "Settler Colonialism and the Elimination of the Native." *Journal of Genocide Research* 8, no. 4 (2006): 387–409.

Wood, Nancy. "Memory's Remains: Les lieux de mémoire." *History and Memory* 6, no. 1 (1994): 123–149.

Wright, J. Leitch, Jr. *Creeks and Seminoles: The Destruction and Regeneration of the Muscogulge People.* Lincoln: University of Nebraska Press, 1987.

Wrobel, David. *The End of American Exceptionalism: Frontier Anxiety from the Old West to the New Deal.* Lawrence: University Press of Kansas, 1993.

———. *Promised Lands: Promotion, Memory, and the Creation of the American West.* Lawrence: University Press of Kansas, 2002.

Young, Alfred F. *Masquerade: The Life and Times of Deborah Sampson, Continental Soldier.* New York: Vintage, 2004.

Yuval-Davis, Nira. *Gender and Nation.* Thousand Oaks, CA: Sage, 1997.

Zerubavel, Eviatar. "From 'Social Memories: Steps towards a Sociology of the Past.'" In *The Collective Memory Reader,* edited by Jeffrey K. Olick, Vered Vinitzky-Seroussi, and Daniel Levy, 221–224. New York: Oxford University Press, 2011.

Ziegler-McPherson, Christina A. *Americanization in the States: Immigrant Social Welfare Policy, Citizenship, and National Identity in the United States, 1908–1929.* Gainesville: University Press of Florida, 2009.

Zimmerman, Jonathan. "Storm of the Schoolhouse: Exploring Popular Influences upon the American Curriculum, 1890–1941." *Teachers College Record* 100, no. 3 (1999): 602–626.

Index

Page numbers in *italics* indicate illustrations.

Immigration, DAR attitudes toward: Cold War era, 175–79, 191; restrictions, favoring, 161, 163, 176, 201; twenty-first century, 208

Immigration Act of 1965, 191

Imperialist nostalgia, 99

Indian Reorganization Act, 120–21

Indians: activism, 126; American Indian Bureau, 114; Aracoma, 119; Bureau of Indian Affairs, 100, 122–23; Cateechee, 107; Cherokee, 116–17; Chief Joseph, 116; citizenship, 113–14; Creek Nation, 94, 101–3; in cultural memory, 99; cultural performances, 98; education of, 114–15; as government wards, 100, 114; invisibility of, 134–35; membership in DAR, 96, 109; Merriam Report findings, 115; music, popularization of, 94; National Congress of American Indians, 126; nationalism of, 113; as nonthreatening, 134–35; and Old Trails Road ceremonies, 83, 85; Ottawa, 117–18; Passamaquoddy, 105; in pioneer memoirs, 73; Pocahontas, 106–7, 109; Potawatomi, 112, 117–18; Sacajawea, 107–8; settler cooperation, 73; Sioux, 97, 100, 102–3, 124; in the US military, 112–13, 124; vanishing race theory, 95–96, 111, 115, 122–23; in the West, 61; and Westward expansion commemorations, 72; women, romanticization of, 106, 118–19; Wounded Knee massacre, 97–98. See also Redfeather, Tsianina

Indians, DAR commemorations of: overview of, 96; admiration in, 116; Aracoma, 119; Battle of Bear's Paw, 116; Cateechee, 107; chapter names, 107, 111, 119; Cherokees, 116–17; communicative memory, use of, 104–5, 107, 118; contradictions in, 99; cooperation and friendship, 95, 99–100, 104, 124; cultural emphasis, 179; cultural memory, shaping of, 104; Depression era, 120; essay contests, 115–16; Fontenelle, Logan, 102; Indian days, 111, 120; Indian participation in, 103–5, 117–18, 179; and integration, 99; interwar period, 112–21; Junaluska, 102–4; McIntosh, William, 101–2; mixed-race leaders, 100–2, 116–17; national unity narrative, 100; playing Indian, 111–12; Pocahontas, 119; postwar era, 179–84; Potawatomi and Ottawa council site, 118; princess figures, 96, 106–7; Progressive Era, 96–112; Revolutionary War, 104–5; Sacajawea, 108; Sauganash,

101; treaties, 95, 100–3, 111–12, 117; of US military support, 102–3; violence, absence of, 179; and white masculinity, 107, 119; women, absence of, 164

Indians, DAR support for: American Indians Committee, 122–23, 126; citizenship, 113–14, 180; as conditional, 10, 13; Conservation and Thrift Committee, 115; cultural preservation, 115–16, 120, 122–23; education, 114, 121–22, 180, 191–92; injustices, condemnation of, 114–15; Living Indians Room, 123; and nationalism, 95, 121–22; political activism, 126; scholarship programs, 122; self-determination, 121; social uplift, 180, 191–92; wartime, 124–26; welfare, 113, 121–22; white wrongdoing, admittance of, 125–26

Indians, DAR views of: admiration, 123–24; versus African Americans, 134–35; and Continental Congress, thirtieth, 94–95, 113–14; fascination with, 96, 109, 111, 163–64, 179; interracial marriage, 96, 109, 119; loyalty to the US, 96, 105, 109, 113, 124–25, 179; meeting, desirability of, 124, 179; mixed-race, 100–1; nationalism of, 113, 179; in nationalist ideology, 95–96; nation-building contributions, 123, 191; playing Indian, 111; Pocahontas, 106–7, 109, 119; prejudice against, 146–47; primitiveness, 72, 98–99, 143, 163, 179–80; princess figures, 96, 106–9, 118–19; romanticizing, 116; Sacajawea, 107–8; vanishing race theory, 95–96, 111, 115, 123; wartime, 112, 124–26; white-Indian friendship, 95, 116; women, 96, 106–9, 118–19

Indians, white views of: cultural fascination, 98–99; as imperialist nostalgia, 99; interracial marriage, 98; mixed-race, 100–1; playing Indian, 99, 111; positive, 114; primitivism, celebrated, 98–99; princess figures, 96, 106–9, 119; racism, 98; warrior stereotypes, 124

Indian-white relations: boarding schools, 98; integration efforts, 97–98; interwar period, 114–15; land reforms, 97; reservations, 97, 100, 120, 134; self-determination legislation, 120–21; and the status quo, 134; treaties, 100–2; World War I, 100; World War II, 124

Interwar period, the DAR during: antiradicalism strategies, 53–54; chapter expansion, 47; children, focus on, 54–55; criticisms of, 55;

male heroes, emphasis on, 50; membership growth, 47; New History, attacks on, 48–49; pioneer commemorations, 87–93; socialism, fears of, 49–50; and textbooks, 48–49, 54; women, commemorations of, 50–53. *See also* Pioneer trail marking

Japanese Americans, 160–61
Jefferson, Thomas, 50
Jews, and DAR membership, 139
Johnson, Grace D., 1
Johnson, Lyndon B., 185, 190
Johnson, Nancy L., 198
Jones, Sara Roddis, 186, 189
Junior American Citizens (JAC), 54

Kaiser, Ramona, 123
Keats, John, 192–93
Kelly, Wilhelmena Rhodes, 207
Kennedy, Jacqueline, 192
Kennedy, John F., 186, 192
King, Martin Luther, Jr., 174
King, Sarah M., 197–99
Ku Klux Klan, 149–50

Ladies' Memorial Associations, 21, 213n8
Lee, Mary Custis, 138
Leimbach, August, 83
Lewis, Victor Alonzo, 68–69
Lewis and Clark expedition, 62–63, 73, 88
Lincoln, Abraham, 85
Lockwood, Mary S.: club experience, 23; Confederate flag protest, 136; and the DAR's founding, 16–17; on immigration, 139; on New History, 48; suffrage views, 42; tribute to Arnett, 16, 37
Luce, Clare Boothe, 168–72, 199

Magna, Edith Scott, 53
Mandoka, Samuel, 118
Manifest Destiny, 61, 64–65, 69
Manual of the United States, 146
Masculinity: and heroism, 10, 50, 59–61, 63, 72, 88; and Indian commemorations, 107, 119; martial, 17–18, 36–39; and memory, 1, 11, 13, 35–37, 63, 71–72, 204; and nationalism, 10–11, 13, 37, 75, 204; and nation-building, 73, 75, 107; and pioneer commemorations, 64, 69, 73–75, 88, 91; and valor, 37–38, 40, 45–46,

191; and westward expansion, 71–72. *See also* Gender politics, the DAR's; Revolutionary War commemorations, men in
Massachusetts, 133
McCarthy, Joseph, 165–66
McDowell, William O., 17
McIntosh, William, 101–2
McKinley, William, 139
McLean, Emily Nelson Ritchie, 35
Membership, DAR: Cold War era, 172, 184; demographics, 5; early, 4–5, 24; Indians, 96, 109; interwar, 47; Jews, 139, 5; photographs of, 6; post-Civil Rights era, 192, 200; post-war, 172; prestige of, 23–24; requirements, 4, 137; southerners, 13; UDC overlaps, 135–36; Western growth, 59. *See also* African Americans, DAR membership
Memorial Continental Hall, 40, *41*
Memorial Day, 20
Memory, communicative: and commemorations, 31; *versus* cultural memory, 12, 212n24; cultural memory connections, 56–57, 59–60, 63–64, 66, 73–74, 181; definition of, 12; of Indians, 104–5, 107, 118; and Nationalism, the DAR's, 13–14; preservation efforts, in Michigan, 90–91; Revolutionary War, 31; and state centennial celebrations, 92; of westward expansion, 87–88, 90–92. *See also* Pioneer trail marking and communicative memory
Memory, cultural: commemoration projects, Westward expansion, 92–93; *versus* communicative memory, 12, 212n24; definition of, 12; democratization of, 201; and essay contests, 54; the Federal government and, 55–56, 92–93, 182, 198, 200–1; heroism in, 47, 66, 128; and immigrants, 142; Indians in, 99, 104, 134–35; and nationalism, the DAR's, 13–14, 23, 25, 49, 54–55, 209; National Old Trails Road, 78; and race, 128, 133–35, 151, 156, 191; women ancestors, 51. *See also* Pioneer trail marking and cultural memory
Memory, historical: antebellum period, 19; and the centennial, 20; of the Civil War, 19–21, 134–38; Cold War era, 191–92; and collective memory, 12; colonial era, 20–21; conservative feminism and, 207; DAR's use of, 12–13, 34–36, 47–48; definition of, 11; elitist, 34–36; the federal government

Revolutionary War commemorations, men in: condemnations of, 38–39; and DAR's goals, 33–34, 38–39; examples of, 34; and gender hierarchies, 33; grave locating and marking, 34; and heroism, democratization of, 34; and hero worship, 34–35, 50; martial ideal of, 36–39; Washington, George, 35

Revolutionary War commemorations, women in: absence of, 180–81; Arnett, Hannah, 37; and communicative memory, 31; Corbin, Margaret, 29–31, 33; in DAR chapter names, 31; and gender hierarchies, 33, 51; and gender roles, 29–30; Hart, Nancy, 30–31, 33; heroism in, 28–29, 32; interwar period efforts, 50–53; and love, 28; male narratives, countering, 28, 31–32; and nationalistic pride, 31; Pilgrim Mothers, 50; Real Daughters, 32; Sampson, Deborah, 31, 33; self-sacrifice in, 28–29

Robert, Sarah Corbin, 154, 158
Robertson, Alice, 94, 113
Rogers, Edith Nourse, 153
Roosevelt, Eleanor, 127, 155, *169*, 173
Roosevelt, Theodore, 61–62, 131, 133
Roots, 207
Russian Revolution, 44, 146. *See also* Bolshevism

Sacajawea, 107–8
Sampson, Deborah, 30, 33
Santa Fe trail, 63
Schlafly, Phyllis, 188, *189*, 203–4
Scott, Hazel, 163, 166–68, 172
Scott, Julia Green, 144
Segregation: attacks on, 158, 160, 168; end of, 174; *versus* government rhetoric, 158; groups favoring, 174–75; protests of, 160; and Roosevelt, Eleanor, 155
Smith, John, 106–7
Socialism, 5, 45, 49–50
Sons of Revolutionary Sires, 20
Sons of the American Revolution (SAR), 3, 16
South Africa, 199–200
Spanish-American War, 39–40
Stanton, Elizabeth Cady, 22
Stevenson, Letitia Green, 24
Story, Daisy Allen, 136
Sullivan, Adele Erb, 187

Talmadge, May Erwin, 166, 168, 171–73
Textbooks: the DAR and, 48–49, 54, 192; diversity in, 201, 203–4
Thurmond, Strom, 186
Trail marking. *See* Pioneer trail marking
True womanhood ideology, 4, 6, 21, 53
Truman, Bess, 168
Truman, Harry, 167
Turner, Frederick Jackson, 61–62

United Daughters of the Confederacy (UDC): overviews of, 4–5, 136; authority of, 21; DAR membership overlaps, 135–36; DAR relations, 128, 136–38, 151; gender ideologies, 138, 238n26; and white supremacy, 136
United Nations, opposition to, 164, 182–83, 209
United Nation's Children's Fund (UNICEF), 183

Walworth, Ellen Hardin, 17, 23
Washington, Booker T., 131, 133
Washington, D.C., 151–52, 207–8
Washington, Eugenia, 16–17
Washington, George, 35, 50, 56, 119
Western frontier: closure of, 59–62, 97; and the national character, 61, 64; nostalgia for, 61–62; perceptions of, 60–61
Western frontier commemorations: Lewis and Clark centennial, 62–63; and male heroism, 61; Old Settler Associations, 62, 71; Pioneer Societies, 62, 71; Roosevelt's plans for, 61–62
Westward expansion, 61, 64–65, 69, 72
Westward expansion commemorations: and communicative memory, 87–88, 90, 92; and cultural memory, national, 92–93; gender binaries, 59–60; government involvement in, 92; impact of, 74–75; Indian-settler cooperation in, 73; Madonna of the Trail, 59–60; male heroism, 59–60, 63, 72, 88; and members' nationalism, 81; nationalistic functions, 81; postwar era, 181; racial politics in, 59–60, 88–90, 93, 95; "savage foe" themes, 72; state line monuments, 68–69; women and communicative memory, 87–88, 91. *See also* National Old Trails Road; Pioneer commemorations
White supremacy, 130–31, 149–50; in popular books, 130; Southern, 131. *See also* segregation

White supremacy, the DAR's: overview of, 10, 13; African Americans *versus* Indians, 134–35, 151; and Appalachian mountaineers, 13, 128–29, 143–44, 149, 178; and Asians, 130, 145, 148–49; attacks on, 152–57; and children, 156–57; and civil rights, 174; and cultural memory, 128; defenses of, 154; and heritage, 131–32; and Hispanics, 176–79; and history, 203–4; and immigrants, 128–29, 148–49, 176, 178; membership policies, 132–33; and miscegenation, 131–32, 135, 174; and nationalism, 128, 130–31, 135, 149, 152–53; and nation-building, 89; objections to, internal, 154–55; as racist amnesia, 128; and Roosevelt, Eleanor, 155–56; and true Americanness, 129; and the UDC, 138

Woman's Relief Corps, 136

Woman suffrage movement: arguments favoring, 41; DAR opposition to, 6, 42, 44–45; early, 22; Sacajawea as symbol, 108

Women: activism of, 21–23; in Americanization campaigns, 147; commemoration absences, 63, 71–72, 164, 180–81; conservative, 2, 205–6; in *DAR Magazine,* 29; historians, 27; immigrants, 147; Indian, DAR views of, 96, 106–9, 118–19; Indian princesses, 96, 106–7; in the military, 190, 202; and nationalism, the DAR's, 3–4, 23, 25–26, 40, 86; and the National Old Trails Road, 82–83, 85–87; New, 6, 25–26; pioneer, 51, 71–72, 91–92; in the Revolutionary War, 1, 27; white elite, 21. *See also* Mothers

Women, commemorations of: interwar period, 50–53; pioneer, 91–92; Westward expansion, 87–88, 91. *See also* Revolutionary War commemorations, women in

Women's rights, DAR opposition to, 42–43

Wood, Grant, 55

World War I: and antiradicalism, 44–45; and historical memory, 47; Indians fighting in, 112–13; and Indian-white relations, 100; nationalism, impact on, 17–18, 44–45; and nationalism, 44–46; and race relations, 144

World War II, 124, 160–61

SIMON WENDT is associate professor of American studies at Goethe University Frankfurt. He is the author of *The Spirit and the Shotgun: Armed Resistance and the Struggle for Civil Rights* and editor or coeditor of a number of books, including *Warring over Valor: How Race and Gender Shaped American Military Heroism in the Twentieth and Twenty-First Centuries* and *Black Intellectual Thought in Modern America: A Historical Perspective.*